# ENGLISH FEMINISM
## 1780–1980

# ENGLISH FEMINISM
## 1780–1980

Barbara Caine

Oxford University Press
1997

Oxford University Press, Great Clarendon Street, Oxford OX2 6DP

Oxford  New York

Athens  Auckland  Bangkok  Bogota  Bombay
Buenos Aires  Calcutta  Cape Town  Dar es Salaam
Delhi  Florence  Hong Kong  Istanbul  Karachi
Kuala Lumpur  Madras  Madrid  Melbourne
Mexico City  Nairobi  Paris  Singapore
Taipei  Tokyo  Toronto  Warsaw

and associated companies in
Berlin  Ibadan

Oxford is a trade mark of Oxford University Press

Published in the United States
by Oxford University Press Inc., New York

First Published 1997

British Library Cataloguing in Publication Data
Data available

Library of Congress Cataloging in Publication Data
Caine, Barbara.
  English feminism, 1780–1980/Barbara Caine.
    p.  cm.
  Includes bibliographical references.
  1. Feminism—England—History.  2. Women—England—Social conditions.  I. Title.
HQ1593.C344  1997
305.4'0942—dc21                           96-51166

ISBN 0-19-820686-0
ISBN 0-19-820434-5 (pbk)

Typeset by Best-set Typesetter Ltd., Hong Kong
Printed in Great Britain
on acid-free paper by
Bookcraft Ltd., Midsomer Norton
Nr. Bath, Somerset

*For Larry, Tessa, and Nicholas*

# Preface

I first became interested in the history of feminism in the early 1970s
when, as a postgraduate student in Britain, the advent of the women's
liberation movement made me aware of the complete neglect of
women in my own historical training and research. As an Australian
spending a relatively brief period at a provincial university, however, it
was not so much the activities of the British women's liberation movement—about which I only became aware when they made media
headlines—as the books that accompanied it which were of direct importance to me. And from the start, American and Australian work was
perhaps more important. Kate Millett's *Sexual Politics* in particular
challenged the conventional understanding of Victorian life and letters
which was my particular field of interest and led me into a variety of
projects dealing with the lives and the dilemmas of nineteenth-century
women. Hence the book is very much a product of the women's liberation movement and its aftermath with which it ends—but it is a product not so much of the British women's movement as of its Australian
counterpart, because it was there that I lived and taught and worked out
how to integrate feminism into my study of history, making regular
forays back to Britain in search of research materials.

It was the teaching of women's history which led to this work: while
my previous research has concentrated on a relatively small chrono-
logical period, teaching undergraduate courses on the history of feminism made me venture outside my accustomed boundaries, moving
backwards into the eighteenth century and forwards to the present.
These courses made me aware that while there are ever-increasing
numbers of wonderful, specific, and detailed studies dealing with particular periods or problems or issues in the history of feminism, there
are few works which explore this history over an extended period, or
which discuss the questions about continuity and change or the connections between different periods in feminist thought that fascinated
my own students.

The absence of such long-term or extended histories of feminism is
not particularly surprising. In a period when historical scholarship is
becoming more and more specialized and in which discontinuities are
of more interest than continuity, general histories and long narratives
seem almost to be a relic from the past. And feminism offers particular

questions and problems of its own which act as a deterrent to such an approach; the very richness of recent scholarship on the history of feminism and of contemporary feminist theory has shown how complex and contested every aspect of the chronology, the meaning, and the subject-matter of feminism are, and how difficult it is to work out how even to approach it. All of these things made me feel very tentative in approaching this subject—while at the same time making it an immensely challenging and exciting one.

As a book which began as a series of lecture and seminar courses, this work has been very much a collaborative endeavour and one in which I am greatly indebted to many people with whom I have worked out or discussed my ideas on feminism. My greatest debt is to the students from both the History Department and the Women's Studies Centre at the University of Sydney who made me try to answer the difficult questions which led to this book. I owe a special debt to Mary Spongberg and to Alison Bashford, both of whom shared my interest in Victorian and Edwardian feminism, but pushed it—and me—in many new directions.

Over the years, I have been very fortunate to be able to share my interest in the history of feminism with a number of others who work in this general field and whose ideas and research have contributed substantially to my understanding of feminism. I would like particularly to thank Christine Battersby, Rosalind Delmar, Moira Gatens, Rosemary Pringle, Martha Vicinus, Sophie Watson, and Glenda Sluga, who have endured endless discussions of my particular obsession with the history of feminism, offering me in turn their vast knowledge, sharp insights, and wonderful judgement. I am also grateful to Sally Alexander, Ellen Dubois and Amanda Sebestyen for sharing their understanding of the history of feminism with me.

While researching and beginning the writing of this book at the University of Sydney, I was greatly assisted in the research by Sarah Benjamin, Pippa Leary, and Suzanne Fraser, all of whom were assiduous in following up leads and in finding me material. I feel the book would not have been finished at all, once I moved to Monash University, had it not been for the research assistance I received from Stuart Bennett. His careful scholarship, his enthusiasm and his sense of humour have been invaluable. I thank him also for preparing the Index.

The book has required substantial periods of research in Britain and I would like to thank the Australian Research Council for the grants which made them possible. Like any one researching the history of

British feminism, I am greatly indebted to the Fawcett Library and the help of David Doughan.

Many people have read or heard part of this book in earlier drafts. I would like particularly to thank the participants at the Gender History Seminar at the Institute of Historical Research in London, the Centre for European History at the University of Michigan, the Humanities Research Centre at the Australian National University and both the History Department and the Women's Studies Centre at the University of Sydney for useful suggestions and comments. Several people have read and commented on part or all of the manuscript and I thank Christine Battersby, Joan Landes, Judith Keene, Robyn Cooper and Stephen Garton for their helpful comments.

Finally, I dedicate this book to Larry Boyd and to Tessa and Nicholas who continue to endure my research and writing—and to make it all so pleasurable to me.

*Melbourne, 1996*                                                Barbara Caine

# Contents

Contents

# Chronology

| Year | Legislation, Insititutional Change, and Public Events | Feminist Lives and Campaigns | Publications |
|------|---|---|---|
| 1792 | | | Vindication of the Rights of Woman |
| 1796 | | Death of Mary Wollstonecraft | |
| 1799 | | | Hannah More, *Strictures on the Modern System of Female Education* |
| 1815 | | | Fanny Burney, *The Wanderer* |
| 1825 | | Establishment of Ladies Society for the Relief of Negro Slaves | William Thompson, *Appeal of One-Half of the Human Race, Women, against the Pretensions of the other Half, Men, to retain them in political and thence in civil and domestic Slavery; in Reply to a paragraph of Mr Mill's celebrated 'Article on Government'* |
| 1837 | Queen Victoria's accession to the Throne | | |
| 1839 | An Act to Amend the Law Relating to the Custody of infants: children of separated parents under the age of seven allowed to reside with mother, provided this privilege was agreed to by the Lord Chancellor and that she was of 'good character' | | |
| 1840 | London Anti-Slavery Convention | | |
| 1854 | | | Caroline Norton, *English Laws for Women in the Nineteenth Century*, London, 1854 |
| 1857 | Matrimonial Causes Act | | Start of *The English Woman's Journal* |
| 1859 | | Establishment of Langham Place circle and of Society for Promoting the Employment of Women | |

# Chronology

| Year | Legislation, Insititutional Change, and Public Events | Feminist Lives and Campaigns | Publications |
|------|-------------------------------------------------------|------------------------------|--------------|
| 1864 | Contagious Diseases Act (Act for the prevention of Contagious Diseases at Certain Naval and Military Stations) passed | | |
| 1867 | John Stuart Mill elected to Parliament | Establishment of London and Manchester National Societies for Women's Suffrage. Women's Suffrage petition presented to Parliament | |
| 1868 | | Establishment of women's suffrage societies in Edinburgh, in Bristol, in Dublin | |
| 1869 | Oxford and Cambridge Local Examinations made available to women | Josephine Butler becomes President of the Ladies' National Association for the Repeal of the Contagious Diseases Acts. Elizabeth Garrett Anderson becomes first woman to qualify as a doctor in England. Hitchin College, forerunner to Girton, opened | Publication of: 1) John Stuart Mill, *The Subjection of Women* 2) Josephine Butler (ed.), *Women's Work, Women's Culture* |
| 1870 | Married Women's property Act gives married women right to their own earnings | | Start of *Women's Suffrage Journal* |
| 1871 | Establishment of Local School Boards: women eligible for election | | |
| 1873 | | Girton College opened | |
| 1876 | Women gain right to register as Physicians | | |
| 1878 | Women admitted to degrees at University of London | | |
| 1882 | Married Women's Property Act | | |
| 1884 | Matrimonial Causes Act makes 'aggravated assault' grounds for judicial separation | | |
| 1885 | Act to make further provision for the Protection of Women and Girls, and for suppression of brothels raises Age of Consent for girls to 16. Also outlaws homosexual acts between consenting male adults | Establishment of Women's Co-operative Guild | Publication of 'Maiden Tribute of Modern Babylon' |
| 1886 | Repeal of Contagious Diseases Acts | Esther Roper becomes secretary of the North of England Society for Women's Suffrage | |
| 1889 | First woman elected to London County Council | | |

| Year | Legislation, Insititutional Change, and Public Events | Feminist Lives and Campaigns | Publications |
|------|------|------|------|
| 1890 | First woman Poor Law guardian elected | | New edition of Wollstonecraft, *Vindication of the Rights of Woman* with Introduction by Millicent Garrett Fawcett |
| 1891 | | Death of Lydia Becker | |
| 1892 | | Death of Barbara Bodichon | Establishment of *Shafts* |
| 1893 | | | Olive Schreiner's *Story of an African Farm*; George Gissing, *The Odd Women* |
| 1894 | Sarah Grand coins the term 'New Woman' | Formation of National Union of Women's Suffrage Societies | Mona Caird's *The Daughters of Danaeus*, and Emma Brooke's *A Superfluous Woman* |
| 1895 | Word 'feminist' appears for first time in *Athenaeum* of 27 April | | Establishment of *The Woman's Signal* |
| 1897 | | | Mona Caird, *The Morality of Marriage and other Essays on the Status and Destiny of Woman* |
| 1898 | Term 'feminist' first used in *The Westminster Review* | | Sarah Grand, *The Beth Book* |
| 1903 | | Establishment of Women's Social and Political Union | |
| 1904 | | WSPU moves to London. Establishment of British National Federation of Women Workers | |
| 1905 | | Start of Militant Campaign | |
| 1906 | | Death of Josephine Butler. WSPU moves to London | |
| 1907 | | Split within WSPU: start of Women's Freedom League | |
| 1909 | | | Start of *The Common Cause* |
| 1911 | | | Christabel Pankhurst, *The Great Scourge* |
| 1912 | | | Start of *The Suffragette* |
| 1913 | | | Margaret Llewellyn Davies (ed.), *Maternity: Letters from Working Women* |
| 1914 | Start of First World War | End of suffrage campaigns | |
| 1917 | Representation of the People Act: grants suffrage to women over the age of 30. First birth control clinic established in North London | | |

| Year | Legislation, Insititutional Change, and Public Events | Feminist Lives and Campaigns | Publications |
|------|---|---|---|
| 1919 | Sex Disqualification (Remocal) Act—admits women to legal profession. Nancy Astor becomes first woman Member of Parliament | NUWSS changes name to National Union of Societies for Equal Citizenship. Eleanor Rathbone becomes President. London National Society for Women's Suffrage becomes London National Society for Women's Service | |
| 1920 | Oxford University admits women to degrees. Marriage bar introduced in teaching, civil service, local government | | Start of *The Woman's Leader* and of *Time and Tide* |
| 1921 | Women sworn in as jurors in divorce courts | Establishment of Six Point Group | |
| 1922 | Married Women (Maintenance) Act allowed women some maintenance under separation orders | | |
| 1923 | Matrimonial Causes Act enabled wives to sue for divorce on the basis of adultery. Guardianship of Infants Act gave divorced women right to custody of children | | |
| 1924 | Ellen Wilkinson becomes first woman in Labour Party to be elected an MP | | Eleanor Rathbone, *The Disinherited Family* |
| 1926 | | Establishment of Women's Service Library (later to be named the Fawcett Library) | |
| 1928 | Equal Franchise Act gives women vote on same terms as men | Death of Emmeline Pankhurst. NUSEC begins setting up Townswomen's Guilds | Ray Strachey, *The Cause*; Virginia Woolf, *A Room of One's Own* |
| 1929 | | Death of Millicent Garrett Fawcett | |
| 1930 | | | *The Woman's Leader* changes name to *The Townswoman* |
| 1938 | | | Virginia Woolf, *Three Guineas* |
| 1940 | | Death of Ray Strachey | |
| 1944 | Marriage Bar for teachers abolished by an amendment to the Education Act of 1944 | | |
| 1945 | Women admitted to Police Force | | |
| 1946 | Marriage bar abolished in Civil Service | | |

# Chronology

| Year | Legislation, Insititutional Change, and Public Events | Feminist Lives and Campaigns | Publications |
|------|-------------------------------------------------------|------------------------------|--------------|
| 1948 | British Nationality Act allowed British women to retain their nationality on marriage. Women admitted to degrees at Cambridge University | | |
| 1952 | Equal pay for men and women teachers | Six Point Group Conference on The Feminine Point of View | Olwen Campbell (ed.), *Report of a Conference on The Feminine Point of View*, London, 1952 |
| 1954 | Equal pay for men and women in Civil Service | | First English edition of Simone de Beauvoir', *Second Sex* |
| 1957 | | | Judith Hubback, *Wives who went to College* |
| 1958 | | | Alva Myrdal and Viola Klein *Women's Two Roles* |
| 1961 | | Women's Freedom League ceases to exist | |
| 1963 | | | Betty Friedan, *The Feminine Mystique* |
| 1966 | | | Hannah Gavron *Captive Wives*; Juliet Mitchell, 'Women: The Longest Revolution' in *The New Left Review* |
| 1968 | Abortion Act allows for legal abortion if two physicians agree that pregnancy dangerous for mental or physical health of woman | Start Of London Women's Liberation Workshop. Re-introduction of International Women's Day | |
| 1970 | | First National Women's Liberation Conference at Ruskin College | |
| 1971 | | First major Women's Liberation street march | Juliet Mitchell, *Women's Estate* |
| 1972 | | Establishment of Women's Aid | Start of *Spare Rib* |
| 1973 | | | Sheila Rowbotham, *Hidden From History* |
| 1974 | | | Juliet Mitchell, *Psychoanalysis and Feminism* |
| 1975 | International Women's Year. UN declares 1975–85 decade for Women, Equality, Development and Peace | English Prostitutes Collective founded | |
| 1978 | | Last National Women's Liberation Conference | |
| 1979 | | | Start of Feminist Review |
| 1980 | | End of Six Point Group | |
| 1982 | | | Hazel Carby, 'White woman listen!' |

# Introduction

The history of feminism has developed into a major field in recent years as scholars from many disciplines and in many countries have sought to explore the ways in which women's oppression has been represented, discussed, and resisted in the past few centuries. This new scholarship and research has revealed the intensity, the extent, the duration, and the complexity of the concern to understand the meaning of sexual difference and to end sexual oppression and hierarchy, which is the core of feminism. Until quite recently, feminist discussion and debate was seen as spasmodic and fragmentary, at least until the mid-nineteenth century, and then as going into abeyance after the First World War. Now, by contrast, it is possible to construct a more or less continuous history of British feminism, showing its persistence in terms of published texts and active engagement at least from the seventeenth century to the present.[1]

This interest in the history of feminism and the sense of its expansiveness has come from a number of different fields. While historians and biographers have explored the ideas, lives, and activities of feminist writers and activists, scholars engaged with literature and philosophical and cultural studies have written about the feminist engagement of literary and philosophical texts. The novels of Fanny Burney, Mary Hays, Jane Austen and George Eliot, and the poetry of Elizabeth Barrett Browning, have thus been encompassed within recent discussions of the history of feminism alongside the novels of Sarah Grand, Olive Schreiner and Virginia Woolf. In a similar way, the importance for feminism not only of Rousseau, John Stuart Mill, and Sigmund Freud but also of Locke and the late eighteenth- and nineteenth-century Political Economists has been explored.[2] The feminist underpinnings, or the implications for feminism of a range of political, social, and philanthropic ideas and activities have also been examined and explored, as recent scholars have stressed the need to recognize the relationship between changing ideas about the public and the private spheres and women's social and political role.[3] Most recently there has developed an immense interest in the relationship between feminism and imperialism, in the endorsement of the racism and imperialist ideals by many white feminists, and the assumption by

British feminists of their own particular version of the 'white man's burden'.[4]

All of this research has served not only to expand but also to transform the history of feminism, making clear both its immense scope and its complexity. On the one hand, it is now clear that feminist ideas and debates have existed and been elaborated more or less constantly over the last three centuries. On the other hand, the question of feminism itself—of what it means and what it encompasses—has become immensely more complex and almost impossible to answer with any degree of certainty. Where once feminism was taken to mean primarily a concern with gaining equal political and legal rights for women, this is now seen as at best a small part of what the term covers. In recent years far more emphasis has been placed on feminist concerns with the sexual oppression of women and the rendering of them as objects of male desire rather than as sexual subjects seeking to articulate and express their own desires. Interrogating the meaning of sexual difference and exploring what it means to be and to live as a woman have now become major feminist interests.[5] This expanded framework has made central to feminist concerns not only questions about marriage, prostitution, and sexual violence, but also those dealing with women's sexuality and demands for recognition of their entitlement either to chastity or to autonomous sexual desire, and indeed the whole question of women's demand to speak for and represent themselves.[6] The desire and capacity for women to speak for and define themselves, to explore and expound their own understanding of the world, and to critique what has stood in the past as objective and neutral forms of knowledge are all now seen as having an important place within any feminist project.[7]

This immense breadth makes it extremely difficult of course to decide whether to classify a particular text or individual or campaign as 'feminist'. Indeed, increasingly, contemporary feminist debates would suggest that such a classification is neither viable nor necessary. The current emphasis in feminist theory and in women's studies on the need to recognize diversity and difference amongst women, and to accept the existence of many different and even conflicting emancipatory projects and feminisms in place of any unitary 'feminism', alerts one to the inevitable prescriptiveness involved in any attempt at definition.[8] It has served also to emphasize the close connection between feminism and particular constructions of the idea of 'women' or of womanhood—and the paradox of the need for feminists to speak on behalf of their sex, despite the problems and inevitable narrowing and exclusive-ness which attend their claims to define or speak for 'women'.[9]

All of these developments necessarily establish a variety of new challenges for anyone seeking to explore feminist ideas and debates, and especially for anyone seeking as I am to trace some of these over a long period. This is not only because of the changing frameworks I have just described, but also because of changes and new developments which have been brought to the study of history from literary theory and from cultural studies. The shift away from authorial intention towards meaning or readings in discussing literary texts, which has been so important in recent literary theory and cultural studies, has had a significant impact on thinking about feminism. It is increasingly clear that particular literary texts have played a part in feminist thinking and in feminist debates because of the ways in which they were read and taken up, rather than because of the intent of the author.[10] In a similar way, it is manifestly evident that many women who were not themselves motivated by specifically feminist aims or ideas play a major role in the construction of feminist traditions or campaigns or possibilities. Feminist rhetoric and feminist arguments have necessarily drawn on and made use of literary, social, and political women who have not themselves been strongly committed to the cause of women's emancipation. Florence Nightingale, for example, had marked reservations about supporting the Victorian women's rights movement or its demands for women's suffrage—or for entry to the medical profession. But her life, her work, and her overall stature played a crucial role within that movement—and indeed it is impossible adequately to discuss Victorian feminism without including her. In a similar way, while any history of modern feminism will necessarily give a privileged place to Mary Wollstonecraft, it needs also to examine the importance of Hannah More, who expanded the range of acceptable activities for women and demanded reform of education and marriage, while at the same time rejecting any suggestion that the prevailing sexual hierarchy warranted change or that women sought or needed legal rights.[11]

It has thus become increasingly difficult to attempt to write a history of feminism which even attempts to encompass the full range of individuals, ideas, and activities which deserve attention. Moreover, any historical definition of feminism, however flexible it might appear, has come to be seen by many historians and feminist theorists as not only difficult, but also impossible. What I have sought to do within this framework, however, is not to jettison all of the accepted ideas about this history of feminism, but rather to show how problematic they now are. I have focused my attention on the ideas, beliefs, and activities of a range of people who devoted much of their lives to articulating their views on the oppression of women and working out ways to ameliorate, resist, or revolt against it. At the same time, I have attempted to show how problematic for later ideas of feminism many of the claims of the ostensible champions of women were—and how important were the ideas and activities of many who had apparently little concern with women's oppression in setting up the 'woman question' and stimulating feminist debate. In this book, therefore, I will also attempt to explore border regions, to look at the difficulties in establishing at any particular period what might fit into a history of feminism and what might be excluded.

I deal with modern feminism in this text and thus begin with the feminist debates of the 1790s. Feminism had of course existed long before the end of the eighteenth century, but the framework of women's protests against the injustices they faced and their ideas and arguments underwent a distinctive change at this time.[12] In the sixteenth century, Christine de Pizan wrote of a mythical city where women ceased to be excluded from education or deprived of power or subject to male disapproval and calumny; a century and a half later, Mary Astell sought to withdraw women from society into educational institutions where they could study, converse, and develop their own interests away from the lures of men, marriage, and society.[13] By the late eighteenth century, however, these concerns with women's exclusion from education and from religious and civic authority were being replaced by the widespread recognition that women's oppression could only be dealt with through legal, political, and social change. The demand for women's *rights* thus seems to me to be the core of modern feminism, connecting it closely, albeit in complex ways, with the Enlightenment, and the revolutionary demands for the Rights of Man.[14]

Although it is impossible to offer a thorough or complete analysis of the context of any particular feminist discussion or debate, I have tried to show the close, if complex, connection between feminist ideas and the social, political, and intellectual context in which they develop. Feminism is not in any simple or direct way a reflection of the prevailing situation of women. Nor is a history of feminism a general history of women. Sometimes the study of feminism requires a recognition of the importance of new possibilities and of potential changes and developments, even if they were never fully realized. Nowhere is the importance of potential change more marked than in regard to the late eighteenth century and the Enlightenment. While the Enlightenment discourse on the rights of man necessarily and immediately raised the possibility of rights for women, at the very moment that the idea of the natural rights was being propounded, some of those men most ardently demanding legal and political rights for men were arguing that the sexual differences between men and women made these rights sex specific and not in any way applicable to women. Modern feminism has thus come to be seen not as a simple outgrowth of the enlightenment and the French Revolution, but rather as a consequence of the new forms of discrimination which women faced at this time when they were explicitly denied rights being granted to men under bourgeois law. It was this new discrimination which provided the stimulus for feminist demands in Britain as in France and America.[15] Modern feminism was thus not the product of any obvious improvement in the situation of women, but rather a response to a changing political and economic framework which affected women in many complex and contradictory ways.

The changes within feminism over the past two hundred years, in its theoretical concern and analysis, its organization and structure, and its rhetoric and tone, provide another principal concern within this work. While there has been continuity in terms of the focus on rights over this period, there have been considerable changes in how these rights were defined, in how they have been seen in relation to ideas about sexual difference, and in perceptions of the extent to which a transformation of the position of women is possible. Thus questions about continuity and change, and about points of discontinuity or of rupture, have been central ones throughout.

Because I have been working on a longitudinal study of feminism, questions about the relationship between any particular individuals or groups of women or any feminist texts and those by which they were preceded have become immensely important. Increasingly I have found that my own interest has come to focus on questions about a feminist tradition: whether such a tradition does or ever has existed, and with the extent to which a history such as the one I am seeking to write serves to enforce—or to invent—such a tradition. Thus the question of history itself, of the sense of history within feminism at various times, and of the importance of memory and the invocation or denial of a feminist past have become major issues.

What becomes clear as soon as one starts to look for a feminist tradition is the very different ways in which tradition has functioned within feminism as compared with many other forms of political and social thought or other political and social movements. Liberalism, socialism, and conservatism, one might well argue, have developed around particular dominating figures and texts, with ideas and beliefs being transmitted from one generation to the next.[16] Feminism is very different. Mary Wollstonecraft may now be widely accepted as the founding figure in modern Anglo-American feminism, but she was rarely even mentioned, let alone venerated, for most of the nineteenth century. On the contrary, most of those concerned to advance the cause of women's emancipation either avoided any direct reference to her or sought deliberately to distance themselves from her name and from the sexual transgressions which that name immediately brought to mind.

Wollstonecraft's curious and ambiguous status in the hundred years after her death points very clearly to the lack of any legitimating tradition within feminism. And this lack of a definite and coherent feminist tradition seems itself to be a result of the oppression and subordination of women that are the target of feminism. For women in general have lacked the resources needed to establish and transmit their ideas. Few women were either substantial inheritors of family income or able to earn the amount that was required to establish a college or even a major journal, hence feminism lacked the institutional framework which allowed groups like the early political economists or the philosophic radicals to become powerful and influential. Even in the mid-nineteenth and early twentieth centuries, when an organized women's movement existed, the financing of journals—like the financing of women's colleges—was a serious problem.

Moreover, feminist writers, activists, and theorists have never had the kind of prestige or patronage which would make later generations seek connection with them as a way of enhancing their own status or prospects. The contrast between feminism and other important late eighteenth- and early nineteenth-century social, political, or philosophic discourses, like that of political economy, is instructive here. Few nineteenth-century political economists ever wrote without indicating their connection to the great tradition stretching through Adam Smith, Malthus, and Ricardo to John Stuart Mill. But even fewer nineteenth-century feminists claimed any direct connection with or descent from Mary Wollstonecraft. Where the claim to a connection with Smith or Malthus or Mill automatically conferred legitimacy and importance on male writers, serving sometimes also to obtain positions for them in a variety of fields of journalism, education, or administration, connection with Wollstonecraft suggested only moral laxity.[17]

The gendered nature of the public sphere is a central issue here. The masculine nature of the public sphere, and the complementary development of a private female sphere in the course of the eighteenth century, went along not only with consistent criticism of any public role for women, but with a sense that, as Rousseau argued, women's involvement in the public sphere was in and of itself immoral and even indecent. The different and gendered meanings of the term 'public' whereby a 'public' man was one understood to be concerned with political and community affairs while a 'public' woman was a prostitute shows how absolute the exclusion of women from the public sphere was—while at the same time pointing to the fact that any public involvement of women was seen as potentially or actually immoral.[18] This meant that the slightest deviation from strict propriety by prominent women was met with complete ostracism. In the case of Mary Wollstonecraft, knowledge of her private life—of her relationship with Gilbert Imlay, her illegitimate daughter, and her unconventional marriage to William Godwin—brought to an end her reputation and made her name a byword for illicit passion and irregular sexual relations. But the fates of some of her immediate predecessors shows how hard it was for prominent eighteenth-century women to avoid having some severe slur cast on their reputations. A second marriage, albeit a perfectly legitimate one undertaken when they were widowed, was enough to ensure not only that Catherine Macaulay and Hester Thrale were subject to scorn and derision, but also that their work ceased to be read.[19] But all of this simply emphasizes the fact that women were always transgressing when they became publicly known, and hence that they lacked the capacity either to bestow legitimacy on each other or to make it worth the while for later women to attempt to connect themselves with earlier ones.

But while feminism lacks any obvious legitimating tradition, Wollstonecraft's place within it suggests that there may be other ways of thinking about and of connecting generations of women with their past. For while not often mentioned and only cursorily discussed, Wollstonecraft was certainly not forgotten in the nineteenth century. She was mentioned in memoirs and essays and private correspondence in ways which show clearly how much she was thought about. Her first name alone—underlined or italicized—was enough to bring her to mind. She was a powerful, haunting, and suggestive presence whose well-known transgressions served always as a reminder of the close link between demands for women's rights and rejection of the prevailing norms of femininity and domesticity. Despite the attempts of many women to emphasize the propriety of those concerned with women's rights throughout the nineteenth century, feminism was always linked to demands for sexual freedom, for the freedom to negotiate sexual relationships without the bonds of marriage, and to explore new ways of living which did not conform to middle-class norms. Mary Wollstonecraft symbolized the connection between these personal and sexual demands and those for political and legal rights. Her life story and the strong interest in it provided a continuous undercurrent through much of the nineteenth century, being retold and reformulated constantly as a backdrop against which later generations of women waged their own struggle to establish new ways of living that met their own desires for and interpretations of emancipation.

Within feminism then, tradition and transgression have been intimately linked as a result of women's marginality on the one hand, and of the personal dimensions in feminist politics and political thought on the other. This complex past and the fact that feminism lacks a legitimating tradition make it appear particularly subject to discontinuities and to breaks and constantly to be in need of revival and rescue. But the uncertainties and the breaks within feminism and the lack of any definite and generally accepted tradition have operated, like so many other developments in feminism, in a way which offers both possibilities and problems for later feminists. On the one hand, the lack of a strong and legitimating tradition has meant that almost every generation of feminists feels that they are either starting from scratch or making up for the errors of previous generations, and thereby hampers their effort to demonstrate the significance of their concerns. On the other hand, the lack of an institutionally based tradition has conferred great freedom on later feminists to break with the past, and thus not only to formulate new theories and programmes, but also to read and reconstruct their feminist past as they choose. Hence a number of different feminist traditions have been created at various significant periods in accordance with the needs of those active at the time. In the present, as feminists emphasize the diversities amongst women and the pluralities which require the recognition of feminisms in place of any unitary feminism, there is also a constant rewriting and reworking of what constitutes the various and different feminist pasts.

Many historians of feminism have pointed to the ways in which their task is rendered problematic by the fact that the term 'feminism' entered into English-language discussions only in the 1890s and was not widely used until the First World War.[20] Much of the discussion depicted in this book occurred before there was any simple or single label to designate a primary concern with women's oppression. But one needs to be aware too that the introduction of the term did not remove the problems: even when the term 'feminism' was introduced and gained currency in the 1890s and the early twentieth century, it did not admit of clear or unambiguous definition. Right from the start, in the 1890s, its meanings and applications have been contentious and its use as a term often divisive and even disruptive.[21] It was, moreover, used in ways very different from those current today. Thus it was often rejected or ignored by groups and individuals who are given a prominent place in the current feminist historical imagination—such as the suffragettes in the early twentieth century, or Virginia Woolf in the 1920s and 1930s—while being claimed by individuals and groups whose ideas are problematic—such as Dora Russell and Janet Chance, who saw it as part and parcel of their celebration of heterosexuality.[22] Thus the application or use of the term and its changing meanings become questions requiring extensive discussion.

Because of my interest in the question of change, of the relationship between one period of feminist activity and another, and in the extent to which one can talk about a functioning feminist tradition, I have chosen to organize this book chronologically rather than thematically. Decisions about chronology are themselves complex ones that carry a considerable interpretive weight. Does one, for example, accept that one phase of feminist debate effectively came to an end with the death of Wollstonecraft in 1796, and if so, how does one deal with the posthumous debate and discussion about her? Does mid-Victorian feminism begin with the start of petitions and the Langham Place Circle in the late 1850s, or with the suffrage campaign and the contagious diseases agitation in the late 1860s? Arguments could be made for any of a variety of different chronologies, and each in turn would produce a different interpretation over continuity and change and over which aspects of feminism were most significant at any particular time or which ones seem most significant retrospectively.

The chronology I have chosen is in many ways a conventional one, beginning with a chapter on feminism during the period of the French Revolution and its aftermath, and then moving on to look at the first half of the nineteenth century. I have taken mid-Victorian feminism to begin with the advent of the first campaigns of the 1850s and to end with the advent of the 'new woman' debate and the new concerns about marriage and sexuality in the late 1880s and 1890s. Thus the period which encompasses the 'new woman', the militant campaign, and the expansions of the suffrage movement up until the advent of the First World War has a separate chapter.

Thinking about the history of feminism in the twentieth century has been dominated by the dramatic nature of the militant campaigns, on the one hand, and by the explosive and energetic nature of the Women's Liberation movement on the other. Inevitably, discussion of the interwar and postwar periods occurs in terms of their relative lack of feminist activity or analysis, as compared with these other times. I have tried here not just to explore whether and to what extent one can find feminist agitation or writing in periods once seen as having none, but also to explore the light cast on these periods by others that have become more dominant in the feminist imaginary. The ways in which the rhetoric of Women's Liberation invokes the suffragettes, but obliterates the decades immediately preceding the 1970s, for example, seems to me to have led to a failure to see the changes which were occurring in the 'woman question' in the 1960s. I have tried to show the changes which occurred within the two decades after the Second World War, and the ways in which the ground was prepared for Women's Liberation through an extensive critique of the project of women's emancipation that developed in many different arenas in the mid- and late 1960s.

The concluding chapter deals with the advent of Women's Liberation and with its aftermath. It does not attempt to encompass the history of the last twenty-five years. Such a project would require not one, but many books. Rather, what it seeks to do is to explore the ways in which Women's Liberation sought to stress its own extreme originality, and at the same time to invoke a particular feminist tradition and to construct and negotiate a history of feminism. It also looks at the ways in which the feminist debates and disagreements of the 1970s and 1980s, and the stress on the need to recognize and encompass the differences amongst women, led to the giving up of any idea of a single feminism or of a dominant feminist project and to an emphasis on the importance of plurality and difference.

# one

# FEMINISM AND THE RIGHTS OF WOMAN

The demand for the Rights of Woman in the late eighteenth century provided the basis and the framework for modern feminism. In Britain its emergence was closely bound up with the broad range of social and economic changes brought by industrialization and urbanization in the later eighteenth century, the expansion in wealth and power of the middle class, and the new emphasis on individualism and economic independence which accompanied it. But it was the political upheaval of the French Revolution and the debates about political rights and citizenship which surrounded it that brought the first extensive discussion of women's emancipation, the central concern of modern feminism.[1]

To say this is not to pretend that the French Revolution brought a general acceptance of the need for women's rights or representation. In the early years of the French Revolution, women both in France and in England actively demanded citizenship and direct involvement in political life—but these rights were not granted. On the contrary, as much recent feminist scholarship demonstrates, feminism arose out of the tensions created by the fact that the political and economic freedoms demanded and gained by men during this period were actively denied to women. In France, as later in England and America in the late eighteenth and nineteenth centuries, the extension of the suffrage to all, or to larger groups of men, went along with the specific gendering of that suffrage so that it was explicitly manhood suffrage that was coming into being.[2] In the century between 1750 and 1850, as Joan Landes has pointed out, women were confronted with a new and previously unimportant form of discrimination: the constitutional denial to them of political and legal rights.[3] The most significant feminist statements of the period were direct responses to new legislation granting men rights which were not being extended to women. None the less, despite the ultimate denial to them of political rights or civic status, the intense debates about the meaning of women's citizenship during the French Revolution meant that women and their situation became a central issue in the political debate of the 1790s. Women thus became a political category and feminism assumed its modern political form through the debates about women's rights during the French Revolution.[4]

That the French Revolution should simultaneously provide the possibility of emancipation and of citizenship for women while denying them any civic existence illustrates the paradoxical and contradictory possibilities and arguments which established the framework for late eighteenth-century and early nineteenth-century feminism, and serves to explain why that feminism itself was sometimes paradoxical. In a similar way, the process of industrialization in Britain, with its expanding middle class and increasing range of professional and commercial opportunities for men, gave new prominence to the ideal of economic independence and to that of a career open to talent. In the process, the possibility of economic independence and the importance of self-reliance for women came to the fore—although such independence was rarely possible and indeed was explicitly denied, 'dependence' becoming as much an attribute of middle-class femininity as 'independence' was of masculinity. In both the economic and the political sphere, however, opportunities were thus simultaneously being raised and denied to women.

In this chapter I will explore the complex interactions between the social and political developments of the late eighteenth century and the rise of modern feminism, paying particular attention to the new definitions of masculinity and femininity which were so central a feature of the Enlightenment, of Romanticism, and of the emergence of an industrial society. But neither the feminist possibilities of this period nor its reconstruction in later histories of feminism are clear cut. Any history of feminism must give a central place to the ideas, beliefs, and struggles of women who consciously committed themselves to the emancipation of their sex. But how one defines or establishes who these women are is far from simple, as the meaning of 'emancipation' has been expanded in recent years to encompass not only political and legal rights, but also sexual freedom and independence. Mary Wollstonecraft clearly has the central place in any discussion of the origins of modern feminism and the chapter will largely focus on her. But increasingly in the last few years, it has become evident that it is necessary to look at her not just as an isolated individual, greatly 'ahead of her time', but rather within the context of the late eighteenth-century expansion in literature as a profession for women. It is not only the *Vindication of the Rights of Woman* that is important in the history of feminism, but also Wollstonecraft's novels, which followed the pattern of many of her contemporaries in their exploration of the wrongs and the sufferings of her sex.

While the late eighteenth century saw nothing that can be called 'a women's movement', it did see debates and discussions about women's nature, rights, and responsibilities that have recently come to be seen as significant feminist debates.[5] At the same time, many literary scholars have insisted on the need to recognize the feminist impulses and concerns evident in the writings of Mary Hays, Fanny Burney, and Jane Austen.[6] Their work raised a series of questions about the need to recognize women's sexuality and their autonomous sexual desire, the possibility of equality in marriage and domestic relationships, and the importance of education for girls and of rational motherhood. In this period, several decades before the appearance of organized feminist groups or campaigns, changing literary ideas and representations of women assume a heightened importance, and especially because of the expansion of literature as a profession for women and one through which many women demanded the right to represent themselves. Hence the emergence of women novelists and the increasing focus of literary works on women's sentiments and sensibilities in the late eighteenth century has also played a part in recent constructions of the history of feminism.

Finally, it is necessary to recognize the importance of the activities and the work of some prominent women who ostensibly opposed feminist aims and objectives even as they served to expand the range of activities and opportunities open to women. Thus evangelicals like Hannah More or Mrs West, women who made very clear their hostility to Wollstonecraft and to the whole project of women's emancipation, none the less have a place in much later feminist writing and in this study because of their demand for reform of some aspects of family life, their insistence on a renegotiation of marriage, their belief in the need to define a form of female citizenship, and because of the importance attributed to them by later generations of feminist activists and writers.[7]

## Social Change and Sexual Difference in the Late Eighteenth Century

Neither the extent nor the nature of the feminist debates of the late eighteenth and early nineteenth centuries can be understood without some recognition of the changing social and economic situation of women, both within the family and in the wider society, which accompanied the processes of industrialization and urbanization. These changes were extremely complex and diverse, varying considerably according to social class, ethnic, and religious origin and regional location.[8] For some women, for example, industrialization brought new possibilities of paid labour either outside or within the home, as factory workers, outworkers, or domestic servants.[9] For others, it brought paid work to an end while care of family and home became a full-time task. But what is most significant at this time in terms of feminist theory and rhetoric is the situation that obtained within the middle class, the class from which most feminists were recruited.[10]

The expansion in trade and manufacture, which was so marked in Britain in the course of the eighteenth century, brought a significant increase in the size and power of the urban middle class. The number of middle-class families increased as did their spending power, and the period from the late eighteenth century to the mid-nineteenth saw immense developments in domestic architecture and in the production of household goods and furniture, as the middle class increasingly sought to mark its new wealth and status by its new suburban way of life. The increasing size and expanding range of opportunities for the middle class were accompanied by a growing sense of the importance of economic independence and of the capacity of a man to establish his social standing through his own effort. Middle-class industriousness was thus accompanied by solemnity and sobriety and by a strong sense of the specific merits and distinctive nature of middle-class concerns with family life, with morality, and with religion.[11]

While middle-class women clearly benefited from the increasing wealth of their families, they were no more given new rights and freedoms by this process than by the French Revolution. On the contrary, the rise of the middle class and the whole process of industrialization in England was accompanied by an end of a traditional idea that families were income-earning units in which all members participated and by a new sense that income should be earned by the male household head, leaving his wife and daughters secure within the domestic realm.[12] For those middle-class men aspiring to the status of gentleman, it was necessary to demonstrate that they could support their wives and daughters in leisure. Thus the period from the late eighteenth century to the mid-nineteenth saw the gradual withdrawal of middle-class women from paid labour. The homes of the middle class were themselves undergoing change, with the development of suburbs and with a massive increase in the production of furniture and household goods. Looking after a home and a family thus came to require considerable amounts of labour and of supervision and was defined as a distinctively feminine activity.[13]

The importance attributed to women's domestic role is closely associated with the late eighteenth-century preoccupation with family life, romantic love, and with the importance attributed to the care and nurture of children.[14] The term 'family' itself changed its meaning at this time, as it came increasingly to refer to the unit composed of parents and children, in contrast to earlier meanings which had stressed either lineage groups or households with apprentices.[15] The role of mothers underwent a considerable expansion with the new emphasis on the importance of breast-feeding and on the importance of direct and close maternal involvement in the care of children. This elaboration of the role of mothers in the works of Rousseau and many of his followers has led to a strong sense that women were the central figures within the late eighteenth- and early nineteenth-century middle-class family.[16] This development has been seen as one which lessened the patriarchal privileges of men while enhancing the status of women and bringing into being a new companionate marriage and family.[17] But the relationship between women and the family which now received so much emphasis was complex and paradoxical, as the enhancement of women's domestic and familial role seemed both to suggest greater power and influence for women, and to re-enforce their economic and legal subordination to men.

This withdrawal of women from paid labour and their immersion in domestic duties was accompanied by extensive discussion both of the innate suitability of women for this sphere and of the importance of domestic life. In France, this view was expounded most powerfully by Rousseau, who stressed the need for female modesty to be protected within the home.[18] In England, the new discourse on maternity, which was more widely accepted, came from the moral and religious concerns of the evangelicals. It was their concern with the moral and spiritual consequences of the capitalist market that made evangelicals insist on the importance of the home as the centre of moral and religious life and on women as the central figures within the domestic religious community. Women's domestic piety became, for the evangelicals, a necessary counterpart to the rationalism and even brutality of the commercial world. Middle-class men would only retain their religious beliefs and their moral centre if persuaded to do so by their pious and beloved womenfolk.[19] The result, as Catherine Hall, Mary Poovey, and several others have convincingly shown, was that late eighteenth- and early nineteenth-century women faced an extraordinarily paradoxical situation. Their position as mothers was enhanced and expanded. Indeed, they were presented with a model of wifehood and motherhood in which the wife was not only charged with educating children, but with being a proper companion to her husband, consulted by him in all matters and having besides her familial tasks her own extensive philanthropic duties which brought her into close contact with the community.[20] This sense of the civic importance of maternity and wifehood, which was strongly endorsed even by the politically conservative Hannah More, created 'a pattern of female domestic heroism, an image of activity, strength, fortitude, and ethical maturity, of self-denial, purity and truth'.[21] But through all of this, women were expected to be the religious and moral guides and leaders of men to whom they were in every way subordinate. They were expected to raise the moral and religious tone of their family, household, and local community, and, through that, of the wider economic and political world—a world to which they were denied any direct access.

This emphasis on the need for women to confine their attention to the private world of family and home was occurring at precisely the moment when the notion of the 'public' world of political and civic concerns was being redefined and expanded. Indeed, this whole period has been seen by Jurgen Habermas as the one in which the concept of 'the public' came into being with the increasing power of public opinion as a major social and political force.[22] In England, the realm of civic activity for middle-class men expanded enormously at this time, as they set up and joined a range of new public and civic institutions, including learned societies and chambers of commerce, as well as becoming active in parishes, vestries, boroughs, and political organizations.

The question of women's relation to the public world at this time is a complex one. As we have seen, there was much theoretical and ideological elaboration of the importance of keeping the public and the private spheres completely separate—although such a separation was ultimately impossible. The involvement of women in family life and family businesses, in social and community activities, inevitably spilled over into the political realm as well. At the same time, the increasing medical, educational, and political concern about childbirth, family life, and education, and about the relationship between domestic order on the one hand and social and political order on the other, served to make women's private activities a source of public debate and discussion that showed the impossibility of these absolute distinctions between the public and the private in the very act of setting them up. The fact that the home became the centre of religious and social life also served to emphasize its connection with the wider social and religious worlds. Indeed, as Linda Colley and others have argued, despite the rhetoric of female domesticity, women's public and political activity markedly increased at this time as women began to appear and to be noted as patriots as well as in the guises of reformers or radicals.[23] The new emphasis on private and public and on the gendering of space served at least as much to make women's activities visible as to restrict their scope.

But while women clearly participated in some aspects of public life, the question of their connection with the political world was one that was the subject of enormous disagreement. For Rousseau, whose ideas were immensely influential in England at this time, the separation of the public from the private sphere, the confinement of women to the private and domestic world, and the establishment of an orderly domestic and familial life were not only important in themselves but were integral to the establishment and maintenance of social and political order. Rousseau's ideas were set out very clearly in his influential educational work *Emile*, which laid out the appropriate education, training, and domestic and familial structure for Emile, the representative male citizen, and for Sophie, his female counterpart. Emile, in Rousseau's view, needs preparation for the intermeshed roles of husband, citizen, and father, as progenitor of new generations of citizens.[24] Sophie, by contrast, requires a training in submission and domesticity in which constraint is central. She inhabits only the world of the private and the domestic because, in Rousseau's view, her complete exclusion from the public realm is the only possible way to ensure order. The confinement of women to the home serves to reform the public world, by withdrawing women from the promiscuous gaze of men—and it thus also reforms masculine behaviour by confining male sexual and emotional needs to monogamous family life. There is certainly no equivalence between public and private for Rousseau. On the contrary, while he emphasized the connection between sexual difference and different spheres, this in turn imposed on women subjection to a rule of silence and denied them any participation in the ethical life of the community, the area which gives value and purpose to actions. Women, in Rousseau's view, lacked any ethical sense and hence could not be guided by their own reason. They had rather to be guided by public opinion and the dictates of men.[25]

Rousseau offered the most detailed argument and discussion of any eighteenth-century *philosophe* to show that the natural rights of men were not general human rights, but were sex specific and appropriate only to men.[26] Where many others disregarded the question of women in relation to the rights of man, Rousseau provided an elaborate analysis of the differences between the sexes in their physical, intellectual, emotional, and moral natures, which, in turn, served to explain the importance of separate sexual spheres, of women's confinement to the home, and of men's dominance and women's subordination. His concern particularly about the sexual powers of women to enslave men made him insist on the need for women's sexuality to be contained within monogamous marriage under the rule of a husband. Moreover, for him the proper recognition of 'natural' sexual differences within the home and family were necessary to ensure the proper conduct of men as citizens within the state.

But Rousseau's views and the whole debate about the rights of man were amenable to other interpretations as well. While Rousseau emphasized the apolitical status of mothers, there were others who reworked his emphasis on motherhood in ways that had a distinctly political cast.[27] The republican political beliefs which accompanied the American and French Revolutions brought both demands from women for the rights of citizenship and a new emphasis on the importance of education, of the connection between domestic order and civic virtue, and a sense of the ways in which women themselves contributed to the public good through their care and education of their children and families. The notion of 'republican motherhood' which was articulated clearly in America and France and echoed in some English writing accepted Rousseau's ideas about the importance of maternal care and nurture, but stressed also the importance of mothers in the education and training of children and their duty to ensure that their families were imbued with civic virtue and patriotic feeling. Members of republican women's clubs in the early 1790s in Paris took oaths to 'persuade on all occasions my husband, my brothers, and my children to fulfil their duties towards the country'.[28] None the less, the subordinate position of women was clear. While the idea of mothers as the active carers and educators of their children was bringing a new sense of the importance and of the responsibilities involved in the private sphere, this feminine private sphere was constantly diminished by contrast with the expanding masculine public sphere of political, civic, and intellectual life, and of industry and commerce. Women might gain a sense of citizenship through careful mothering, but it was a limited citizenship, especially when contrasted with the growing demand for—

and in some cases the granting of—universal enfranchisement and direct political representation for men.

Recent scholarship in the history of feminism has stressed the need to see not only the ways in which liberal ideas and demands for natural rights could be applied to women, but also to recognize the extent to which discussion about the 'natural rights' of men was accompanied by a growing emphasis on the differences between men and women, in anatomy and physiology, and in intellect, emotions, and moral capacities.[29] The new scholarship in this field does not deny that the Enlightenment any more than the French Revolution or the process of industrialization were important for the development of ideas about women's rights. Rather, it rejects the idea that the spirit of the Enlightenment or indeed any of the central tenets of liberalism could be applied directly to the situation of women by exploring the complex and contradictory Enlightenment discourse on sexual difference. The Enlightenment insistence on human rationality and its connection with natural rights inevitably suggested the need to assert the rationality and the natural rights of women. But at the very moment that this suggestion was being made, the intellectual, moral, and physical differences between men and women were constantly being asserted and elaborated. At the same time, women were being directed along new paths and required to undertake new and special duties in the private and domestic sphere which re-enforced their dependence and demonstrated its connection with their physical and emotional nature.

Interest in eighteenth-century discussions about sexual difference has also served to highlight the redefinition of masculinity which was occurring at this time. Indeed, the whole debate about the rights of man, and the specific and clear gendering of those rights, is best seen in the context of the extensive redefinition of manliness and of masculinity which occurred in the course of the eighteenth century and which provided a counterpart for the new ideas on femininity. This redefinition of masculinity was very evident in discussions about the public sphere, but it was equally evident in much of that which centred on the family.

It is by now almost an axiom within the history of the family that the eighteenth century brought a decline in patriarchal authority, as an older authoritarian family, in which marriage was based on lineage and family interest, gave way to a closer-knit unit in which marriage involved ties of affection.[30] But arguably, this change brought a transformation of the form of patriarchal authority without reducing its power. The changing but none the less still-dominant role of men within the private sphere has recently become the subject of extensive historical interest as scholars have begun to look at the ways in which not only mothering but also fathering underwent significant changes, with the increasing eighteenth-century emphasis on the importance of the home as the site of education and of civic virtue. The emerging sense of a childhood as a special stage of human development, and one requiring particular kinds of care and attention, is important here. Locke's psychology and his educational theories, stressing as they did the need for parents to understand and care for their children, ensuring obedience through inculcating a sense of filial obligation, respect, and loyalty, indicate the nature of this new concern. Only by imprinting loyalty on a child's mind first by 'fear and awe' and later by 'love and Friendship', he argued, will the parent rest secure in the child's continuing fidelity.[31] Mary Wollstonecraft was one of many who greatly approved of Locke's educational ideas. 'A slavish bondage to parents cramps every faculty of the mind', she wrote, 'and Mr Locke very judiciously observes that, "if the mind be curbed and humbled too much in children; or their spirits be abased and broken by too strict a hand over them; they lose all vigour and industry".'[32] She believed that this excessively strict parental hand might itself account for the weakness of women, who were held under it more than boys.

But while these new educational ideas demand that fathers become less concerned with discipline and more involved in the education of their children, they do not bring any diminution in paternal authority. Looking at the family life and childhood of several women writers, including Fanny Burney and Maria Edgeworth, both Margaret Anne Doody and Beth Kowaleski-Wallace have argued that the girl child was especially vulnerable to the effects of Locke's programme. Although Locke's plan assumed that parents would work together, in fact the dominant educational role was that of the father, with the mother's role being purely ancillary. She acted as intermediary between father and child, but had no voice of her own. Because of her perception of the disproportionate status of the father in the domestic setting, a young girl would be particularly susceptible when her father turned his attentions to her tutelage. This transformation of fatherhood served to make the father the central and most important figure not only in the home but also in the emotional lives of children. Women's maternal and domestic activities provided necessary services, but offered nothing comparable to the knowledge or education offered by men. This, in turn, rendered educated women extraordinarily docile and dutiful—almost as a recognition that their education was a privilege which allowed them insights into and connection with the world of men.[33] Fanny Burney and Maria Edgeworth both provide examples of women who were not only closely identified with their fathers, but who subordinated their own talent and their work to paternal demands—and who shared the concern their fathers held about the need to control female sexuality and disorder.[34]

While men clearly had an honoured and even dominant place within the private sphere, women were excluded from any recognition within the public or economic sphere. Political Economy offers a particularly significant example here, in view of its importance in defining British social, economic, and political thought. Political Economy was concerned with defining and ascertaining the laws which operated in the market and hence with delineating in economic terms the 'public sphere'.[35] In the writings of the political economists, the public sphere was a fundamentally gendered one, the seat of masculine enterprise and activity, which contrasted with the private world of family and home—the proper location of women and children.[36] Hence political economy served in a powerful way to emphasize the distinctions between the public and the private spheres. Despite the qualms expressed by Adam Smith about the human and social consequences of industrialization, the basic assumptions of political economy provided a strong re-enforcement of the significance of masculine economic activity. If the wealth of nations was simply the accumulated wealth of individuals, each individual male was simultaneously benefiting his society and himself by every business or professional success he enjoyed. The emphasis on individualism which was so integral to the middle classes was thus automatically connected with a sense of social and civic responsibility.

Women had no place in this process. The preoccupation of political economy with the accumulation of wealth and with production, distribution, and exchange went along with an emphasis on industry and on manufactures: on factories and workshops, which were predominantly male places of work, rather than on the continuation of domestic and small-scale production in which women were engaged.[37] As a result, political economy had almost nothing to say about women's paid work or about their role in providing the capital, the techniques, and the sources of labour.[38] At the same time, and as an almost necessary consequence of the concern of political economy with the measurable wealth of nations, women's domestic and reproductive activities began to be classified as 'unproductive'. Despite John Stuart Mill's later attempts to insist that the term was used in a purely technical way, and

**21**

that 'unproductive' did not mean 'useless', Mill's very defensiveness serves to show how effective political economy had been in suggesting that in their domestic and familial roles women did not contribute to social and economic well-being.[39]

This claiming for men of the province of productive labour had its counterpart in the world of art and aesthetics, in new definitions of genius. As recent feminist philosophers have pointed out, Edmund Burke, in his *Philosophical Inquiry into the Origin of the Sublime and the Beautiful*, set up a contrast between the sublime and the beautiful which depends on the language of sexual power and sexual difference. The 'sublime', a term which had earlier been used to describe any natural phenomena which induced terror or awe, came through Burke to link natural greatness with masculine power, so that the awe which is produced by great creations is exemplified by powerful men—discharging their terrible strength and overcoming all obstacles—or by the awesome grandeur of the Alps, which themselves become masculine. By contrast, the beautiful, which is lesser both in its actual importance and in its capacity to inspire, is described in explicitly feminine terms as small, delicate, and graceful. The beautiful is the province of women, and is defined in terms of male heterosexual desire. This high evaluation of the sublime was accompanied by the increasingly prevalent assumption that creative power and genius required male physical strength and stamina. As Christine Battersby has argued: 'By the end of the eighteenth century, the Romantic idea of genius transformed it from a kind of talent into a superior type of being who walked a "sublime" path between "sanity" and "madness", between the "monstrous" and the "superhuman". The driving force of genius came from male sexual energies—connected to female emotions and sensitivity.'[40] The genius epitomized the male appropriation of female qualities—at the same time suggesting that these very qualities were more significant in men than was ever possible in women. Thus, while some eighteenth-century writers and many contemporary historians would argue that importance of women as wives and mothers was being greatly enhanced at this time, others would rather emphasize the changing balance between the sexes, as the world of middle-class men was expanding while that of their womenfolk was contracting and being focused more and more narrowly on the home.

These broad-ranging social and intellectual developments had a number of somewhat contradictory implications and results, in terms of the position of women and the demands for women's rights. On the one hand, there was a massive new emphasis on the importance of home, as the centre of consumption and of family life, both of which were presided over by women. Moreover, this very family was seen to have great importance in the civic world. On the other hand, every aspect of women's familial role served to emphasize their dependence. Mothering became a more important occupation involving more direct care of infants and more social and community responsibility. And yet, as Dorothy Thompson has recently argued, during this period, middle- and upper-middle-class women lost a lot of the power and influence they had wielded, both at a local and a national level.[41] They might have gained power in the home, but they did so at the very moment that their menfolk were demanding power in the public realm and the state. A new and more serious ideal of womanhood was emerging, but, at the same time, manhood was being exalted in new ways and in ways which served to emphasize the extent to which men embodied all human excellence. Modern feminism certainly made use of the enhanced role of mothers and of the domestic sphere as a gendered realm which gave women special duties and an expertise on which to claim rights and authority. In addition, however, it sought to contest prevailing ideas about sexual difference and gendered spheres and to combat the sense not only of the dominance, but also of the superior abilities of men, in which much of the late eighteenth-century adulation of motherhood was embedded.

## Mary Wollstonecraft and the Origins of Modern Feminism

Mary Wollstonecraft's *Vindication of the Rights of Woman* has long been recognized as the central text in late eighteenth-century British, or even Anglo-American, feminism. Despite the growing interest in the whole range of Wollstonecraft's work—including her published novels, reviews, travel writings, histories, and her letters—in terms of the broader history of feminism, it is the *Vindication* which remains her most important work. This is so partly because of its scope. It offers a powerful critique of women's education and of the assumptions surrounding marriage and family life. But even more important is its complex discussion of sexual difference and its elaboration of the ways in which constructions of femininity, both at an ideological level and in terms of the conduct of everyday life, serve the interests of male sexual desire. This work is significant also because of its extraordinary energy and its sense of the possibilities of change. For ultimately, it is the belief that a change in the gender order and a transformation of the sexual hierarchy is both desirable and possible that serves to differentiate feminism from a mere concern with the 'woman question'.

In the *Vindication*, Wollstonecraft set out the fundamental feminist demand that women be recognized as sharing with men the capacity and the right to be regarded as autonomous beings, entitled to recognition as citizens in the civic sphere. While demanding rights for women, Wollstonecraft made no attempt to deny sexual difference. On the contrary, she saw women as having quite specific social and familial duties. What she sought was rather the recognition that sexual difference occurred within a common humanity, and that it should cease to be seen and expressed in hierarchical terms.

Wollstonecraft's importance as the founding figure of modern feminism is accorded higher recognition now than it has ever been before. While the scope of her intellectual importance is constantly being extended, her life continues to stand as a symbol of the feminist revolt against constraint and convention. Virginia Sapiro and Barbara Taylor have perhaps made the most expansive claims for Wollstonecraft, demanding recognition not only of her place in the history of feminism, but also in the history of political theory. Wollstonecraft, Sapiro argues, added a new dimension to political theory by offering a 'means of stretching the liberal temperament to incorporate into political thinking explicit concern for the quality of personal relations and day-to-day conditions of the ordinary citizens'.[42] Taylor makes a similar claim in stressing the need to recognize the political dimension in Wollstonecraft's redrawing of the boundaries of political discourse to encompass personal relations and emotional experience.[43]

It is this insistence on the political dimension of personal and emotional relations which is the core both of Wollstonecraft and of modern feminism, and which makes Wollstonecraft's *Vindication* the 'founding text' of Anglo-American feminism. But it is necessary to stress the fact that the political and social turmoil of the 1790s provided the framework in which this connection between the situation of women and the political world would be made. Indeed Wollstonecraft's *Vindication* is emphatically a product of the French Revolution, directly inspired by that event and filled with revolutionary optimism in its sense that political revolution could bring a transformation of the social and domestic worlds. Wollstonecraft makes no explicit reference in her text to the other works which raise questions similar to hers—Olympe de Gouges' 'Declaration of the rights of

Woman' or the Marquis de Condorcet's essay 'On the Admission of Women to the Rights of Citizenship' which preceded it—and there is no evidence to suggest that she read these works. If she had, it is more than likely that she would have been repelled by their general political approach. De Gouges' appeal to Marie Antoinette, for example, would scarcely have appealed to her. But these works, like hers, serve very clearly to emphasize the ways in which the political debates about rights and citizenship during the revolution brought immediately to the fore the question of women's rights.

It was not only because of the political debates that it inspired that the French Revolution was important for Wollstonecraft. It marked an epoch in her personal life as well. The year 1791 was a particularly important one for her both politically and personally. Not only did it still seem as if the *ancien regime* could be overthrown and replaced relatively easily with a government concerned to institutionalize the rights of men, but it was also the year in which Wollstonecraft herself emerged as a leading figure, through the publication of both *The Rights of Men* and then through the *Vindication of the Rights of Woman*. *The Rights of Men*, which contains Wollstonecraft's strongest defence of the French Revolution, was written in response to Edmund Burke's critical *Reflections on the Revolution in France*. It gave Wollstonecraft a central place in the British debate about the revolution and thus served to bring her out of obscurity and to catapult her onto the national political stage.[44] A *Vindication of the Rights of Woman*, written in six extraordinary weeks after this, confirmed her position and established her as an independent author. She had recently become a regular journalist and reviewer for Joseph Johnson's *Analytical Review*, but her new fame meant that she could now turn to writing as her sole source of an income, rather than having to continue the hated tasks of being a paid companion, a governess, or a schoolmistress. Through her writings about the French Revolution, Wollstonecraft was thus able to make the question of women's oppression a major political issue. At the same time, her early enthusiasm for the Revolution changed her own life. Her later experiences in France in 1792 when, having journeyed alone to France, she not only witnessed the King going to his trial and the Terror, but also began her passionate affair with Gilbert Imlay, give a whole new meaning to the idea that 'the personal is political' and make Wollstonecraft's life as important as her texts in the history of feminism.

Wollstonecraft's enthusiasm for the early stages of the French Revolution was almost unbounded.[45] *The Rights of Men* shows very clearly her sense of the revolution as the embodiment of the central tenets of the Enlightenment and of liberalism. Her somewhat eclectic approach meant that she saw the revolution as enacting the ideas both of Locke and of Rousseau and thus as bringing about the liberal, tolerant and rational society for which she yearned.[46] In explaining her support for the revolution, she emphatically endorsed Locke's belief that: '[T]he birthright of man is such a degree of liberty, civil and religious, as is compatible with the liberty of every other individual with whom he is united in a social compact, and the continued existence of this compact.'[47] She was also a strong believer in natural rights. 'It is necessary', she insisted, 'emphatically to repeat, that there are rights which men inherit at their birth, as rational creatures who were raised above the brute creation by their improvable faculties; and that, in receiving them, not from their forefathers but, from God, prescription can never undermine natural rights.'[48]

Believing absolutely that society and social institutions should be grounded on reason, Wollstonecraft deplored Burke's appeal to tradition and to sentiment. 'I perceive from the whole tenor of your argument', she wrote to Burke, 'that you have antipathy to reason—want *feelings* to lead us.' But this was simply to ensure the continuation of traditional privilege and injustice. Burke might laud existing cultural and social institutions for their moral and aesthetic values, but in her view,

the civilisation which has taken place in Europe has been very partial, and, like every custom that an arbitrary point of honour has established, refines the manners at the expense of the morals, by making sentiments and opinions current in conversation that have no root in the heart, or weight in the cooler resolves of the mind.—And what has stopped its progress?—hereditary property—hereditary honours.[49]

As a radical democrat, Wollstonecraft believed very strongly that any profession or institution 'in which great subordination of rank constitutes its power, is injurious to morality' and makes men foolish and vicious.[50] Aristocrats and monarchs, like the army, the navy, and the Church, professions which depended on hierarchical structures, were thus all subject to her attack.

Wollstonecraft took issue particularly with Burke's sexual stereotyping and his depiction of women. In *The Rights of Men*, she singled out for particular comment the sexual attitudes behind some of his 'rhetorical flourishes'. She decoded his description of the return of the Royal family to Paris—' "amidst the horrid yells, and shrill screams, and frantic dances and infamous contumelies, and all the unutterable abominations of the furies of hell, in the abused shape of the vilest of women"'—somewhat acidly: 'Probably', she explained, 'you mean women who gained a livelihood by selling vegetables or fish, who never had any advantages of education; or their vices might have lost part of their abominable deformity, by losing part of their grossness.'[51]

Wollstonecraft's intense enthusiasm for the liberatory programme of the early years of the French Revolution, and her assumption that women, like men, were rational beings, explains the absolute fury which she felt when it became clear that women were being denied rights and freedom by those very revolutionaries who were demanding that men be liberated from traditional hierarchical structures and given new freedoms. The *Vindication* was specifically a response to the legislation which established a new system of education for boys, but not for girls. While demanding freedom and the right to judge for themselves as men respecting their own happiness, Wollstonecraft argued, French legislators were quite happy to subjugate women. 'Who made man the exclusive judge', she asked, 'if woman partake with him the gift of reason?' The argument that men, in denying women rights, thought they were acting to promote the happiness of women was only too familiar:

In this style argue tyrants of every denomination from the weak king to the weak father of a family; they are all eager to crush out reason; yet always assert that they usurp its throne only to be useful. Do you not act a similar part, when you *force* all women, by denying them civil and political rights, to remain immured in their families, groping in the dark?[52]

But what precisely were the rights of woman that Wollstonecraft sought to vindicate? There are two aspects to this question. First, she demanded a revolution in manners, based on a rethinking of conventional ideas about women's conduct and moral qualities in accordance with her belief that there was only one standard of human virtue and that it must be the same for men and women. The gendering of moral qualities appalled her. She singled out for particular critical comment 'modesty', the term that was so central to the discussions of women amongst Rousseau and his followers. The sexed meanings of 'modesty', so that in men it referred to 'that soberness of mind which teaches a man not to think more highly of himself than he ought to think,'[53] while in women it referred to a specifically sexual demeanour, infuriated her. Wollstonecraft sought to deny the existence of sexed virtues, demanding instead a single set of human virtues with the same meanings for men and women.[54]

But alongside the discussion of moral questions, Wollstonecraft also argued for the institutional and legal changes which followed from the recognition of women's moral autonomy: an education based on rational principles and which combined intellectual training with useful skills; an end to the sexual double standard; reform of marriage; and the admission of women to a range of fields of study and of paid employment which would allow them to be economically independent—Wollstonecraft specified the study of medicine and of business as possible professional pursuits, while recommending the study of politics and history as intellectual pursuits. Such activities would allow women an alternative to marriage, which was greatly needed.[55]

Although questions of rights and of citizenship were central concerns for Wollstonecraft, she did not go so far as to demand the enfranchisement of women. She hinted at her belief 'that women ought to have representatives, instead of being arbitrarily governed without having any direct share allowed them in the deliberations of government',[56] but did not pursue this in the *Vindication*, feeling that the very idea would 'excite laughter'. She pointed out, ironically, that women 'are as well represented as a numerous class of hard-working mechanics, who pay for the support of royalty when they can hardly stop their children's mouths with bread'. The very limited franchise which obtained in England at the time she was writing made her seek a definition of citizenship in other terms, ones which were more closely connected with family and local community. Hence what she argued for was a larger and more responsible role for women in the home—but one which would bring them independence from men and a direct role within the community. Thus, while not demanding the vote, Wollstonecraft connected every discussion of women's education, of motherhood, and of women's work in the *Vindication* with independence and citizenship.[57]

The novelty and radicalism of Wollstonecraft's ideas have long been the subject of debate and discussion. The importance of improving women's education, of emphasizing their minds and souls rather than their bodies, of redirecting that education away from accomplishments and towards a training of the intellect along rational lines, had long been advocated as a way of improving the situation of women. As Mitzi Myers and several others have shown, Wollstonecraft's educational ideas were shared by many of her contemporaries. Educational reform was advocated not only by Catherine Macaulay, with whom she was closely identified, but also by others, like Maria Edgeworth, who rejected any notion that they were champions of the rights of woman, but were concerned 'to determine what is most to our general advantage',[58] and even by some of those who believed in women's subordination, like Hannah More or Mrs West. The presentation of women as rational and educable, and the importance of education as a basis of prudent and successful marriage and of wise motherhood, was, moreover, the subject of much late eighteenth- and early nineteenth-century fiction: several of the novels of Jane Austen and Susan Ferrier's *Marriage*, for example, stress the connection between rational education and the training and control of feeling, having as central themes the contrast between education and wise marriage on the one hand, and ignorance, frivolity, and destructive imprudence on the other.

And yet while it is undoubtedly worth pointing out the resemblance between Wollstonecraft's ideas on education and the broad progressive current of her day, it is equally important to recognize where her views differed from those of her contemporaries. While many shared her sense of the importance of education, few accepted her belief that by carrying out their specific maternal duties properly, women were showing their entitlement to independence from men and to citizenship. For Wollstonecraft, the question of female citizenship remained a central one, connected in the *Vindication* with every discussion of women's education, of motherhood, and of women's work.

The being who discharges the duties of its station is independent; and, speaking of women at large, their first duty is to themselves as rational creatures, and the next, in point of importance, as citizens, is that . . . of a mother. . . . But to render her really virtuous and useful, she must not, if she discharge her civil duties, want, individually the protection of civil laws; she must not be dependent on her husband's bounty for her subsistence during his life, or support after his death—for how can a being be generous who has nothing of its own? or virtuous, who is not free?

In order to render women's 'private virtue a public benefit', Wollstonecraft argued, women needed 'a civil existence in the state' whether they were married or single, both as a means of improving their private circumstances and as a means of contributing to the common good.[59]

While her sense of the importance of women's social and civic contribution is a crucial aspect of Wollstonecraft's feminism, an equally important one is her explosive anger over the treatment of women in her day. Indeed, the *Vindication* is most powerful and interesting when read, not as a feminist programme, but rather as a passionate and angry protest against women's subordination and against prevailing ideas of sexual difference. The anger, which was the source of such concern to Virginia Woolf a century and a half later, seems to have been Wollstonecraft's driving force. It is almost palpable as one reads the *Vindication*. Her anger is only too easy to understand. Much of her own intellectual development had consisted of encounters with philosophers whose work she admired and found inspiring—but who denied to women intellectual capacities, education, and independence, and even, in some cases, any direct connection with human nature. The most important of these encounters was that with Rousseau, by whose writings she was initially entranced but many of whose ideas on women she deplored. She read him often and with pleasure, admired much of his work, and often identified closely with him, but, as she commented in the *Vindication*, 'indignation always takes the place of admiration, and the rigid frown of insulted virtue effaced the smile of complacency . . . when I read his voluptuous reveries'[60] on the subject of women. As a one-time teacher with a passionate interest in education, Wollstonecraft was particularly engaged with Rousseau's *Emile*. She greatly admired the educational ideals set down in the first four sections of *Emile*, but the contrast between Emile's broad education and Sophie's narrow training, devised explicitly to render her docile and obedient, appalled her. It was, as Christine Battersby has shown, 'her outraged reaction to this discovery that turned Wollstonecraft into a professional author. She wrote and wrote as a way of trying to work out how to modify and extend Rousseau's conclusions so as to include women.'[61]

But at almost every turn, well-versed as she was in eighteenth-century scientific and educational literature, Wollstonecraft confronted works devoted to establishing the bodily differences between the sexes and to showing how these differences led in turn to contrasting natures, capacities, and spheres of action. Her planned abridgement and translation of Lavater's *Essays on Physiognomy*, for example, a work which she greatly admired, presented her with lengthy analyses of men, while women were represented almost entirely in terms of their charm, beauty, gentleness, and grace, all serving to demonstrate their lack of gravity or capacity to take in information. Lavater acknowledged his own lack of understanding of women, shuddering at how 'contrary to my intention, the study of physiognomy might be abused, when applied to women'. He was thus engaged in writing a 'science of human nature', in which it was to him unproblematic that he had little to say about 'the female part of the human race.'[62]

Wollstonecraft's anger was also aroused by many of her personal experiences and observations: by the ways in which women were belittled and humiliated in so many aspects of everyday life, sometimes under the guise of 'gallantry'; by the suffering, the inadequacy, and the cruelty of her own mother and of the various women in whose houses she had worked; by her own sorry family history. Personal anger and anguish informed and gave life to her condemnation of the situation of women and to her demand for a radical reform in manners and morals that would be the sexual and domestic counterpart of the political revolution currently under way in France.

Wollstonecraft's criticism of Rousseau, and indeed of many other contemporary writers who set out to explain the nature and the duties of women, centred on their implicit and explicit denial to women of reason. As reason was the privileged signifier, differentiating humans from animals, the denial to women of reason was a denial of their very humanity. And this was extended through the denial to them of personality and character. Men, Wollstonecraft argues, 'are allowed by moralists to cultivate as nature directs—various temperaments, but all women are to be levelled, by meekness and docility, into one character of yielding softness and gentle compliance.'[63] As rational creatures, Wollstonecraft argued, women were essentially similar to men in their mental and moral make-up. They possessed both the reason and the passions of men. And Wollstonecraft was almost as critical of the denial to women of active sexuality or the capacity for sexual pleasure as she was of the denial of reason.[64]

But while rejecting so insistently the idea of sexual difference as applying to intellectual or moral faculties, Wollstonecraft none the less accepted the consequences of this belief when she endorsed Rousseau's belief that there is a natural division of labour between the sexes and that women's proper location and duties centre on family and home. Like many of her contemporaries, she supported Rousseau's insistence on the importance of direct maternal care, including breast-feeding, and of the role of mothers in the education of young children, seeing these activities as making mothering into a larger and more important function. Indeed, Wollstonecraft was scathing about those women who neglected the care of their homes and children in order to undertake other pursuits. Thus, while condemning Rousseau, Wollstonecraft herself offered an image of woman that was primarily located within the private world and largely reduced to a single bodily function. And for all her personal hostility to conventional family life, Wollstonecraft's own text included a set piece idealizing the family in very Rousseauian terms. Often, she wrote, when fatigued with insipid grandeur,

I have turned to some other scene to relieve my eye . . . I have then viewed with pleasure a woman nursing her children, and discharging the duties of her station with, perhaps, merely a servant maid to take off her hands the servile part of household business. I have seen her prepare herself and children, with only the luxury of cleanliness, to receive her husband, who returning weary home in the evening found smiling babies and a clean hearth. My heart has loitered in the midst of the group, and has even throbbed with sympathetic emotion.[65]

Motherhood was only occasionally bathed in this kind of sentimental and sexual glow, however. More often, as we have seen, it was connected with a form of female citizenship. But even while insisting on the civic nature of motherhood Wollstonecraft did not, as Moira Gatens has argued, challenge the asymmetrical relation between the citizen/father/husband on the one hand and the citizen/wife/mother on the other.[66] Moreover, this acceptance of sexual difference as the basis of social duty bound her to a view of women's duties which was as narrow and uniform as that which she protested against—and one which did not, in fact, allow for her own aspirations for women, or indeed for the life which she wanted for herself. She acknowledged this difficulty briefly: 'to avoid misconstruction,' she wrote, 'though I consider that women in the common walks of life are called to fulfil the duties of wives and mothers, by religion and reason, I cannot help lamenting that women of a superior cast have not a road open by which they can pursue more extensive plans of usefulness and independence.'[67] But at no point did Wollstonecraft elaborate on the need for such a road or the ways in which it might occur. Thus while Wollstonecraft's critique of Rousseau and his contemporaries is powerful and cogent, her own acceptance of some of their central tenets prevented her from setting out the future possibilities for women which she really wanted to see.

Wollstonecraft's belief in the possibility that sexual distinction could be overcome and that men and women could share the freedoms and the rights endorsed by eighteenth-century liberalism has been the subject of considerable criticism amongst recent feminist scholars. Her view that women could share the same rights as men ignored the extent to which liberalism itself presupposed a form of sexual hierarchy, in which men participate in the public worlds of politics and the market, not simply as individuals, but as male heads of households. The assumption within liberalism that there is a natural sexual division of labour, in which women remain predominantly within the home, caring for children and subject to the control and authority of husbands, is as much evident in the works of Locke as it is in the writings of Adam Smith and the political economists.[68] Although Rousseau was unusual in spelling out in detail the extent to which women's immersion in domestic and family life established the private world which guaranteed the stability and order of the public world—and hence the possibilities for men to be active citizens—the picture he drew is one that was assumed in various different forms in the whole liberal tradition on which Wollstonecraft drew.

Wollstonecraft was trapped here in what has remained one of the insoluble dilemmas for feminism. In seeking to recognize the importance of sexual difference and to explore the conditions and the needs of women, she focused necessarily on mothers. In so doing, she reduced all women to a single function—something not so very different from the levelling of all women to a single standard of meekness and docility of which she was so critical. And yet there was no other way in which she could insist both on the importance of sexual difference and on the needs for women to have a form of citizenship that incorporated or recognized that difference. Wollstonecraft sought to make motherhood as much as possible like a profession—hence her insistence on the active engagement of mothers in the nursing, educating, and training of their children. She sought also to separate motherhood from the sexual relationship of husband and wife, in her insistence that marriage should be based on friendship, that sexual passion was necessarily transient and, indeed, that it should be in order to allow both husbands and wives to carry out their social duties and responsibilities, in her argument that unhappily married women often made the best mothers—having more time to devote to their children—and above all, in her insistence that in order for women properly to carry out the duties of mothers they needed not only education, but also financial independence. Unless women were independent of men, she argued, it was impossible for them to develop virtue, to follow their own sense of duty, or properly to meet the needs of their children. But there was no way open to her to demand this without confining women in some way to a narrowly defined sphere. Thus even her dream of a future civic utopia included it. She hoped 'that society will some time or other be so constituted, that man must necessarily fulfil the duties of a citizen or be despised, and that while he was employed in any of the departments of civil life, his wife, also an active citizen, should be equally intent to manage her family, educate her children, and assist her neighbours'.[69]

Although Wollstonecraft attacked the masculinist assumptions prevailing in France in the 1790s and strove to develop a larger and more expansive sphere for women, her very language undermined her attempt to reconstruct womanhood. She followed the common practice of radical writers by using as her ultimate measure of praise or condemnation terms derived respectively from manliness or masculinity on the one hand or from femininity on the other. Thus she contrasted the 'effeminate court' of the *Ancien Regime* with the 'enlightened sentiments of masculine and improved philosophy' evident in 1790; or the effeminacy and sensuality of France with the masculinity of England: Louis XIV, she argued, inadvertently did his country some good, for by 'introducing the fashion of admiring the English, he led men to read and translate some of their masculine writers, which greatly contribute to arouse the sleeping manhood of the French'.[70] In the *Vindication* itself, dissolute aristocrats, like members of standing armies, were all described by her as emasculated or effeminate—lacking in the nobility of the common man. Wollstonecraft's insistence that it was hierarchical institutions and lack of fulfilling occupation which produced 'effeminacy' in men illustrates clearly her belief that character traits were determined by environment. This belief was important because it allowed her to be extremely critical of the women of her own day, without ever suggesting that women were inherently weak or inadequate. Rather, the characteristics which she deplored could be shown to derive from their lack of proper employment and their dependence, for these qualities were shared by groups of men who were similarly circumstanced. Yet at the very moment that Wollstonecraft was insisting that much of the weakness of women, like that of standing armies and aristocrats, resulted from their lack of education or of employment, her language inevitably served both to connect these dissolute beings with women and to re-enforce the idea that strength, nobility, and rationality were concomitants of certain forms of masculinity.

Wollstonecraft was not unaware of the problem posed for feminism through this privileging of masculinity, which in turn made it almost impossible to find adequate terms in which to praise women. She faced this problem when attempting to make clear her very high estimation of the historian and educational writer Catherine Macaulay.[71] Macaulay was an exceptional writer remarkable especially amongst her own sex. Her work, Wollstonecraft argued, 'displays a degree of sound reason and profound thought which either through defective organs, or a mistaken education, seldom appears in female productions'.[72] But she could only show how highly she thought of Macaulay by describing her as a 'masculine and fervid writer'! Her sense of the enormity of this appellation was made evident two years later. While writing the *Vindication*, Wollstonecraft was extremely troubled by the implications of her earlier article, refusing to call Macaulay's understanding masculine, 'because I admit not of such an arrogant assumption of reason'. What she wanted now was to claim Macaulay as a model of what women could be. Her judgement was 'the matured fruit of profound thinking, was a proof that a woman can acquire judgement in the full extent of that word'.[73] Macaulay was, in Wollstonecraft's view, 'the woman of the greatest abilities, undoubtedly, that this country has ever produced.—And yet this woman has been suffered to die without sufficient respect being paid to her memory.' And Macaulay also functioned as Wollstonecraft's imaginary friend and the only other woman of stature whose intellectual project resembled her own.

But this praise of Macaulay is unusual: unlike many later feminists who engaged in much adulation of womanhood, Wollstonecraft combined a defence of women's rights with critical, even hostile comments about specific women and indeed about the whole female sex. Barbara Taylor is surely right to comment on Wollstonecraft's capacity to speak '*against* her sex . . . sometimes with a misogynist intensity which appals the modern reader'.[74] Certainly Wollstonecraft's writings are filled with bitter denunciations of women who lavish more affection on their lap-dogs than on their children, or of women who play upon their physical weakness and delicacy, using their ostensible powerlessness and their sexual attractiveness as a means of gaining enormous and, in her view, completely irresponsible power. Far from seeing all women as powerless victims, Wollstonecraft feared that some, like 'despots, have now, perhaps, more power than they would have if the world . . . were governed by laws deduced from the exercise of reason'.[75]

Wollstonecraft's bewailing of the effeminacy of the French serves also to illustrate her strong sense of national and racial hierarchy. Wollstonecraft's European travels enabled her to expound at some length not only on the inadequacies of the French, but also on the uncouthness and lack of culture and civilization evident in Norway and Sweden. But, however lacking the rest of Europe was when compared with Britain, it was infinitely superior to Asia or North Africa. Originating what has come to be called 'feminist orientalism', Wollstonecraft could find nothing more telling to show her sense of the degradation of women in Europe than to compare it with that of women in China or the Middle East.[76] The picture of a desirable woman presented by Rousseau or Drs Gregory or Fordyce, Wollstonecraft argued, was similar to all intents and purposes to that of the inmates of a harem. Rousseau's ideas on women's education are for her the moral equivalents of Chinese foot-binding.[77]

Many of the ideas in the *Vindication* have been criticized by later feminists. Her refusal to deal more explicitly with the issue of political representation for women, for example, was a source of great concern to nineteenth-century feminists. From the 1820s until the 1890s, commentators constantly referred to the limitations of Wollstonecraft's approach. Her concern with questions of morals and mores, of behaviour, custom, and culture was hard to understand during a period when women were seen as moral arbiters, and when feminism was becoming increasingly programmatic in its concern with actual campaigns for reform and with parliamentary representation and legislation to bring about specific changes. By contrast, in the 1920s, once the vote was finally won, Wollstonecraft's *Vindication* was seen as a much more important work than any nineteenth-century text—precisely because of its concern with questions about the sexual double standard and the ongoing problems of sexual relations and family life.[78]

More recently, her reticence on questions about women's sexuality and need for sexual freedom have been the source of concern.[79] While mid-Victorian feminists found common ground with Wollstonecraft's emphasis on maternal duty, several contemporary scholars, most notably Cora Kaplan, Mary Poovey, and Joan Landes, have commented on the insistence on sexual restraint so evident in the *Vindication*, with its acceptance of women's sexuality as a destructive force, rather than any plea for greater sexual freedom for women.[80]

This is all the more significant because Wollstonecraft's own life came to represent for many the sexual revolution and the demand for sexual subjectivity implicit in the demand for women's rights. But it raises also a question about the relationship between the analysis and diagnoses of the nature of women's oppression on the one hand and the suggestions for change or reform on the other. As Kaplan argues, Wollstonecraft provides an extensive analysis of sensibility and pleasure as instruments of patriarchal control, showing how women's sexuality and dependency are constructed both in the existing state of society and in the writings of Rousseau. For her, women's sexuality is central to their oppression. However, rather than attacking the patriarchal construction and control of women through a demand for women's control of their own sexuality, Wollstonecraft insisted on a puritan sexual ethic for women centring on denial and familial duty rather than on active female desire.

This sense of the limitations of the *Vindication*, especially when it comes to discussing the questions about sexual difference and sexuality that have been so central to contemporary feminism, has directed the attention of a number of recent scholars towards Wollstonecraft's other writings, particularly her novels. For as Claudia Johnson has recently argued, while the *Vindication* and Wollstonecraft's other political writings insist repeatedly that virtue has no sex, the very form of the novel requires the representation of sexual difference and extensive discussion of the specificity of the female body.

Discussion of Wollstonecraft's novels has also brought to the fore the need to recognize that, in the very process of offering a radical critique of the social structures and conventions of her day, and of the sexual oppression of women, she was none the less closely enmeshed within a range of prevailing beliefs, assumptions, and ideas, some of which were embedded in the very forms she used. In *Mary*, her first novel, Wollstonecraft sought to explode the conventions of sentimental fiction, choosing to tell the story and to display 'the mind of a woman who has thinking powers' and whose desires extend beyond the bounds of a romantic plot. Nevertheless, as Patricia Myer Spacks has argued, the novel relies on many of the structures and devices common amongst the women who wrote romantic fiction in the late eighteenth century. Wollstonecraft subjected her heroine to the traditional series of hardships of such fiction, showing her compliance with parental wishes and her helplessness to go against the demands of her father; she follows the conventional pattern of heroines, doing only what is good, and manifesting intense loyalty to her friend and to her platonic lover. Thus in her novels, as Mary Poovey suggests, Wollstonecraft sets out to challenge the delusiveness of the 'romantic expectations' that trivialize women, only to be herself seduced by versions of those expectations within her own writing.[81]

Wollstonecraft's novels pushed conventional discussions of women's lot to extremes thereby problematizing them in new ways. Thus Spacks insists that *Mary*, while replicating many of the standard tropes of romantic women's fiction, none the less enforces a point not made in any other work: for Mary's goodness is not in any way rewarded, and her story serves rather to demonstrate that virtue finds adequate reward only in heaven. Wollstonecraft shows that the emphasis on women as marriageable and sexual beings can result in intense sexual loathing. Hence the novel contains the revolutionary message that happiness and marriage bear no relation to each other. Her heroine seeks the reverse of the conventional reward: the absence of marital ties. Therefore, while conforming in many ways to other similar fiction, *Mary* depicts clearly Wollstonecraft's 'fierce detestation of woman's lot. . . . More vividly than any fiction preceding it, *Mary* reveals how the novel might lend itself to a woman's purpose of complaint and opposition.'[82]

More recently, Claudia Johnson has argued the need to see the importance of the homoerotic element in the novel, to recognize the primacy of the relationship between Mary and her friend Ann—although the 'swerve' away from this primary relationship and its replacement by Mary's love for Henry, which is required by the sentimental romantic form, transforms a possibly emancipatory fiction back into an oppressively gendered novel.[83]

The question of heterosexual love and its possibilities is dealt with more directly and more powerfully in Wollstonecraft's final and unfinished novel, *Maria or the Wrongs of Woman*. This work is regarded by many as her most extensive and significant feminist work because of the ways in which it addresses questions about marriage and sexuality, and the problems faced by working-class women as well as those of their middle-class counterparts, and because of its concern with the relationships of women to each other: namely, the structures that make for their rivalry and the possibilities that exist for friendship.

In the Preface to *Maria*, Wollstonecraft insists that the novel is really one in which 'the history ought rather to be considered, as of woman, than of an individual'.[84] What is perhaps most significant about this is its sense of the absolute impossibility of satisfactory heterosexual relationships for women. After leaving a terrible and dissolute husband who sought only her money, and indeed for gain was happy to offer her to his friends, Maria loses and is finally locked in a lunatic asylum. There she meets and falls in love with an apparently very different man—who embodies the virtues of republican masculinity, in contrast to the dissolute aristocratic cast of her husband. But when she escapes from the asylum, helped and supported by the asylum wardress, Jemima, who has become her close friend, Maria is abandoned by her lover, Darnford. She plans suicide, but desists when her child is returned to her by Jemima. Eschewing heterosexual passion, she settles for female friendship, declaring that she will now live for her child. In this novel, as Claudia Johnson argues, Wollstonecraft reworks her earlier idealization of republican masculinity.[85] While the *Vindication* deals with Wollstonecraft's own hope for the emancipatory potential of this form of masculinity, *Maria* represents this hope as the madness from which she must be emancipated. The novel in this way demonstrates Wollstonecraft's own complete disillusionment with the French Revolution, both in terms of its general democratic potential and in relation to the position of women.

In planning this work, Wollstonecraft intended 'to show the wrongs of different classes of women, equally oppressive, though, from the differences of education, necessarily various'. Much of this is done through the story of Jemima, which offers a litany of the problems of poor women, detailing the perils and difficulties of domestic service, street prostitution, and work in a brothel. This novel explores intensely the ways in which women are forced to hurt and destroy each other: the asylum wardress, Jemima, tells of her remorse over an incident in which she insisted that her new lover force his previous mistress out of his house, even though the woman was pregnant and utterly dependent on him. For Jemima, too, this house was the only available shelter, and while she regretted her action later, she saw it at the time as her only way to survive. But as her telling of her own story shows, Jemima is herself able to recognize the ways in which women are set up as rivals and hence to overcome them. Subsequently Jemima befriends Maria and assists her in escaping from the asylum.

The Gothic form of this novel is extremely important in emphasizing Wollstonecraft's sense of the connection between marriage and incarceration. Both rape and prostitution are central to Wollstonecraft's discussion. Both are involved in the marital relationship itself, with its assumption that husbands need do nothing to render themselves attractive or desirable to their wives. Maria has no right to her body, to her inherited property or to her child, suffering as one of her greatest wrongs that of having a small baby torn from her breast. Marriage is itself a prison leading to other forms of imprisonment. The only escape, and the only alternative that is possible, comes through women's friendships with and loyalty to each other. The form of friendship envisaged here has few of the erotic overtones suggested in *Mary*. Rather it is a relationship which centres on maternal bonds, suggesting them as the central humanizing influence. Jemima not only engineers Maria's escape from the asylum, but she also finds her lost child, thus repairing Mary's blighted motherhood, and enmeshing herself in a relationship which will help repair her own blighted childhood. The three women constitute a new form of family, centring on maternal love and domesticity—but eschewing connection with paternal figures or heterosexual love.

The sexual restraint and the emphasis on the need for controlling and containing women's sexuality evident in Wollstonecraft's writings fits oddly with the image she has long had, as a romantic rebel, rejecting conventional moral norms and demanding unprecedented sexual and emotional freedom. Indeed, for most of the nineteenth century, Wollstonecraft's mere name was enough to invoke ideas of political anarchy and sexual impropriety. The moderation of her texts, and their initially favourable reception came to an abrupt end when the story of her life was published by William Godwin in his *Memoirs of the Author of the Vindication of the Rights of Woman*. Written as a way to assuage his grief after Wollstonecraft's tragic and unexpected death after the birth of their child, Godwin's intended tribute managed at one stroke to destroy Wollstonecraft's reputation and to ensure her infamy for nearly a century.

What most shocked both contemporaries and later readers of Godwin's book was the frank discussion of Wollstonecraft's emotional and sexual life: her infatuation with the painter, Henry Fuseli; her passionate and short-lived relationship with Gilbert Imlay, which ended unhappily, leaving her to care for an illegitimate child—and after which she twice attempted suicide—and finally her unconventional, happy, but tragically short-lived relationship with Godwin himself, which ended in her death after the birth of their child. The immediate impact of this work has been traced by Claire Tomalin and Claudia Johnson and it certainly resulted in a widespread condemnation of Wollstonecraft by anti-feminists and anti-Jacobins alike.[86] Indeed, for those seeking to demonstrate that advocacy of women's rights involved the destruction of the family, of morality, and of social order, Godwin's book was a positive gift.

But the power of Godwin's *Memoirs* should not be underestimated. His version of Wollstonecraft's personal story was a haunting and memorable one, from which she emerged as a great and tragic romantic figure, a martyr to feeling and sentiment, and a woman who had sought above all to live according to her own needs and ideals. She may not have been a radical democrat or a revolutionary, but she was certainly a larger-than-life, almost heroically tragic, romantic figure. At the same time, both in his emphasis on her powerful emotions and in his discussions of her written work, Godwin managed to question her intellectual capacities and interests and to undermine completely her own feminist project. Indeed, read in the light of most recent Wollstonecraft scholarship, what is most noticeable about Godwin's *Memoirs* is not so much its indiscretion about her personal life as its construction of her intellectual framework and outlook—its resolute refusal in any way to take seriously Wollstonecraft's ideas about sexual difference and sexual character or her insistence on the need to recognize women's capacity for reason. Wollstonecraft's extensive discussions and criticisms of prevailing views of sexual characteristics have no place in Godwin's work. Rather, Godwin used the most conventional of sexual terms and stereotypes to contrast himself and Wollstonecraft, arguing that each of them embodied in an extreme form the characteristics of their sex: he was the man of reason; she the woman of feeling. Her feelings, he argued,

had a character of peculiar strength and decision; and the discovery of them, whether in matters of taste or of moral virtue, she found herself unable to control. . . . her education had been fortunately free from the prejudices of system and bigotry, and her sensitive and generous spirit was left to the spontaneous exercise of its own decisions. The warmth of her heart defended her from artificial rules of judgement; and it is therefore surprising what a degree of soundness pervaded her sentiments. In the strict sense of the term, she had reasoned comparatively little; and she was therefore little subject to diffidence and scepticism. Yet a mind more candid in perceiving and retracting error when it was pointed out to her perhaps never existed.[87]

Godwin emphasized this picture of Wollstonecraft as enmeshed completely in emotions by describing her repeatedly as a 'female Werther'. Her letters, he insisted, particularly those to Imlay, 'may possibly be found to contain the finest examples of the language of sentiment and passion ever presented to the world'.[88] And Godwin used what he saw as the emotional tone and obsessive nature of Wollstonecraft's letters to Imlay to establish the framework through which he saw the whole of her life. Thus, in his memoirs of Wollstonecraft, the relationship with Imlay followed a pattern earlier evident in her passion for her adolescent friend, Fanny Blood, her painful entanglement with her family, and her feelings for Henry Fuseli. While emphasizing that she was a romantic completely immersed in emotion, he seemed to deny her interests or even feelings outside the circle of personal passion and desire. He explained her trip to France in 1792 purely in personal terms. 'The single purpose she had in view', he argued, was 'that of an endeavour to heal her distempered mind' after having become too closely involved with Henry Fuseli.[89] Her book on *The Rights of Men*, and her commission to write about the French

Revolution for Joseph Johnson were not sufficient for Godwin to recognize that she might have had other reasons for her visit, such as a deep interest in and commitment to the French Revolution. Predictably then, for Godwin, Wollstonecraft's French experience centred entirely on her personal relationship with Gilbert Imlay. Her interest and involvement in the French political upheavals of 1793 do not even warrant a mention.[90]

Godwin's emphasis on Wollstonecraft's femininity and her intensity of feeling also provided the framework for his reading of her work. Thus, while insisting that she be recognized as a genius, he used the term most clearly in relation to her early novel *Mary*, because of its sentiment and its 'true and exquisite feelings'.[91]

By contrast, he found the *Vindication of the Rights of Woman* wanting when 'tried by the hoary and long-established laws of literary composition'. It was too 'amazonian'. Although it showed a 'luxuriance of imagination, and a trembling delicacy of sentiment which would have done honour to a poet' it also contained sentiments of a rather masculine description and 'occasional passages of a stern and rugged character, incompatible with the true stamina of the writer's character'.[92]

Godwin unquestionably lessened Wollstonecraft's claim as a feminist theorist or as one claiming the political high ground for women. The fact that his views on both her life and her text provided the framework through which she was seen for much of the nineteenth century helps to explain her low reputation. When the *Vindication* was republished in 1844, his *Memoir* was incorporated into its Preface. The *Preface* also set what became a familiar tone in the second half of the nineteenth century in its critical approach to the work. The haste of its composition was seen as explaining its unwieldy style and the work was abridged:

some few passages that exhibited an unnecessary prolixity, or that had reference to circumstances that no longer exist, have been greatly abridged, and on one case wholly expunged. Care has been taken, however, not to enervate the author's masculine and nervous style, nor unnecessarily to soften down the strength and plain speaking of certain passages, because they might possibly give offence to the fastidious taste who have been imbued with the sentiments and feelings of a false morality. The object has been to make the work what the author herself would have made it, had she taken time and thought to do so, rather than to improve it.[93]

It is hard at present not to see Wollstonecraft as a somewhat larger-than-life figure who not only wrote the first modern feminist text, but who also symbolizes modern feminism in her personal revolt, her political involvements, and her constant struggle to live a full life which allowed her some autonomy, while meeting her sexual, emotional, and intellectual needs and desires. But Godwin's story served also to show the close connection so feared by conservatives between feminist political demands on the one hand, and personal immorality, chaos, and despair on the other. Godwin's portrait provided opponents with a perfect illustration of the ways in which unrestrained female passion was not only destructive of family life and social stability, but led to despair, attempted suicides, and a complete breakdown of any semblance of orderly life. At the same time, Godwin made Wollstonecraft a martyr to the cause of personal feeling and emotional honesty. For some, this made her also a martyr to the woman's cause. Hence, while accepting that in many ways Godwin did his wife a considerable disservice, I am also inclined to think that he gave her a power within nineteenth-century feminism which her published texts alone would not have produced. Through Godwin, Wollstonecraft's personal revolt, her refusal to comply with existing social and sexual mores, came to symbolize an undercurrent of feminism and an insistence on its connection with personal revolt and transgression that remained an undercurrent even in periods in which propriety was deemed to be the chief feminist virtue.

## Feminism and the Woman Question

While the French Revolution and the discussions about rights and citizenship provides one important context for the emergence of modern feminism, it needs also to be seen in relation to the widespread debate about women's nature, roles, and responsibility, which was so extensive in Britain in the late eighteenth century. Rebutting the ideas contained in an extensive array of the books which attempted to lay down for women their true nature, as well as outlining appropriate conduct and demeanour, was a primary target of Wollstonecraft's *Vindication* and serves to suggest how popular, and in her view how damaging, such works were. At the same time, there were significant critiques of and challenges to prevailing ideals of femininity in fiction and in a variety of other literary forms. All of this discussion made the 'woman question' an extraordinarily topical one, re-enforcing the close connection between the gender order and the social and political order and providing the framework which allowed for the emergence of feminism by the weight that it gave to discussions about women and about sexual difference.

Nowhere is the close connection between social and economic change in the late eighteenth century on the one hand, and concern with the gender order on the other, more clearly evident than in the massively expanding field of fiction. For every aspect of women's lives and a range of issues including seduction, rape, and prostitution, as well as marriage, motherhood, and family life were extensively dealt with in fiction. Moreover, while discussion of women's rights was frequently met with hostility and contempt, the wrongs of woman had become almost the staple subject-matter of fiction.

This exploration of the sufferings of women and of their subjectivity in the late eighteenth century, while clearly very significant, had a complex relationship with feminism. It was evident in the writings of both male and female novelists and did not necessarily raise questions about the legal status of women or the need to alter the sexual hierarchy. Samuel Richardson, after all, was the first major author to explore women's sufferings when subjected to male sexual violence, but *Clarissa* did not significantly enhance the status of women or offer an expanded view of their characters or capacities.[94]

What was probably more significant was the emergence of the woman writer at this time. The expanding literary market came to offer a paid occupation to substantial numbers of women, offering one of the few ways in which women could take advantage of the new opportunities which came with industrialization. Fiction allowed great scope for women because of its concern with the domestic world of family and private relationships and because it did not require the knowledge of classical literature still deemed essential for poetry and drama. This of course meant that, for the first time, large numbers of women were themselves engaged in the discussions, definitions, and delineations of femininity and of the lives, experiences, and sufferings of women. Some would even argue that women writers came to dominate the literary scene.

But the implications of this expansion in female authorship for feminism are complex. Looking at the work and at the social position of women authors, Jane Spencer has argued, that women only achieved their acceptability as writers at a very high cost. Unlike their predecessors, Aphra Behn or Eliza Heywood, writers like Fanny Burney and Ann Radcliffe gained considerable renown and even respectability. But their very acceptance weakened the earlier link between women's writing and feminism; once women's writing was no longer considered unfeminine, it ceased to offer a challenge to male domination. Rather women were confined to specific subjects—explorations of female characters and of the female condition. Women writers ceased to be censured as improper women, receiving instead 'tributes to their feminine modesty and morality'. In the process, they 'exchanged the freedom of the outcast for the conformity of the lady accepted on carefully defined terms'.[95] One the other hand, as Alice Brown suggests, fictional discussions and the very existence of fantasies about female heroines, unquestionably expanded the range of ways in which women could be thought about, allowing the potential to explore not only female sensibility, but also women's ideas, resources, and strengths in contrast with male weakness. Fiction written by women served, moreover, both to expand the range of attributes exhibited by women and to focus on women as subjects with their own point of view.[96] The Gothic novels of Ann Radcliffe are a case in point; as Marilyn Butler has argued, Radcliffe pushed further than anyone had previously done the novel's technique for seeing the world through explicitly female eyes.[97]

Increasingly literary scholars are suggesting the need for more complex ways of assessing this development. Patricia Spacks, for example, argues that eighteenth-century women employ the writing of novels both to affirm and to resist the social order that limits them. Most eighteenth-century novels by women dwell at length on the ways in which the outside world impinges on the personal, expressing also the fantasies through which women combat that impingement. Hence they offer an enthusiastic endorsement of the system, at the same time comprising a subtle mode of combat.[98] In a similar vein, Mary Poovey has argued that there is a constant and difficult negotiation between the ideal of female propriety and the activity of writing for women in the eighteenth century. The 'Proper Lady' cast a shadow across the careers of women who became professional authors in defiance of the strictures of propriety.[99] In her view, 'the very act of a woman writing during a period in which self-assertion was considered "unladylike" exposes the contradiction inherent in propriety: just as the inhibitions visible in her writing constitute a record of her historical oppression, so the work itself proclaims her momentary, possibly unconscious, but effective defiance.'[100] The difficulties of even trying to classify all late eighteenth-century women novelists in relation to feminism, or of establishing a clear feminist agenda within fiction are thus immense. Claudia Johnson has recently termed Burney, Radcliffe, Jane Austen, and even Wollstonecraft as 'equivocal beings', pointing to the ways they simultaneously attempted to imagine gender anew, reinventing masculinity as well as femininity, while at the same time remaining immersed in prevailing and traditional gender ideals and values. Johnson, as Catherine Stimpson suggests, shows the ways in which a writer's voice, viewed historically, will 'fragment into many voices—some imprisoning, some freeing, and some whistling in the dark'.[101]

Mary Wollstonecraft herself had a very strong sense both of the importance and of the limitations of the women writers who were her contemporaries. Her book notes and reviews for the *Analytical Review* make it clear that she was well acquainted with the work of many contemporary women writers. She read Fanny Burney and Ann Radcliffe with great pleasure, favouring especially Burney's early works, *Evelina* and *Cecilia*, which evinced 'the sagacity and rectitude of the author's mind, reflecting equal credit on her heart and understanding'.[102] Radcliffe's 'uncommon talent for exhibiting with picturesque touches of genius, the vague and horrid shapes which imagination bodies forth' was also something she admired.[103] She found in the writings of both women useful depictions of women's lives and heartening demonstrations of women's literary and intellectual capacities. Unquestionably, these women established part of the context in which she thought and wrote, helping also in her own attempt to insist on women's creative and imaginative capacities. At the same time, however, when writing the *Vindication*, Wollstonecraft made very clear her sense that she was writing alone: that while there were many women who repeated the strictures of Rousseau and who rendered women objects of contempt, the only woman whom she saw as engaged with the question that preoccupied her was the late Catherine Macaulay.

Wollstonecraft's rejection of the idea that women writers, by virtue of their very existence, contributed to the woman's cause has been reenforced recently as a result of new developments in literary biography. The once widely accepted idea that any expansion in women's range of activities was important for feminism has been powerfully questioned by a number of fascinating studies of late eighteenth-century women. Recent work on Fanny Burney, Hannah More, and on Maria Edgeworth have all pointed to the paradoxes evident in these women: in their abilities and achievements, on the one hand, and their denial of their own abilities or those of women generally, on the other. All three women were characterized by dedication and devotion to either actual or literary fathers, in the face of whom they were completely self-abnegating. Burney's desire to do no wrong and to gain parental approval for her work, Edgeworth's subordination of her own wishes and desires as a writer and More's infatuation with Milton and construction of literary fathers, all served to enmesh these women within patriarchal structures, which they, in turn, endorsed, seeing themselves as privileged by the care they received from fathers and internalizing the concern with women's unruliness and sexuality, which was so much a part of their literary and familial inheritance. Thus, while showing new avenues available to women, many of the notable women of the late eighteenth century set their faces firmly against any significant change in the prevailing gender order.

But while the feminist aims and intentions of women writers are more and more open to question, the eighteenth-century feminist agenda has become more extensive and more complex, suggesting the need to include works once largely ignored within it. In recent years, the importance of discussions about prostitution, together with questions about female desire and friendship, have come to be seen as a central feminist concern of the 1790s, alongside the preoccupations with women's education, rational marriage, and appropriate standards of motherhood.

The issue which has been subject to most discussion and disagreement in recent years, however, is the question of women's sexuality and their autonomous sexual desire. For some, this has become a matter of considerable concern—and discussion of it automatically entitles the discussant to feminist status. To others, the texts in which this issue is discussed are so problematic as to question profoundly their feminist leanings. This question, or rather the sufferings of desiring women through unsought—and unreciprocated—sexual desire, was a subject of particular concern to Mary Wollstonecraft's friend, Mary Hays. Hays' novels have been seen as feminist in their concern to depict women's sexuality and to deal with their demands to be recognized as sexual subjects rather than merely as the object of male desire.[104] But this reading is constantly countered by others which share Mary Wollstonecraft's own impatience with Hays' excessive emotionalism and see in her novels, not a feminist statement or demand, but rather 'the nuances of her own unregulated, openly confessed, and one-sided sexual passion for William Frend'.[105]

And Hays' novel *Emma Courtney* is a difficult one in terms of the history of feminism. The sufferings of Hays' eponymous heroine Emma make up the subject of the novel, but they seem almost to be self-inflicted and to result from Emma's own complete immersion in her emotions. Emma's sexual subjectivity is closely connected with her reading of Rousseau. Coming upon the *Nouvelle Heloise* in her father's library as a young woman, Emma was entranced by this 'dangerous, enchanting work'.[106]

In after years, when the death of her father deprived her both of a stable home life and of financial dependence, Emma is left prey to material hardship and to the powerful feelings unleashed by the reading of Rousseau. She conceives a violent passion for Albert Harleigh, the son of one of her friends, and is unable to do anything but suffer grievously and continuously in the face of Harleigh's refusal or inability to return her feelings. Attempts to reveal her own feelings or to elicit his produce nothing but humiliation. While Hays details Emma's feeling, she also makes it clear that this passion is not strengthening or energizing, but merely debilitating. Thus, while *Emma Courtney* serves to show the ways that women suffer from unrequited love, its quivering heroine seems to suggest no alternative possibilities for women. At the same time, Hays' novel does show how hard it was within the literary conventions of the late eighteenth century to deal in any acceptable or sympathetic way with women's sexual passion.

This question of women's sexuality, and indeed the broader one of how to read eighteenth-century women novelists, have also frequently been raised in relation to Fanny Burney. The question whether or not Burney should be seen as a feminist novelist has been subject to much debate in recent years. Some scholars argue that only her last novel, *The Wanderer or Female Difficulties*, is unquestionably a feminist one, while others insist that the concern with female difficulties—difficulties in gaining an income, in establishing their identity, in escaping unwanted male attention—is central to all her novels, pointing to her concern about the central feminist issues of the time. But this view is countered by opponents, who maintain that even in this last novel Burney upholds traditional notions of gender, even as she protests them, and that the themes of all her novels are really determined by their genre, rather than by their preoccupation with gender.

Burney's final novel, *The Wanderer* (which was written in the 1790s, but not published until 1814), continues and extends the themes evident in *Evelina* and *Camille* in its concern with women's uncertain social location and their personal vulnerability. But it adds to them a detailed discussion of the problems women face when suddenly penniless and friendless, of the tyranny which is exercised over women by conventional assumptions about propriety, and of the question of women's own emotions and desires. Burney's work, too, is a difficult one, with plot contortions that are almost impossible to understand. In this case, it is not the heroine, but a subsidiary character, Elinor

Joddrell, who rejects a proffered suitor, falling in love instead with his brother, and demanding the right to love and to speak her love. Elinor explicitly connects her passion with the Rights of Woman.[107] Why, she asks, for so many centuries,

has man alone been supposed to possess not only force and the power for action and defence, but even all the rights of taste? . . . Why, alone, is woman to be excluded from the exertions of courage, the field of glory, the immortal honour of death? . . . must even her heart be circumscribed by boundaries as narrow as her sphere of action in life? Must she be taught to subdue all its native emotions? . . . Must her affections be bestowed but as the recompense of flattery received; not of merit discriminated? Must everything that she does be prescribed by rule? . . . Must nothing that is spontaneous, generous, intuitive, spring from her soul to her lips?[108]

Elinor's questions do not persuade the man she loves to do anything but pity her. On the contrary, they serve if anything to confirm his love for the docile Juliet. Thus these questions remain unanswered in the novel and the comic form in which they are asked suggests that they are not only unanswerable, but somehow ludicrous.

However one reads Burney's novel, it adds another vital element to the whole question of the history of feminism through the very fact that it takes up and reworks some of the ideas of Wollstonecraft and of Hays. In its use of names, its selection of specific incidents, and its general themes, the novel makes constant references both to Wollstonecraft's *Maria—or the Wrongs of Woman* and Hays' *Emma Courtney*, thus very clearly showing not only the importance of female literary traditions, but also the ways in which questions about women's status and oppression and feminist demands were being consciously addressed within fiction and were thus being made current to a wide reading public.

During this period, before the advent of an organized women's movement, the fictional discussion of feminist questions and texts is particularly important. For while Wollstonecraft's name was rarely mentioned during the period of anti-Jacobinism and of conservative reaction after her death, her influence and importance can still be seen in the various literary works that discuss and rework her ideas—even though, as in Burney's case, this reworking serves almost to undermine them. In the works of Jane Austen too, one can see what has been called a 'conservative recuperation' of Wollstonecraft, as Austen extolled the female education and showed the superiority of the kind of rational motherhood possible only to educated women compared with the sentimental and misdirected motherhood evident in women who lived through their emotions and emphasized their own femininity.[109] But while Austen may have offered a critique of prevailing ideals of masculinity, and a sense of the need to remake manhood, far from criticizing marriage or questioning the possibilitie of heterosexual relations, most of her novels seem to be directed towards a new and improved companionate marriage and thus towards a modest reform of the status quo.[110]

While a concern to discuss Wollstonecraft's ideas or preoccupations within fiction clearly makes them important within the history of feminism, equal weight probably also needs to be given to some of those who most disliked and most emphatically rejected Wollstonecraft— and spoke out most strongly against her ideas, and indeed against the notion that women were oppressed. The key figure here is Hannah More. For while More stands out as one of the most conservative of late eighteenth-century women writers, insisting on both the benefits and the importance of their subordination, and advocating an education which stressed obedience, patience, and humility and which taught them to 'distrust their own judgement', she has long been seen as an important figure within the history of feminism.[111] In part, this is because of the example of her life and the importance of her own work. Just as the emergence of women writers has clear implications for feminism, so too has More's work to expand the role of women in philanthropy and in education and to set up Sunday schools become part of the history of feminism. Ray Strachey, in her classic history of British feminism, commented on the irony involved in the fact that Miss Hannah More, Mrs Trimmer,

and the other good ladies who started the Sunday School and cottage-visiting fashions were the founders of a movement which would have shocked them so profoundly; but it is clearly true. When Hannah More and her sisters began personally to teach the wild children of the Cheddar Hills they opened up a new field of activity for women. It is true that their educational ambitions were extremely limited. . . . But all the same . . . she [sic] was marking out a new sphere for the young women of the middle classes, and their revolt against their own narrow and futile lives followed as a matter of course.[112]

Strachey was of course right that More would have been outraged at this suggestion that she was a pioneer in the women's movement. She regarded any discussion of women's rights as 'impious', maintaining that she had more than enough freedom for herself, and that women desperately needed and greatly benefited from their subordinate position.[113] A single woman herself, More was adamant about the need for women to marry and to be contained within a home and family. She was appalled at the anarchic sexual and social possibilities open to women, explaining at great length, both in her *Strictures on the Modern System of Female Education* and in her novel *Coelebs in Search of a Wife* how important it was for women to have proper education and guidance at home, to obey their parents completely, trusting to their wisdom in the choice of marriage partners, and devoting their attentions to family matters. Young men, in turn, were severely warned of the dangers they would face if they contemplated marriage with a woman met in a public place, rather than in a known family circle.[114]

Hence More, both in her activities and in her actual arguments, gave greater scope to the issue of women's emancipation than she wished ostensibly to do—and in the process served to show how difficult it was to broach the 'woman question' at all without raising questions about women's emancipation. In More's case, one might see this as connected with an underlying ambivalence in her own position, but the issue extends beyond her to the point where it is necessary to recognize the extent to which the very proliferation of discourses on femininity and the obsession with defining precisely the proper education, role, and conduct appropriate for women served to undermine the idea that the prevailing role of women was part of the natural order and to render it problematical. Every time the necessary inferiority and subordination of women was insisted upon, repressed alternatives were also evident.

At the same time, some would argue that More was herself both reflecting and advocating a rising standard of education for women, based on rational training and moral principles rather than show and inculcating self-restraint and self-discipline. While she was appalled by and reacted strongly against Wollstonecraft, seeing both her work and her life as abhorrent, More shared with Wollstonecraft a sense of the importance of raising the status of women within the domestic and familial sphere. Mitzi Myers and Marilyn Butler have both insisted on the need to see More, like Maria Edgeworth, as similar to Wollstonecraft in their demand for improved education for women, their ideal of a marriage based on friendship and on duty, and in their insistence on the importance of women's activities and role within a local community.[115] While none of this makes one wish to claim More as feminist, the similarity between her and Wollstonecraft on some points serves in turn to suggest the conservatism of some of Wollstonecraft's ideas and of her approach to questions about women's education and family life.

Overall, More serves like Fanny Burney and Jane Austen, to show how important it is to go beyond those specifically committed to the project of women's emancipation in writing a history of feminism. The debate about them and their work shows how complex the borders of feminism are, while indicating the extent to which feminist concerns or their refutation became part of the dominant middle-class culture at this time—thus keeping alive feminism, even though it was advocated only by a very few.

## two

# FEMINISM AND THE WOMAN QUESTION IN THE EARLY NINETEENTH CENTURY

The period after the death of Mary Wollstonecraft raises many complex issues for historians of feminism. It is generally accepted that feminist debate and discussion ceased completely at this time. The French Revolution and the wars that followed them brought a powerful conservative reaction which made any suggestion of political and social reform all but impossible. And within this context, any suggestion of the need for women's rights or for changes in sexual relations or family life invoked developments in France and raised fears, not only of revolution, but of contaminating British ways of life with French ideas. The sense of Britain as exemplified by manliness, which was accepted even by Wollstonecraft, had as its counterpart a sense of France as excessively feminine and as a country in which women had too much power. Thus traditional family structures and ideals of masculinity and femininity came increasingly to be seen as a central and defining part of British life.[1] Godwin's revelations about Wollstonecraft confirmed both the anti-French sentiment and the counter-revolutionary belief that the discussion of women's rights·was inseparable from political subversion and personal immorality, ensuring that Wollstonecraft's ideas were not generally discussed or elaborated for some decades.[2] But this very conjunction of France with a fear of femininity and of women's power raised sexual anxieties and made questions of gender central political ones.

It was not until the 1820s, with the emergence of utopian socialist ideas of social transformation and the renewal of interest in broad-scale social, parliamentary, and legal reform, that radical demands for the emancipation of women were put forward. But this is not to say that there were no significant feminist developments in this period. On the contrary, the intense debate about the nature of women, marriage, and family life, and the increasing emphasis on the rationality, seriousness, and moral capacities of women, which was evident both in serious fiction and in much religious literature, continued to raise questions about the nature and the situation of women.[3] The discussion that made up the 'woman question' at this time offered a redefinition of womanhood which was central to much nineteenth-century feminism.[4] In this period too, women were becoming increasingly active in a range of public activities. During the wars with France, women became involved in patriotic endeavours, raising money for objects that ranged from statues of the Duke of Wellington to shoes for the militia, and, in the process, establishing a civic role for themselves.[5] At the same time, women were becoming increasingly involved in British philanthropic and abolitionist circles, moving beyond a supportive role by setting up their own groups and organizations. Few philanthropic or abolitionist groups voiced feminist demands at this point, although they were beginning to emerge.[6] But as Claire Midgley has recently shown, abolitionist activity both expanded the range of women's public involvement and provided women with 'the skills, self-confidence, connections, sense of collective identity, and commitment to public and political activism' that provided the basis for organized feminism.[7] Thus this period was one in which a number of new activities for and ideas about women came to the fore, many of which had a bearing—albeit a complex one—on later feminist activity.

The development of British feminism during this period, as in the preceding one, was closely linked to events and developments elsewhere, particularly in America. In the 1790s, France had the commanding position in establishing the framework for the demand for women's rights. French developments continued to be important: the ideas of Fourier and of the Saint-Simonians in particular were known to and influential for many radicals and Owenites.[8] But the size of their following was small. Increasingly from the 1820s onwards, British feminism was more strongly influenced by the American abolitionist movement.

It was no more the case in England than in America that feminism and anti-slavery were simply two sides of the same coin.[9] Opposition to slavery and to the slave trade had been voiced by many prominent women at the turn of the eighteenth and nineteenth centuries, including radicals like Mary Wollstonecraft, Helen Maria Williams,[10] Unitarians like Anna Letitia Barbauld,[11] and conservative and evangelical women like Hannah More.[12] But as even this rudimentary list of concerned abolitionists makes clear, opposition to black slavery did not necessarily entail rejection of the prevailing sexual hierarchy. On the contrary, many abolitionist organizations perpetuated existing ideas about the appropriate sphere and behaviours of women, welcoming them as subscribers but rarely permitting them either to be on committees or to petition Parliament.

None the less, abolitionist activity provided a positive focal point for women's organization and political involvement, with the first specifically female Anti-Slavery Society being formed in 1825.[13] Such societies proliferated in the next two decades, often providing the 'cement' of the networks, the labour and the funds which kept the whole abolitionist movement going.[14] While some women took pains to stress that their abolitionist involvement was an extension of their religious and philanthropic work, and consonant with the strictest codes of female propriety, the very existence of women-only societies, with their petitions, their distribution of tracts, and their attempts to organize and expand support for the movement as a whole, made women more visible by extending their range of public activities. In some societies, such as the pivotal Female Society for Birmingham, the situation of female slaves, and the particular need for women to address the sexual side of slavery, was explicitly addressed and, as Claire Midgley has argued, the women's abolitionist societies that emerged at this time marked 'the change from abolition as an individual woman's commitment to antislavery as a collective female endeavour'.[15]

The problematic nature of the feminism of the 1820s can be seen most clearly if one focuses on the outspoken criticisms of women's oppression and of the legal and social institutions which perpetuated it amongst radical liberals, radical religious groups like the Unitarian followers of W. J. Fox, and some Owenites involved in the Cooperative movement. These groups have always had a central place in histories of British feminism, and deservedly so.[16] Some of them were very much influenced by Wollstonecraft. Indeed the connection between personal rebellion and feminist commitment, which Wollstonecraft had already come to represent, had a strong resonance with the experiences and the ideas of many of those involved both in the Owenite movement and in Unitarian circles who were seeking greater personal and sexual freedom as well as social, legal, and political reform of the situation of women. At the same time, the central point of Wollstonecraft's emphasis that she was protesting for and on behalf of her own sex had only a little echo at this time. There were, as Barbara Taylor has shown, able and eloquent women within the Owenite movement, who spoke and wrote at length about the oppression of women, amongst their own community as well as in the wider society.[17] And yet their voices even then were muted, heard by few and short-lived, while the most powerful and longest-remembered voices raised to protest against women's oppression were male ones—and male voices, moreover, which were critical of Wollstonecraft and of the efforts of actual women to bring about their own emancipation. William Thompson's *Appeal*, for example, was reread throughout the nineteenth century, while Anna Wheeler was known only through the comments that he made about her.[18] Thompson's only comment on Wollstonecraft was a pitying one, referring to her martyrdom—a comment which fitted well with his overall depiction of women as absolutely enslaved and pitiful and hence as unable to resist in any effective way their oppression.[19] While his work showed great sympathy with the plight of women, like John Stuart Mill, he tended through this very sympathy to deny women the agency and autonomy which is integral to feminism.

This emphasis on women's enslavement and incapacity to assist or defend themselves was evident also in the writings of other sympathetic men, including the Unitarians W. J. Fox and W. B. Adams. The dominance of male voices was accompanied by a sense of priorities which were determined by the personal needs and predicaments of the men themselves—rather than by any recognition of the priorities of their female associates and companions. W. J. Fox, for example, wrote at great length and very movingly about the enslavement of women in loveless or brutal marriages which they were unable to end. But Fox was himself facing the problem of how to end a marriage which had become irksome—and to enter into a relationship with a younger woman whom he loved.[20] And while he was eloquent on this subject, he was much less concerned with other aspects of women's oppression.

This sense of a masculine voice expounding the truths of feminism was not only the result of the interest taken in the subject by sympathetic men. For women too adopted male personae in writing about their sex. The most prominent woman to address the question of women's oppression at this time, Harriet Martineau, mostly wrote under a male persona—adopting in her early essays the *nom de plume Disciplus*, the masculine form of Latin for 'learner', and only much later actually identifying herself as a woman speaking for her own cause.[21] And there were few countervailing female voices speaking directly of women's experience or plight with any self-conscious attempt to write on behalf of their sex. The woman who dramatized and protested most eloquently against her own sufferings, Caroline Norton, was, like Florence Nightingale a couple of decades later, completely disinclined either to speak on behalf of her sex or to use her own experiences to demand women's rights in any broad way.[22] Rather, Norton made a point of accepting that women were weak and inferior to men—seeking from men the chivalry which was appropriate to their strength—rather than demanding justice for her sex.[23]

In thinking about feminist traditions, and about the importance of the ideas and activities of one generation of women for their predecessors, it is necessary to move beyond the radical circles either of Wollstonecraft and Godwin or of the Owenites and the Unitarians. For the currency of radical ideas was limited, within later middle-class feminist circles, which were much better acquainted with the very wide-scale debate about women's nature and their domestic, social, and religious duties that constituted the early nineteenth-century discussion about 'woman's mission'. The almost continuous discussion of women's sphere, of the meanings of sexual difference, and of the whole gender order which was so widely canvassed in scientific, religious, and literary circles, generated a language and a series of ideas about women which later feminists sought both to appropriate and to oppose. The growing emphasis on the moral and religious aspect of women's domestic responsibilities, the shifts in ideas about the proper basis of marriage and in the activities which constituted responsible motherhood were clearly reflected in mid-Victorian feminism. Indeed, the feminist heritage of the early nineteenth century, at least in so far as it was taken up in the mid and later part of that century, seems to comprise almost more of the evangelical and conservative elaboration of women's domestic role and duties than it does of the radical criticisms of women's economic, political, and sexual subordination to be found in the radical and socialist press.[24]

## Men in Feminism: William Thompson and the Unitarian Radicals

The first dramatic new note which was sounded in British feminism in the 1820s was the demand for political representation for women. This issue had been broached but not developed by Wollstonecraft. It became a matter of much more concern in the 1820s with the renewal of interest in parliamentary reform. As in the late eighteenth century, the explicit exclusion of women from the rights and privileges being demanded for men provided the stimulus for the writing of feminist texts. Where Wollstonecraft was responding to Rousseau and to the political and educational developments in France in the early 1790s, in England in the 1820s and 1830s it was James Mill's influential 'Article on Government' which provided the necessary goad, becoming the central focus for William Thompson—and also for Harriet Martineau.

Mill's essay, as Barbara Taylor has argued, serves to demonstrate the narrowing of liberal ideas which had occurred since the 1790s.[25] Neither women nor working-class men needed to be granted political rights in a representative system, Mill argued, women because 'the interest of almost all . . . is involved either in that of their father or in that of their husbands',[26] while working-class men would be looked after by 'the most wise and virtuous part of the community, the middle rank'.[27] The needs and interests of working-class women did not even rate a mention.

Mill's ideas about women were powerfully attacked by William Thompson, whose *Appeal* remains the best-known feminist text of the early nineteenth century. Thompson was appalled by the contempt Mill expressed for women, which was well illustrated by Mill's assumption that women ranked alongside children with no entitlements or rights. His anger and disgust serve to make the *Appeal* into a passionate attack on what he saw as women's complete sexual and domestic slavery. Writing within the context of the sexual radicalism of the Owenites, Thompson clearly felt a greater freedom to deal with questions about women's sexuality than had been evident a couple of decades before, and his open assertion of women's sexual desires and their entitlement to sexual satisfaction is one of the most interesting aspects of his work.

Thompson began his attack on Mill by pointing to the internal contradictions in Mill's argument. Mill himself had insisted on the natural tendency of men to seek to increase their power over the actions of others, so that, unless restrained by external checks it would 'reduce each and all, . . . to the condition of Negroes in the West Indies'.[28] In view of this, Thompson argued, it was absurd to suggest that the interests of either women or workers would be safeguarded and protected by others. Disputing Mill's assumption that the interests and happiness of women and children were bound up with those of men, Thompson set himself to inquire in detail as to whether such an identity of interest did in fact exist between women and their husbands or fathers. Not surprisingly, he concluded that it did not.

Thompson's work stressed the need to see and understand the different situations and problems faced by different groups of women. He thus continued the disruption of the general category 'women' which was evident in Wollstonecraft's final work, *Maria*. Thompson divided women into three separate categories: wives, adult daughters in their father's establishment, and women without either husbands or fathers. His formal purpose was to show how, in each case, Mill's claim that women did not need direct representation was wrong. But it allowed him also to look at the different situation of each group and to explore the particular dimensions of their oppression. Where Mill assumed that all women were wives, Thompson delineated with care the situation of daughters, one of the central categories of concern in much nineteenth-century feminism. He insisted that the interests of daughters were no more contained in those of fathers than were the interests of sons—and no one thought to deny adult men political rights because their fathers had them. Adult daughters suffered almost as much as wives: shut out from education, they were denied purposeful activity and kept confined within the domestic world.[29] Their daily misery was similar in many ways to that of wives, resulting from the same cause: the denial to them of the enjoyment or development of their full human potential. But the case of wives was even worse and Thompson joined the long line of those who compared the situation of married women to slaves. Working closely with Mill's image of Negro slavery in the West Indies, Thompson insisted that married women lived under a contract which was very similar to that of a slave contract. Women had no more capacity than slaves to determine the nature or conditions of the marriage contract and, like slaves, on marriage, they became 'the movable property, and ever obedient servant to a husband who was also their master'.[30] Anticipating John Stuart Mill, Thompson insisted that the position of married women in England was even worse and more degrading than that of some West Indian slaves because of their personal bondage to their master—and because they were required not only to be obedient, but to appear voluntarily to accept, even to desire, their subordination.[31]

Hence while James Mill insisted that the happiness of women was contained in that of men, Thompson argued the reverse. Women, in his view, and particularly married women were '*more in need* of political rights than any other portion of human beings'. Through marriage, they were in a situation in which they were controlled by the superior strength of men as well as 'having been reduced, by the want of political rights to a state of helplessness, slavery, and of consequent unequal enjoyments, pains, and privations'.[32] Political rights were essential if women were ever to emerge from this state.

Like Anna Wheeler, whose ideas he claimed to be articulating, Thompson was an Owenite, sharing Robert Owen's belief in the need for a complete transformation of society by ending competitive capitalism and developing a harmonious system of co-operative labour. He believed that women's oppression would end only with the establishment of complete equality in all matters of civil and criminal law, the opening to women of all public offices, and a transformation of society on the lines of co-operation. Hence while the form of Thompson's work was dictated by his desire to provide an exhaustive refutation of Mill's argument, its ultimate aim was the advocacy of a co-operative system as the only one which could emancipate women. Thompson saw the competitiveness required by capitalism as particularly damaging to women because their 'permanent inferiority of strength, and occasional loss of time in gestation and rearing infants—must eternally render the average exertions of women in the race of the competition for wealth less successful than those of men'.[33] The greater capacity of men to accumulate wealth contributed to their view of themselves as more important than their dependent wives. This emphasis on wealth served also to deny proper acknowledgement of or compensation for the pains and privations women suffered in childbirth.

By contrast, the system of 'Labour by Mutual Co-operation' centred on community rather than on individual household units. It would thus incorporate both working and living arrangements, allowing all men and women to contribute in the way most appropriate. Co-operative living would end women's domestic drudgery and confinement to a home by offering a community-based form of child care; and it would also end women's financial dependence on their husbands. It was, in Thompson's view, the only scheme of social arrangements 'which will completely and for ever insure the perfect equality and entire reciprocity of happiness between women and men'.[34] The co-operative system would also solve one of the other great problems women faced: their exclusion from education, which, in turn, meant that they 'lose the immense accession to their happiness which intellectual culture would afford'.[35]

Thompson's attack on marriage and on the overall situation of women followed Wollstonecraft in its emphasis on the role of male sexual licence and profligacy in the degradation of women. He was scathing of the ways in which men directed women's lives solely for the gratification of their animal appetites. But he was rather more outspoken than Wollstonecraft in his condemnation of the ways in which existing sexual morality privileged male desire while refusing even to recognize its existence in women. Woman, Thompson argued, and especially if married, 'is more the slave of man for the gratification of her desires than man is of woman'. Where men could seek sexual pleasure and gratification outside marriage, existing moral codes made this impossible for women—indeed there was no recognition even of women's entitlement to sexual activity or fulfilment within marriage. In marriage, man was the master and commanded; woman obeyed. In consequence, 'woman must case nature, or feign to cast it, from her breast'.

She is not permitted to appear to feel, or desire. The whole of what is called her education training her to be the obedient instrument of man's sensual gratification, she is not permitted even to wish for any gratification for herself. She must have no desires: she must always yield, submit as a matter of duty, not repose upon her equal for the sake of happiness: she must blush to own that she enjoys in his generous caresses, were such by chance ever given.[36]

Thompson's radical programme was clearly based on a sense of the connection between the public political world and the private world of home. However, while he assumed that end of competitive capitalism and the introduction of a system of co-operative labour would transform the position of women, he never noticed the extent to which the ideas of sexual difference which underlay capitalism were equally evident amongst Robert Owen and many of his followers. Nor did he enter into the struggles within the Owenite movement between those women who espoused feminist views and the majority who opposed them.[37] Thompson, like Mill, entered occasionally and as it suited him into feminist debate, writing always in the persona and with the authority of male experience. Hence Thompson's work raises a similar problem to Mill's *Subjection of Women* in terms of how one assesses or describes the role of men within feminism.

In his 'Introductory letter to Mrs Wheeler', with which he began the *Appeal*, Thompson makes it clear that he was acutely sensitive to this problem. He was indebted to her ideas, he explains, and keen that she should 'take up the cause of your proscribed sex, and state to the world in writing, in your own name, what you have so often and so well stated in conversation'. He had thought much about the situation of women, but her life contained direct experiences of the wrongs he sought to end.[38] Yet as we have seen, in the complex process of explaining why, despite his hesitation at writing and claiming authorship of their joint ideas, he had none the less decided to write the book, Thompson used the familiar ploy of praising Wheeler's personal and intellectual merits—by denigrating the work and abilities of both Mary Wollstonecraft and Mary Hays. In the process, he used terms redolent with existing stereotypes of sexual differences, describing Wollstonecraft as lacking 'comprehensiveness of mind' and Hays as being unable to attract attention because of 'the timidity and impotence of conclusion accompanying' her 'gentle eloquence'.[39]

Thompson's comments about his debts to Anna Wheeler do seem to be borne out in the text. In his powerful critique of women's marital and domestic slavery, and particularly in his lengthy discussion of the ways in which the existing situation in regard to marriage refused to recognize women's sexual and emotional needs, it is hard not to see him as drawing on her life and experiences. For Wheeler had experienced many of the trials and miseries, against which Thompson protested, in her own married life. Coming from an 'enlightened family of Anglo-Irish landlords', Anna Wheeler was the daughter of Archbishop Doyle, and the god-daughter of the Irish nationalist leader, Henry Grattan. A girl of spirit and beauty, she married the dissolute son of a local landowner at the age of 15. Wheeler averaged one pregnancy every two years of the twelve she spent with him, in a marriage in which there seems to have been neither affection nor companionship. While her husband hunted, drank, and let the estate fall into ruin, she turned her attention to her own education, spending her days reading. Finding herself no longer able to tolerate this life, she finally fled with her only two surviving children in 1812, going to France and then living a somewhat peripatetic life moving amongst radical groups in England and France. After her husband's death in 1822, she returned to Ireland.[40]

William Thompson was not the only man to take up the cudgels on behalf of women in this period. An indignation and fervour similar to his was expressed also within the radical Unitarian group which surrounded W. J. Fox. He, like his friend R. B. Adams, shared both Thompson's hostility towards male libertinism and his belief that, in their treatment of women, men were driven not by passion but by base sexual desire and animal appetites. Like him, Fox and Adams argued forcefully that men kept women subordinate in order to ensure their own greater sexual privilege and licence.

In a moving piece which drew on a recent history of the Wesley family, Fox turned his attention to Mehitabel, a younger sister of John Wesley, whose 'primeval calamity was that of being born into what is called a well-regulated family'. Her mother followed 'the law, order, and duty system, the fear, honour, reverence and obey plan in its most complete development. Everything is summed up in submission'.[41] Mehitabel was apparently prevented by her parents from marrying the man she loved, being pressured instead into marrying a violent and unaffectionate plumber with whom she had nothing in common. She lived with him for twenty-six miserable years during which time all her children died (she thought their deaths were a result of the white-lead involved in his trade). Although she wrote to her father about her unhappiness, there was no thought that anything might be done. With an emphatic, even violent tone, which suggests that he was in fact referring to his own situation, Fox insisted that her

marriage was an immorality. So was her continuing through life in a sexual companionship where mutual affection was impossible; not that she was conscious of viciousness, but the contrary; she no doubt thought her misery was her duty. . . . For women so situated there ought to be redress, open and honourable redress, in every country that calls itself civilized. Her situation was even worse than if she had committed that act which, by the law of Moses, would have subjected her to death by stoning; for then she might have been liberated herself from an enforced and intolerable bond, and even have entered on a new state, perchance of the affection and enjoyment for which she was framed.

She could not do so because 'her mind was enslaved; it had been scourged into the faith that she was a property and not a being'.[42]

Fox's condemnation of the ways women were ensnared in loveless marriages was extended in a general way by Adams in his overview of the relations between the sexes. Offering a brief survey of human and social development, Adams argued that,

savage man kicks and beats woman, and makes her toil in the fields; semicivilized man locks her up in a harem; and man three-quarters civilized, which is as far as we are got, educates her for pleasure and dependency, keeps her in a state of pupillage, closes against her most of the avenues of self-support, and cheats her by the false forms of a contract into a life of subservience to his will.[43]

This demand by men that women devote themselves to serving male sexual desire had evil results on society as a whole. Women, regardless of social class, were 'as much slaves as the inmate of a Turkish harem, though after a different fashion'. The prevailing system of marriage reduced women to the position of animals, 'bidden to sit, and to walk, and to recline, . . . just as a horse is put through its paces'.[44] As a result, marriage itself was but a matter of bargain and sale. Using the oriental idiom which characterized so much nineteenth-century criticism of British marriage, Adams likened British husbands to harem masters, buying wives in something akin to an oriental slave market, and wandering forth in search of fresh excitement when they tired of them after a few weeks. Discarded wives had children to care for and could not behave as their husbands did, but they too were corrupted by the expectations and behaviour of their husbands and would seek whatever dissipation they could find for themselves and ignoring their children.[45]

In behaving in this way, Adams argued, men made a bad bargain, gaining neither companions for themselves nor adequate mothers for their children. Offering women no viable financial alternatives to marriage meant that marriage itself was 'at best but prostitution clothed in the robes of sanctity'. We make women bond slaves, argued *Junius Redivivius*, 'and with their milk they breathe the self-same spirit into our children'.[46]

While Adams and Fox, like Thompson, presented very powerful critiques of masculine privilege and searing analyses of marriage and of the colonization of women, all of them presented women as absolutely controlled, defined, and victimized by men. There was no suggestion that women could resist this domination—and, those, like Wollstonecraft or Mary Hays, who had sought to do so, were both pitied and dismissed because of their personal sufferings and the narrowness of their views. Interestingly, the sufferings of women provided these men with a way to address the problem of divorce without revealing their own direct interest in it. Fox, for example, was unhappily married and unable to divorce or to marry the young woman with whom he was in love. His heartfelt discussion of the prison-like bonds of marriage are all done in terms of the sufferings of women rather than of men, but his very tone served further to render women victims, incapable even of protesting on their own behalf.

The question of how women were represented was taken up and discussed at this time by women like Anna Wheeler and by the journalist and novelist Mary Lemane Grimstone. They disputed the view that women were 'not capable of that self-abstraction—that concentration of the powers of the mind—that calm deliberate sobriety of contemplativeness, indispensable to statesmanship'.[47] Such a view of women,

Mary Lemane Grimstone argued, was itself an illustration of male privilege and reflected the fact that men had far more opportunity to publish their views on women than women had to write about themselves. 'If lions and tigers ever learn to write,' Grimstone commented,

> what counterstatements we shall have to put against the descriptions of gallant hunts in which tigers turned tail and lions turned pale before the potent eyes of their human pursuer! Some such an effect will, I fear, follow when women come to fill the chair of oral anatomy; a different view will then be taken and given of some of the leviathans of fame, from Milton to Montgomery! How little was the conduct of the great Napoleon to Madame de Stael.[48]

In a similar way, Anna Wheeler argued that the prevailing belief that women's social position reflected their 'moral incapacity' and intellectual inferiority was completely false. Like Wollstonecraft in her final work, *Maria*, Wheeler argued that women's enslavement to male desire and their apparent antipathy and antagonism to each other was a result of their economic situation. Once women were entirely dependent on male pleasure for subsistence, they were necessarily set up in competition with each other and had to ensure their master's favour in order to survive. At the same time, Wheeler shared with Wollstonecraft a very critical approach to many women and a sense of extreme anger at the ways that women seemed not only to accept, but even to relish their enslavement.[49] She frequently expressed her disgust at women's passivity, even going so far as to argue that 'the love of rational liberty forms no part of the nature of this willingly degraded sex' whose personal courage was 'chiefly exhibited in the endurance [sic] of oppression'.[50]

While the prevalence of male voices raises questions about the nature of feminist debates in the 1820s and 1830s, it was none the less the case that male support was very necessary for those women concerned about the oppression of their sex. Anna Wheeler never managed to write the major text Thompson wanted her to. Yet it does seem to be the case that his work and the success of his *Appeal* gave her the encouragement she needed to expand her own feminist lecturing and writing. Throughout the late 1820s and the 1830s, she gave a number of lectures to radical and Owenite groups, many of which were subsequently published in *The Co-operator*. But while never addressing why this might be so, Wheeler felt increasingly bitter and disillusioned over the failure of women to band together or organize in order to challenge the laws and institutions which oppressed them.[51]

## The Tragic Tale of Caroline Norton

Wheeler's disgust at women's passivity and acceptance of their subordination could find no better illustration than that of Caroline Norton. Where Wheeler managed to flout English law, leaving a hateful marriage and taking her children with her in pursuit of a new life amongst radical, socialist, and high political circles, Norton was absolutely trapped by that law, which denied her access to her children and her property. But while protesting vociferously and powerfully against her own sufferings, and seeking reform of certain of the laws which denied her custody or the right to her own income, Norton always posed her demands in terms of a need for greater protection of women by men—rather than a need for legal and political rights which would give them autonomy.

Legally, the status of married women was defined by the common law doctrine of coverture which dictated that when a woman married, her legal personality was subsumed by her husband. The best-known formulation of this doctrine was that contained in William Blackstone's *Commentaries on the Laws of England*, which stated the rationale of the law as follows: if husband and wife were 'one body' before God, they were 'one person' in the law and that person was represented by the husband.[52] This doctrine meant that a married woman could not enter into contracts, sue or be sued, or make a valid will without the consent or participation of her husband. Moreover, he assumed legal rights over any property she might have at marriage and any property that came to her once she was married. A husband could not alienate his wife's real property, but any rents or interest belonged to him as did any savings or earnings she had before her marriage or obtained during it. The husband also had other rights in law: he decided the family domicile, and he had the right to correct his wife physically, albeit 'not in a violent or cruel manner', and to confine her, if necessary, to ensure her compliance with his domestic and sexual needs.[53] Women who were unhappily married had no redress: prior to the Divorce Act of 1857, the only way to end a marriage—other than by ecclesiastical annulment—was by private Act of Parliament, which was an extremely expensive and costly undertaking. Even when that Act came into force, divorce was difficult and expensive, especially for women, who had to prove adultery aggravated by some enormity such as bigamy or incest, while men had only to prove adultery.[54] The husband was also the sole guardian of his children and had the right to sequestrate them, punish them, take them away from their mother, and entrust them to a third person of his choice, including his mistress, refusing their mother any access to them.

Many feminists in the 1830s and 1840s, like those later in the century, commented on the extraordinary irony of the Anglican marriage ceremony in which a husband promised to endow his wife with his worldly goods—while in the very process of appropriating hers without binding his to her in any way.[55] In her *Plea for Women*, Mrs Hugo Reid argued that the Anglican ritual would only be brought into line with the truth if the bridegroom said henceforth 'what is yours is mine; and what is mine is *my own*'.[56]

Some of the injustices in the existing laws came to the fore in a dramatic way during the 1830s through the case of Caroline Norton. Norton came from an upper middle-class family with an extensive range of contacts in the political, legal, and literary worlds. But none of them could protect her from the savage treatment which the law permitted for married women. After years of marital misery, characterized by violent scenes followed by partial reconciliations, Norton returned home from a short trip away to find that her husband had not only ended their marriage, but had also removed their three sons, the youngest of whom was aged 2, and had barred the house to her. He initiated divorce proceedings by bringing a case of 'criminal conversation' against Lord Melbourne, one of Caroline's close friends. The case was dismissed as George Norton was unable to demonstrate that his wife had been adulterous. But the failure to obtain a divorce did not bring a reconciliation and the couple remained separated. George Norton kept the children away from his wife, sending them to live with distant relatives for some of the time and keeping them on his Yorkshire estate. Caroline Norton managed to see them very occasionally, but was never permitted either to spend a night with them or to care for them, even when they were ill. Instead, she waited in anguish, knowing them to be neglected and fearing that the drunkenness, violence, and moodiness of her husband would result in the brutal treatment of their children. Her fears were only too well justified: in 1842, six years after the children had been removed from her, the youngest died after a riding accident—which Caroline felt would have been avoided had the children been under proper supervision. After this, she was allowed access to her older sons, but was never able to make a home for them.[57]

When forced to recognize that the law gave her children absolutely into the hands of their father, and that none of her social or political contacts could help her, Caroline Norton set about attempting to demonstrate publicly her own suffering and to change the law. She worked with a young Whig barrister, Serjeant-at-law Talfourd, who had specialized in infant custody cases and was himself well aware of the need for legal reform. He, in turn, apprised Caroline of several other cases similar to her own, and all demonstrating the inability or unwillingness of the courts to interfere with the rights of fathers.

Norton used her considerable literary skills to produce pamphlets on the question, which became the source of intense debate. There was some support for her position, but much hostility was directed against her by the conservative press. Eventually, in 1839, an Infants Custody Act was passed, according to which, children of separated parents under the age of 7 were allowed to reside with their mother, provided that her appeal for this privilege was agreed to by the Lord Chancellor and that she was of 'good character'. The law availed Norton herself very little for her own children were now living in Scotland—and hence outside the jurisdiction of the Lord Chancellor.

Norton's battle continued into the following decades. Her lack of money was another ongoing source of grievance, as the same laws which deprived her of a legal identity and hence of her children also meant that her husband was entitled to all the earnings she received from her writings. He was, moreover, disinclined to pay her even the allowance he had agreed to, especially when she was left a couple of small legacies by her mother and by Lord Melbourne. The courts upheld his right to refuse her an allowance—and to refuse any liability for her debts. She, in turn, attempted to gain public support and to reform the laws, smarting all the while from the way in which her reputation was tarnished by the separation, even though there was no evidence against her and her husband had been unable to show her as an adulterer.

Norton's much-publicized case—which she expounded upon at great length herself—had a significant impact on many later feminists.[58] But like so many other nineteenth-century feminist heroines, she posed a distinct problem to later feminists because of her refusal to enter directly into any form of feminist protest. At the very moment that she was protesting against the provisions in the laws affecting women, she rejected any appeal to women's rights or the idea of sexual equality, emphasizing rather her belief in 'the natural superiority of men', in which she believed as firmly 'as I do in the existence of God'.[59] It was this belief that made her insist on the importance of men's realizing their obligation and duty to protect women. Women, she argued, 'have one *right* (perhaps only that one). They have a right—founded on nature, equity, and religion—to the protection of man. *Power* is on the side of men—power of body, power of position. With that power should come, not only the fact, but the *instinct* of protection'.[60]

And yet, Norton's own work serves not only to demonstrate her importance for feminism, but to question her own disclaiming of feminist intent. Her book, *English Laws for Women*, served, as it was intended, to generalize her complaint and to point to the legal and structural injustices suffered by women. She was not, she insisted, concerned merely to 'prove merely that my husband has been unjust, and my fate a hard one', for this would be but a poor ambition.

I aspire to a different object. I desire to prove, not my suffering or his injustice but that the present law of England cannot prevent any such suffering, or control any such injustice. I write in the hope that the law may be amended; and that those who are at present so ill-provided as to have only Truth and Justice on their side, may hereafter have the benefit of Law and Lawyers.[61]

Norton thus used her own experience as a way of dramatizing the plight of all women and their need for legal reform. Her life and her writings served to galvanize a younger generation, who saw her sufferings, 'transmuted by her sympathetic nature into the will and the power to plead for others', as the start of their campaign to reform the laws which deprived married women of their property.[62] But in using her own personal situation in this way, Norton was in many ways following a path much closer to twentieth-century feminism than to its nineteenth-century counterpart. For her, the personal was deeply political and she connected closely her own sufferings, and the private sufferings of many other women, with the public world of law. In the process, as Mary Poovey argues, she broke the barrier between the private sphere and the public domain, elevating her personal complaint to a political demand.[63]

In one sense, then, Norton offers a complete contrast with Mary Wollstonecraft, pleading not for her sex, but rather for herself. But the specific plea she made was very similar to that contained in Wollstonecraft's last work, *Maria*, with its detailed analysis of men's power over their wives and particularly in regard to their children and their property. Moreover, as a wronged wife, and one against whom no charge of adultery or illicit sexual behaviour could be sustained, Norton had a standing and could become a name and a known figure within later feminism around whom a younger generation could gather. Her writings were very influential in turning the attention of the next generation of feminists to the question of married women and their legal disabilities. Her dramatic statements about her own wrongs and her personal anguish fired the imagination of younger women with a zeal to extend her battle to reform the situation of married women— and to gain for them the very rights which Norton herself claimed to disdain.

## Harriet Martineau and the Slow Development of Feminist Consciousness

Just as Caroline Norton necessarily plays a part in any history of nine-teenth-century feminism, so too does Harriet Martineau, although both pose enormous problems in thinking about a feminist tradition.[64] As the recent republication of many of her articles and letters makes clear, Martineau wrote constantly about women's oppression and about the 'woman question' throughout her adult life.[65] Her first pub-lished article—as a very laudatory late nineteenth-century biography claiming her as a feminist pioneer pointed out—was about women's contributions in religion.[66] And over the decades she wrote about al-most every aspect of women's oppression in regard to education, po-litical rights, marriage laws and social customs, health, clothing, and particularly their sexual exploitation through prostitution and in marriage.

But while the subject-matter of Martineau's work adhered to and even helps define much of the nineteenth-century feminist pro-gramme, her tone and many of her specific comments were often at odds with the dominant feminist approach and even unsympathetic to it. Her use of a male pseudonym emphasized her disinclination to see herself or her own position as illustrative of the broader situation of women. Even some of her most courageous writings—her early attacks on the idea of regulating prostitution, for example—were written as if she were a man appealing to the better nature of other husbands and fathers, rather than with any of Josephine Butler's sense of the need for women to join together to fight against their sexual exploitation.[67]

Martineau's autobiography sets up both sides of this dilemma. Like Caroline Norton's writing about her own personal misfortunes, Martineau simultaneously exposes the private and familial sufferings of an intelligent middle-class woman, and disassociated herself from any recognition of the ways her life resulted from the disabilities of her sex. Her autobiography offers a moving story of her own personal un-happiness as the little understood and often neglected daughter of an insensitive and unloving mother. But her life also exhibits many of the problems faced by most middle-class women. The denial to her of the education given her brothers, the lack of any interest in her abilities, the refusal to let her follow a chosen career path—even when she had shown herself quite capable of doing so—and the insistence that she return home to be a companion to the mother with whom she was so ill at ease, offer an extreme version of the miseries common amongst in-telligent nineteenth-century women.[68]

The telling of her life story, her deafness and chronic ill health, particularly the illness which threatened to be terminal—until mir-aculously cured by hypnotism—cry out for psychoanalytic readings. But what is of particular interest here is the way in which Martineau, like Norton, simultaneously reveals the power structures which brought such suffering in her private life, and at the same time refuses in any overt way to see her life as in itself making a case for feminist rebellion.[69]

Martineau was associated with the radical circles which produced most of the other feminists in the 1820s and 1830s, and published her own early work in the *Monthly Repository*. She took little part in either the personal rebellions or the personal plights of the other men and women associated with that circle, however, showing little sympathy with their criticism of the existing sexual hierarchy. Her earliest writ-ings on women were published in the 1820s, when the *Monthly Reposi-tory* was still largely a religious periodical and before it had adopted the outspokenly radical tone that characterized it in the early 1830s. Her ideas fitted well with the views of its then editor, Edward Fox, with his espousal of philosophic radicalism and his concern about educational reform for women as well as men. Her contact with the journal dimin-ished, however, in the 1830s when under the editorship of W. J. Fox its religious content was reduced and its critiques of marriage and of the political and social subordination of women became increasingly outspoken.[70]

Her first article on women's education illustrated the moderation and limitations of Martineau's early views. Extolling the great boon brought by Christianity to women, she sought improved education in order to enable them better to carry out the duties which fell to their lot in Christian England. Women required a better system of schooling and improved private education, she argued, not because 'great stores of information are as necessary to women as to men', but because 'their own appropriate duties and peculiar employments' would be better performed. 'If the whole mind be exercised and strengthened, it will bring vigour to the performance of its duties in any particular province.'[71] There is no suggestion here that education might allow women not to marry or that it might give them the capacity for action. Rather her views bear a very close connection with those of Hannah More in seeking a more rational and solid education to better enable women to carry out their domestic tasks.

Martineau's acceptance of the domestic framework of women's lives and her concern to ensure that women undertake their duties with proper seriousness immediately marks the contrast between her approach and those either of Fox's Unitarian followers or of the Owenites, all of whom declaimed against the enslavement of women to marriage and domestic life. Where Fox, like Thompson or Wheeler, deplored the nature of marriage and the permanency of marital ties, Martineau accepted absolutely the prevailing sexual double standard, refusing to associate with any woman guilty of sexual irregularity— although she continued to acknowledge and see men guilty of the same behaviour. Moreover, where William Thompson and Wheeler saw women's emancipation as possible only with a change in the whole economic and social order, Martineau combined her discussion of women's oppression with her powerful advocacy of political economy. She was probably the best-known popularizer of political economy in the nineteenth century, finding a moral basis for its dictums and helping to ensure its position of pre-eminence in political and economic terms.

The different frameworks adopted by Martineau on the one hand, and by the radicals and Owenites on the other, did not mean that they had nothing in common. On the contrary, there were a number of significant meeting points and common arguments between them. Martineau had very much the same objections as William Thompson to the ideas of James Mill—and refuting his views, produced the strongest feminist statement which she made in her book on *Society in America*.[72] Similarly, she shared with Anna Wheeler the view that women needed to band together and organize in order to end their oppression. But the very points of contact illustrate also their differences.

Although some of Martineau's objections to James Mill were similar to those of Thompson, her tone could not have been more different. Where Thompson made his essay the occasion for a diatribe against the enslavement of women in marriage, Martineau kept strictly to the narrow grounds of political theory. She focused her attention on two prominent liberal theorists, Thomas Jefferson and James Mill, castigating both for their failure to recognize that the democratic spirit by which governments derived their just power from the consent of the governed required that women be enfranchised. In their refusal to accept the need for women's suffrage, these two

most principled democratic writers on government have . . . sunk into fallacies, as disgraceful as any advocate of despotism has adduced. In fact, they have thus sunk to being, for the moment, advocates of despotism. Jefferson in America, and James Mill at home, subside, for the occasion, to the level of the author of the Emperor of Russia's catechism for the young Poles.[73]

In her view, governments could not make just laws, or laws which women should obey, concerning their taxation, their property, or their legal status, without women's direct involvement through parliamentary representation. Mill's belief that the interests of most women were represented by their fathers or their husbands was completely unacceptable to her. It left fatherless single women like herself without any form of representation and hence clearly did not deal with the interests of all women. Martineau was a strong critic of the existing legal and social framework of marriage, but where Thompson centred his argument on this question, she simply castigated Mill for his complete failure to recognize that 'the interests of women who have fathers and husbands can never be identical with theirs, while there is a necessity for laws to protect women against their husbands and fathers. The statement is not worth another word.'[74]

It would seem clear too that while Wheeler and Martineau both wanted women to organize protests against their subordination, they would have chosen neither the same targets nor the same type of organization. In the late 1830s, Martineau wrote to her publisher, E. J. Fox, of her hope that an organization would be established which would 'obtain a revision in parliam' [sic] of all laws regarding Woman; & to expose her whole state, from her bad nursery training to her insulted wifehood in palaces, & and her wretchedness in prostitution'. She enjoined him to secrecy about the plan, however, because 'We are not secure enough of all our apparatus for any boasting yet'. The problem that had to be solved was 'whether able women enough can be found to aid our beginnings: for women must work for their own redemption'.[75] But while Martineau regretted the lack of women with the courage to fight, she was very anxious to ensure that only the right kind of women should attempt to do so. In 1849, for example, she refused to send an address to a Woman's Rights Convention in the United States because, 'I do not approve of the tone used by some of the public advocates of Woman's Rights; & I do not think that any good will be attained by the formation of such a society as you tell me of. I therefore do not wish my name to be connected with its proceedings by any act of my own.'[76]

Nowhere is the contrast between Martineau and Wheeler more evident than in their response to Mary Wollstonecraft. While Wheeler's decision to leave her husband and begin an independent life was attributed by her daughter at least in part to her being 'strongly tainted' by revolutionary poisons emanating from Wollstonecraft's *Vindication*, Martineau insisted that she was completely immune to that work or to the influence of its author. Wollstonecraft, as a 'poor victim of passion', was not someone she could regard as 'a safe example, nor as a successful champion for Woman and her Rights'. Indeed, any woman who pleaded her own cause or referred to her own wrongs was for Martineau an enemy of the women's cause. Like Lydia Becker in the 1860s, she argued that

[t]he best friends of that cause are women who are morally as well as intellectually competent to the most serious business of life, and who must be clearly seen to speak from the conviction of the truth, and not from personal unhappiness. . . . the happy wives and the busy, cheerful, satisfied, single women, who have no injuries of their own to venge, and no painful vacuity or mortification to relieve.[77]

But while Martineau was disgusted by Wollstonecraft's emotional and sexual excesses, she could not ignore her. Indeed, even while rejecting the idea that Wollstonecraft was important to her, she invoked her name whenever she talked about her own involvement in the cause of women's emancipation. In the late 1840s, for example, Martineau wrote a series of letters dealing with the exclusion of women speakers from the World Anti-Slavery Convention held in London in 1847.[78] Martineau was grieved that, 'after battling so many long years for the liberties of African slaves, I can take no part in a convention that strikes down the most sacred rights of women'. She greatly admired Garrison's refusal to sit on the floor from, which women were excluded, and his insistence on joining them in the gallery. His act had done much for the woman question. Martineau still felt concern as to how the movement would develop: 'what with the vices of some women and the fears of others, it is hard work for us to assert our liberty.' She proposed to do so until her death, however, 'and so make it easier for some few to follow us than it was for poor Mary Wollstonecraft to begin'.[79]

As Deirdre David has shown, the career of Martineau, as of some other Victorian women intellectuals, was constituted by an ensemble of discordant, harmonious, and complex relations between different politics, texts, and imperatives, all of which sometimes complement and sometimes contend with each other. David is interested in the fact that Martineau made her name as a popularizer of the ideas of Political Economy, a form of thought which served powerfully to justify Victorian capitalism, and the dominance of men within it. And yet while herself so powerfully buttressing Victorian patriarchal institutions, she constantly reiterated her concerns about women's oppression.[80]

But even within her writings about women themselves, one can see changes, conflicts, and contradictions. Martineau trod a difficult course, sometimes posing as a particularly well-informed and neutral individual who was above the battle and claimed the right to assess and adjudicate the women's cause. She re-enforced her distance and neutrality by choosing male pseudonyms. At other times, however, she made clear her own involvement with the women's cause, writing and speaking as a woman and joining in the protest of her sex. This switch from male to female persona, and from neutral spectator to involved participant, went back and forth throughout her life.

It was Martineau's trip to America which first brought a direct statement of her own sense of injustice and oppression. In her widely read book *Society in America* she first wrote of her own anger as a woman at being denied political representation.[81] Indeed, this work marks a turning-point for Martineau, both in terms of how she wrote about herself and in terms of making her recognize the importance of working closely and publicly with other women for the cause. It was her contact with the women abolitionists, by whom she was immensely impressed, which first made her recognize the importance of writing as a woman and of campaigning with others over their shared grievances. While Martineau refused to be associated with radicals like Mary Wollstonecraft, she found in the course of her travels in America women like the Grimke sisters, Lucretia Mott, and Lydia Child, who combined their passionate opposition to slavery with an equally passionate commitment to fighting against the oppression of women.[82] For Martineau, these women were 'safe' advocates of the women's cause and under their influence she made her first unequivocal feminist statements, pointing to the similarities between the position of women and slaves and demanding political rights for women.[83] It was in regard to the activities of the American women abolitionists that Martineau most strongly challenged ideas about women's appropriate sphere of activity, insisting that 'fidelity of conscience' must take precedence over false ideas of female modesty.[84]

Martineau was one of a number of British women abolitionists who became closely involved with their American counterparts and with feminist campaigns through transatlantic travel. As a result of their visits to America, many British women were inevitably drawn into the debates and discussions about women's participation and women's rights which were occurring in the American abolitionist movement at this time. Although British women had pioneered the formation of all female abolitionist groups, by the 1830s their American sisters had moved a stage beyond this in directly including discussions on sexual equality and on the need for white women to break their own bonds in order to be able to campaign more effectively against slavery. The speeches and letters of Angelina and Sarah Grimke, which initiated a new stage of discussion about women's rights in America, were widely reported in England and found many sympathizers there.[85] The image of women as slaves, which had been elaborated by Thompson, was reworked and expanded by many women who were drawn through opposition to slavery into articulating a demand for women's rights—and strengthened those demands by indicating their sense of the similarities between women and slaves. As Claire Midgley has shown, Harriet Martineau was but one of the women who became concerned about women's rights through abolitionism at this time. A number of other women, including Owenite women like Mrs Lemane Grimstone, made constant references to the analogy between women and slaves. And several other women who later became prominent in feminist causes, including Anne Knight and Mary Estlin, also found this the channel through which they became feminist activists.[86]

While abolitionism provided a bridge to direct feminist involvement for Martineau, some of her views on slavery are extremely troubling for contemporary feminists. When it came to the question of sexual relations between slave-owners and slaves, for example, she seemed concerned more with the deleterious consequences of this practice on marriages amongst whites than with the sexual exploitation of women slaves! Wives were ill-treated by this practice, she argued, because the 'licentious intercourse with the lowest of the sex' unfits men for appreciating the highest.[87] At the same time, she was only too aware of 'the management of the female slaves on estates where the object is to rear as many as possible, like stock, for the southern market', and of 'the boundless licentiousness caused by the practice: a practice which wrung from the heart of a planter, in the bitterness of her heart, the declaration that a planter's wife was only "the chief slave of the harem"'.[88] Martineau's abolitionism was thus combined with very pronounced racism.[89]

The connection between abolitionism and feminism became closer and closer in the 1830s and 1840s, culminating in the event which some still see as the stimulus to the development of both the American and the mid-century British women's movements: the World Anti-Slavery Convention which the British and Foreign Anti-Slavery Society held in London in 1840. The story of this convention is well known, and particularly its salient feature: the refusal of the organizing committee to permit the women delegates sent by the Garrisonian Abolitionists to take their seats in the convention hall. The women were forced to sit behind a curtain, where they could hear the proceedings, but not take part. This event sparked heated debate, both at the Convention itself and then increasingly within the Quaker community and all the various participating societies.[90] After it was over, the American women delegates, who included Lucretia Mott and Elizabeth Cady Stanton, toured the country giving public speeches and meeting many women abolitionists. There was much opposition to them from Quakers on sectarian grounds, but everywhere they went, the question of their right to speak as women was discussed. In their talks they met and got to know many women who became important in the setting up of the women's movement, including Mary Howitt and Elizabeth Reid.

Although Martineau continued to advocate caution in regard to women's rights, once she had broached the question of women's suffrage and identified herself with the feminist cause, she continued to address it, often breaking quite new ground. In the eyes of many, she initiated a whole new campaign in her writing on women's employment. Martineau's writings on employment were frequently commented on by mid-Victorian feminists, some of whom argued that they had no idea of the extent of women's paid labour until she pointed it out. The plight of middle-class women who lacked the kind of stable home assumed to be the location of their sex and needed to support themselves had been a serious cause for concern to feminists of all kinds, from Mary Wollstonecraft and Mary Hays in the late eighteenth century through to Josephine Butler and Millicent Garret Fawcett in the nineteenth. Like women novelists, including Fanny Burney, Jane Austen, and Elizabeth Gaskell, they protested at the lack of employment opportunities open to women, arguing that the assumption that all women would be financially supported by men left women no option but prostitution.

Harriet Martineau was well aware of this problem. She, like the Brontës and, for that matter, Mary Wollstonecraft, had only escaped the fate of a governess by virtue of her literary ability, and she watched her sister forced into it as her only means of becoming self-supporting. But she did not direct her attention to the plight of the governess, claiming rather to be 'wearied' with 'the incessant repetition of the dreary story of spirit-broken governesses and starving needlewomen.' Martineau sought rather to show 'the full breadth of the area of female labour in Great Britain', and to demand recognition of the varieties of work done by women and of the huge numbers of working-class women forced to be self-supporting.[91]

Like other facets of life in the modern age, Martineau argued, the conditions of female life have sustained as much alteration as the fortunes of other classes by the progress of civilization. The Census results and various major surveys now revealed that, contrary to popular beliefs, 'a very large proportion of the women of England earn their own bread'. There was no saying, she argued, 'how much misery may be saved by a timely recognition of this simple truth'.

We go on talking as if it were still true that every woman is, or ought to be supported by her father, brother, or husband: we are only beginning to think of the claim of all workers,—that their work should be paid for by its quality and its place in the market, irrespective of the status of the worker . . . We are (probably to a man) unaware of the amount of the business of life in England done by women; and if we do not attend to the fact in time, the knowledge will be forced on us in some disadvantageous or disagreeable way. A social organisation framed for a community of which half stayed at home, while the other half went out to work, cannot answer the purposes of a society of which a quarter remains at home while three-quarters goes out to work.[92]

The Census of 1851, she argued, showed the increase in the numbers of women involved in paid employment. 'While the female population has increased (between 1841 and 1851) in the ratio of 7 to 8, the number of women returned as engaged in independent industry has increased in the far greater ratio of 3 to 4.' Women were now employed in many forms of agriculture, in mining and extractive industries, in many industries concerned with 'the produce of the waters', including catching, curing, and selling fish, in a wide variety of crafts and trades, and in domestic service. New occupations for women included manufacturing, especially the textile, lace, and ribbon industries, as well as telegraphy and clerical. Increasing numbers of women were also engaged in the keeping of lodging houses.[93]

Martineau's position in regard to these issues remains a difficult one. On the one hand, she asserted absolutely her belief that these developments needed to be accepted and seen as inescapable and indeed as beneficial. She would not accept that factory labour in itself brutalized either women or men, but rather that they were harmed by 'the state of ignorance in which they enter upon a life of bustle and publicity'.[94] Education was needed to enable girls both to work in factories and to carry out the traditional duties of women. The independence of women simply had to be accepted, she insisted, especially by men. But while making this claim, unaltered in substance throughout the feminist debates until the 1880s and 1890s, Martineau continued to write as a man—even quoting herself within her text—thus again making the feminist case while not allowing herself in any simple way to be included within the feminist campaign.

Like all the feminists of the 1860s and 1870s, Martineau saw one of the main problems of women to be the 'jealousy of men in regard to the industrial independence of women:—it shows itself with every step gained in civilisation; and its immediate effect is to pauperise a large number of women who are willing to work for their bread; and, we need not add, to condemn to perdition many more who have no choice left but between starvation and vice'.[95] Women needed to be able to expand drastically their range of professional employments as well as to have access to new ones in manufacturing and trade.

Out of six millions of women above twenty years of age, in Great Britain . . . no less than half are industrial in their mode of life. . . . With this new condition of affairs, new duties and new views must be accepted. Old obstructions must be removed; and the aim set before us, as a nation as well as in private life, to provide for the free development and full use of the powers of every member of the community. In other words we must improve and extend education to the utmost; and then open a fair field to the powers and energies we have educed. This will secure our welfare, nationally and in our homes to which few elements can contribute more vitally and more richly than the independent industry of our countrywomen.[96]

While Martineau's discussion of women's employment provided a basis in terms of information and a stimulus for the whole employment campaign of the late 1850s and 1860s, she was not herself involved in that campaign. She acknowledged the papers given at the National Association for the promotion of Social Science by Bessie Parkes and others on the subject, and continued to express her own interest in and concern about the need for women's work and for an education which would prepare them for it, but she had no actual connection with the Society for Promoting the Employment of Women. The situation was very different, however, when it came to the Contagious Diseases Acts. Here one can see a distinctive shift in Martineau's rhetoric and in her self-presentation as she became, for the first time, closely associated with a powerful feminist campaign, working alongside other women who were passionately committed to their cause.

Martineau had long feared the possibility of legislation to regulate prostitution and, when discussion on the subject began in the 1860s, she argued strongly against it both privately in her own correspondence and publicly in a series of leaders in the *Daily News*. In these letters, she voiced her fears about the ways in which the regulation of prostitution stimulated vice and led to overall moral decay. For the first time, Martineau signed herself 'An Englishwoman', and wrote unequivocally about her own commitment and that of many other women to fight against the subjection of women 'to the caprices of police and the oppression of the law'. [97] Attempting to show simultaneously the strength of feeling of those involved in the campaign, and their vulnerability, Martineau insisted that it was 'the way of Englishwomen to give themselves to a good work, not without counting, but without too much heeding, the cost'. Indeed, like Josephine Butler, Martineau almost exulted in the vulnerability of the women engaged in the campaign, as frequent references to Lady Godiva show.

That representative Englishwoman, Godiva of blessed memory, could not but have counted the cost of her deed; and so, no doubt, it has been with her countrywomen of every age between her and us. So it assuredly is with these honourable women who are now putting away the most sensitive of personal feelings, to help us out of the peril we have incurred, and to destroy the risk for all future time. Their deed is of a kindred quality to Godiva's, while its scope is wider and its import infinitely deeper. She pitied starvation in poor men's homes. These are striving to save home itself, and to preserve the most sacred of institutions, and one hitherto pre-eminently our own—the Family. [98]

This celebration of women's self-sacrifice, which is seen as having the capacity to bring social and moral transformation, alongside a protest against the prevailing sexual hierarchy and an endorsement of rather conservative familial and moral values is a quite common feature of much Victorian feminism. But what is most striking about Martineau's comments is the sense of admiration, even veneration, she showed for those women devoting themselves to this cause. And it seems clear that Martineau was carried away by it, so that she lost all her earlier hesitancy and prevarication. As Frances Yates has shown, Martineau initially set up the conflict over the Contagious Diseases legislation in terms of the interests of opposing groups of men: those who sought their 'atrocious objects' through legislation on the one hand, and 'the strong determination of the fathers, brothers and husbands of Englishwomen to leave no rest or peace to their rulers till their wives, sisters, and daughters are securely sheltered under the law of the land' on the other.[99] But she was very soon recognizing also the need for women to battle against the acts on behalf of their sex and themselves.

Martineau had long recognized the implications for all women of the legal enforcement of the sexual double standard involved in the Contagious Diseases Acts and protested against them. But it was her meeting with Josephine Butler and the Ladies' National Association for the Repeal of the Contagious Diseases Acts which brought her to see the importance of having women actively and publicly fight against their own oppression even when their actions were deemed improper and immoral. As a signatory to all the early protests against the Acts made by the Ladies' National Association, Martineau clearly accepted the views put forward by Butler, Elizabeth Wolstenholme Elmy, and the others concerning the manifold political and social injustices involved in the Acts—and the extent to which they affected all women by removing 'every guarantee of personal security which the law has established and held sacred, and put their reputation, their freedom, and their persons absolutely in the power of the police'.[100] But more importantly, she was brought through this agitation to identify with the sufferings of women and to connect herself unequivocally with the fight for women's emancipation. Her development shows some of the complexities of crossgenerational contact within feminism: while she was hesitant to connect herself with an earlier feminist like Wollstonecraft, the emergence of an organized women's movement which actively sought her assistance and support and looked to her as an empowering and even legitimating figure made her much more prepared to declare herself and to connect herself with the cause. As Simone de Beauvoir was to do in the late twentieth century, Martineau became a feminist more or less retrospectively in response to the enthusiasm and urgency of a younger generation of women whose views and activities she supported and from whom she in turn gained recognition and support.

## Feminism, Evangelicalism, and 'Woman's Sphere'

Although it is tempting to look for feminist heritages and influence only in radical and progressive quarters and amongst those overtly protesting or rebelling against the oppression of women, it is impossible to do so. For such an approach ignores the importance to feminists of conservative women and of some conservative stereotypes of femininity which they used so effectively in making their arguments, demands, and claims.[101] For much of the nineteenth century, feminists reworked and rethought conventional ideas and images as a way both of articulating and gaining widespread acknowledgement of their views.

The central issue which had to be dealt with in the nineteenth century was the middle-class assumption that the proper location for women was in the home, providing care, nurturance, and comfort for a family. The importance of home life for women was elaborated in a never-ending series of tracts, sermons, and handbooks designed to explain to women the nature and the importance of their moral and religious duty to family and hearth. All of this came to be termed 'woman's mission'—and the literature and the general discussion of 'woman's mission' also serves to illustrate the paradoxical nature of the relationship between feminism and its surrounding culture and environment. On the one hand, the tracts and books on this subject which proliferated in the early and mid-nineteenth century served to re-enforce the idea of women's necessary domestic seclusion, and their inferiority to men, best exemplified in the fact that they were only ever defined in relative terms as wives, daughters, or mothers. Their primary duty was to subordinate their own wishes and desires to the needs of their family and of the wider society. On the other hand, the very formulation of this duty came in terms of a mission to transform morally and in the interests of religion and order not only their immediate family, but also potentially the whole society.[102] Hence the idea of 'Woman's Mission' served at one and the same time to discipline women and contain their demands—and to offer them a vastly new and extended scope for action. It was this evangelical and transforming impulse that provided both the framework and the energy which enabled later women like

Josephine Butler and even the Pankhursts to set about attempting the radical transformation of their society.[103]

The very idea of 'woman's mission' was a consequence of the evangelical revival of the late eighteenth century. Evangelicalism in turn was a significant factor in establishing the outlook and the power base of the provincial middle class. As Leonore Davidoff and Catherine Hall have shown, evangelicalism set up a new standard by which members of the middle class could demonstrate their gentility and their entitlement to status and respect.[104] At the same time, evangelicalism, like Wesleyan Methodism, set up a dilemma which was soluble only through a particular configuration of sexual difference and gendered behaviour. For the very religious and moral beliefs established by these fundamentalist religions were threatened by the competitive and amoral market in which middle-class men earned their living. The only way to prevent this was to ensure that the home could be protected as the basis of a new moral order in which religious piety and family affection were protected.

This greatly increased emphasis on the family as the central unit in religious observation brought a new sense of how the family functioned. The centrality of the family in religious observance had always been integral to Protestantism. But the evangelical family of the late eighteenth and early nineteenth centuries was somewhat different from the Reformation family described by Luther. Where the sixteenth-century Protestant family centred on the father as the chief religious guide and inspiration, the evangelical family of the late eighteenth and early nineteenth centuries centred on the mother who became the embodiment of piety, the moral and spiritual guide, and the centre of care and affection. Jane Austen's *Mansfield Park* provides a particularly clear illustration of this shift as the moral centre of the Bertram family moves in the course of the novel away from Sir Thomas—the head of the family, but a man who is too distant, too stern, and too often away to know sufficiently about the education of his children or the tenor of their daily life—and towards Fanny Price who is always there and hence can see how closely the questions of proper mothering, a sound education, and an orderly household are integrated with the development of sound religious and moral beliefs. Fanny exemplifies the sense that a woman could only perform this function of ensuring stability, morality, and piety if she remained at home, and far away from the corrupting knowledge and temptations of the public worlds of the market, of politics, and of improper entertainments and promiscuous sexuality.

Evangelicalism, then, established a framework for seeing the home as the natural sphere for women and for giving a religious basis to male dominance and female subordination. It provided the framework for an essentially conservative reformulation of the status, the nature, and the duty of women while carrying within itself the basis for a new assertion of women's rights. As Davidoff and Hall have shown, the need for women to provide the distinctive religious and moral base for middle-class families and the moral and spiritual guidance for their menfolk meant that women were seen at one and the same time as naturally subordinate to men—and as the most appropriate leaders and guides of those men in religious and moral matters. They were both to confine themselves to the home and to transform that home—and through it the whole world—by virtue of their religion and piety.[105]

The central contradiction in the ways in which women's duty was seen and understood is evident both in the evangelical writings of the late eighteenth and early nineteenth centuries and in the literature about women's role and duty by writers like Sarah Lewis, Mrs John Sandford, and, best known of all, Sarah Ellis, which proved to be so popular in the 1830s and 1840s. It can be seen most clearly in the way in which discussions of women's domestic activity move imperceptibly on to the question of 'woman's mission'. From a statement of the limitations women face and of their necessary domestic confinement, all of these writers move to the demand that women carry first into their homes and then into the wider society something of the religious zeal and fervour which other missionaries were taking to the heathen in foreign lands. Of course, the methods suggested to women had to be entirely different from those of other missionaries: women were to use charm and domestic comfort to make religious values appealing and pleasurable to their menfolk. Women were instructed almost to seduce their husbands into religion and virtue. Mrs John Sandford, for example, insisted that women of piety should not give rise to the reproach that religious persons are often vulgar or awkward. 'On the contrary, they imbibe more deeply the spirit of their lovely religion, when they carry its charm into the detail of life, when they are fascinating as well as faithful, agreeable as well as good.'[106] But the missionary role is none the less there—and it leads inevitably to discussions about women's power and about their public role.

Sarah Ellis, who ranked second to none in her insistence that women understand their relative status and their duties to family and home, also insisted that they 'have the social morals of their country in their power'.[107] Later in the century, Ruskin gave this a slightly different twist when he argued that it was women, through their immense domestic influence who were responsible for all the evil, disharmony and even war within society.[108]

The influence allowed women through the notion of their moral and religious 'mission' became a new source of contention in the 1830s. In that decade, a series of pamphlets and sermons appeared which raged against the excessive influence claimed by or on behalf of women. Clergymen, like James Burgon, preached sermons in which they stressed the secondary nature of female creation and hence the fact that woman was intended as man's helper.[109] Woman, as one anonymous author argued, 'has managed to overstep her sphere—she has usurped the dominion of the head, when she should have aimed but at the subjection of the heart; and the hand which ought to be held out to man, only to sustain and cheer him on his journey, now checks his steps and points to the way he is to go!'[110]

But all of this in turn led the way for more consciously feminist sentiments to be articulated and the 1830s and 1840s saw a spate of anonymous tracts and pamphlets which either took up ideas of woman's mission in their title, like Anne Richelieu Lamb's *Can Woman Regenerate Society?*, or in their arguments. An anonymous tract entitled *Domestic Tyranny, or Woman in Chains*, for example, took up the Scriptural injunction so beloved of evangelicals, 'Wives, submit yourselves to your husbands, as is fit in the Lord', to argue that this statement did not imply that women were inferior or degraded, but was 'particularly addressed to them as responsible and self-governing agents, who are also required to search the Scriptures to know the will of the Lord'.[111] Lamb addressed herself not to the Scriptures, but rather to the notion of *Woman's Mission* as articulated by Sarah Lewis in her popular book, and argued powerfully that women could not regenerate anything until they had first regenerated themselves through gaining an education and being allowed to exercise their full humanity. In terms quite similar to those of Harriet Martineau, Lamb criticizes the arbitrary confinement of women to a particular 'sphere' designated as appropriate to them, while not allowing them any capacity to develop their own abilities or potential. Her book follows both Wollstonecraft and Martineau both in its condemnation of the constant infantilizing of women in order to ensure that they devote their lives to the service and entertainment of men, and in its anger at the ways in which women accept social mores and the dictates of fashion rather than asserting themselves to attack the sexual double standard and the other forms of conventional morality which serve to limit and circumscribe women in ways not done to men. This little-known text makes many interesting points—some of which recurred in mid-Victorian feminism—concerning the extraordinary contradictions evident in contemporary ideals of femininity, not least in terms of extolling marriage as the only career for women, when, in fact, women might find much more pleasure in celibacy. But what is most significant about it here is precisely the ways in which it used that conventional framework of women's capacity to regenerate society to attack the prevailing situation of women— not least because while women were charged with the powers of guardian angels, whatever power or influence they had was rendered void by the obstacles placed in their path. When a woman 'leads the way to pleasure or amusement,' Anne Richelieu Lamb argued,

she is followed for a day, a short-lived day, and is admired; when she points to stern duties, and speaks of man as the being of immorality, rather than the mere pleasure-hunter, or lover of the world; when she reasons of self-government, or the principle of self-regulation; what is the result? She is tolerated, perhaps, but laughed at for her pains; she may dance, sing, and be a child as long as she pleases, write pretty stories, string rosy words in rhyme,—but to help in devising or practising such schemes, as may be for the real benefit of mankind, becomes in her a matter for ridicule, a subject of merriment.[112]

The very idea that women can and should serve their family and society in terms of raising moral standards becomes necessarily the basis for demanding education, a wider sphere of employment and independence from men.

The emphasis on the moral and religious importance of women's domestic role took a particular form in England in the early nineteenth century because of its connection with evangelicalism. But the move towards this concentration on women as mothers and towards seeing maternity as the basis for a claim for full citizenship on their behalf had been made earlier by Wollstonecraft as by other feminists involved in the French Revolution. All of them accepted with Rousseau that a home life which contained sexual demands while providing for the proper care of children was fundamental to political order. But where Rousseau—like the evangelicals—saw that home life as ensuring women's seclusion from the political world, Wollstonecraft, like later feminists, saw it both as legitimating women's claim to citizenship and as showing how important sexual difference was in thinking about political representation.

While feminism could never escape its connection with personal rebellion against the constraints of family, society, and conventional morality, feminist theories and programmes inevitably weave a path between, firstly, the radical rejection of convention involved in this personal rebellion, and secondly, the apparently more moderate demands for women to be seen as fully human by being given equality with men, not only before the law, but also in terms of access to resources and institutions. In the early nineteenth century, the emphasis on personal rebellion and social transformation evident in the ideas of William Thompson and Anna Wheeler were contrasted constantly with the emphasis on moderation, pragmatism, and social conformity evident in the writings of Harriet Martineau. That it was Martineau and not Wheeler who became important for mid-Victorian feminism tells us much about the nature of that feminism—and about the increasingly small place in it for personal rebellion.

# three
# MID-VICTORIAN FEMINISM

The 1850s and 1860s saw the emergence of the first women's movement in Britain, with headquarters, journals, and a host of different campaigns aimed at the emancipation of women. Beginning with a petition to reform the laws which oppressed married women and deprived them of any property, the early feminist activists soon turned their attention to expanding the range of employment open to women, to improving secondary education and making higher education accessible to women, and then to the suffrage.[1] The campaigns were accompanied by the establishment of a number of feminist periodicals, some of which spelled out in graphic detail the full extent of women's economic, sexual, and political oppression while spreading the ideas and publicizing the activities of those who worked for women's emancipation.[2]

The advent of organized feminist campaigns was accompanied by a marked shift in feminist ideas and outlook. The most significant feature of this new outlook was its high evaluation of women and of what they could be and do. Mary Wollstonecraft's angry and bitter complaints about women have long been the subject of comment from historians. Mid-century feminists by contrast developed a powerful image of sexual difference, based on exalting the general qualities of womanhood on the one hand, and praising the activities, demeanour, and character of particular women on the other. Florence Nightingale was a central figure here. But the merits of many other active British philanthropic, literary, intellectual, and artistic women, including Elizabeth Fry, Mary Carpenter, Louisa Twining, and Mary Somerville, all served to show what women were capable of and what might be hoped for by emancipating the whole sex.[3] Queen Victoria too was seen as an exemplary woman, and was written about at length by feminists.[4] Overall, then, where Wollstonecraft—like Mill—set men up as the highest standard of human achievement, mid-Victorian feminists rejected this view, arguing that the very idea that women wanted to become like men was a sign of male arrogance. They set up instead a model of female excellence which combined accepted ideas about women's morality, chastity, and nurturance with an assertion of their intelligence, their independence, and their personal strength. As a result, they demanded and sought not simply political rights for women, but also that women be able to use and exercise their specific moral qualities in all areas of life.

This new element reflects the way in which mid-Victorian feminism actually developed. While both Wollstonecraft and Martineau were isolated in and by their concerns about women, the emergence of mid-Victorian feminism coincided with an increasingly large public and philanthropic role for women that involved organized activity undertaken in close association with groups of other women.[5] The importance of female friendships and of familial support groups increasingly came to be recognized and even celebrated at this time, and many early feminist campaigns were organized through close networks of female friendships and family groups.[6] The web of friendships that made up the Langham Place group or the Ladies' National Association for the Repeal of the Contagious Diseases Acts have been explored in detail.[7] Indeed, Philippa Levine has argued that the close and interlinked networks of friends that made up the movement provided the social and personal counterpoint to the 'woman-centredness' that defines its overall theoretical and political approach.[8]

But while the 'woman-centredness' of mid-Victorian feminism brought a new sense of the values and virtues of womanhood, it also entailed a particular and somewhat restrictive idea of who the women were whose emancipation was being sought. In its origins and its outlook, mid-Victorian feminism was a middle-class movement, drawing many of its ideas from the liberal economic and political beliefs that were so important for the middle class, and making extensive use also of a distinctively middle-class ideal of womanhood. Although there was some disagreement amongst feminists over the extent and nature of the differences between men and women, all accepted the idea that women were innately more chaste, compassionate, virtuous and dutiful than men, and used this image of women as a means of arguing that women needed and were entitled to a larger public role. Their qualities and merits, feminists argued, were such as were vitally needed in public organizations and in the state.[9] While aware of and concerned about the problems of working-class women, mid-Victorian feminists both understood these problems and posed solutions to them in terms of their singular sense of womanhood, and in terms of their beliefs that all women were basically in need of the same remedies: the removal of artificial barriers which limited their educational and employment opportunities and denied them full adult status in family and political life.[10] Their assumption that all women shared the same qualities and problems gave them little insight into their own privileged position, or into the ways in which the class structure, which they took for granted in itself, constituted part of the oppression of working-class women.

Just as mid-Victorian feminism was specific in its class base and worked with social and sexual ideals derived from that class, so too it was very specific in its sense of both national and imperial identity. Like Mary Wollstonecraft, many mid-Victorian feminists possessed a powerful sense of themselves, not so much as British, but as English women. Feminist developments encompassed Scotland and Ireland in this period, with the emergence of women into a range of public activities and the advent of suffrage organizations. But the movement was always seen as one centring in England: either in London or in the north, in Manchester or Liverpool, and with branches elsewhere. This period also saw the advent of a new form of imperial feminism. The general sense of the superiority of the West, in terms of the status of its women—which was so central for Mary Wollstonecraft and caused a particular form of 'feminist orientalism'—gave way to a specific concern with the status of Indian women, who were seen as being in particular need and were regarded as the special responsibility of their more enlightened and more fortunate English sisters.[11]

For all the new developments of the mid-century period, it is clear that many of the concerns and preoccupations of the 1850s and 1860s were ones with a very long history. Moreover, the nature of the early feminist organization, in which small committees of respectable women held meetings and circulated petitions in the hope of gaining parliamentary support for their views, makes it hard to see this development as more than an incremental change from earlier discussions and debates. Feminists during this period participated in drawing-room gatherings, addressed small conferences, and attended and spoke at larger public meetings, but always in ways designed to show their own acceptance of Victorian codes of propriety. The sense of dramatic change suggested by the advent of a women's movement is undercut by the caution and moderation of that movement. Indeed, some would argue that the real turning-point was not so much the early campaigns of the 1850s and 1860s as the contagious diseases agitation, which began in 1869 but dominated much feminist consciousness during the 1870s.[12] This campaign, directed against police regulation of prostitution, soon involved a national movement with a substantial membership, working through large-scale public meetings and demonstrations, direct political intervention in by-elections, and by producing effective propaganda. Drawing on the model of the abolitionist movement, it also developed a powerful religious rhetoric which tied its specific legal objective, the end of the Contagious Diseases Acts, with an ideal of moral and religious transformation—and the end of the sexual double standard.

That feminist ideas became the basis of a movement for political and social reform at this time reflects the increasing numbers of women concerned about their own oppression and that of their sex, but it also points to the widespread interest in political, legal, social, and educational reform that was so marked in British society in the mid-nineteenth century. The women's movement thus worked closely with other reformist groups. Those concerned to reform the laws pertaining to the property of married women turned in the 1850s to the Law Amendment Society as a means of having their views heard within Parliament.[13] The establishment of the National Association for the Advancement of Social Science in 1856 provided another venue where questions which were of concern to women could be publicly aired and debated.[14] This, in turn, paved the way for organized groups of women seeking to become directly involved in sanitary reform, in philanthropy, and in a range of other public projects which required their mobilization to reform social ills. In the 1860s, those concerned about the state of girls' education made their concerns known through the large-scale commissions of inquiry, such as the Taunton Commission set up to investigate secondary education and endowed schools generally.[15] Some also made common cause with those like Henry Sidgwick seeking reform of the university curriculum.[16]

As was so often the case with feminism, however, the apparent allies often provided as much hindrance as help in the realization of feminist goals. In regard to the question of marriage, for example, the fact that the Law Reform Commission had already taken up the question of divorce meant that those addressing the marital problems of women had a ready-made forum. But the very fact that there was a move to reform divorce, thereby enabling some unhappily married women to leave their husbands, provided an excuse for ignoring the wider question of the legal disabilities of all married women. That the new divorce law of 1857 itself enshrined the sexual double standard by allowing men to obtain a divorce on the grounds of their wife's adultery, while women had to prove that their husbands were not only adulterous but also cruel, bigamous, or incestuous, shows that divorce reform did not fundamentally question the hierarchical nature of marriage.[17] In a similar way, the alliance between those feminists seeking university education for women and the better-known university reformers was always very fraught.[18]

Ironically, while the development of feminism was hampered as much as it was helped by its connection with other reform organizations, it was unquestionably helped more than it was hampered by the formalization of the idea of separate spheres during the period. The question whether one can in fact talk about separate spheres in the nineteenth century, and what precisely the separation involved, is becoming increasingly complex.[19] None the less, at an ideological level, the doctrine of separate male and female spheres was widely accepted and, indeed, served to provide much of the framework for feminism. By the mid-nineteenth century one can see the completion of the process begun in the later eighteenth century of withdrawing middle-class women from paid labour in the home or family business and the consequent ending of a family economy and its replacement by a family dependent on a single (usually male) income earner. But this decline of women's capacity to act openly as partners to their husbands in business did not mean that they did not contribute financially and managerially to income-earning activities.[20] At the same time, the recognition that many women lacked family duties or financial support brought a demand for paid employment or public involvement through local and charitable institutions for these women.

While some historians argue that the increasing emphasis on the separation between the public and the private spheres reduced the range of activities that were open to women in pre-industrial societies and limited the community power they had exercised by virtue of their connection with family farms and businesses, others stress the way in which this new discourse also provided the framework that enabled women to take a more active part in politics.[21] In this process, traditional female activities which had been undertaken without comment as an extension of the role of wives and daughters, such as local philanthropy and parochial educational, became designated as 'public' activities—and hence became part of the growing demand for a proper voice for women in the public sphere. Those seeking legal rights and political citizenship pointed to women's philanthropic activity as one of the justifications for their claims, showing through this rhetoric the ways in which many female activities which had once been a part of women's private and familial role were now serving to mark out their independent public one.[22]

The emergence of feminist campaigns was both preceded and followed by a great expansion in theoretical discussions of women's rights and wrongs, their needs and entitlements, and their abilities and weaknesses. The early nineteenth-century discussions about women's nature, duties, and role expanded greatly in the mid-nineteenth century with an enormous increase in the numbers of periodical articles, pamphlets, tracts, and novels dealing with the woman question in general and exploring the pros and cons of feminist demands. The earlier discussions of women's education, of their disabilities on the one hand and their moral and religious mission on the other, developed considerably, as did debate about the problems involved in marriage and the possible alternatives for women. Not only was women's entitlement to a better education debated, but also the precise kind of education and the extent to which it should be identical with or different from men's at primary, secondary, and tertiary levels. In regard to marriage too there was a change: although the problems women faced in marriage continued to be aired, there was much discussion also of all the many alternate ways in which single women might find themselves a fulfilling life without marriage.[23] The great scope offered single women in philanthropy, in religious life, or in education was set beside marriage. Unquestionably amongst some feminists, the sexual radicalism of the late eighteenth and early nineteenth centuries was lost—but the emphasis on the possibilities open to celibate women went along with an insistence on the need to combat the sexual double standard and to recognize women's autonomy, while at the same time serving to displace sexuality as the main focus in regard to women.[24] By the mid-nineteenth century, the 'woman question' involved not only a catalogue of women's sufferings, but also a recognition of their capacity to organize and manage their own lives.

## The Langham Place Circle and the Ghost of Mary Wollstonecraft

The importance of women's friendships within mid-Victorian feminism is immediately evident within the first centre of feminist activity in the 1850s, which developed in London around two close friends: Barbara Leigh Smith and Bessie Rayner Parkes.[25] In 1854, both women published feminist pamphlets: Smith's *Brief Summary in Plain Lan-*

*guage of the Most Important Laws of England Concerning Women* and Parkes' *Remarks on the Education of Girls.*[26] A year later, they were working on a petition to reform the laws pertaining to married women, and drawing many of their friends and relatives into this venture by organizing a committee to help draw it up and circulate it for signatures.[27]

Seeking to publish their views on women and to extend discussions of women's activities, Parkes and Smith established the *English Woman's Journal*, which was financed by Smith and edited by Parkes. The journal brought them into contact with other women also seeking fulfilling activities and some way to improve the position of women.[28] Soon they were joined by other women: Isa Craig, Adelaide Proctor, Maria Rye, and Jessie Boucheret, all equally dedicated to the emancipation of their sex. Boucheret and Proctor set up the Society for Promoting the Employment of Women while Boucheret also held classes in arithmetic and bookkeeping; Maria Rye set up an office copying legal documents; Emily Faithful established the Victoria Press.[29] At first, they worked out of a room in Cavendish Square, but as their numbers and their activities expanded, they moved in 1859 to the house at 19 Langham Place, where the offices of the *English Woman's Journal* were located.[30] The house which gave them their name as the Langham Place circle was indeed central to their plans as it provided not only offices from which all their activities could be run, but also a space for teaching classes, a library, a dining-room, and the facilities for a ladies' club. Indeed Langham Place provided everything that could be desired by a new reform or lobby group, including a coffee shop, an employment list, job training, new social networks, and information for interested women.[31] It also played a leading role in recruiting women to the movement, offering a base and a social network for those increasing numbers of middle-class women who were feeling and expressing discontent with their own lives and opportunities. Emily Davies, for example, set up an office there from which she organized the campaign to have her friend, Elizabeth Garrett, admitted to the medical profession before developing the broader campaigns to expand secondary and tertiary education for women.[32]

The Langham Place women worked closely with the newly formed National Association for the Promotion of Social Science, using its annual conferences and proceedings to expand their sway and raise their public profile.[33] While the NAPSS provided them with a forum, they in turn took up some of the favourite projects of the association. When a Ladies' Sanitary Association was set up in conjunction with the NAPSS, for example, Bessie Parkes encouraged all her readers to participate in its activities and to spread knowledge and enforcement of the laws of health throughout the community.[34]

One of the most remarkable features of the Langham Place group was its capacity not only to attract younger women, but also to appeal to an older generation of women who, although well aware of the problems women faced, had never felt inclined to involve themselves directly in feminist campaigns. The two most notable women in this category were Anna Jameson and Mary Howitt.[35] Both women had established independent lives for themselves, Jameson by leaving an unhappy marriage and supporting herself by writing, Howitt through a close and companionate marriage which involved shared religious beliefs and joint literary endeavours.[36] Jameson's writings on art made her an influential figure for Bodichon's own artistic work, and her interest in questions about women's work and about the marriage question was closely connected with Bodichon's. But while Jameson and Howitt were both concerned about the situation of women, Howitt, being involved with many of the Quaker women active in both abolitionist and feminist causes, neither gave the question of women's oppression pride of place until they were swept up by Bodichon's enthusiasm and brought into the committee she organized to help with her petition to reform the Married Women's Property Laws. Both became signatories to the petition and worked hard to find others.[37] Thus, while it has often been remarked that mid-Victorian feminists were more likely to have supportive fathers than mothers, the movement itself offered a version of maternal support through its own generational structure.[38]

This close connection with an older generation of women gave mid-Victorian feminism the appearance of harmony and of continuity with earlier feminist concerns. And this sense of cross-generational continuity was expanded by the importance given by mid-Victorian feminists to the work of both Caroline Norton and Harriet Martineau. The publication of Norton's *English Laws for Women in the Nineteenth Century* in 1854 was an important event in the intellectual formation of Barbara Leigh Smith, turning her attention immediately to the need for reform.[39] In a similar way, Harriet Martineau's extended discussion of women's employment, and her insistence on the range of work women did and of the need for broad social recognition of women's need for economic independence, played a significant part in the Langham Place employment campaigns.[40]

This direct connection with older women had a counterpart in the very considerable concern evident within most mid-Victorian feminist journals to develop some sense of women's history and of their own connection with prominent, active, and able women of former times. Working within the conventional parameters of their day, their interest in 'women's history' centred on an effort to explore the ways in which women had excelled or been notable in the artistic, literary, social, or political world of the past. Prominent women artists, such as Artemesia Gentilesschi and Angelica Kauffman, for example, were described in the pages of the *English Woman's Journal* alongside well-known writers such as Maria Edgeworth, Mary Russell Mitford and Elizabeth Fry.

While mid-Victorian feminists did their best to link themselves with a tradition of prominent women whose claim to prominence was based on their own talents and endeavour, rather than on their family of origin or marriage, they did not construct themselves as part of an extended feminist tradition. Women of ability, not those seeking an amelioration of the sufferings of their sex, featured in their pages. Thus they had little to say about Mary Astell, or 'Sophia'—or Mary Wollstonecraft.

The prominence of Wollstonecraft for contemporary feminists and her now widely accepted status as the 'founding figure' in modern British feminism makes her omission from the writings of mid-Victorian feminists particularly striking—and seems to demand some further examination.[41] And indeed, an attempt to locate knowledge of Wollstonecraft and of her importance at this time brings to the fore elements of mid-Victorian feminism which are otherwise only too easy to ignore. Although Wollstonecraft was rarely named, it is difficult to accept that she was either unknown or unimportant to mid-Victorian feminists. On the contrary, one cannot but feel that she is a silent presence in many of their texts, haunting them with her apparent disregard for much that they held dear. And it is soon clear that Wollstonecraft was not simply omitted from mid-Victorian feminist writing—she was specifically rejected and disdained. One of the few articles to mention her in the *English Woman's Journal*, for example, drew a clear contrast between the solid merit of Maria Edgeworth and 'the wildness of the Wollstonecraft school, and all its ultra-theories'.[42]

The reasons why Wollstonecraft would be avoided and disdained by mid-Victorian feminists are not hard to find. The impact and the continued currency of Godwin's *Memoirs of the Author of the Vindication Of The Rights Of Woman*, meant that Wollstonecraft's very name symbolized the connection between personal and sexual revolt on the one hand and feminist conviction on the other, a claim which many Victorian feminists sought totally to deny. Mid-Victorian feminists were much more concerned to ally themselves with Florence Nightingale and Louisa Twining, women who combined intellect, ambition, and ability with social and philanthropic concerns and blameless personal lives, than with a political and sexual radical like Wollstonecraft.

But this public disdain does not tell the whole story: while Wollstonecraft was disdained in public, she seems to have held a very different position in private. Thus, at the very time that Bessie Parkes was publishing scathing comments about Wollstonecraft in the *English Women's Journal*, she was writing to Barbara Leigh Smith to express her immense delight at hearing that one of their friends had received a letter from Wollstonecraft's daughter, Mary Shelley. In this letter, Mary Shelley was described simply as '*Mary's* daughter, *his* wife' as if the first name of Wollstonecraft alone sufficed to identify her in intimate correspondence.[43]

This curious discrepancy between public and private responses to Wollstonecraft seems to highlight a central dilemma within mid-Victorian feminism between its respectable surface and its underlying rebelliousness. Many mid-Victorian feminists were quite explicit about their sense that unless they proceeded in a decorous and cautious way, they would have no chance of succeeding in their objectives. And such caution clearly demanded that they eschew any connection with Wollstonecraft. At the same time, Victorian feminism itself was constantly threatened by personal revolt and sexual transgression—and such transgression was always accompanied by some discussion of Wollstonecraft. It comes as little surprise that it was in the correspondence of Bessie Parkes and Barbara Leigh Smith that Wollstonecraft should be such a familiar figure, for both were very much involved in sexual and familial conflicts at the very time that they became active in feminist causes. The friendship between them, as Jane Rendall has shown, was itself a cause of considerable concern in Parkes' family, because of its intensity, especially for Parkes—who found no prospective male suitor as engaging as her beloved Barbara.[44] And indeed several other writers have recently explored the way that questions about cross-dressing, 'female marriages', and lesbianism were raised in relation to feminist circles with whom the Langham Place group were connected in England as well as in Europe in the 1850s and 1860s. In some cases, close women's friendship was readily and easily accepted, but as Martha Vicinus has recently shown, lesbian relationships were quite explicitly seen as a threat to heterosexual and marital harmony. The citing of Emily Faithfull in the Codrington divorce trial brought this whole question into considerable public prominence.[45]

The Langham Place group and its friends and associates were also closely involved in heterosexual scandals of several different kinds. George Eliot, after all, was a very close friend of both Barbara Leigh Smith and Bessie Parkes, as she was of other pioneering feminists, like Clementia Taylor. Her dramatic decision to defy convention and to live with G. H. Lewes as his wife, even though she was not able to marry him, had been taken in the early 1850s, just before the Langham Place group was established, but it was clearly known about and discussed in feminist circles. Indeed, Parkes seems rather to have relished what she saw as Eliot's demand for sexual freedom—writing to her and even daring to visit, despite paternal prohibitions.[46] Interestingly, it was George Eliot who wrote the one essay on Wollstonecraft that connects her directly with the early stages of the women's movement. Eliot's essay also, albeit in a rather masked way, suggests the close connection between Wollstonecraft's life and the conflicts faced by a number of mid-Victorian women. Eliot published her essay on Mary Wollstonecraft and Margaret Fuller in *The Leader* in 1855, the year after she had made her decision to live with G. H Lewes—and also the year in which she probably suffered most intensely both from social ostracism and from anxiety about her status and her future. It was just at the time she was contemplating writing fiction, but before she had published any. This context seems to me to help explain this somewhat curious essay. Indeed, the main point of Eliot's essay seems to be its insistence that Wollstonecraft's scandalous private life had nothing to do with the lack of interest or attention paid to her work. 'There is in some quarters', wrote Eliot, 'a vague prejudice against the *Rights Of Woman* as in some way or other a reprehensible book, but readers who go to it with this impression will be surprised to find it eminently serious, severely moral, and withal rather heavy—the true reason, perhaps, that no edition has been published since 1796, and that it is now rather scarce.'[47]

Eliot saw none of the imagination or eloquence in Wollstonecraft lauded by Godwin, arguing that Wollstonecraft was nothing if not rational. 'She has no erudition, and her grave pages are lit up by no ray of fancy.'[48] But Eliot followed Godwin in her denial to Wollstonecraft of intellectual passion or of serious ideas—or indeed, of seriousness as a writer. Wollstonecraft, in her view, lacked both literary skill and interest in literature as an art. She could not and did not in any way commend her work. Indeed, Eliot seems to be engaged in the rather unusual task of attempting to revive interest in Wollstonecraft by assuring readers that she is intensely dull! But the underlying argument in Eliot's essay, and the one that seems to explain why she wrote it at all, seems to lie in her insistence that Wollstonecraft's text was not contaminated by her private life—and conversely, that her scandalous life had no effect on the reception of the text.[49] Ironically, Eliot's essay serves to confirm the view that Wollstonecraft was widely known about and discussed: it assumes that the basis and nature of the 'vague disapproval' provoked by any mention of the *Vindication* are sufficiently well known to her readers to make it quite unnecessary for her to provide any details of this or of the usual grounds given for the failure to reprint the *Vindication*. Indeed, the essay would have had little meaning if these things were not known. Eliot seems to be displacing her own anxiety about the impact of her private life on her own planned career by suggesting that in Wollstonecraft's case it was lack of literary merit—rather than personal scandal—which determined her standing. Her essay thus serves simultaneously to distance her from Wollstonecraft and to suggest an underlying sense of close affinity.

Eliot's essay seems to me to fix Wollstonecraft closely within the dominant framework for feminist discussions about private life and personal rebellion. Moreover, by focusing on Wollstonecraft, one gains a somewhat different perspective on Victorian feminism. Rather than developing simply out of a sense of women's moral and domestic virtue, one can see that it was surrounded on all sides by questions of personal and sexual rebellion, and that it had constantly to battle to assert its moderation and propriety.

In view of the framework from which mid-Victorian feminism emerged, what is perhaps most surprising is the conservatism and moderation which Langham Place seems to have bequeathed to later London-based feminist activities. The unconventional lives and lifestyles which many early feminists—including not only Leigh Smith, Parkes and Faithfull, but also Frances Power Cobbe—had shared and relished were hidden beneath a proper and decorous exterior and subordinated to educational and political campaigns.[50]

Perhaps one reason for this is that Barbara Leigh Smith, although the galvanizing force behind the group, exercised relatively little influence on it and certainly did not set its dominant tone. Her 'essentially progressive and bold' vision was in marked contrast to the much more timid and conventional ones of her close friend, Bessie Parkes, or of the other women who were attracted to the group, including Emily Davies.[51] Where they sought reform of the laws pertaining to married women, Smith went further, demanding also an autonomous sphere of action to enable married women to pursue their own interests and activities. Where they sought to expand the range of paid jobs available to unmarried women, but hesitated about paid work for married women, she insisted that women's need for work was exactly the same as men's—and that almost all professions and occupations should be open to them. When they were cautious and hesitant about advocating the need for women's suffrage, she was in no doubt about the need to campaign for it as publicly as possible.[52] But few of these ideas were transmitted or communicated in a sufficiently powerful way to make an impact. Indeed, while feminist activists of the next generation, like Millicent Garrett Fawcett, commented on the importance of earlier women such as Harriet Martineau, they did not draw attention to the ideas of Bodichon. Her early work in regard to the reform of the married women's property laws was generally acknowledged, as was her support for Girton College, but there is no sense amongst other mid- and late nineteenth-century feminists of her as having been a powerful or influential figure.[53]

Bodichon failed to impress the women's movement with her own sense of the urgency of suffrage or the importance of allowing women a wider scope for independent action. Similarly, her own personal rebellion, her attempt to work out a private and a professional life which was quite outside the bounds of Victorian convention, also failed to become in any way part of the framework of Victorian feminism. Bodichon was one of the very few mid-Victorian feminists who sought to defy prevailing sexual and moral norms, seeking for a time to live with John Chapman—who was already married and unable to get a divorce. This project, however, was hastily ended by her father who, for all his own experience of sexual irregularity, would not permit it amongst his daughters. Under the strain, Barbara suffered a breakdown and was sent to Algiers to recover. While there, she met and married a French doctor, Eugene Bodichon.[54] Given the history of Chapman's sexual liaisons, one cannot but doubt that living with him would have been catastrophic for Bodichon.[55] At the same time, it is interesting to see the ease with which she was made to conform to patriarchal familial norms. In some ways, her marriage to Bodichon offered a life to her taste. The marriage was in every way an unconventional one. On their honeymoon trip to America, she painted and explored—while he kept house. His work, she explained to a friend, was 'head work' which made it 'good for him to have a little marketing and housework'. Her work, mostly sketching, was, however both 'head work and hand work' and so could be pursued all day long!'[56]

After the honeymoon period, Smith established a pattern of spending half the year with him and half in England, where she could live in her own house, see her friends, paint, and live the life of an affluent single woman. This pattern anticipated some of the marital experiments of the twentieth century, and while many people knew about it, the eccentricities of Eugene Bodichon and his complete inability to get on with Barbara's friends made it also seem as if she chose this pattern simply in order to escape a marriage that was becoming somewhat onerous.[57] Hence it did not serve as the basis for any broader discussion of alternatives to conventional marriage. Unlike Wollstonecraft and Wheeler, Bodichon's life was never the subject or the inspiration of an important literary or feminist text, nor did she urge her own course of action on anyone else. Thus while her life was known about and often commented upon, it remained a singular example of an unusual life pattern rather than setting the framework for a debate about ways of negotiating married life. It was a personal solution which was never transformed into any form of political action. But for all this, Bodichon, like Wollstonecraft, made very clear the connection between personal rebellion and feminist commitment—a connection which remained largely buried, but was always troubling and threatening to Victorian feminism.

Barbara Leigh Smith was not the only sexual radical of the mid-nineteenth century, and she was tamer than some others. While family pressure put an end to her planned indiscretion, a few years later another prominent feminist, Elizabeth Wolstenholme, actually did set up house with her lover, Ben Elmy. Wolstenholme was one of the most prominent mid-Victorian feminist activists.[58] A central figure in the campaigns for reform of the laws pertaining to married women's property and of custody, she was also very active in the Contagious Diseases Agitation and in the suffrage campaign. Almost single-handedly, Wolstenholme also ran a campaign against marital rape, arguing that the laws which allowed a man constant access to his wife's body reduced married women to the position of sexual slaves.[59] In Wolstenholme's view, the new criminal code of 1880 which defined rape as 'the act of a man, not under the age of 14 years, having carnal knowledge of a woman, *who is not his wife*, without her consent,' reduced 'every English wife to the legal position of the purchased slave of the harem'.[60]

In deciding to live with Elmy, Wolstenholme was specifically and explicitly rejecting the marriage laws—and was also apparently intentionally following Wollstonecraft's example. Her behaviour was intensely distressing to many of her feminist colleagues, one of whom persuaded her to marry Elmy before the birth of their child.[61] But despite several attempts to remove Wolstenholme from the various committees on which she sat, she remained a prominent feminist—because there were always at least as many of her feminist colleagues willing either to support her, or to regard her private conduct as her own affair, as there were others desiring that she be ostracized.[62]

The link between Wollstonecraft and mid-Victorian feminism is emphasized in the fact that controversy about Elmy in the early 1870s occurred at almost the same time as the first major efforts to revive Wollstonecraft's reputation were being made, with the publication of Kegan Paul's *William Godwin and his Friends*. Two decades later, she was finally and decisively rehabilitated and claimed as the great feminist pioneer—just at the moment that the 'New Woman' debate again raised the whole question about feminism and women's sexuality.[63]

## Feminism, Liberalism, and the Problem of Sexual Oppression

It was not only through personal rebellion that sexuality became an issue in mid-Victorian feminism. On the contrary, while some feminists were critical of Elizabeth Wolstenholme, many agreed that it was women's sexual oppression, even their sexual slavery, that was the central question. Recognition of this point has brought a considerable revision of the once strongly held idea that the English women's movement was concerned primarily, even exclusively, with gaining access for women to the public sphere, and has directed attention to the concern of Victorian feminists with the oppression of women in domestic life, as daughters within families, as wives in marriage, and in all forms of sexual relations.[64] But while there was often considerable agreement about the basic structures of women's oppression, there was considerable disagreement over how best to deal with women's need for autonomy, and for rights and recognition both in terms of their familial and domestic life and in the economic and political spheres.

For the most part, mid-Victorian feminists, regardless of their party affiliation or specific views and ideas, accepted the broad liberal political and economic ideas which were so widespread amongst the Victorian middle class. Millicent Garrett Fawcett, a leading campaigner both for women's suffrage and for equal education and employment opportunity, for example, placed particular stress on the very close connection between feminist demands and liberal economic theory, arguing that the demand for the removal of the barrier that excluded them from higher education was only a 'phase of the free trade argument'.[65] Liberal economic arguments were also used to argue against the barriers women faced in employment and against any attempt to restrict their hours or conditions in ways which were not deemed suitable for men. In a similar way, liberal political beliefs, especially those centring on the importance of representative government as a way to ensure good government for all and to raise the educational level of the governed, were constantly repeated by those demanding women's suffrage.[66]

But while it is necessary to stress the close connections between liberalism and feminism in the mid-Victorian period, it is equally necessary to recognize that similarity is not identity, and indeed, that there were substantial areas of conflict and disagreement between liberalism and feminism. Liberalism itself was of course extremely complex and embraced considerable diversity in terms of its philosophy, its history, and its temper. Thus, while Millicent Garrett Fawcett stressed the pragmatism of liberalism in her support of its economic principles, other feminists, most noticeably Josephine Butler and some of her supporters, fought against what they saw as the excessive encroachment of government on personal life and stressed the moral and religious impetus of the great liberal reform campaigns, especially that for the abolition of slavery.[67] Such campaigns sought both freedom and moral transformation. For Butler, the great central issue for feminism was the enslavement of women, especially by the legal regulation of prostitution. She strongly supported broad liberal and economic principles, and opposed government intervention in many aspects of economic and family life. But she saw herself not so much engaged in a particular political conflict, but rather as fighting a fundamental struggle for the freedom of women against laws and regulations which not only oppressed, but degraded and enslaved them.[68]

While feminism drew on and sometimes used the language and rhetoric of liberalism, it also critiqued and showed the serious inadequacies of liberalism, especially when it came to dealing with women. Many of those who strongly espoused liberal ideas and beliefs found at some point that their liberalism and their feminism came into conflict. For while liberalism certainly offered a language and a framework for the statement of some feminist demands, it had no way of acknowledging or integrating the feminist concern with exploring the meaning of sexual difference or for analysing the dimensions and dynamics of sexual oppression. For the most part, historically, liberalism accepted as natural the existing sexual division of labour, and thus regarded the hierarchical relations of marriage and the confinement of women to the domestic realm as unproblematic.[69] By contrast, those liberals most strongly committed to women's emancipation, like John Stuart Mill, tended to believe and to argue that prevailing sexual differences were a result of women's inadequate education and legal and political confinement, and that as women were given the opportunities available to men, they would become more and more like them.[70]

Indeed the tensions between liberalism and feminism in the mid-nineteenth century can best be illustrated by examining the contrasts and even the conflicts between Mill's ideas and approach and that of some of the women who were most active and vocal in advocating the cause of women's emancipation. In fact, Mill's position within mid-Victorian feminism was always a contentious one. From the very start, there was pronounced disagreement regarding his importance, Millicent Garrett Fawcett made the most exalted claims for him when she argued that 'Mr Mill's influence marks an epoch in the women's movement. . . . Just as in art, a master forms a school and influences his successors for generations, so the present leaders and champions of the women's movement have been influenced and to a great extent formed by Mr Mill.'[71] By contrast, for Josephine Butler, Mill's views on women were 'but the somewhat tardy expression of a conviction which has been gaining strength in society for the last twenty years'.[72]

For Mill, the basic framework for women's oppression rested on custom: the long continuing tradition whereby the natural position of women was that of dependent wife, with no source of independent income and no independent legal or political rights.[73] The position of women at the current time, Mill argued, still bore all the signs of its origin in a primitive form of slavery and bondage—and women were still the main group in society whose opportunities and whole life framework was determined solely by birth.[74] They were assumed to be lesser than men and designed for wifedom and maternity by nature and by their own wishes—but were denied the opportunity to choose some other path. Every aspect of women's education, Mill insisted, directed them towards acceptance of their lot, for men sought in their wives not only slaves, but willing slaves.[75]

Mill saw the central oppressive relationship for women as that of marriage, and *The Subjection of Women* offers one of the most searing and critical pictures of marriage to emerge in the nineteenth century, with its emphasis on the moral and physical degradation marriage entailed both on women and on men.[76] But ironically, Mill continued to see marriage as the normal state for the majority of women, and to see family duties, rather than paid employment, as the centre of their active life and as providing their chief social contribution. Thus Mill sought neither to end nor radically to transform marriage, but rather to improve and reform it through legal changes and through the granting of political rights to women which would not only give them some say in the legal structures which determined their lives, but would also enhance their status both in society at large and within the family.[77]

Though powerful, Mill's analysis is extremely narrow. His ideas, while used by some feminists, covered a far more limited range than theirs. Unlike William Thompson, Mill had almost nothing to say about single women. His entire discussion of the domestic problems of women focused on the situation of wives. The situations of daughters and sisters, of single women living either alone or under a paternal roof, were thus matters which Mill totally ignored. His omission of these other groups of women immediately separates him from most of the women involved in the women's movement. For them, the plight of single women was of the utmost importance. The demographic imbalance of the mid-nineteenth century and the increasing numbers of single women requiring an occupation and a means of supporting themselves has long been seen as one of the underlying reasons for the emergence of a women's movement at this time.[78] Many of those who came into the women's movement were single women or had sisters and friends who were, and their sense of the restrictions and difficulties faced by such women in economic terms, because of their limited employment opportunities, and in terms of their often restricted lives, was a crucial aspect of their feminism. They concentrated considerable attention on the problems of daughters in particular—thereby addressing the one situation and relationship which all women shared, and the one which was of pre-eminent concern in a society which did not accord daughters much independence. The centrality of the role of daughters for Victorian feminists is evident in the lengthy discussion which the Kensington Society held on the question, 'What is the true basis, and what are the limits of parental authority?' For many Victorian feminists were unable even to undertake their activity in the women's movement without going against parental wishes, and therefore the question whether and to what extent they were entitled to demand moral autonomy—even while accepting daughterly duty—was a significant one.[79] For some, like Frances Cobbe, this question occupied a pre-eminent place in all moral and social discussion.[80] Focusing on daughters, moreover, provided an appropriate framework for discussing the power of fathers and for delineating the basis of patriarchy. At the same time, it made marriage into a secondary relationship rather than the primary one for which all women were designed.

Seeing marriage as the key to women's oppression, Mill did little in the way of exploring the ways in which the sexual double standard operated either inside or outside marriage—in relation to men's sexual privilege on the one hand, and to single women and prostitutes on the other. Thus, when many feminists came to believe that the legislative regulation of prostitution symbolized the centrality of the sexual double standard in women's oppression and that the fight against it should be seen as closely connected with that for women's suffrage, Mill refused to countenance this position. Although he opposed the regulation of prostitution, he continued to argue that it was women's suffrage that was the key: once women could participate in the political process, he argued, they would prevent the passage of legislation injurious to themselves and to their sex. The need for women themselves to confront the sexual double standard or to condemn male sexual privilege and its many institutional forms was not something he was ever able or prepared to recognize.[81]

In essence, Mill's approach to feminism involved an attempt to use the public and legislative sphere to bring in reforms which he believed would inevitably trickle down into family and domestic life. The moral and educational effects of the suffrage were for him immense and would raise both the educational level of women and the whole tone of society. But he saw no particular need for women themselves to take a significant or dominant role in the struggle for their own emancipation. *The Subjection* clearly minimizes the extent of feminist organization and activity that was evident by the time of its publication in 1869 and often tends to belittle those women engaged in it.[82] Where, for many feminists, activity and involvement was itself part of the whole feminist project, Mill seemed more concerned to ensure that women whom he regarded as unreliable did not engage in anything that could be considered unwomanly behaviour than he was to give or allow them their own voice.[83]

Mill's lack of interest in women's own contribution to their emancipation reflects his very equivocal ideas both about sexual difference and what women could contribute to society at large. He certainly believed that women had certain intellectual characteristics denied to men, and that their 'sensibility to the present' and capacity for intuition would be of great benefit in the public domain, where it would complement the male tendency to think only in terms of general principles.[84] But he was disinclined to accept that women had any moral qualities different from men—and certainly none that were superior to them. Thus, while all mid-Victorian feminists argued that the very domestic experiences shared by most middle-class women both developed and exhibited qualities greatly needed in the public world, Mill spoke rather of his concern about the extent of their current social and political influence. He expressed great reservations about the expanding role of women in philanthropy. While accepting that educated and experienced women might be able to administer charities competently, he feared that most women simply gave money in a charitable spirit,with no idea of the consequences of their actions. Being unfree themselves, women did not understand the importance of independence for the poor and hence contributed to their demoralization.[85] In his view, the distinctive sphere of womanhood had no positive consequences for women. It merely served to isolate women from education and from any form of public activity. As a result, it led only to a selfish concern with the welfare and well-being of those closest to them and prevented them from developing the public-spiritedness which was for Mill so important.[86]

As we have said, Mill's ideas and approach were very influential for some feminists and certainly played a notable part in establishing the dominance of the suffrage campaign in the late 1860s and early 1870s. His sense of the importance of feminist campaigns being run along decorous lines and in ways which challenged as little as possible the prevailing ideals of womanly conduct was also endorsed by a number of feminists, including Emily Davies, Elizabeth Garrett Anderson, and Millicent Garrett Fawcett. All of them accepted, too, his sense of the importance of men taking a prominent part in feminist campaigns as a means of showing how well men and women could work together.

But even some of those most impressed by and devoted to Mill, like Millicent Garrett Fawcett, ultimately found that addressing the importance of women's suffrage did not fully meet their sense of the centrality of questions about sexuality, the sexual double standard, and about women's sexual exploitation and enslavement in their oppression. Therefore, while not initially participating in the big national campaigns around the Contagious Diseases Acts or the need to recognize the existence of rape within marriage, Fawcett and some of her supporters attempted to combat the sexual exploitation of women through becoming involved in social purity movements and through exposing individual men whom they saw as particularly heinous in regard to their conduct to women.[87] Such an approach lacked a clear theoretical foundation—but served well to express a certain frustration with attempting to use accepted political procedures as the only appropriate means for dealing with the oppression of women.

While Mill demonstrates both the importance and the limitations of liberalism, even when sympathetically applied to women, it is Josephine Butler who most clearly illustrates both what feminists themselves derived from liberalism and the areas and issues over which they came into conflict with it.[88] As one might expect, the conflict came to the fore most immediately when questions about women's sexual oppression were explicitly raised. Butler herself was strongly imbued with liberal economic and political theory and made many of her feminist demands in these terms. She demanded an end to all Factory Acts and industrial legislation which applied to women, but not to men.[89] In addition, she sought legal and political reform: the end of the system of coverture and of the laws which deprived married women of their property; the extension to women, whether married, unmarried, or widowed of the right to vote at parliamentary, local and other elections on the same conditions which qualify men; and complete equality of civil and political rights between women and men. These liberal views were also evident in the early stages of the Contagious Diseases agitation. It was the hostility to central government intervention in private life or morality, which Butler shared with her provincial radical liberal friends and associates, that gave the political cast and framework to her opposition to the Contagious Diseases Acts and which provided a clear way for her to differentiate her concerns from those of rescue workers seeking to redeem or care for individual prostitutes.[90]

It was the Contagious Diseases Acts which brought Butler to prominence in the women's movement and which also caused her to develop and extend her feminist analysis and ideas. The Acts, which were passed in 1864 and extended in 1866, were designed to reduce venereal disease in the army and navy by establishing a system of compulsory medical examination for any woman thought to be a 'common prostitute' in a naval garrison or port. If found to be diseased, the woman could be confined to a lock-hospital for treatment.[91] Butler had long been preoccupied by the sexual double standard and by the fate of young prostitutes, whom she saw as victims of male lust and of society's endorsement of the double standard.[92] The Contagious Diseases Acts went further than anything previously in actually embodying the double standard in legislation. The Acts assumed that men, acting on their own natural sexual impulses, required the provision of prostitutes, and that to meet this need, the government should find ways of providing a supply of 'clean' and healthy women. These women, in turn, were de-

nied the most basic of civil rights: prostitution was not a criminal offence, but none the less, under the Acts, even the suspicion that a
woman was a prostitute could result in her arrest, arraignment before a
magistrate, and imprisonment for a lengthy period. Far from outlaw-
ing prostitution, Butler—and later historians—have argued that the
Acts and the police procedures encouraged it by enforcing the label on
women and then ensuring that they were unable to escape from it.

Initially, the Contagious Diseases campaign combined in a very easy
way Butler's great hostility to excessive government interference in the
lives of individuals and her concern about the double standard in
sexual morality. She frequently presented the Acts as a 'slave code' imposed on women, thus drawing even more closely the parallel between
her concern and that for the abolition of slavery.[93] But for her, as for so
many mid-Victorian feminists, the prostitute symbolized women's
oppression through her lack of educational and employment opportunities and her absolute dependence upon male sexual desire for her
survival. Thus the laws themselves became for Butler a symbol of the
ever-growing encroachment of masculine sexual privilege on the lives
and freedom of women. In the course of the campaign she became
more and more aware, not simply of the ways in which the Acts denied
women legal and civil rights, but even more of the ways in which they
set up new structures of male authority that ensured men's unimpeded
access to women's bodies and offered men a range of new ways to hu-
miliate and degrade them. In the course of her reports on the operation
of the Acts, Butler pointed to the venial and indeed sexual investment
which many men had in the whole process and which she saw as evident
in the fact that the men could switch roles—so that the man who was
the client one day was the magistrate sentencing prostitutes to lock-
hospitals on the next.[94] Nor had Butler any faith in the disinterested approach of the medical profession, arguing rather that there was 'a
deadly fight on the part of us women for our bodies' against 'medical
lust'.[95] The 'diabolical triple power' of police, magistrates, and doctors
was a fundamental theme for Butler, who saw these groups as creating a
whole network of men who were engaged in the systematic surveil-
lance, degradation, and oppression of women.[96]

Through the Contagious Diseases campaign, Butler came increasingly to recognize the importance of female solidarity and of woman
being the primary actors in fighting for their own oppression. 'Sys-
tematized prostitution will never be overthrown', she argued, 'till it is
attacked by women.'[97] The redress of any great social wrong required
that those opposed to it identify with the downtrodden class. In her

view, the Contagious Diseases Acts, like any form of regulated prostitution, 'secured the enslavement of women',[98] and effectively constituted
a 'slave code'.[99] Many women in the past had groaned secretly over the
sufferings of their sex, but 'the distinctive feature of our time is that they
do more, they *openly* proclaim and pertinaciously *assert* their opposition to the slavery of their own sex in the interests of vice.'[100]

For Butler, the Contagious Diseases agitation was not simply a battle
for the repeal of unjust legislation, but also one directed towards an imperative moral transformation. She sought through the repeal of the
Acts an end to the whole sexual double standard—and hence placed
great stress on the symbolic importance of having women stand together in support of each other and in opposition to sexual exploitation
and 'vice'.[101] Butler's many comments on the need for female solidarity
and support point to her awareness of the tensions evident within the
abolitionist movement. Judith Walkowitz has explored the gender
conflict within the overall movement for the repeal of the Contagious
Diseases Acts, illustrating the way in which women had to wage a double battle: their public fight to obtain the right of women to control their
own persons was matched by a private struggle for recognition of their
rights and authority within their own movement.[102] Male supporters
and organizers on many occasions actively discouraged the participation of women, especially when it came to policy formulation or to
public appearances. Butler wrote to the executive of the Ladies'
National Association, expressing her disquiet over the

tendency which I see among men to allow women to drop out of the foremost
ranks in this crusade, the general tendency both at home and abroad to
consider that our question having now attained the rank of a scientific and
international question advocated by distinguished and learned men, it is less
necessary that women should be the inspiring and even the guiding power.[103]

Butler's approach was thus diametrically opposed to that of Mill.
While Mill himself used the language of slavery in regard to married
women, regarding their sexual slavery as particularly horrific, he continued to believe that the admission of women to the suffrage was the
solution to all other problems. Butler and many of her supporters and
close colleagues focused rather on the need to confront oppressive
sexual relations directly, fighting against the laws and judicial processes
that allowed them and against the social and cultural representations
which appeared to legitimate them. For Elizabeth Wolstenholme Elmy,
as we have seen, women's sexual slavery was not simply a remaining
relic of a barbaric earlier time, but rather 'the root of all slavery'.[104]

Combating it, in her view, required not only women's suffrage, but also specific campaigns directed towards the marriage laws, which denied women's right to property or to custody of children, and against the criminal law, which denied the possibility of rape in marriage, and the Contagious Diseases Acts.[105] But these issues needed to be fought, not only through reform of laws, but also in terms of judicial processes and popular beliefs. The need for change in these areas demonstrated the importance of women's suffrage, but they still needed to be fought for separately—and indeed, they were given priority, suffrage only becoming their central issue after some gains had been made in these other matters.

The whole question of violence and brutality to women, as evident in marriage, and in police and court procedures, as well as in sexual and physical assaults, was dealt with by feminists both in terms of specific cases and in terms of the broader question of why violence towards women took the particular forms that it did. One particularly brutal case, in which the murderer hacked and sawed the body of his victim (with whom he had previously had an illicit sexual relationship) into sixteen pieces, prompted Frances Cobbe to ask the question, 'Why are these particularly revolting murders always committed against women—women who have invariably borne to their cruel assassins those intimate relations on which are supposed to be founded so much of the tenderness of *men* for their sex? Why do the murderers of men, who have often just as much reason to wish to make away with the evidences of their guilt, shrink from hewing a man's corpse as if it were the carcass of a sheep?'[106]

While insisting on the need for women to act in concert and to fight together to end their oppression, Butler's unspoken assumption was that the women so engaged would all be middle-class ones like herself. Although she solicited the assistance of working-class men in her battle against the Contagious Diseases Act, Butler did not attempt to bring working-class women—and especially not prostitutes—into the campaign. Prostitutes were spoken for rather than being invited to speak, and they were always represented as young, vulnerable, and helpless women, more sinned against than sinning, and needing the support and help of other women in their dreadful plight.[107] Butler's powerful campaign drew very strongly on its use and manipulation of a number of particular views and stereotypes of women, all of which served both to empower her and her supporters and to make it unnecessary even to ask whether any women might choose to enter prostitution as a career.[108] Women, in Butler's view, were naturally chaste, compassionate, and virtuous in a far greater degree than were men. Reproducing almost exactly the views of conservative upholders of Victorian domestic ideology, Butler believed absolutely that 'home is the nursery of all virtue' and that women were instinctively home-makers.[109] Hence for her, all prostitutes had been deprived of their natural centre and their proper location, and had suffered as a consequence.

Butler's radical attack on the sexual double standard moved her well beyond the framework of liberalism, but it also had its conservative side. It was based on a strong and very particular idea of sexual differ-ence, and on one which assumed that all women actually had the char-acteristics central to a dominant mid-Victorian feminine idea. Her views on the distinctive characteristics of women were quite unlike those of Mill and very similar to those of much more conservative femi-nists, like Frances Cobbe. With Cobbe, she believed not only that women were home-makers by instinct, but also that it was home which best developed their outstanding qualities, and that emancipation would not bring a diminution of the distinctive—and admirable—qualities of womanhood. Those who feared such an outcome did not understand the strength of Nature.

Every good quality, every virtue which we regard as distinctively feminine, will, under conditions of greater freedom, develop more freely, . . . It will al-ways be in her nature to foster, to cherish, to take the part of the weak, to train, to guide, to have a care for individuals, to discern the small seeds of a great fu-ture, to warm and cherish those seeds into fullness of life. 'I serve', will always be one of her favourite mottos, even should the utmost freedom be accorded her in the choice of vocation.[110]

'It would be wise of the State', Butler insisted, 'to avail itself of this abundance of generous womanliness, of tender and wise motherliness which lives in the hearts of thousands of women who are free to bring their capacities to bear where they are most needed.'[111] Her veneration for this version of womanhood did not stop her demanding complete legal and political equality for women, but it did make her reject the idea that women should have the same education or even the same range of occupations as men. Thus, while becoming involved in the campaign to extend university education to women, Butler did not fa-vour the admission of women to degrees as she did not really want women's university education ever to approximate to that of men's. Indeed, she disliked the women who had received a college education, complaining of their want of womanly 'grace'.[112]

As this shows, questions about how to classify or label feminism in this period raise very considerable difficulties—in part, because those feminists whose ideas and approaches appear most radical, and most accord with our own concerns, combine these ideas with others which appear extraordinarily conservative. Thus Butler's capacity to confront and to find a language to discuss questions about sexuality and sexual oppression works often through the manipulation of a feminine ideal which seems as oppressive as do the laws against which she was protesting. By contrast, some of those feminists who were most hesitant and cautious in their overall approach, and who seem most narrow and conservative to twentieth-century eyes in terms of their specific campaigns and values, like Emily Davies or Millicent Garrett Fawcett, were the ones who argued most strongly that it was the very framework of sexual difference, and the acceptance as natural of one very particular and exaggerated cultural construction of femininity which was at the base of women's oppression.

Emily Davies, for example, eschewed not only the Contagious Diseases agitation, but even the suffrage cause for some time, disliking its radical tone and preferring to put her energies into the struggle to have women admitted to a university education. In this campaign, she could find support from the churchmen and respectable folk with whom she was most at ease. But along with her refusal to broach unacceptable subjects went a complete rejection of the sentimental ideals of womanhood so beloved of Butler. Where Butler gloried in the Victorian feminine ideal, Davies rejected both the idea that all women were by nature philanthropic or self-sacrificing and that they were innately home-making and home-loving creatures. She was neither of these things herself and hence could not accept them in others. Taking no pleasure in domestic activities and lacking any appreciation of the purported wonders of womanhood, she also had little sympathy with the ideal of female solidarity or separateness. Women had long had this, she argued, and now needed to be able to work with men on equal terms.[113] She was concerned not to stress difference or the need for segregated and separate spheres of action, but rather to emphasize the shared qualities and the common humanity of men and women. In her view, the differences between the sexes were absurdly exaggerated in contemporary societies, producing a sense of masculinity and femininity which, while not without aesthetic appeal, bore no relation to actual people or their characters. In her opposition to the conventional beliefs of her society, Davies turned frequently to her religious beliefs and to the teachings and practices of the Church of England.

In baptism, in confirmation, in the catechism the same duties are laid down for men and women. This principle is evident in the Scotch Church as well. The Shorter Catechism teaches that God created man, male and female, after His own image in knowledge, righteousness, and holiness, with dominion over the creatures.[114]

In a similar way, Elizabeth Garrett rejected the view currently being put forward by medical specialists that adolescent girls were harmed by undergoing the same educational processes as boys or that they obviously needed special treatment to ensure their physical and sexual maturation. While accepting that investigation of this question should be undertaken, she insisted that people realise the 'improbability of any organ or set of organs requiring exceptional attention; the rule certainly being that, when people are well, their physiological processes go on more smoothly without attention than with it'. She pointed out too that while the care which girls required during menstruation was cited as a reason why they should not go to school, no one ever felt that domestic servants should be given special treatment during their menstrual periods—nor was there any evidence that working-class women suffered as a result of this.[115]

But Davies and Garrett were both quite unusual in their insistence on the need to question existing ideas of sexual difference and to allow women the freedom to be or become what they chose. Quite large numbers of other feminists tended rather to stress their own acceptance of the full extent and importance of sexual difference, and to put forward their own ideas about the unique contributions which women could make to society, in a framework very similar to that of Victorian domestic ideology—the frame of mind which is so often seen as the one against which they were protesting. The point for them, of course, was that domestic ideology, with its emphasis on the importance of the domestic sphere and of women's dominant role within it, was the only language in the nineteenth century which offered the basis for asserting the sexual differences between men and women, not in terms of women's inadequacy, but rather in terms of their distinctive merits and virtues. It was this ideology which enabled them to claim a significant place in both the public and the private spheres. Victorian feminists, like their French and American counterparts, asserted the need for female public participation in terms of the particular nature of women and the specific contribution they could make as a consequence of their sex and of the familial duties. But where American and French women asserted the importance of republican motherhood and of having women capable of educating the citizens needed by the new republics,

English women drew on the evangelical tradition and on the religious and moral duties of women in an industrializing society. It was ironic that this should be so because it meant that Victorian feminism was imbued through and through with the values of its conservative opponents.

Even Millicent Garrett Fawcett, who tended slightly more towards the views of Davies and her sister, Elizabeth Garrett, responded to the charge that feminists were attempting to unsex women and hence to undermine the sacred role of women within the home, by stressing her belief in the importance of motherhood and the sanctity of women's domestic role. This belief, Fawcett argued, was a central part of feminism.

From Mary Wollstonecraft and Miss Martineau, the spokeswomen for women's freedom have always held in the highest esteem the value of women's work in the home. The fact that to the mother in nearly all classes is consigned the training of children in their most impressionable years in itself is one of the strongest claims that has ever been made for the emancipation of women.[116]

Elsewhere, Fawcett even went so far as to argue that the women's movement had been accompanied by a new emphasis on women's domestic role and by the establishment of higher standards in all areas of women's work.[117]

## Feminist Campaigns and Feminist Strategies

While the manipulation and reworking of Victorian ideals of femininity were an important aspect of mid-Victorian feminist theory and rhetoric, the disagreements amongst feminists about this ideal and about its importance became a central issue in questions of strategy. Several of the principal disagreements, concerning which issues should become the focus of feminist campaigns and how those campaigns should be run, centred on questions about what precisely the emancipation of women meant and about how much should be done, not only to remove particular restrictions from women, but to open to them all the economic, social, and political opportunities available to men.

The first campaign in which the issue of sexual difference, especially in terms of the intellectual differences between men and women, came to the fore was that over higher education. All mid-Victorian feminists agreed that educational deprivation was an essential feature of women's oppression, and one, as many of them would argue, bearing particularly harshly on middle-class women who were denied access to the schools and universities attended by their brothers. But there was profound disagreement as to how best to alter this situation. Some, like Emily Davies, believed that any education designed specifically for girls entailed the arbitrary imposition of a particular view of their nature and capacities. The only way to let women develop their full potential, in her view, was to offer women the best education currently available, which was that currently offered to boys. Hence she sought the raising of the standard of girls' secondary schooling to that of boys and the admission of women to universities and colleges where they would be able to have an education identical to that already available to boys.[118] Davies attempted to secure these aims by ensuring that girls' schools were included in the terms of reference of the Taunton Commission and thus that the quality of education to girls came under proper scrutiny. She also sought to have the Oxford and Cambridge Local Examinations opened to girls as a means of providing external assessment. Her main achievement was the establishment of Girton College at Cambridge, but she did not live to see her ultimate aim realized: namely, the admission of women to Cambridge, and indeed to all university degrees.

But as we have seen, other feminists did not agree with Davies' approach. While she was working in London, a North of England Council for Promoting the Higher Education of Women was set up in Liverpool, with Josephine Butler as its president and Anne Jemmies Chough as its moving force. This group eventually joined up with those who had been working at Cambridge with Henry Sidgwick, to set up an alternate form of education for girls from that offered by Girton. Newnham College, which was founded shortly after Girton, involved the provision of special lectures and classes for girls who had the benefit of university tutors without being required to follow the syllabus or sit the examinations undertaken by their brothers.[119] The issue of special education for girls at this time raised many other questions—not least, about the merits of and the need for more general reform of education. But basically it went to the very heart of the question whether and to what extent feminists really believed in the intellectual equality and mental similarities of men and women, and the differing answers to it make very clear the differing ideas about this most fundamental matter evident amongst Victorian feminists. Henry Sidgwick, in opposing Davies' approach, demanded to know why girls should be exposed to an existing university education which was so seriously flawed?[120] Davies, who never set up to be an educational reformer on a grand scale, countered by insisting that any form of education for girls which differed from that available for boys would be seen to be inferior. 'We are not fighting for the existing Little-Go any more than for one part or another of the Tripos Examinations', she insisted. 'What we are fighting for is the common standard for women and men without in the least committing ourselves to the opinion that the ultimate best has as yet been reached in any examination.'[121]

Davies's position imposed a particularly rigid regime on Girton students.[122] But, as she was well aware, the irony in the whole situation was that those who saw themselves as liberal educational reformers were the ones arguing for a special education for women—one which would not have prepared them for degrees, and which had as one of its aims a perpetuation of that very separation between men and women to which she was so hostile. That this sense of the importance of femininity was central to those who preferred a special scheme of education for women was made very clear, even in the language that they used. Thus, for example, Josephine Butler regarded Davies as one of the 'masculine aiming women' who sought to obliterate sexual differences. She saw Davies attempt to introduce the same education for men and for women as one that was bound to fail—and which made life harder for those of 'us who are driving towards a different and a higher goal'.[123]

But here, as elsewhere, there were very different understandings of what 'womanliness' was, and of how it should be encompassed or negotiated within campaign strategy. Thus while Davies rejected the idea of sexual difference in terms of education, she was every bit as strongly imbued with the importance of accepting prevailing ideals of womanhood when it came to the actual conduct of feminist campaigns, and this, in turn, made her refuse to participate in a large-scale suffrage campaign where she would have to work with radical women whose behaviour she found completely lacking in decorum.[124] Questions about femininity and the appropriate behaviour of women were very important. At a time when the very idea of women speaking on a platform was regarded as not only indecorous, but even indecent, managing a public campaign which needed to persuade male Members of Parliament to take action was seen by some as a very delicate matter.

The suffrage campaign began in the late 1860s with the establishment of two suffrage committees in 1867, one in London and the other in Manchester. They were followed a year later by similar committees in Edinburgh, in Bristol, in Dublin, and then in a number of other provincial cities. From the start there were concerns about how the suffrage question should be handled. Although Davies regarded it as impossibly radical, the London National Society for Women's Suffrage set up a model designed to deviate as little as possible from accepted middle-class standards of womanly behaviour. It organized drawing-room meetings, and public lectures—at which male speakers pre-dominated—and worked hard to show that the women concerned about parliamentary representation were in all other respects perfectly feminine. The importance of demonstrating that 'the championship of woman's cause is not confined to women who have no qualifications for success in the more beaten track' was stressed particularly by John Stuart Mill, who was its President for some years in the late 1860s and early 1870s. Thus Mill insisted that the corresponding secretary of the society always be a married woman, and concurred in the general plan of stage managing public meetings to ensure that only attractive and docile-looking women could sit in the front row, and that anyone who looked 'strong minded' sit at the rear of the hall.[125]

This approach was very different from that taken in the north of England where there was much less concern with decorum and ladylike behaviour and more interest in establishing a large-scale campaign along the lines of the anti-Corn Law League. The establishment of a national suffrage movement was largely the work of Lydia Becker who travelled the countryside speaking at suffrage meetings and provided regular reports on all suffrage activity through the *Women's Suffrage Journal*, which she began in 1870 and edited until her death in 1881.[126] In some ways the contrast between the London-based approach and the Manchester-based approach is illustrated by Becker herself: with her solid figure, sensible shoes, and thick spectacles, Becker typified the 'strong-minded woman' that Mill and Emily Davies would have made sit at the back of the hall—but instead, she sat on the platform and spoke, however nervously.[127]

While some of those in London also sought to keep each campaign separate, The *Women's Suffrage Journal* showed very clearly Becker's sense of the close connection between the campaign for women's suffrage and the disabilities of women in the educational, legal, and domestic realms. It dealt graphically with the kinds of assault and abuses women suffered in the home and on the streets, pointing frequently to the parallels between the situation of women and that of Negro slaves. It used images and language rarely found in the education campaigns carried out by Davies or in the speeches and articles in support of women's suffrage emanating from the London-based feminists. Thus the *Women's Suffrage Journal* kept up a continuous attack on the traditional laws pertaining to the property and legal rights of married women and on the 1870 Married Women's Property Act, which had completely failed to bring into effect the feminist demand of safeguarding all the inherited property and earnings of married women for their own use. It also dealt at length with the question of child custody, reporting on a number of cases in which screaming children were torn from their mothers and handed to their fathers, and commenting on the fact that the position of married women with children was very similar to that of mothers under slavery in that they were not recognized as having any legal rights at all in regard to their children.[128] In regard to the discussion of married women's property, the existing laws and the sufferings of women under them were seen as the background for the reform campaigns currently under way, and the progress of these campaigns was regularly reported. The Married Women's Property Act of 1882 'which secures the women subjects of Her Majesty henceforward and for ever indefeasible legal right to their own property, irrespective of and independent of any husband to whom they may be married', was hailed as 'the Magna Carta for women'.[129]

Although there were clear differences in approach to feminist campaigns, they cannot only be seen in terms of the contrast between London and Manchester. Much of Becker's material came from London-based feminists. Thus the extensive coverage which she gave to the issue of marital violence drew heavily on the writing of her friend, Frances Power Cobbe. Becker was closely associated with Cobbe's campaign to have aggravated assaults against women made grounds for judicial separation. Becker also helped to publicize Cobbe's appeal for Isobel Grant—a woman sentenced to death for killing her husband during a drunken fight. In the very same week, a habitual wife-abuser who killed his wife was sentenced to one week in prison. Cobbe insisted that she was not seeking exceptional leniency for Grant, but was rather arguing against exceptional severity. Why, she asked, should a woman be 'hanged for stabbing her husband in a sudden tipsy quarrel, when homicides of like kind by men are almost uniformly punished as "manslaughter" only?'[130]

But the question of how campaigns should be run, and of how to work for women's emancipation in ways that would gain the endorsement and support of the male Members of Parliament whose action was required proved a very difficult problem for all feminists. Becker herself, while doing things which would not have been approved by Mill or Davies, none the less exercised considerable caution in terms of the issues she dealt with and the ways in which she organized her campaigns. For instance, while she provided detailed coverage of many other campaigns in *The Women's Suffrage Journal*, she drew the line at the Contagious Diseases agitation. Although a supporter and some-time participant in the Contagious Diseases campaign, she never mentioned it directly in her journal. On the occasions when she referred to it, it was in terms so inexplicit as to be meaningless to anyone who did not already know all about it. The first reference to the Contagious Diseases agitation, in 1871, for example, offered a summary of what was being done while Parliament was not in session. This included a 'cry for repeal of recent oppressive legislation'. Readers were told that a committee had been formed for amending the law on points wherein it is injurious to women and that 'the immediate occasion for engaging in this duty has been the introduction of some and the foreshadowing of other proposals of an oppressive and injurious nature as regards the liberties and personal rights of individuals—more especially of women'.[131] Even when the Acts were suspended in 1883, readers were informed that,

the most important question relating to women that came before the House of Commons during the session was the resolution carried by Mr Stansfeld on April 20. . . . It is beyond the province of this *Journal* to enter into any details respecting legislation on this painful subject, but we expressed at the time and reiterate now our solemn conviction that when questions of public morality and matters touching the safety, honour, and welfare of women are under discussion in the House of Commons, members would be greatly strengthened and guided in forming a right conclusion if they were directly responsible to women among other electors in their constituencies.[132]

Becker's sense of propriety was so great that, while the *Women's Suffrage Journal* made a point of marking the deaths of prominent women, it did not even mention that of George Eliot in 1881.

Becker's caution and moderation served ultimately to alienate many of her erstwhile northern colleagues who could not accept her caution on the question of women's suffrage. Becker always worked closely with the parliamentary supporters of women's suffrage, seeing their support as essential if the measure were ever to be gained. In the early years of the suffrage campaign, this meant working with Jacob Bright and other liberals and radicals strongly committed to women's emancipation. But there were times when it meant working with conservatives or with men who were reluctant to see too much change in the existing sexual order. After the election of 1874 and again in 1884, the main parliamentary supporters of the women's suffrage bill insisted on including in the bill a clause explicitly excluding married women from the suffrage. In fact, as everyone was aware, the legal doctrine of coverture probably meant that married women could not vote anyway. But, as Becker herself explained, those campaigning for women's suffrage did not want to 'introduce the marriage question into the electoral law'. They wanted rather to leave the operation of common law to the courts, advocating a measure that would enfranchise all women who met the requirements which entitled men to vote. Despite her opposition to this provision and her regret that it had been inserted, Becker argued that the suffrage movement should support the 1874 women's suffrage bill put forward by William Forsyth Q.C. It was the only bill before the House; if passed it would give women some representation—and its actual workings, in terms of which women it enfranchised, would ultimately be the same as Bright's bill.[133]

Becker's position on this matter was endorsed by the London leader of the suffrage movement, Millicent Garrett Fawcett, who was becoming increasingly important in the whole suffrage campaign. What mattered to them both was that some women were enfranchised and hence could ensure that women's interests were protected in the legislative process. 'If I am right in believing that the enfranchisement of single women and widows would lead to the gradual removal of laws oppressive to women, and would ensure to women fair play in future legislation,' Fawcett argued,

I really don't care whether married women have votes or not. I cannot enter into the feelings of those who violently object to married women having votes. I do not think that there would be an end to domestic virtue and domestic affections if they had votes; but I do recognise that there is a strong feeling in the country against married women's suffrage, and that there is not a strong feeling against the suffrage being exercised by single women and widows who possess the necessary qualification; and believing as I do, that all practical grievances will be removed by the enfranchisement of single women, I, for one, should be perfectly contented with a Women's Suffrage Bill which did not enfranchise married women.[134]

But while Fawcett could accept the idea that all women shared the same interests, and hence that single women would act in the interests of their married sisters, Elizabeth Wolstenholme Elmy saw the explicit exclusion of married women from the franchise as something which reenforced the doctrine of coverture and hence contributed to the oppression and the degradation of married women. She found it a bitter irony that, having devoted most of her adult life to the women's cause, she should be 'spending my last efforts in trying to prevent gross injustice being done . . . by English women to other English women. It is too absurd, and I would laugh at the whole comedy, but for the burning indignation.'[135] This subject surfaced briefly in the 1870s, but became a key issue in the late 1880s when Elmy and Ursula Bright ceased working with Becker, forming instead their own organization, the Women's Franchise League, to press for the full emancipation of all women married as well as single.[136]

As Sylvia Pankhurst later commented, although ostensibly guided by pragmatic considerations, neither Becker's nor Fawcett's strategies paid off.[137] Their preparedness to compromise, to work closely with any parliamentary supporters, and to accept the most minimal suffrage for women did not overcome the opposition of those, like Gladstone, who were implacably opposed to women's suffrage and nor did they serve to make those who claimed to sympathize with their cause actually fight for them in Parliament. The substantial increase in the size of the male electorate served to underline the extent to which the disabilities of women were ones based entirely on sex—while at the same time emphasizing the importance of full political citizenship in men's eyes. Moreover, the failure to have women included in the 1884 Reform Act, despite the extensive outside lobbying and work within Parliament, left a large question mark as to how the suffrage was to be achieved.

The slow pace and lack of success of the suffrage campaign contrasts strongly with the extraordinary success and impact of the campaign most feared and disliked by those conscious of the need for decorum, the Contagious Diseases agitation. Under the charismatic leadership of Josephine Butler, the Ladies' National Association for the Repeal of the Contagious Diseases Acts established a powerful national movement. It began in 1869, and by 1871 had fifty-seven branches.[138] The branches were welded together through a central organizing committee and a periodical, The Shield, which also provided constant and graphic information about the horrors of the Acts and reported the debates and deliberations of Parliament and of the various Royal Commissions set up to investigate the Acts. The movement to oppose the Acts gained enormous support amongst some religious groups, and amongst large numbers of working-class men as well as from many middle-class women.[139] Butler's religious fervour and enormous public appeal served to make it into something of a mass movement, which she and some of her followers saw as one that would not only involve the repeal of these laws, but also bring a great moral and social transformation.

Much of the success of the repeal campaign seemed to derive from its religious and moral overtones, something which was emphasized by

Butler's own sense of herself as having responded to a call from God in undertaking the work and in her powerful use of religious language and rhetoric. The campaign also derived a great deal of its power from its careful manipulation of Victorian ideals of femininity. Taking up the model of the American temperance movement, with its vigils in which genteel women, clad in white, would stand outside bars and brothels and thus make clear the private damage wrought by public vice, Butler engaged also in this symbolic use of feminine purity. Prayer meetings and vigils were regular features of the Contagious Diseases campaign, used as a means of contesting public space and of questioning the different standards operating in public and private spheres.[140] This dramatic use of femininity, and of having perfectly clad middle-class women talking about prostitution and sexual violations of women, had an impact both on women and on men which was far greater than that of the staid suffrage campaign. Indeed, it was only when these techniques began to be used by the militant suffragettes that the suffrage movement itself became a mass campaign that gained national attention. It allowed for a much more direct, and potentially violent confrontation with masculine privilege: on occasion, Butler and her followers were threatened with violence and even death, but this, in turn, only exalted their sense of potential martyrdom. At the same time, however, it was remarkably successful, suggesting that while feminist campaigns did well to utilize images of femininity, they could not properly be conducted by those who sought never in any way to transgress accepted boundaries of feminine behaviours.

## Nation and Empire in Victorian Feminism

In the past few years, increasing attention has been paid to the fact that organized feminism in Britain emerged in the context of Victorian imperialism and to the significance of the imperial discourse and concerns evident in the writing of many feminists. Millicent Garrett Fawcett was particularly outspoken when she described herself as a 'worshipper at the inner shrine, the holy of holies, all that England stands for to her children, and to the world', but she was not alone.[141]

The very nature of nineteenth-century feminism made the question of imperialism a central one; in seeking to establish the political basis of women's oppression and to demand the recognition of women's place in the nation, mid-Victorian feminists embraced existing ideas of that nation, and, by extension, of the empire. The question of women's

rights and of citizenship had been raised by Wollstonecraft, but her understanding of citizenship had been confined to participation in local
and neighbourhood matters. She had hesitated over the suffrage and
refrained from demanding full political rights. By the mid-nineteenth
century, women's participation in local matters, especially in philanthropic and church activities, was dramatically increasing. Feminists
sought to extend this still further, moving into the area of local
government and beyond, into national and imperial politics. By the
mid-nineteenth century, the 'public sphere' and the nation had become almost synonymous for them.[142] Thus, for example, Barbara
Bodichon argued that giving women the vote would increase their
public spirit and their patriotism, by producing 'a lively, intelligent
interest in everything which concerns the nation to which we
belong'.[143]

The demand for inclusion in national political life reflected the class
basis of mid-Victorian feminism. The mid-Victorian women's movement was predominantly a middle-class one with a membership drawn
almost exclusively from the professional and upper middle classes and
from the gentry. Many of those active within it had come to political
consciousness through the historical campaigns, such as that to end the
Corn Laws, through which their fathers and husbands had demanded
recognition of the political rights, needs, and power of the middle class.
Women had been drawn into the anti-Corn Law League in the 1840s
and many had taken a close interest in mid-nineteenth-century political developments. This sense of their own activities as having national
significance is evident in the very naming of the first suffrage committees, all of which claimed to be 'national', even if located in a specific
city, and all of which later combined to form the National Union of
Women's Suffrage Societies.[144] The connection of women with the nation and with national political concerns was extended in the later part
of the century as they were drawn into parliamentary campaigning and
party organizations on an ever-increasing scale. The passage of the
Corrupt and Illegal Practices Act of 1883 increased this trend. The Act
outlawed the use of paid agents and their customary usage of bribery,
treating, assault, or abduction to ensure that electors turned up on polling days and that they voted the right way. This, in turn, made it necessary to find new ways of organizing parliamentary campaigns—and
the wives, mothers, and daughters of candidates provided an obvious
source of labour and assistance.[145] To expand the base of party support
and to co-ordinate the activities of women, a number of party organizations and auxiliaries were established, including the Tory Primrose

League and the Women's Liberal Federation in the mid-1880s, followed by the Women's Liberal Unionist Association and the Conservative and Unionist Women's Association.[146]

The establishment of these party organizations led to considerable debate within feminist organizations, most of which sought to remain independent of specific party affiliation, while recognizing that their members had close party ties.[147] At the same time, the emergence of the party auxiliaries raised a range of questions about how precisely women fitted within the nation: they were expected to campaign, to make speeches, to understand national elections and issues, and to persuade others to accept their views—and yet those very parties which sought to make such extensive use of them opposed the idea of giving women the vote.[148] Feminists sought to pressure the party auxiliaries to support women's suffrage—but many women who felt that these organizations allowed them an immense sway, and that they could have more influence working through them without the vote, were closely involved in these auxiliaries and in parliamentary campaigns.[149]

This demand for the inclusion of women within the nation went along with the frequent insistence that women and their participation were essential for national strength and greatness. The idea that 'British womanhood' was superior to any other, and was indeed a primary illustration of British superiority, was frequently stated, and increasingly from the mid-1850s onwards, in articles which set out to describe or examine the women of different countries. European women, particularly French and Italian women, were the subject of great interest— and served almost as much as articles on the Colonies to demonstrate the excellence of things English. Frances Cobbe's article on 'Women in Italy in 1862' is an interesting example. It reads like a kind of natural history of Italian women, in which they are placed under a microscope in order that their strange ways might be revealed. The article is in large part a list of the inadequacies of Italian women: their lack of education; the rigidity of their Catholicism and its effect on their intellectual and moral development; their lack of reflection and self-consciousness; their lack of true religious feeling; and the sad limitations of their lives, make up the bulk of Cobbe's discussion. Cobbe's hatred of Catholicism dominates her discussion, providing the basis for her view of the degradation and limitations of Italian women. Even though they engage in charity, for example, they know nothing of the English spirit of philanthropy: rather, their actions are determined by 'the great moral plague of Catholicism', so that they treat charity as a matter of spiritual earning to the giver rather than natural benefit to the receiver.[150] Italian women thus do not engage in workhouse visiting or in any of the philanthropic activities that were becoming so prominent in England in the mid-nineteenth century. Those of the wealthy classes tend to frivolity—but amongst the humbler classes of servants, Italians 'are no worse and no better than French, Swiss or Irish servants'. They are, however, particularly prone to creating myths since 'truth, *as a virtue in itself*, is barely recognised at all by Catholic nations'.[151]

This belief in the inferiority of other nations augmented the emphasis in feminists' arguments about the need for women to be allowed to act as a bulwark against the instability and the threats posed by other seekers of political rights—especially working-class men and migrants. Indeed, the full measure of the class assumptions of mid-Victorian feminism are often found stated most clearly in these comparisons, which take it for granted that only middle-class women typify British womanhood. The working class, male or female, were thus as much of a threat to British values and British political stability, in the eyes of some feminists, as were foreigners. A sense of the alienness of the working class is made very clear in the work of Frances Cobbe, for example, as she fulminated against the opening of 'the gates of our sacred polis to a rabble of illiterates' in 1884. She sought to show the contrast between

proposals to admit the dregs of a population to the franchise, and those to admit the mothers, daughters and sisters of the men who already exercise it; and again between proposals to admit aliens of another race, and those to admit women who have the same hereditary tendencies and attachments, creeds and interests; and who are the inevitable partakers of the nation's prosperity, and the deepest sufferers by its disasters and misrule.[152]

Lack of desire to include workers or foreigners within the constitution did not mean that there was no interest in them or their well-being. The women's movement was in many ways very concerned about the needs and the problems faced by working-class women. Several of the first papers given by members of the women's movement at the National Association for the Promotion of Social Science addressed the question of women as industrial workers and as manual labourers in non-industrial fields, for example, and many of the campaigns to improve the lot of married women as well as the Contagious Diseases agitation took working-class women as their focus.[153] This concern with working-class women was the more easily expressed because feminists assumed that working-class and middle-class women faced the same problems in terms of their subjection to husbands and masters and to the various legislative restrictions that reduced their economic freedom. Thus middle-class women were well able to speak for their less fortunate 'sisters'.

For Frances Cobbe herself, feminism was always closely connected with philanthropy and she was one of many Victorian feminists who saw themselves as 'happily circumstanced women' whose duty it was to campaign on behalf of their suffering sisters. But this in turn involved a strong sense of herself as knowing and understanding what other women needed. Cobbe became concerned particularly with the question of domestic violence, using all her journalistic skills to publicize the frequency of its occurrence and the leniency with which its male perpetrators were dealt with in the courts. She was a central figure in the campaign to have aggravated assault recognized as a ground for judicial separation. But for Cobbe, as for John Stuart Mill, it was within the working class that domestic violence was most widespread, serving further to show how uneducated and lacking in the values most respected within polite society this class was. Cobbe thus campaigned for reforms on behalf of working-class women, but rarely thought of them as able to campaign or organize on their own behalf.

The close connection between feminism and philanthropy in the mid-nineteenth century established the framework through which feminism expanded to incorporate imperial projects and ideals. The rate and the importance of imperial expansion in the mid-nineteenth century meant that the needs of the colonies became significant almost as soon as the widespread involvement of women in philanthropy came to be accepted. As Antoinette Burton has argued, 'our magnificent colonies' became the natural ground for the practice of British women's philanthropy, offering a whole new range of avenues which provided relief from the constraints on their reform activities at home. Philanthropic work within the colonies also became a source of collective national pride.[154]

Mary Carpenter, whose pioneering work in the setting up of 'ragged schools' and in the campaign for industrial schools made her a heroine amongst mid-Victorian feminists, also played a leading role in setting up the concern with Indian women which has recently been described as the 'special burden' of British feminists. As a result of a close family association with the Bengali reformer, Raja Rammohan Roy, Mary Carpenter became deeply interested in India and very concerned with the oppressive conditions for women which Roy outlined. Roy's unexpected death so moved Carpenter that she decided to visit India and to work there, 'with the spirit of my beloved father and the noble Raja for the elevation of women, and perhaps also for the planting of a pure

Christianity'.[155] Carpenter toured India in 1866–7, where she visited jails, asylums, and girls' schools as well as observing society generally. On her return, she published *Months in India* in which she paid particular attention to the deplorable state of girls' education and the institution of child marriage. Carpenter developed a lifelong concern about India, lecturing frequently on it, writing to Indian authorities, and lobbying both the Queen and the India Office. She returned to India several times and kept up her pressure for reform until her death in 1876.[156]

While Carpenter's schemes and her pressure were unwelcome both to colonial administrators and missionary societies, she was accorded immense attention and respect by feminists. Her ideas on India were presented in the *Englishwomen's Review* as offering the 'regime of truth' about India, and she was held up both as a feminist ideal and as an imperial heroine—thus immediately connecting the two, and indicating the importance of imperial questions for feminism. Carpenter's deep-seated concern about Indian women went along with an unquestioning assumption that she understood them and their needs absolutely, and that it was the special duty of British women to assist and guide their Indian sisters. 'The capabilities of Hindoo women are not inferior, under proper development, to their western sisters,' she wrote, and moreover, 'the natives work well under the English, if . . . they fully realize the superiority of the British character and yield to its guidance with willingness'.[157]

Following on from Carpenter's particular concern about the education of Indian women, she planned a scheme with Anna Gore-Langton to send trained British 'lady teachers' to India to preside over a number of girls' schools. Carpenter's enthusiasm was effective in raising money, and in interesting British women both at home and in India in the reform of girls' schooling. After an initial emphasis on sending British women to India, scholarships were provided to train Indian women as teachers as well.[158] The concern about education was followed by one about women's health and about the need for the provision of women doctors to Indian women who would not countenance male doctors. Here too, money was raised both in Britain and in India to provide training, initially for British women, but also for Indian women to become doctors.[159] As Antoinette Burton points out, there was throughout all of this some recognition of the abilities and the achievements of specific Indian women. But overall, the schemes directed towards India were seen as ones necessarily begun and mainly carried out by British women on behalf of their less educated and passively suffering Indian sisters.[160]

While education and medical care were the predominant feminist concerns of the 1860s and 70s, they were replaced by questions about the Contagious Diseases Acts and child marriage in the later decades of the nineteenth century. Josephine Butler signalled the need for the Ladies' National Association to address itself to the Indian situation in 1886, and Butler then led a campaign in India very similar to that which she had organized earlier in Britain, seeking repeal of the 'Cantonment Rules' which permitted the operation of brothels within regimental lines and enforced the regular medical examination of prostitutes.[161] At much the same time, the question of child marriage along with that of suttee became a matter of immense concern to British feminists and there was considerable press discussion of the degraded state of Indian women which these practices illustrated. While the situation of Indian women therefore came to concern British feminists, in some cases it was something of an afterthought. Josephine Butler, for example, took up the question of the Contagious Diseases Acts in India only after she had dealt with the European situation, which was so much closer to her heart.[162]

The whole question of British women in India in the nineteenth century has become the subject of increasing debate and discussion. On the one hand, it is clear that the established idea of the 'memsahib' as an imperious exponent of British culture with no interest in India has to be revised to take note of the significant numbers of British women who became immensely concerned about the condition of Indian women and worked, sometimes quite effectively, to keep alive in the public mind their needs and interests. On the other hand, while some of these women came to know and appreciate Indian women, and to make themselves mouthpieces for the goals that Indian women set, others both in India and in Britain assumed that their own high level of education and development made them the ones best suited to know what Indian women needed.[163] In general, they assumed that the aims and objectives sought by feminists in Britain set the framework for women's emancipation everywhere. Mary Carpenter regarded herself as an expert on India after a short visit, and neither Josephine Butler nor Millicent Garrett Fawcett ever visited India at all, although both became very closely involved in campaigns directed towards Indian women. Their campaigns simply involved the application of British programmes to the Indian situation.

Moreover, in some cases, campaigns ostensibly aimed at reforming the conditions of Indian women were directed at least as much towards ensuring the maintenance of imperial stability. Thus behind Butler's concern to repeal the Cantonment Acts was both a concern about the degrading effects of the Acts on Indian women, and a sense that it was necessary to end the state regulation of vice in view of 'the great responsibility which England has for India'. Butler was in many ways critical of the behaviour of British administrators and of the ways in which imperial expansion was undertaken. But what she sought was not an end to empire as much as a more ethical form of imperialism, operated in a truly Christian spirit. While seeking participation and close connection, therefore, between Indian women and the British-led repeal campaign, and attempting to dispute prevailing ideas about the sensuality of Indian women, Butler still represented Indian women as 'helpless, voiceless, hopeless'. Their helplessness appeals to the heart, she wrote,

in somewhat the same way in which the helplessness and suffering of a dumb animal does, under the knife of a vivisector. Somewhere, halfway between the Martyr Saints and the tortured 'friend of man', the noble dog, stands, it seems to me, these pitiful Indian women, girls, children, as many of them are.[164]

Ultimately, for her as for many of the others who became concerned about Indian women in the nineteenth century, each new venture served more fully as a means for British feminists to show their own fitness for political rights and responsibilities through their prepared-ness and capacity to take on their own particular imperial burden.

# four
# THE 'NEW WOMAN'
# AND THE MILITANT

In the 1890s and more particularly the early twentieth century, the question of women's rights finally became a matter of intense public and political debate. After decades of discussion of the 'woman question' amongst activists, writers, artists, scientists, moralists, and educators, questions about the nature and the situation and the demands of women began to feature in the popular imagination—as *Punch* cartoons of the late 1880s and 1890s, featuring powerful and athletic women on bicycles or cricket fields, or bullying effeminate men at cocktail parties, serve to show.[1] Public discussion and press coverage became even more extensive with the advent of militancy and the massive suffrage demonstrations which developed after 1907.[2]

The nature of the 'woman question' changed in this period too: extensive discussion of the 'new woman' in the 1890s raised a number of questions about marriage and sexuality that had rarely been publicly debated previously.[3] The new methods of campaigning used by militant suffragettes and moderate suffragists alike, with the ever-expanding use of banners, posters, pageants, plays, and marches, ensured that the battle for political rights was accompanied by an equally powerful battle of representations. In the course of this, the conventional Victorian feminine ideal was challenged by contrasting images of women: as militant and martyred in the style of Joan of Arc; as strong and composed professional women, especially doctors, lawyers, and Members of Parliament; or, for anti-suffragists, as drunken slatterns, shrewish housewives and neglectful and immoral wives and mothers.[4]

The increasing prevalence of images and discussions of the 'woman question' at this time bore witness to a massive increase in feminist organization, agitation and activity. This was most notable in the rapid increase in suffrage societies and suffrage activity in the early twentieth century.[5] But it was evident also in the campaigns to expand the role of women in local government and education, and in the widespread discussion of women's work, their needs and their duties as mothers, and their contribution as citizens.[6] It was not only those who supported women's suffrage who became more organized, but also their opponents. There had always been large numbers of vocal and influential opponents of the women's movement in general, and of women's suffrage in particular. But now there was the establishment of an Anti-Suffrage League with elected presidents, a periodical, and a large number of public meetings.[7]

But while feminist campaigns and debates expanded enormously in this period, some of these developments brought new conflicts and new problems. Conflict centred on a number of different issues. One of the most prominent was simply that of age cohort or generation. This period was an unusual one in the history of feminism because it contained a number of different generations working at the same time. Some prominent mid-Victorian feminists including Elizabeth Wolstenholme Elmy, Millicent Garrett Fawcett, and Emily Davies were still actively involved in feminist activities, often continuing to follow the paths and approaches which they had adopted in their earlier lives and activities. But their outlooks were in many ways very different from those of a new generation whose ideas, values, and approach to strategy encompassed new social and political possibilities. Generational conflicts were evident in many different areas: in ideas about sexuality and about the nature of womanhood; in attitudes towards the labour movement and the situation of working-class women; in ideas about politics and about how best to organize the suffrage campaign; in disagreements over questions about nationalism; and in pacifism, which surfaced in almost every organisation during this period.[8] Some of these divisions also illustrate the expanding scope and range of feminism, which, for the first time, lost its largely middle-class identity.[9] The growth of the labour movement, the expansion in the number and scope of trade unions, the establishment of the Independent Labour Party and the Fabian Society, all led to a new set of debates about working-class women and about whether their needs and interests were best served by a predominantly middle-class women's movement or by the labour movement.[10] This period was, moreover, the first one in which working-class women emerged in sufficient numbers and with sufficient force to articulate their own concerns and to express their own demands. New organizations, like the Women's Cooperative Guild, or the Lancashire and Cheshire Textile and other Workers Representative Committee began to express their own views and to enter into debate both with the labour movement and with the women's movement as they sought to address their own needs as working-class women.[11]

The involvement of working-class women also brought to the fore new questions and problems which had not previously troubled middle-class feminists, but which became primary concerns in the twentieth century. The most notable of these was child care and the question of how to combine paid employment and political agitation with family responsibilities. Although there was no agitation for child care as a feminist demand at this time, the question of how working women managed was a matter of concern to the Women's Co-operative Guild, which undertook surveys to gain information. This question was also one of great moment to those working-class women who devoted their time to feminist and other political activities, but without the luxury of being able to leave their children with servants.

Debates about whether women constituted a specific group or whether their situation was determined rather more by their social class led in turn to a recognition of differences amongst women and to a broader analysis of the meaning of the category of 'women'.[12] Imperial questions also came to the fore at this time. The question of the relationship between English feminists and their Irish, Indian, and South African 'sisters' was one which was raised—although not resolved, since many British feminists combined a sense of the importance of internationalism with an often unquestioned acceptance of imperialist assumptions.[13] The national and international crises of the period were all reflected within feminism. Both the Boer War and the First World War brought into a new prominence questions about the relationship of feminism to nationalism and militarism on the one hand, and to internationalism and pacifism on the other.[14]

The expanding range of feminist and anti-feminist activities and campaigns was anticipated by the 'new woman' debate in fiction, drama, and in the popular press in the 1890s. The 'new woman' debate raised to a high profile questions about whether or not women wished to reject marriage and family ties. Feminist interventions in this debate, both in fiction and in terms of discussions about femininity, marriage, sexuality, and women's autonomy, added a new dimension to feminist theory. At the same time, new intellectual and scientific developments brought a rethinking of women's sexuality. For some recent commentators, what is most noticeable about late nineteenth-century ideas on sexuality, Social Darwinism, eugenics, and national efficiency is the ways in which they re-enforced the centrality of women's biology, elevating motherhood to an altogether new height and making it central in women's contribution to racial health and prosperity.[15] But increasingly, historians have come to see that in the eyes of late nineteenth-century feminists, there was often much that was attractive in these 'progressive' developments, which allowed for the assertion of women's sexual needs, offered a powerful way for thinking about female citizenship, and provided a new basis for demanding an end to the sexual double standard.[16]

## Feminism and the 'New Woman'

While the late nineteenth century obviously saw continuity with mid-Victorian feminism, there was also much that was new. Many of the new issues can best be seen in the emergence during the 1890s and the early twentieth century of a series of new terms—including 'feminist', 'suffragist', and 'suffragette'—which replaced the clumsy phrases which mid-Victorian women had been obliged to employ in order to signify their connection with the women's cause. Thus while Frances Power Cobbe referred to herself as 'a woman's rights woman', and Millicent Garrett Fawcett wrote in the 1870s about 'the camp of what is called, for want of a better term, "the woman's movement"', Cicely Hamilton and Dora Marsden described themselves simply as 'feminists', while the Pankhursts and their followers gloried in the term—first applied to them as one of abuse—'suffragette'.[17]

The first term around which considerable discussion and redefinitions of feminism occurred was that of 'the new woman', which dominated much literary and social debate in the mid-1890s. The term 'new woman' burst onto the English literary and journalistic scene in 1894,[18] after several decades during which a series of other terms had been used in an attempt to describe what many regarded as the worrying changes in the behaviour, the activities, and the demeanour of women. The 'Girl of the Period', whose behaviour caused such distress in the 1870s, was followed by a debate about the 'Revolt of the Daughters' in the late 1880s. But both fell into disuse in the 1890s, when the 'new woman' emerged to state her case for change with the *fin-de-siècle* questioning of so many institutions, assumptions and beliefs, particularly those centring on sexuality, marriage, and family life.

The 'new woman' aroused passionate feelings within the women's movement; for some, the 'new woman' was almost synonymous with the advocates of women's rights, but many of those active within the women's movement hated both the term and qualities which it seemed to describe. The discussion about the 'new woman' showed very clearly the extent of generational conflict within the women's movement, as some young feminists played a significant part in naming and defining the 'new woman', using her to attack some of the Victorian ideals of marriage and womanliness which had been upheld by their mid-Victorian predecessors. These predecessors attempted alternately to deny that there was anything new in the womanhood of the 1890s and to suggest that the 'new woman' was simply a better-educated woman than had been common in earlier decades.

Although it was obviously just a matter of time before someone added 'woman' to the growing list of people and institutions character-ized as 'new' at the turn of the century, Sarah Grand was the first to at-tempt to define it in 1894 and Grand unquestionably put a particular stamp on the discussion with the extraordinarily violent and confron-tational language that she used to describe and to praise the 'new woman'.[19] Allowing no place for Victorian ideals of femininity, Grand distinguished between 'the cow-woman and the scum-woman' on the one hand, and the 'new woman' on the other. The former, in her view, were treated by 'the bawling brotherhood' either like domestic cattle or as prostitutes; the latter rejected the idea that 'Home-is-the-Woman's-Sphere' and sought a wider world of thought and activity.[20]

In a series of later articles, Grand redefined her ideas, showing them to be rather less critical of traditional womanly demeanour than she had first suggested. But throughout she made clear her own sense that the existing form of sexual relationship and existing sexual stereotypes were no longer possible. Grand also foreshadowed what was later to become a central theme for many feminists when she insisted that the 'Modern Girl' must choose,

whether she should be the gentle namby-pamby, of little consequence, never at ease, incapable of independent action, unfitted for liberty, a dependent and a parasite from the cradle to the grave, or that nobler girl who is not the less ten-der because she is self-reliant, nor the less womanly because she has the power to resent insult and imposition.[21]

Independence and self-reliance became central issues in this whole at-tempt to define what women should be, while dependence, especially financial dependence, was seen as parasitic.[22]

The 'new woman' was a vital preoccupation in a range of English fiction in the 1890s, most notably in Mona Caird's *The Daughters of Danaus*, Emma Brooke's *The Superfluous Woman*, Sarah Grand's *The*

*Beth Book* and *The Heavenly Twins,* Olive Schreiner's *Story of an African Farm,* Grant Allen's *The Woman Who Did,* George Gissing's *The Odd Women,* and Thomas Hardy's *Jude the Obscure.*[23] For Gissing, Hardy, and Allen, what differentiated the 'new' woman from her mother or older sister was her rejection of marriage, either because she condemned it as a degrading institution for women—preferring free sexual unions—or because she was a cerebral creature who lacked sexual or maternal desire. Olive Schreiner also followed this approach, making the refusal to marry a central theme in her *Story of an African Farm.* But she was unusual amongst the women who dealt with this subject, most of whom concentrated on detailing the appalling sufferings of those who married rather than on depicting women who sought alternate forms of relationship.[24] Grand, Brooke, and Caird all depicted the moral and physical sufferings and degradation which married women suffered at the hands of their husbands and families.

It was Mona Caird who took up the question of marriage in the most critical way, insisting that it involved the enslavement of women and the atrophy of their intellectual abilities and personal identity. Marriage, in her view, still carried the marks of its barbaric origin, involving the sale and enslavement of women and the binding of them to a man for his personal use and for the procreation of his children.[25] For Sarah Grand, as for Emma Brooke, and later Christabel Pankhurst, there was also the more specific problem of the sexual double standard, symbolized by the threat to their own health and that of their children which women faced as a result of their husband's sexual indulgence.[26] In their novels, innocent and ignorant women faced the terrible suffering which came from venereal disease and which was a result both of their own sexual ignorance and of the past sexual excesses of their husbands. Constant ill health for themselves—and the even greater horror of giving birth to children with congenital syphilis—served for them, as for many others in the course of the 1890s, to show why existing marriage was impossible and why masculine sexual privilege and female sexual ignorance had to stop. In using venereal disease to mount a powerful feminist critique of marital and family life, writers like Grand and Brooke served to demonstrate an important shift in thinking about venereal disease that had come about since the mid-nineteenth century.[27] In the 1850s and 1860s, the widespread concern about venereal disease in the army and the navy targeted women, particularly prostitutes, as the source of contagion.[28] By the 1890s, it was congenital syphilis and the infection of innocent women and children which was the focus of concern, while profligate men were seen as the source of contagion.[29] Although there was talk about reintroducing contagious diseases acts in the 1890s, the medical profession and the many social commentators concerned about social efficiency and eugenics united with feminists in their opposition to it and in their insistence that the group needing protection was not men, but their wives and families.[30]

This focus on disease brought a new sharpness and bitterness to the whole feminist critique of marriage.[31] Mid-Victorian feminists criticized the legal and economic basis of marriage, but accepted that individual marriages and 'true' marriages based on love could be happy ones. By contrast, Grand and Brooke argued that male sexual licence made a happy or even viable marriage almost impossible, and that women's sense of bodily integrity and their self-respect often made it imperative for them to leave husband and home. In a similar way, Mona Caird argued that conventional marriage brought spiritual death for women, involving as it did enslavement to domestic labour and child care, and the complete sacrifice of their own intellectual, emotional, and physical needs.[32] In her view, women's economic dependence on men and men's sense of possession of women served to demean and denigrate both sexes, making conventional marriage into a morally deleterious institution for individuals and for society. For her, marriage would not be tolerable until it was completely transformed and became an institution in which men and women were equal, and guaranteed their right to privacy, freedom, and to terminate the relationship on equal terms.[33]

In its focus on sexuality, marriage, and venereal disease, feminism reflected the growing preoccupation with these questions in much of the social and scientific thought at this time.[34] Imperial expansion and social Darwinism combined towards the end of the nineteenth century to produce an immense interest in eugenics and in the whole question of 'healthy' reproduction. The falling birth rate and the lamentable state of health amongst ordinary working-class men led to a very considerable concern for the health of the British 'race' and even a fear of 'race suicide'.[35] Although eugenics has long been seen as antithetical and indeed harmful to feminism, because of its emphasis on women's reproductive role rather than on their rights or individual freedom, in fact many feminists in Britain and elsewhere espoused eugenic ideas, joined eugenic societies, and included eugenic aims and objectives within their own platform. The apparently progressive nature of eugenics clearly made it appealing, as many feminists saw their aims as necessarily consonant with scientific developments and ideals. But feminists were also attracted by the elevated status of mothers that was implied in eugenic arguments and in the attack on a sexual double standard which degraded women.[36] By adopting eugenic concerns about healthy progeny, feminists could attack the sexual double standard in terms of science and public well-being; their concerns could therefore not simply be denounced as the prejudices of individual women. In aligning feminists with those who expressed their concern about the health of the nation, eugenics served to validate and expand long-standing feminist concerns with male sexual behaviour.[37]

The discussion about the 'new woman' both in fiction and non-fiction during the 1890s also reflected the emphasis on sexuality and sexual relations which accompanied the emergence of sexology and psychoanalysis at this time. Havelock Ellis, in particular, argued that sexuality was the core of personal identity, and that women's sexuality in particular needed to be acknowledged. He went further than this, insisting that sexual relations provided the basis for mental health and emotional balance.[38] All of this served to establish a new ideal of femininity and a new understanding of womanhood.[39] There has been much discussion recently of the ways in which sexology undermined the nineteenth-century feminist ideal of celibacy by making it appear sexually abnormal. The further suggestion that female friendships were not 'innocent' but were sexual implied that such relationships were deviant and perverse.[40] However, several historians have pointed rather to the positive effects which accompanied a recognition of women's sexuality and which allowed it to be acknowledged in more open ways.[41] What is most evident, however, is the way in which feminism at this point began to shift its focus away from the needs of single women and towards questions about sexual morality, maternity, and personal autonomy in marriage. Single women did not disappear from the feminist framework, but their needs and interests increasingly seemed to take second place to married women and, particularly, to mothers.

While the 'new woman' debate focused on issues and ideas which were surfacing for the first time in the 1880s and 1890s, it was accompanied by discussion and new perspectives on earlier feminist developments. This period saw a significant rehabilitation of Mary Wollstonecraft, with a series of biographies and critical studies as well as a number of new editions of the *Vindication*.[42] Wollstonecraft's life came to be treated in an increasingly sympathetic manner at this time:

both Elizabeth Robins Pennell and Florence Fenwick Miller commended her 'because she had the courage to express opinions new to her generation, and the independence to live according to her own standard of right and wrong'.[43] Wollstonecraft's martyrdom was still emphasized, but she was now coming to represent a demand increasingly apparent amongst 'new women' to be able to work out and live a life which met her own needs and sense of morality, rather than one that accorded with social convention and respectability.

The extent of this revival of interest in and sympathy for Wollstonecraft made it impossible for even the most conservative wing of the women's movement to ignore her. This was made clear in 1891 when Millicent Garrett Fawcett wrote an introduction to a new edition of the *Vindication*. It is both telling and ironic that Fawcett should have felt compelled to confront Wollstonecraft in the early 1890s, just three years before the 'new woman' burst onto the literary scene.[44] One cannot help thinking that Fawcett sensed the tensions simmering under the surface of Victorian feminism and attempted to deal with them by domesticating and taming Wollstonecraft, and by stressing the extent to which in her writing she had been concerned with women's duties. Fawcett refused to discuss Wollstonecraft's personal life, merely expressing her own disgust for it. 'In unravelling the curious tangle of relationships, intrigues, suicides and attempted suicides of the remarkable groups of personalities to whom Mary Wollstonecraft belonged,' she wrote, 'one is sickened for ever . . . of the subject of irregular relations.'[45]

But irregular unions combined with a powerful new critique of marriage and of the enslavement of women within it were central issues in the feminism of the 1890s, and shortly after this, Fawcett found herself defending the women's movement from the suggestion that it was associated with the 'new woman' or with 'the perfidious barque of free love'. She savaged Grant Allen's *The Woman Who Did*, which suggested that feminism was first and foremost concerned with asserting women's rights to free sexual unions without marital ties. Fawcett began her attack by insisting that, while Allen purported to be writing in support of the enfranchisement of women, he 'has never given any help by tongue or pen to any practical effort to improve the legal or social status of women. He is not a friend but an enemy, and it is as an enemy that he claims to link together the claim of women to citizenship and social and industrial independence, with attacks upon marriage and the family.'[46] But Fawcett's claims were unavailing and while few feminists demanded 'free love' as a specific goal or ideal, feminist discussions were inevitably and extensively coloured by the new sexual pre-occupations of the 1890s.[47]

The complexity of the relationship between the 'new woman' and feminism can perhaps best be seen in the different ways in which it was discussed in two leading feminist papers of the 1890s, the *Woman's Signal* and *Shafts*. The latter was unquestionably the more radical of the two, directing itself as it did to the interests of women and the labour movement and to the introduction of 'shafts of thought' into the dark corners of life.[48] It provided critical but sympathetic reviews, not only of the women who wrote about 'new women', but also of the ideas of Edward Carpenter and the writings on sexuality and birth control published by Elizabeth Wolstenholme Elmy under the pseudonym 'Ellis Ethelmer'. *Shafts'* approach was in marked contrast to that of the *Woman's Signal*, which never lost its associations with mid-Victorian feminism or with temperance and purity, even when taken over in 1895 by Florence Fenwick-Miller.[49] Where *Shafts* attracted the support and regular participation of the most radical of the mid-Victorian feminists, Elizabeth Wolstenholme Elmy, the *Woman's Signal* kept up a regular discussion of and had contributions from Millicent Garrett Fawcett, Frances Power Cobbe and Josephine Butler. The *Woman's Signal* certainly dealt with new issues: rational dress and cycling clubs featured very prominently indeed, but it did not and could not take on board with any ease any wholesale recasting of feminine behaviour or morals.

Because of its close connection with mid-Victorian feminism, it is in the *Woman's Signal* that one sees most clearly the attempt to redefine and to reappropriate the 'new woman' so that it accorded with earlier feminist beliefs and values. Part of the strategy here involved criticizing or condemning fictional portrayals as false representations of a 'real' New Woman, while pointing rather to the way a new generation joined new activities with an older feminine ideal. Thus the first article entitled 'The New Woman' castigated the portrayal of the 'new woman' offered in mainstream journals, such as the *Quarterly Review*, which presented her as someone 'who condemns law and contracts, is in complete accord with the anarchist and demands emancipation from religion, law, custom and authority'. This version of the 'new woman' was a slander and libel. To oppose it, the *Woman's Signal* offered its own definition, insisting that 'the new Womanhood is not primarily an affair of divided garments, private latch-keys, and treatises on the pathology of vice; but that it is essentially an arm, novel and puissant, of the forces of militant righteousness'.[50]

Accepting that the 'new woman' brought a hitherto unknown directness and militancy into discussions of women's position and of sexual morality, the *Woman's Signal* insisted people should recognize that the revolt of the new woman was 'Puritan and not Bohemian, . . . an uprising against the tyranny of organised intemperance, impurity, mammonism and selfish monopoly'.[51] In later articles, the paper rather toned down its emphasis on the militancy and radicalism of the 'new woman' by calling all women engaged in education or in paid occupations, especially ones recently opened to women, 'new women' and by stressing the demand of the 'new woman' for economic independence. By 1896, the *Woman's Signal* was arguing that the new woman was 'simply a creature endowed with a little more strength of body and mind than we have in times past looked to see in our women'. It was 'in the natural course of evolution' that the woman of today would be stronger than her predecessor—and that she would adopt somewhat more of the outlook, manner, and even clothing of her male counterparts as her conditions of existence required more independence.[52] In the following year, even girls attending Board school cookery kitchens became 'new women' because of the care and thoroughness with which they learnt their tasks.[53]

While domesticating and normalizing the concept so that all young women became 'new women', the *Woman's Signal* was very critical of many fictional or literary discussions of the subject. Sarah Grand's *The Beth Book* was deemed excellent when it dealt with Beth's childhood, but tiresome and dull when it dealt with her adult life or opinions.[54] Grand's attack on male sexual behaviour was questioned: was she not doing the other sex an injustice?[55] While the state of the English divorce law was recognized as unjust and wicked, the reviewer could not believe that there was any point in seeking reform of the divorce law until women had the vote.[56] Mona Caird's views on marriage were regarded as excessive and extreme, and *The Morality of Modern Marriage* was criticized as repetitive and hard to read.[57] Overall, the *Woman's Signal* accepted that, while the tone of the woman novel is 'unhealthy', it was better that the poison and distemper which arose from women's legal and social disabilities should come to the surface than that they should remain hidden. But it clearly sought reform and improvement through conventional legal and political channels rather than through challenging ideas of marriage and morality.

In view of Mona Caird's close involvement with *Shafts*, its position on all these questions offers a complete contrast. *The Daughters of Danaus* was described in *Shafts* as a book of 'revealings' and 'awakenings', liable to be misunderstood by the timid and conventional, but in fact a book which 'rings a peal that . . . will be the death knell . . . of that awful slavery of women'. The review included pages of the text—and indeed, became effectively a serialization of the novel.[58] Caird's essays on *The Morality of Marriage* were also serialized in *Shafts*.

The correspondence provoked by Caird's essays suggested that most readers of and contributors to *Shafts* agreed with her, as letters and articles repeatedly attacked conventional marriage, demanding the right for women to have control of their own bodies and lives. The importance of birth control and of voluntary motherhood, the need for an equal moral standard and for new forms of sexual union or marriage, as well as the need for divorce law reform, were all discussed and approved in *Shafts*. It incorporated into its pages many of the demands evident in 'new woman' novels for women's sexual autonomy within marriage. It also published letters and outlines of the beliefs and programme of the 'Legitimation League' with its support for free love and its desire 'to educate public opinion in the direction of a higher relationship between the sexes'.[59] Where the *Woman's Signal* supported the activities of the National Vigilance Association, *Shafts* strongly opposed censorship or the attempt of other newspapers and organizations to boycott supposedly immoral works, like George Moore's *Esther Waters*.[60] *Shafts* thus approved of the portrayal of the 'new woman' even in the novels of men who extolled 'free love'. In 1895, readers of *Shafts* were asked to answer the question, 'Does the modern type of novel help or retard the cause of woman?' While some readers argued that it was necessary to distinguish between Caird's *Daughters of Danaus* and Grant Allen's *Woman Who Did*, others insisted that both Allen and Olive Schreiner, whose novels upheld and even celebrated the decision not to marry, were helpful to feminism in making people think through these questions.[61] *Shafts* also dealt with socialist ideas—and especially with the insistence by all British socialists 'that in order to be on a footing of equality with her husband, the wife must be economically independent of him, and the grown-up resident daughter must be independent of her parents'.[62]

The contrast between the *Woman's Signal* and *Shafts* centred as much on questions about how the situation of women should be approached as it did on specific differences about ideals of femininity. The *Woman's Signal* welcomed the expanding range of activities for women, but it was primarily concerned to ensure that information and support should be generated for the legislative and reform campaigns of the women's movement. By contrast, *Shafts* was more concerned with matters of thought and of lifestyle and with issues of representation. Its cover design, a woman archer, stood as its motto as it wished 'to carry "shafts of thought" to give rise to myriad germs of purity and good intent'. It preferred discussions of language and meaning to those of particular campaigns. Thus where the *Woman's Signal* wrote about girls' education, *Shafts* had a regular column entitled 'What the girl says', which used the figure of the young girl to show the ways in which language usage and social convention had privileged men and rendered women invisible—until now, when the girl's voice can be heard, compounded of present laughter and of an anguished undertone which 'comes up to us from past centuries like a wailing cry—terrible in its meaning'.[63]

Discussion of the term 'feminism' followed closely after the 1890s debates about 'the new woman' and were inevitably coloured by them. The first British article which attempted to define 'feminism' was written by 'Ellis Ethelmer', the pseudonym used by both Ben and Elizabeth Wolstenholme Elmy, in 1898.[64] The actual definition offered in this article is an extremely vague one, and one which suggests that there was a marked contrast between an 1890s understanding of nineteenth-century 'feminism' and that of our own day. Ethelmer lists Words-worth, Tennyson, Ruskin, and Huxley as 'feminists', because of their demand for women's education—and their dependence on the individual women in their families![65] None the less, the use of the term and Ethelmer's insistence that it referred to a very broad-ranging set of ideas, and even to a *zeitgeist*, does suggest that there was a link between the introduction of the term and the emergence of a new kind of feminist identity which extended beyond political and social attitudes and into personal identity and daily life. Other new sexual, cultural, and political identities also began to be discussed at this time. The increasing use of the term 'socialist', for example, reflected not only the revival of socialism, but also the proliferation of socialist organizations which engaged in a range of social, educational, and recreational activities. Fabian summer schools, and *Clarion* caravans and cycling groups brought a sense also of the connection between socialism, private life, sexual relations, and personal and political identities.[66] The widespread discussion of sexual questions also brought a closer sense of the connection between personal liberation, comradeship, intellectual challenge, and new lifestyles on the one hand, and social and political transformation on the other.[67]

The introduction of the term 'feminism' coincided with a marked new interest in the exploration of the history of feminist thought and activity.[68] It was not just Wollstonecraft who was revived at this time: the *Woman's Signal* followed its serialization of the *Vindication of the Rights of Woman* with that of Sydney Smith's essay on 'Female Education',[69] and then with William Thompson's *Appeal*, constructing thereby a rudimentary feminist tradition.[70] At the same time, Elizabeth Wolstenholme Elmy was offering an education in feminist history to readers of *Shafts* by republishing the first protest against the Contagious Diseases Acts issued by the Ladies' National Association in 1870.[71] From the time of Mary Wollstonecraft to that of Harriet Taylor, Elmy argued, there was 'a brilliant-succession of women writers, claiming for the mother-half of the human race that full equality with the other-half of the race which is sometimes supposed to be the original demand of the present day'.[72] She also offered strong encouragement to her close friend Harriet McIlquham to explore the lives and ideas of Mary Astell, 'Sophia', and Lady Mary Wortley Montague in order to demonstrate that the feminist tradition extended back over two centuries.[73]

It is important to note, however, that the introduction of the term 'feminist' did not bring unity or unanimity amongst feminists. On the contrary, the term first came into being just at the point when a mid-Victorian consensus was breaking down, bringing an unprecedented range and diversity of views, not only about feminist strategies and goals, but also about the nature of women and about what their emancipation meant. Hence the enormous energy that went into defining and debating the meaning of the terms 'new woman', 'feminist', and 'suffragette' serve, then, not so much to centralize feminist ideas as to exhibit their range, diversity, and complexity. In some of the earliest uses of feminism as a label, moreover, the term was defined and applied, not as a way of encompassing all those concerned with the emancipation of women, but rather as a means of differentiating some of those fighting for the cause from others. The term was first claimed and used extensively by Dora Marsden, the editor of the *Freewoman*. Feminism, in her view, was a term of great praise, to be guarded and used only to designate those women committed to fighting for and ensuring their own personal, sexual, and economic independence.[74] Marsden and her colleagues called themselves 'feminists' quite specifically as a way of criticizing the militant campaign and the centralized and authoritarian structure of the Women's Social and Political Union (WSPU). The suffrage movement, Marsden argued, had no intrinsic connection with feminism. Indeed, in her view, and in that of Cicely

Hamilton, it was antithetical to the democratic and libertarian values which underlay feminism. As Marsden commented acidly of the WSPU, apart from its concern with the vote, 'its constitution, its temper, its organisation are all anti-libertarian. It is therefore, the nearest thing to a negation of the real Woman movement.'[75] The WSPU was not part of the wider feminist movement because it 'merely asks for a trifling political adjustment—the vote! rather than fighting for the full humanity and the economic, social and sexual freedom of women'.[76]

'Feminism', Marsden insisted, was a hard doctrine, demanding that women take responsibility for themselves and their lives. Where suffragists guard the rear, taking their stand 'upon the weakness and dejectedness of the conditions of women', feminists, imbued with the 'cult of the freeman', emphasize their growing strength.

If the Freewoman is not going to be the protected woman, but is to carve out an independence for herself, she must produce within herself strength sufficient to provide for herself and for those of whom Nature has made her the natural guardian, her children. To this end, she must open up resources of wealth for herself. She must work, earn money, she must seize upon the incentives which have spurred on men to strenuous effort—wealth, power, titles and public honour.[77]

But of course many of those involved with the WSPU saw the question entirely differently, seeing the vote itself as the symbol of precisely the spiritual freedom and personal independence sought by Hamilton and Marsden. Emmeline Pethick-Lawrence, for example, saw Christabel Pankhurst as centrally concerned not with the vote, but with the full emancipation of women.[78] She

was inspired not by pity but by a deep, secret shame—shame that any woman should tamely accept the position accorded to her as something less than a full human being . . . Christabel cared less for the political vote itself than for the dignity of her sex, and she denounced the false dignity earned by submission and extolled the true dignity accorded by revolt. She never made any secret of the fact that to her the means were even more important than the end. Militancy to her meant putting off the slave *Spirit*.[79]

For Pethick-Lawrence herself, the women's movement, as symbolized by the militant campaign, meant 'the coming into the world of new and noble race-ideals; it means the release into the world of a new Soul—the Soul of women hitherto held in subjection and captivity'. She yielded nothing to Marsden on the religious question, for in her view, the women's movement meant 'a new religion, or rather a return of religion to its source—to the sacred Altar of the Hearth; to the

Fount of birth and being. It means the beginning of a new morality, especially of that morality between women and men hitherto determined by the immediate convenience and interest of one sex only.'[80] The WSPU also demanded of women enormous strength and endurance—albeit endurance of pain—and precisely the kind of self-sacrifice which Marsden loathed. WSPU militancy, as both contemporaries and later commentators have recognized, required extraordinary courage and determination. But it did so in pursuit of a demand for sexual and moral transformation which would bring to an end male sexual vice. Its freedom for women was a freedom from sexual subordination—and often from heterosexual involvement.[81]

What differentiated the 'feminists' from the 'suffragettes' and the WSPU, then, was not so much the sense that the woman question involved personal and spiritual questions as well as economic and political ones, for all were agreed about that. They disagreed, rather, about what these personal questions were. For Marsden, the contributors to the *Freewoman*, and to those who attended the discussion circles which the paper ran, questions of independence and of sexual freedom were central; for the WSPU, the issue was rather sexual purity—or at least the withdrawal of women from heterosexuality.[82] Christabel Pankhurst had as a slogan 'Chastity for Men', but it was recognized within the WSPU that marriage and indeed any form of heterosexual relationship was frowned on for women.[83] Pankhurst's discussion of venereal disease in *The Great Scourge* followed the lines of argument of earlier discussions of male profligacy, but took them to an extreme whereby heterosexual relations of any kind were seen as impossible for women.

The late nineteenth and early twentieth centuries then saw a development of earlier criticisms of marriage taken far beyond previous limits. There had long been agreement amongst feminists that existing legal and social structures made marriage impossible, but now this effectively brought into question the possibility of marriage or of heterosexual relationships, while for others it served rather as the basis to demand freer and more open sexual unions in which the partners could be equal. Both arguments were central to feminism and to the emergence of a sense of feminist identity because they served so closely to connect the need for a re-evaluation of ideas about personal morality and private conduct with the overall situation of women and with their demand for emancipation. While the terms 'feminist' and 'suffragette' were used as contrasting ones, therefore, both serve equally to indicate the increasing importance of feminism as involving a personal revolt against conventional norms of womanhood. This contrasts with the mid-Victorian attempt to insist that support for women's rights was a political matter, not necessarily threatening to conventional marriage or lifestyles. But of course it harkens back to Mary Wollstonecraft and serves again to suggest that the question of personal life is always an integral part of feminism, although it is not always equally overt.

## Feminism, the Labour Movement, and Working-Class Women

While some women gloried in the capacity to call themselves 'feminists', others saw the term as very limited. Writing in a special supplement of the *New Statesman* in 1913, for example, Beatrice Webb argued that the 'Awakening of Women' would never be understood until it was recognized that 'it is not mere *feminism*'. Rather, Webb insisted, 'it is one of three simultaneous world-movements towards a more equal partnership among human beings in human affairs.' The question of whether and to what extent these simultaneous movements were part of each other was, she thought, something that should be left to future historical philosophers. 'For the moment it is enough to note that the movement for woman's emancipation is paralleled, on the one hand, by the International Movement of Labour . . . and, on the other, by the unrest among subject-peoples struggling to develop their own peculiar civilisation.'[84]

Recent historians have been extremely vexed over how best to interpret the relationship between the women's movement and the labour movement.[85] Unquestionably, the rise of the organized labour movement and the emergence of new socialist organizations in the 1880s brought new questions and new political and social analyses to the fore. The economic problems and the political oppression of the working class was addressed with renewed intensity.[86] Some socialists at the end of the century, like their utopian counterparts in the early decades of the nineteenth century, also sought a new sexual morality and new sexual relationships.[87] These developments expanded the range of feminist discussions, but they also raised the fundamental question about whether women's primary identity was derived from their economic and class position or from the common interest they shared with other women by virtue of their sex. There was conflict on this issue within the women's movement and the labour movement as both sought and even demanded the adherence of working-class women— while neither was able or prepared to meet their specific needs.

As we have seen, although the mid-Victorian women's movement was predominantly a middle-class one, it was neither ignorant of nor unconcerned about the needs and the problems faced by working-class women, particularly in regard to paid and unpaid labour, domestic violence, and sexual exploitation. This was the more easily expressed, however, because members of the women's movement assumed that their working-class sisters shared the same values as themselves and faced the same problems in terms of their subjection to husbands and masters and to the various legislative restrictions that reduced their economic freedom. Hence Victorian feminists assumed that their demands for an end to legislation which imposed double standards either in sexual matters or in regard to hours and conditions of work would simultaneously meet the needs of all women.[88]

During the 1880s, this assumption that middle-class women faced the same problems as working-class ones was subjected to powerful challenge—often, ironically, from other middle-class women. The overall expansion in factory production and in the industrial employment of women gave a new urgency to questions about women's paid labour. Many women who were concerned with welfare, and particularly with the welfare of working-class women, argued that the needs of working-class women were not adequately understood or met by the existing women's movement, most of whose members came from and shared the attitudes of employers. A graphic illustration of their argument was provided by the match girls' strike of 1889 during which Millicent Garrett Fawcett, who was a shareholder in Bryant & May, supported the employer against the striking 'match girls' who were demanding higher pay, better working conditions, and adequate health safeguards.[89] This highly publicized strike led a number of women to become very concerned about the problems women faced at work and to seek immediate ways to improve their working conditions.

The growing concern about working-class women can be seen most clearly in the proliferation of organizations concerned with women's work and working conditions in the 1880s and 1890s. These decades saw the development of the Women's Trade Union League and the Women's Trade Union Association as well as the Women's Co-operative Guild.[90] In the 1890s, these were added to by the Women's Industrial Council and then by the Women's Labour League and the Fabian Women's Groups. These organizations had a number of different aims: the Women's Trade Union League, for example, sought to ensure the proper organization of women workers and the close connections between these organizations and the Trade Union Congress in the hope that the union movement would protect women workers. Others, like the Women's Industrial Council, attempted rather to research fully and accurately the facts of women's work, to scrutinize parliamentary bills and official reports, and to lobby and pressure governments to protect the interests of women engaged in industry.[91] This attempt to gather information on women's work and on their economic and social problems was later taken up by the Fabian Women's Group, which aimed 'to study the economic position of women and press their claim to equality with men in the personal economic independence to be secured by socialism' and 'to hasten the establishment of equal citizenship for men and women'.[92] These organizations, all of which were composed largely of middle-class women, contrast markedly with the Women's Co-operative Guild, which was 'the very first separatist working-class women's organization' working to bring women into the co-operative movement, to provide education and information for them, and to provide a forum where they could express and debate their own views. Although established and led by middle-class women, its membership and its concerns were solidly located within the working class.[93]

To some extent, the shift in approach to the question of working-class women which came with the advent of the labour movement in the 1880s and 1890s can be seen in the changing names and outlook of organizations like the Women's Trade Union League. Originally named the Women's Protective and Provident League, it was set up by middle-class feminists in 1874 to promote and co-ordinate women's societies in specific trades and industries, but became an integral part of the trade union movement. It illustrates clearly both the ways in which an interest in the labour movement drew the discussion of women's work away from the women's movement, and the problems faced by women within the labour movement itself. Thus its founder, Emma Patterson, attended the annual meetings of the Trades Union Congress, but always rejected the approach of the TUC, vigorously opposing industrial legislation for women which was not applied equally to men. After her death in 1886, the League was renamed the Women's Trade Union League.[94] Under the leadership of Lady Dilke and Gertrude Tuckwell, it established much closer links with the labour movement, continuing to attend annual congresses, setting up women's meetings at the congresses, and working to establish direct and close links between the League and the trade unions which catered for women.[95] The League appointed Mary Macarthur as paid secretary in 1903 and she worked tirelessly to increase unionization amongst women workers, establishing the National Federation of Women Workers in 1906.[96] As a member of the Independent Labour Party, Macarthur furthered the view that the interests of women were tied up with the labour movement rather than to the goals and ideals of the women's movement. She herself rejected women's suffrage in favour of adult suffrage, which was feared by feminists who believed it would produce universal manhood suffrage and make it even harder for women to get the vote. At the same time, Macarthur herself was in constant battle with the TUC and the labour movement as she tried to get a minimum wage established for all workers, rather than go on 'protecting' women by restrictive sex-based legislation.[97]

For many of the middle-class women preoccupied with labour questions, the vote came to assume a secondary place as they sought changes in women's working conditions as an immediate goal. The term 'social feminists' has been coined to describe this group of women[98] who were united in their belief that better pay and conditions of work could only be provided by industrial legislation and trade union agitation. This brought to the fore a direct conflict between their interventionist ideas and the old-style economic liberalism of the women's movement.[99] Many older members of the women's movement, including Millicent Fawcett and Josephine Butler, continued in the 1880s and 1890s, as they had in the 1860s and 1870s, to oppose sex-based industrial legislation. Such legislation, in their view, denied that women were rational adults capable of ascertaining or following their own interests. It served also to reduce the employment opportunities and the income-earning capacity of women.[100]

The economic ideas of the women's suffrage movement were opposed by large numbers of influential women, including the Fabians Beatrice Webb and Barbara Hutchins and the Secretary of the Women's Co-operative Guild, Margaret Llewellyn Davies, all of whom bewailed the economic and social ignorance and the outmoded ideas of 'the able and devoted ladies who have usually led the cause of women's enfranchisement', but who lacked any understanding of the problems of industrial labour.[101] 'We do not', Llewellyn Davies insisted,

find that women have lost their places in the textile trades, and we cannot see how a shop-girl, standing from 70 to 80 hours a week, often in a most unhealthy atmosphere, often only allowed odd times to bolt her food, is a 'freer' woman than the mill-hand, with her legal 56 hours a week, her two hours for food, her half-holiday, and her ventilated and whitewashed surroundings.[102]

Some mid-Victorian feminists accepted the idea that trade union agitation was necessary to improve the pay and conditions of women workers, but others, including Fawcett, retained an implacable hostility to both protective legislation and to the role of trade unions in regard to women's work.[103] There was some truth in Beatrice Webb's insistence that Fawcett's opposition derived from her mid-nineteenth-century economic ideas and her inability to see that there were now new theories and new approaches which had to be applied to women.[104] But for all this, Fawcett was quite correct in her view that much protective legislation was not only sex-based, but devised in order to exclude women from certain categories of highly paid work—and that it was supported by many trade unionists precisely because they believed that women had no real place in the paid workforce.[105] Moreover, as Butler argued, women's paid work was by no means their heaviest labour—and every hour of paid work which was taken from them meant another hour during which they could do unpaid work as the servants of their husbands or in the home![106]

While industrial legislation clearly was necessary to protect the health and well-being of women workers, those who supported such legislation also sometimes attempted to use it as a means of ensuring better sexual morality or a particular kind of family life. Some women in the labour movement shared the views of those working-class men who saw paid work for married women as disastrous for family life. Some even accepted the views of those philanthropic groups which supported restricting the work opportunities of women in order to protect their morals. This question came to the fore in the early years of the twentieth century, when there was a concerted push to reduce and limit the work of women as barmaids. Working alongside the British Women's Temperance Union and the National Union of Women Workers, Margaret Macdonald, the wife of Ramsay MacDonald, attempted to persuade the government to limit employment of women as barmaids as part of its new licensing act of 1901. She sent a memorial to the Prime Minister seeking his support and showing clearly the moral basis of her request. She and her co-workers sought to limit the work of barmaids, believing that their surroundings carry with them special dangers and temptations to which barmen are not subject.

From the great majority of advocates in trade papers, it is evident that the great majority of barmaids are engaged on account of their attractions to men customers, whilst the record of the magistrates and other Courts give convincing statistical proof of the disproportionate number of barmaids whose career ends in drunkenness, immorality, misery and frequent suicide.[107]

The labour movement itself was deeply divided on this issue, but many of the most vocal working-class women were opposed to restrictive legislation which closed an avenue of work to approximately 100,000 women. Barmaids, like chain-makers and pit-brow women, were concerned to ensure a continued source of employment and income. They found some allies in the labour movement and in some of the organizations specifically concerned to safeguard working women—and others in the women's suffrage movement, which fought for their rights as individuals to engage in the paid labour that was available to them.[108]

While middle-class suffragists joined with working-class women to defend the right to work, they were less concerned with the question that this issue of work raised for many working-class women: that is, how to combine paid work with child care and family responsibilities. The pronounced hostility to married women's work evident in many parts of the labour movement—and perhaps most truculently expressed by John Burns—was countered by a number of working-class women and by the Women's Industrial Council, The Fabian Women's Group, and the Women's Co-operative Guild, all of whom insisted both on the entitlement and on the need of many married women with children to engage in paid employment.[109] Questions about the effect of maternal employment on infant health and mortality were widely discussed at the time and many women's groups sought to ascertain how at the present time working-class women dealt with the pressing and sometimes conflicting needs they faced in providing income for and tending to the needs of families. The Fabian Women's Group debated the question of women's work at length, within the framework of the society's support for family endowment on the one hand, and the question of how working-class families managed their overall budgets on the other.[110] In 1908, the Women's Industrial Council began a detailed investigation of married women's work, the results of which were published in 1915. Clementina Black, who edited their report, insisted that their investigation showed clearly the need that many working-class women had to supplement the incomes of their underpaid husbands. The effect of this labour on the well-being of children, Black argued, depended upon whether or not the child was adequately cared for in the mother's absence. Neglect of children was obviously harmful. At the same time, many children, she insisted, might be better off in a properly run nursery or crèche than under the constant care of their mother.[111]

The need for the proper provision of child care and for a rethinking of the assumption that child-care responsibilities were automatically those of the mother was demanded most strongly by Ada Nield Chew, who knew their importance from personal experience. As a married trade-union organizer with a small child, Chew retained almost sole responsibility for child care, taking her daughter with her whenever she had to be away from home.[112] The economic independence of married women was, Chew insisted, imperative if women were to be able to develop their humanity to the full. This, in turn, required the state provision of nurseries for all babies and children, staffed by trained women. This development would simultaneously free mothers from the present enslavement to their children and provide a new form of training and professional employment for those women who particularly enjoyed working with children.[113] The idea of state provision of child care was anathema to many middle-class feminists, although they too recognized the needs and difficulties of working-class women—most directly through the working-class women, like Chew or Selina Cooper, who were paid organizers and speakers for the National Union of Women's Suffrage Societies (NUWSS). Their solutions to this problem, however, were entirely directed towards meeting individual needs, rather than to addressing the question as it affected all working women. Thus, for example, when Selina Cooper expressed her anxiety about leaving her small daughter when she was engaged in campaigning on behalf of the National Union, their solution was to pay for her to have a live-in housekeeper![114]

Many early socialists, particularly those who became concerned with the Independent Labour Party, often felt strongly about the injustices in the sexual hierarchy and sought the emancipation of women alongside the freeing of the working class from the stranglehold of capitalism.[115] None the less, while women's unpaid labour and their active involvement was often welcomed, those women's organizations which developed within the labour movement often had to battle in ways similar to those affiliated with the Liberal and Conservative parties if they wanted not just to campaign for their male colleagues, but also to have their own voices heard and their feminist demands acknowledged. In England, as in Germany and Russia, many of those who sought to bring women into the Labour Movement wanted to educate them to the importance of masculine views and male goals and to show how they could help to attain them. This aim was clearly shown in the formation of the Women's Labour League, which sought, as Margaret Macdonald explained at its inaugural conference, 'to show the wives of trade unionists and co-operators . . . what they have not yet fully discovered, that the best way of looking after their homes is by taking an interest in the life of the community . . . that to improve their conditions it is necessary to take up their cause with earnestness on the same lines as men have done'.[116]

The primacy of women's familial role was thus exalted over their individual wishes or their needs as workers. Even those organizations which rejected this assumption of the primacy of family life for women and took particular interest in women's work and in the overall situation of working-class women, like the Fabian Women's Group, remained small and marginal groups, unable to alter the outlook of their male colleagues for whom the goal of social efficiency and concern about the size and quality of population meant that women were thought about primarily in terms of their reproductive capacities, rather than in terms of their rights.[117] As Olive Banks has pointed out, the decline in the number of feminists with a predominantly liberal national political orientation and the rise in the number of feminists who were also socialists at the end of the nineteenth century was accompanied by a shift away from concern with issues centring on the autonomy of women, the importance of choice and dignity for single women, and the sexual double standard.[118]

The struggle women had if they sought to determine the structure, aims, and policy of their own organizations was well illustrated in the Women's Co-operative Guild. Established in 1883, the Guild was a self-governing body within the Co-operative Union.[119] Policy matters were usually decided at its large annual congress. As Margaret Llewellyn Davies, its long-time secretary, explained in 1920, the Guild was

both an educational and propaganda body. It may also be said to be an army of agitators. Being composed of *married* women who are co-operators, it has naturally become a sort of trade union for married women, and it not only works for Co-operation helping to shape its policy, and secure definite action, but it also takes in hand the reforms needed by wives and mothers.[120]

Guild women demanded the right to determine their own policies, a demand they were only able to make effective because they had independent sources of finance and were prepared, when necessary, to do without financial assistance from the parent body, the Co-operative Union.

Almost from the start, the Guild was engaged in confrontation with the general Co-operative Union. Although the Co-operative Union supported the education and involvement of women and ostensibly sought to assist working-class women to improve their working conditions, an inquiry into the employment practices of 169 member societies undertaken by the Guildswoman and the suffragist, Sarah Reddish, indicated that the Co-operative movement discriminated against its women employees, making them work excessive hours for very low pay, and imposing on them very different conditions than those obtaining for male employees. The Guild was thus soon campaigning to make the Co-operative Union adopt a minimum wage for both men and women. It took ten years before the Co-operative movement agreed to a minimum wage—and then another five years before women were finally included in the scale for minimum wages in 1912.

The largest and most bitter battle fought by the Guild, however, was over the question of divorce. When the Royal Commission on Divorce Law Reform was set up in 1909, evidence was sought from the Guild as a representative working-class women's organization. In order to meet the request, circulars were sent round to all the branches. The responses were collated and published in *Working Women and Divorce* in 1911. They demonstrated very clearly the overwhelming demand amongst married working-class women for sweeping reforms in divorce law. 'No other subject in the life of the guild has aroused such immediate response,' argued Margaret Llewellyn Davies. 'It is impossible to exaggerate the strength of the feeling that there should be an equal moral standard for men and women, and that the grounds of divorce should be the same.'[121] Not a single woman gave a negative view on this point. The women expressed great indignation at the existing legal situation in which a man could divorce his wife if she committed adultery, but she could not divorce him unless cruelty, desertion, or some other offence was added to his adultery. Overall, the majority of Guild members supported cheaper divorce which should be available on a range of grounds: cruelty was seen as the most important, next came insanity, then refusal to maintain and desertion. Some Guild members believed that communication of disease, especially sexually transmitted diseases, should be included within the category of 'cruelty'.[122]

The position of the Guild on this matter was strongly opposed by many Co-operative Societies, especially those with a strong Catholic membership. The Manchester and Salford Catholic Federation, which had close connection with the Co-operative Union, wrote to the Guild, objecting to their stand, and arguing that the matter was one properly dealt with by the Church. The United Board of the Co-operative Society asked the Guild to give up their work on divorce law reform because they feared it might be disruptive to the Co-operative movement as a whole. When the Guild refused, the Board withdrew its annual grant of £400. The Guild was able to withstand this pressure only because its secretary, Margaret Llewellyn Davies, was able to make a personal loan sufficient to cover running costs while the branches worked to raise enough money to make up for their normal grant. The grant was withheld until 1918, by which time the fervour surrounding the divorce question had abated. None the less, the overall point remains that some of the most fundamental feminist battles fought by the Women's Co-operative Guild were for its own autonomy within the national (male) body.[123]

The problems and tensions faced by working-class women attempting to remain within the labour movement, but concerned about citizenship and political rights, can be seen most clearly in the activities of the 'radical suffragists'. These women, based in Lancashire and Cheshire, often began their working life labouring in factories and mills where they had become closely involved in union activities and sometimes also in socialist politics. But increasingly, they became discontented with the lack of attention paid to women's rights—and with the assumption that they would both work alongside male colleagues and provide the hearty teas needed to sustain masculine discussion. Hence they were attracted to the suffrage activities of Esther Roper and Eva Gore-Booth, who, while belonging to the very sedate and proper North of England Society for Women's Suffrage, were attempting to create a mass movement for women's suffrage by holding meetings and trying to gain members in the cotton towns of Lancashire.[124] They established a large following of working women in Lancashire, but found increasingly that these women, while passionately convinced of the importance of women's suffrage, could accept neither the idea of a property-based suffrage nor the genteel tactics of the existing suffrage movement. Hence along with Ada Nield Chew, Hannah Mitchell, Selina Cooper, and Sarah Reddish, they set up an independent organization that attempted to increase working-class support for women's suffrage but still kept in close contact with the Labour Party, the Women's Co-operative Guild, and the trade union movement.[125]

Unquestionably, the radical suffragists helped provide a new impetus to the suffrage movement, gaining wide-scale support as they worked full-time to organize large public meetings and constantly attempted to increase their membership. At the same time, they engaged in agitation to persuade trade unions, the Women's Co-operative Guild and the Labour Representation Committee to support women's suffrage, and to arrange petitions and deputations to Parliament. They were welcomed by the NUWSS and provided the example which fired Christabel Pankhurst with enthusiasm to revitalize the suffrage movement on a national scale. They did, moreover, succeed in gaining support for women's suffrage from the Women's Co-operative Guild, the largest organization of working-class women, and the Labour representation committee. But they were never able to overcome the opposition to women's suffrage within the TUC. Indeed, when the issue of women's suffrage was first raised at the TUC congresses of 1901 and 1902, an adult suffrage amendment was put forward in order to defeat it.

The conflict between adult suffragists and women suffragists dominated the debate about political rights within the labour movement up until the war. The issue was undoubtedly a complex one. The demand for the enfranchisement of women as it was then formulated by the women's suffrage movement sought women's suffrage on the same terms as were currently enfranchised—that is, as property-holders and ratepayers. This demand, as women like Ada Nield Chew and Mary Macarthur argued, would mean that, while

the entire class of wealthy women would be enfranchised, that the great body of working women, married or single, would be voteless still, and that to give wealthy women a vote would mean that they, voting naturally in their own interests, would help to swamp the vote of the enlightened working man, who is trying to get Labour men into Parliament.[126]

On the other hand, some of the most vociferous proponents of adult suffrage, including Philip Snowden, Ramsay Macdonald, and the Social Democratic Federation leaders, Harry Quelch and H. M. Hyndman, were convinced opponents of women's suffrage.[127] Their advocacy of the measure serves to support the fear amongst many feminists that adult suffrage would turn out to mean universal manhood suffrage—and hence would make it even harder for any women to be enfranchised. In contrast, those who supported women's suffrage on a limited basis but still identified with the labour movement did so in the belief that the issue of sex-prejudice had to be dealt with as a matter of principle. They accepted a property-based demand for women's suffrage on the grounds that once any women were enfranchised, the task of expanding the base of women's enfranchisement would be much easier. Women within the labour movement were themselves deeply divided on this matter with some, like Margaret Bondfield and Margaret Macdonald, arguing that women must give their first support to the Labour Party and hence accept adult suffrage, while others, like the 'radical suffragists', sought the vote for women, in the hopes that it would give them more power in the workplace, improve their pay and conditions, and increase their independence.[128] But the demands of the radical suffragists threatened the primacy of the family wage, a deeply entrenched value of the labour movement—and one which assumed that the man was the chief breadwinner, who needed to be able to provide for his dependent wife and child. Thus it was not only women's suffrage, but the whole goal of women's emancipation, which was opposed by many within the labour movement.[129]

The desertion of women's suffrage and of the issue of women's freedom by the labour movement had a powerful impact on many women. As we will see, it was of fundamental importance in the formation and policies of the WSPU. It also drove the radical suffragists into an ever-closer alliance with the women's suffrage movement. Needing both financial and moral support, they increasingly came to work with the women's suffrage movement. Radical suffragists were initially attracted to the WSPU because of its early connection with the ILP and its militant tactics, but the growing political conservatism of the WSPU and its attempts to distance itself from working-class women, combined with the opposition of northern women to violent forms of militancy or to the campaign of deliberately courting arrest, made a separation between the two groups inevitable.[130] The National Union of Women's Suffrage Societies, by contrast, offered constant aid and assistance, including the money to enable the radical suffragists to employ full-time organizers. But the relations between the northern working women and the London-based middle-class suffrage societies were always difficult and strained because of their lack of common understanding and experience. Ultimately, the radical suffragists were neither able to convert the Labour movement to feminism, nor able to find an adequate approach to the needs of working women within the suffrage movement. What they did, however, was to bring into national political and social life a very remarkable group of women, to add the voices of working-class women to the debate, and to show how very complex the situation of working-class women was.

## Militancy

The years between 1890 and 1918 saw the suffrage movement go from a period of torpor and exhaustion to one of extraordinary energy and activity. The militant campaign of the Women's Social and Political Union, which brought about this revival, met with angry opposition from street rowdies and from establishment institutions and individuals—but it also served to stimulate a range of new organizations, new strategies, and new methods. The activities of the WSPU and their genius for publicity meant that all suffrage organizations now experienced rapidly growing memberships and waves of enthusiasm. The suffrage movement became increasingly diverse, with the formation of several broad national societies alongside a huge number of smaller ones that were organized around specific localities and institutions, professions, or religious beliefs. And suffrage ideas and ideals were elaborated and dramatized, not only in demonstrations and meetings, but also in songs, plays, poems, novels, pageants, banners, and paintings.[131]

The Women's Social and Political Union was established in Manchester in 1903. The creation of the Pankhurst family, it was set up to campaign for women's suffrage when the Pankhursts withdrew from the ILP—on discovering that women were not to be admitted to the new branch being established in Pankhurst Hall. Its name was suggested by Christabel Pankhurst who was at the time closely involved with Eva Gore-Booth and the radical working-class suffragists with whom Gore-Booth was working in Lancashire, and it was initially intended to combine suffrage work with some of the social goals of the Labour women, including improved maternity provision.[132] The WSPU worked quietly for two years in Manchester before being catapulted to national prominence when Christabel Pankhurst and Annie Kenney began the militant campaign by interrupting an election meeting being addressed by the Liberal Home Secretary, Sir Edward Grey, to ask whether the Liberals would grant votes to women—and then, to ensure their arrest, spat at the policemen who escorted them out of the building.[133] The resulting court appearance and imprisonment of both women for seven days was featured prominently in the national press. Millicent Garrett Fawcett commented on the fact that newspapers which had previously been 'very chary of admitting that there was any demand on the part of women for political freedom, now blazoned forth with tremendous energy' their indignation against the two women.[134]

The success of this first, and very mild, militant action in gaining national press coverage set the pattern which the WSPU was to follow for the next few years. The election campaign of 1906 provided much opportunity for members of the WSPU to interrupt election meetings, showing 'Votes for Women' slogans and asking for a statement of the intentions of the new government. Rejecting the traditional practice of seeking to gain suffrage through a private member's bill, the WSPU demanded that the government take up the question, hence they directed their attention towards Liberal ministers, appearing whenever possible when one was making a speech.[135] The violence these interruptions met with served to raise the whole emotional temperature of the suffrage campaign. In 1906, the WSPU moved its headquarters to London and continued to find more and more ways of staging dramatic and effective meetings, in or around Parliament, or in a range of open-air locations. They held thousands of meetings, campaigned against government candidates at every by-election, and issued immense numbers of pamphlets and papers.[136]

Under this stimulus, the whole suffrage movement began massively to expand. The National Union of Women's Suffrage Societies, which was established in 1897, had brought together all the older societies in a loose confederation, but it had not dramatically altered the tenor of their work. The National Union had allowed local and regional societies enormous scope to organize and campaign as they chose—hence allowing for the early work of the north of England committee. But its procedures and its complex rules to ensure adequate consultation with local bodies before national policies were reached had been so cumbersome as to prevent any large-scale or concerted action. It had continued to hold meetings, both in public and in drawing-rooms, to send deputations to Parliament, and to lobby MPs. But the effectiveness of these activities, as its leaders well knew, was very limited.[137]

The advent of the WSPU changed all that. Ironically, it was the NUWSS which was the greatest beneficiary of militancy in terms of its increase in vitality, membership, and money. The WSPU was never a large organization. The increasingly autocratic rule exercised by Christabel Pankhurst led to the departure of many members, but in any event the Pankhursts had never sought a mass movement, aiming rather to have a small one able to work with military precision. But many of those stirred by accounts of the militants chose anyway to join the other societies. As Millicent Garrett Fawcett later recalled, the start of militancy brought an immediate increase in activity for the non-militants.

The Secretaries and other active members of the older Suffrage Societies were worked off their feet; every post brought applications for information and membership; Women's Suffrage was the topic of conversation in every household and at every social gathering . . . Money rolled in in unexpected ways; where we were formerly receiving half-crowns and shillings, we were now getting £5 and £10 notes.[138]

Between the years 1907 and 1910, the number of societies affiliated with the NUWSS increased by more than 400, while its total membership increased by more than 50,000 and its income quadrupled.[139]

It was not just in size that the NUWSS changed, but in approach. Even before the WSPU had begun to stage its outdoor meetings, the NUWSS had begun to diversify its activities, with 'suffrage stalls' selling educational material and distributing propaganda in market-places, and with the first large suffrage procession, the 'mud march' of 9 February 1907, in which 3,000 women marched from Hyde Park Corner to Exeter Hall. This was the start of many outdoor marches, pageants, and demonstrations featuring the banners and costumes through which militants and constitutionalists served to transform the suffrage movement, making its public demonstrations eye-catching and memorable. Women artists and writers were drawn into the movement as exhibitions were mounted to draw further attention to the movement and its activities, while suffrage songs were sung and plays staged. The pageantry and sheer scale of suffrage demonstrations now brought extensive news coverage even to the older societies, which were increasingly coming to be called 'constitutionalist' in contrast with the militants.[140]

The vitality of the suffrage movement was both demonstrated and enhanced by the emergence of an organized movement to oppose women's suffrage. In the course of 1908, a Women's National Anti-Suffrage League came into existence, followed shortly after by its male counterpart, the Men's Committee for Opposing Female Suffrage. The *Anti-Suffrage Review* and their frequent public meetings served at one and the same time to mobilize opposition to women's suffrage and to show how serious an item it had now become on the political agenda.[141]

The increase in suffrage activity also brought new conflicts. The advent of the WSPU was welcomed by many in the women's movement, and for a number of years some women belonged both to constitutionalist groups within the NUWSS and to the militant WSPU. But it was not long before the new society became very troubling and very divisive. There were very different responses to it from the veterans of the mid-Victorian women's movement. For Elizabeth Wolstenholme Elmy, who had become increasingly despondent about what she saw as the ineffectiveness of the NUWSS, the advent of the militant WSPU was almost an answer to her prayers. She became a devoted follower of the Pankhursts, a member of their executive committee, and a staunch supporter almost until her death in 1911. For others, like Emily Davies, even the early acts of militancy were unacceptable, and she did her best to ensure that the constitutionalists had no connection with the militants. More significantly, for the northern radical suffragists who had been the inspiration for the WSPU and had also served to revitalize the NUWSS, the militant tactic of courting arrest, the scuffling with police, and the deliberate seeking of imprisonment were deeply offensive and unacceptable. They saw it as demeaning to women's dignity—and as a very blatant display of class privilege. Imprisonment might be quite acceptable for middle-class women with households full of servants, but for working-class women with children to care for, it was the height of irresponsibility.[142] The main body of the constitutionalists led by Millicent Fawcett, despite some misgivings, publicly defended the militants in the early years, sometimes arranging or participating in celebrations when they were released from prison.[143]

But increasingly, there were divisions evident within the suffrage movement as a result of differing ideas about strategy and about overall political beliefs and ideals. The escalation of militancy after 1908 led to a complete break between the constitutionalists and the militants. This escalation began with symbolic protests of a more dramatic kind, like women chaining themselves to the Ladies Gallery in Parliament, but was followed by the start of violence and damage to property: the throwing of acid at polling booths, the destruction of sporting fields and letter boxes, and the breaking of windows. In part, this escalation was the result of spontaneous acts by a number of women seeking arrest and finding that the breaking of shop windows or other forms of damage to property secured the desired result.[144] The WSPU leadership subsequently came to endorse these actions and initiated other new types of campaigning involving calculated threats to public order: groups of women began rushing the Houses of Parliament or acting in concert to break up public meetings. All of this activity aroused considerable opposition from many within the women's movement as well as from those outside, and brought a complete break between the WSPU and the other suffrage organizations. When there was yet another escalation of militancy, with the start of an arson campaign in 1913, the WSPU was completely isolated within the broader suffrage movement.

While the WSPU had begun by attracting large numbers of enthusiasts, its size began quite quickly to decline. Shortly after the Pankhursts moved their headquarters to London, there were murmurings of concern about the increasing concentration of power in the hands of Emmeline and Christabel Pankhurst. The close-knit group at London headquarters, consisting of the Pankhursts and Fred and Emmeline Pethick-Lawrence, had little contact with and gave no recognition to those others who had been very active from the inception of the movement, but were now regarded as outsiders. Charlotte Despard, Teresa Billington-Greig, and Edith How-Martyn were the first to voice opposition.[145] The Pankhursts regarded Billington-Greig as the primary malcontent, and she was certainly the most outspoken in her criticism of them and their approach. Having given up her teaching job to devote herself to the WSPU, she powerfully resented her increasing sense of marginalization. Matters came to a head at the annual conference in September 1907. At this meeting, the constitution and organization of the WSPU was supposed to be discussed. Instead, as she later recalled, there was 'an announcement of dictatorship with all the eloquence and feeling of which Mrs Pankhurst was capable. The draft constitution was dramatically torn up and thrown to the ground. The assembled members were informed that they were in the ranks of an army of which she was the permanent Commander-in Chief.'[146] The WSPU became more and more like an army thereafter, with members being required to pledge themselves to support its objects and expected to give unquestioning obedience to decisions of its leaders. Its processions, too, paralleled traditional armies with their emphasis on precision, use of regalia, and marshals and captains. Flora Drummond, who led many of them, was called the General and rode at their head, dressed in a white military-style costume (designed and presented by Selfridges) and wearing epaulettes and a cap.[147]

The defections from the WSPU led to the formation of new suffrage organizations: Billington-Greig, Despard, and How-Martyn formed the Women's Freedom League, which continued to engage in militancy, but under the presidency of Charlotte Despard developed a democratic organization that allowed participants to organize their own campaigns if they so chose. The WLF also continued to espouse some of the socialist and labour views which had been evident at the beginning of the WSPU, but which had increasingly fallen into abeyance as the Pankhursts sought financial and political support from wealthy women and came to find their working-class followers something of a liability. Following a line of argument not dissimilar from that evident in *The Freewoman*, Theresa Billington-Greig argued that the 'emancipation-in-a-hurry spirit' of the WSPU had ultimately destroyed its own spirit of emancipation.[148]

Daring to advertise in an unconventional way, the movement has dared nothing more. It has cut down its demand from one of sex equality to one of votes on a limited basis. It has suppressed free speech on fundamental issues. It has gradually edged the working class out of the ranks. It has become socially exclusive, punctiliously correct, gracefully fashionable, ultra-respectable, and narrowly religious. It pays for its one breach of decorum with additional circumspection in all other directions. 'I do interrupt meetings, but I am a perfect lady,' expresses the present spirit.[149]

While the WSPU was transforming itself into an army, increasingly celebrating both its small size and its separation from other parts of the women's movement, quite the reverse procedure was evident elsewhere. The NUWSS continued to grow in size and to welcome other new organizations. Its own expansion and its immersion in new and far more picturesque and dramatic forms of demonstration did not in any way reduce its contacts with other political groups or parties. On the contrary, they increased. In part, this was a result of their own strategy: while the militants concentrated their energies on opposing all government candidates, the NUWSS took up the opposite approach, working to support any candidate who had declared his support for women's suffrage. In the process, the NUWSS, while still a non-party organization, made itself an integral part of party politics, receiving considerable support from some male MPs.[150]

Both the extent of support for women's suffrage within parliamentary circles and the impossibility of obtaining women's enfranchisement unless the government came to support it was made evident in the course of 1909–10, during which time male supporters of women's suffrage attempted to gain sufficient support in Parliament to enable the passage of a women's suffrage bill that would give the vote to women on the same basis as was then used in municipal elections. This 'Conciliation Bill', as it was called, was supported by all the suffrage societies except the WSPU. Caution was still the order of the day, and H. N. Brailsford, the originator of the scheme, went to great lengths to impress on Mrs Fawcett and others the importance of ensuring that the women's suffrage societies showed their unity in support of the measure. The WSPU refused to participate, having no faith in the Conciliation Bill or in the government's word. It continued to engage in window-breaking and in confrontations with MPs. Ultimately, the Conciliation Bill failed and, while it brought new bitterness into the relationship between the suffrage societies, as some blamed the WSPU for its failure, it also served to show that women had little to hope for from the Liberal Government.[151] As Leslie Hume argues, one can see in retrospect that this failure of the Liberal Party yet again to grant women's suffrage brought a final disillusionment with the party, making an alliance between the NUWSS and the Labour Party possible.[152]

In fact, while the WSPU was breaking its ties with the labour movement, the NUWSS was forging new ones. Although Millicent Garrett Fawcett was its president, much of the energy and initiative in the NUWSS came from a younger generation of women, who saw their feminism and their concern about social questions as closely linked. Women like Helena Swanwick, Catherine Marshall, and Kathleen Courtney, who were later to break with Fawcett over the response of the NUWSS to the war, were central in formulating its policies in the early twentieth century. Termed 'democratic suffragists' by Sandra Holton, these were women for whom the question of women's suffrage was necessarily tied to a demand for universal suffrage and for proper representation for workers.[153] All of them had pronounced sympathies with certain aspects of socialism and with the Labour Party, and they worked hard to give these sympathies voice within the women's movement. They differed from the women whose primary identification was with that movement in the primacy they accorded their work for the emancipation of women.

Their capacity to work both for women's suffrage and for the labour movement came in 1912, when Arthur Henderson managed to gain support at the Labour Party Conference for a resolution which, while retaining adult suffrage as the ultimate goal, committed the party to supporting any women's suffrage measure. As the Labour Party was now the only party committed to supporting women's suffrage, the democratic suffragists managed to persuade Fawcett and others on the executive that the NUWSS should now support Labour candidates—previously it had supported any candidates who favoured women's suffrage. Although her own sympathies were not with the Labour Party, Fawcett agreed, and an electoral fighting fund was set up whereby the NUWSS would contribute funds and help organize electoral campaigns for Labour men. This move brought the radical suffragists back into the labour fold.[154] Although Fawcett continued to maintain that the NUWSS was a non-party organization, this position became harder to maintain. But while the electoral fighting fund brought a few resignations, it worked at the same time to bring the NUWSS right into the central framework of twentieth-century rather than nineteenth-century politics. As the WSPU had recognized earlier, women's suffrage would only be possible if it was a government measure—and, in view of the constant duplicity of the Liberal Party, Labour seemed the only viable choice. The central executive of the National Union did not have to carry with it the bitterness of some of the radical suffragists who had seen the refusal to accept women's autonomy both within the TUC and on the part of many members of the Labour Party. On the contrary, they entered into an alliance from a position of strength because both their money and their expertise were greatly welcomed. They were, moreover, treated with much greater courtesy and respect than was accorded to labour women. The war brought the electoral fighting fund to an end before it is possible to see what the alliance between the NUWSS and the Labour Party might have meant.

How one assesses the suffrage movement in the period leading up to the First World War remains a very difficult question. The long-standing dominance of the WSPU in studies of this period has recently been questioned by new work showing the importance of the radical suffragists, the immense size and activity of the NUWSS, and the great energy of the many smaller suffrage organizations. By contrast, the relatively small size of the WSPU, as it shed first the women who formed the Women's Freedom League, then Sylvia Pankhurst and her East London Federation, and finally the Pethick-Lawrences, has also been stressed.[155] But while the many and varied activities of the 'constitutional' and moderate suffragists and their increasingly important role in both local and national politics is now recognized, the overall importance of this is called into question by the fact that their goal, the enfranchisement and granting of full citizenship to women, while obviously of great importance, did not in fact serve to emancipate women. No one wishes to turn back the clock, or to deny the political or symbolic importance of enfranchisement, but it is none the less clear that discrimination against women in legal, political, and economic terms continues, as does their subordination within the home. Increasingly, feminists are coming to recognize how deep-seated this discrimination is and to feel that its cultural roots and its powerful hold even on psychic structures and on the unconscious need to be addressed.

It is here that the power and importance of the WSPU and the Pankhursts has again been asserted. While there continues to be much disquiet about the political tendencies of the WSPU, it continues to hold a central place in the feminist historical imagination. The actions of the WSPU served to dramatize both the brutality and the fundamentally sexual nature of male domination—and the complex ways in which women could resist it. As Martha Vicinus has shown, militancy offered women a new kind of freedom and expression, and the capacity to engage in suffering and self-sacrifice of a potentially transforming kind. The tactic of the hunger strike, originated not by the Pankhursts but spontaneously by a number of their followers, provides, as Jane Marcus has argued, the primary image in the public imagination concerning the 'meaning' of the suffrage movement—and it serves to endow that movement with a complex series of associations with women's vulnerability and with an emphasis on female purity, spirituality, and self-denial violently contrasting with both institutional and individual masculine violence and power, and with the refusal of the traditional female functions of nurturance and motherhood.[156]

The capacity of the WSPU to provoke masculine outrage and aggression at the very moment of protesting against it irritated moderate feminists at the time, but serves in retrospect to provide a most powerful representation of the nature of women's oppression. The WSPU drew on an exaggerated version of femininity, ostensibly demanding a chivalrous masculine response, but in the process managing to unleash considerable masculine brutality. Other suffragists resented their doing this as it made their struggle harder and possibly more dangerous.[157] The question whether the militants aided or retarded the gaining of women's suffrage, always an unanswerable and unhelpful question, has ceased to be asked. Hence, while many historians have worked hard to show the actual numbers of women involved in the suffrage struggle and to explore its political and social dimensions, the popular fascination with the Pankhursts and the WSPU has been, if anything, enhanced by a series of cultural studies exploring the dynamics and the nature of their power. They resemble Josephine Butler in their concern to transform sexual morality and relationships and in their brilliant mobilization of idealized images of femininity in the fight against male sexual exploitation. Like them, her actual legal and political target had little bearing on her ultimate aim—and again like them, she continues to fascinate later generations. This fascination has something to do with the charismatic personality of all these women, but more with their capacity to represent sexual oppression in such powerful and millennial ways, demonstrating in the process that the fight against masculine privilege might be a fight to the death.

## Feminism and Imperialism

Just as British feminism responded to and encompassed the late nineteenth-century discussions about sexology and eugenics, so too it was deeply affected and influenced by imperial developments. Many of those who had participated in ruling the empire strongly opposed women's rights, arguing that maintenance of the empire required masculine and not feminine qualities, and stressing how ridiculous was the very idea of having 'the women of England governing India'.[158] But this did not set up any obvious antagonism between feminists and supporters of imperialism. On the contrary, many feminists devoutly supported imperial ambitions, employed imperial rhetoric, and saw their own struggle as gaining greater significance because of the special position British women occupied in relation to other women in the empire. The idea that British women were fighting, 'not just for English women alone, but for all the women, degraded, miserable, unheard of, for whose life and happiness England has daily to answer to God' was quite widespread.[159] Even a woman as radical in her critique of male power and as outspoken in her condemnation of the British government as Elizabeth Wolstenholme Elmy argued that 'the enfranchisement of the women of Great Britain and Ireland will hasten the enfranchisement of the women of all civilised nations, and will thus lead to the development of a higher social and political morality all the world over'.[160] Indeed, neatly inverting the anti-suffrage sense that women could not possibly be involved in governing India, *The Common Cause* insisted that the 'responsibilities of Empire . . . rest on women as well as men. If it were only for the sake of India, women here in great Britain would be bound to demand the vote'.[161]

While for many anti-suffragists it was 'the empire' which provided the strongest arguments against women's suffrage, imperial conflict led to the first major political engagement of women by the government. The outcry that followed the revelations of conditions and mortality figures in the concentration camps in which British interned Boer women and children in Natal during the Boer War led to the appointment of a group of women, under the leadership of Millicent Garrett Fawcett, to investigate the camps. Public debate arose largely as a result of the work of Emily Hobhouse, a pacifist and feminist who had visited South Africa and written extensively about the inhumanity of the British internment of Boer women and children in these camps, pointing particularly to their appalling conditions and their high mortality rates.

Millicent Fawcett was an obvious choice for this task. She had come to national prominence through the leading role she took in the campaign against Irish Home Rule in the late 1880s, and this campaign had brought her into close contact with many members of the Conservative Government. She was outspoken in her patriotic sympathies, accepting absolutely that the Boer War was a just one, 'caused by President Kruger's persistent refusal to admit Englishmen and other "Uitlanders" long settled in the Transvaal to any share in its citizenship'. While many suffragists opposed the war, in Fawcett's view, as in that of Josephine Butler, there was a close parallel between the demands of the 'Uitlanders' and those of suffragists.[162]

Fawcett's support for the war caused immense tension with her feminist colleagues, many of whom opposed the war, seeing it as an act of imperialist aggression. Indeed, hostilities within the NUWSS were such that executive commitee meetings were virtually suspended in 1899.[163] In the eyes of her colleagues, Fawcett was 'unspeakable during the Boer War—till she went to the Camps', and she did not attend meetings of the executive commitee on her return until the war was over.[164] Fawcett's ideas about racial and imperial hierarchy are clearly evident in her report on the camps. There is no suggestion here of sisterly solidarity. On the contrary, in her view, the excessive infant mortality within the camps was largely the result of the superstitious practices and lack of knowledge about health and hygiene of the Boer women, whom she regarded as ignorant peasants.[165] In her discussions of and responses to them, Fawcett asserted again and again the superior knowledge of scientific and hygienic principles which fitted British women for political and public office, but which also made them fitter mothers. Fawcett's support for the Boer War was not shared by many of her colleagues, but her sense of the centrality of Britain, as the 'mother of parliaments' and as having a special place in the women's movement, clearly was.[166]

This assumption of imperial predominance was made very clear in every step British feminists took towards connection with other women's movements or towards internationalism. In the late 1890s, for example, in recognition of the energetic suffrage developments evident in various parts of the empire, the NUWSS decided to invite colonial suffrage organizations to attend its executive meetings—albeit without voting rights. Somewhat to their surprise, none of the suffrage movements in the colonies took the matter sufficiently seriously to appoint representatives. Australian suffragists were mildly interested, because it offered women visiting England the chance to meet other feminists, but they never really took up the offer.

The sense of an imperial hierarchy shifted slightly in regard to Australia and New Zealand in the early years of the twentieth century, when they obtained women's suffrage and hence were in a position to lead their British counterparts. As the suffrage battle became more heated, British feminists regularly pointed to the fact that in these two colonies, the enfranchisement of women had none of the deleterious consequences which the anti-suffragists feared. Many Australian feminists went to England during this period, most notably Vida Goldstein, the leader of the suffrage movement in Victoria, who was invited to tour England by the WSPU in 1911. Goldstein travelled all around the country, insisting on how important the gaining of women's suffrage had been in Australia in improving standards of family and social welfare and in bringing them to national prominence.[167] Goldstein and her Australian followers could not resist a certain smugness at the fact that she had gone 'in response to repeated invitations . . . to assist the suffragettes in England to teach Englishmen, by militancy of speech and the logic of experience, that the road to chivalry is the road to justice'.[168]

Goldstein argued strongly about the benefits and advantages enjoyed by Australian women in comparison with their British sisters. British women suffered from forms of institutional discrimination which appalled her. She was particularly outraged by the metal grille behind which women who attended parliamentary debates were required to sit. Goldstein explained to her English audience that she found it deeply humiliating to see women sitting listening to parliamentary debates sitting behind the grille, which she saw as revealing 'the true English conception of woman. The mother of the race. I am amazed that English women have tolerated that symbol of their slavery and degradation for so long, and yet I should not be amazed for slave conditions and slave minds must go together.'[169]

In the late nineteenth century 'the Indian woman' continued to be the special burden of British feminists, and the campaigns for an end to the Cantonment Rules and to the practices of child marriage and of suttee continued with great vigour, but were often couched in terms which served to belittle or infantilize Indian women. Thus, when the *Woman's Signal* reprinted a paper on the bill to fix the age of marriage in India, it commended the article as one 'written with tact and judgement, and yet firmness' and which provided valuable information 'on the position and prospects of our poor little Indian sisters'.[170] By this very process, as Burton has argued, British feminists constructed 'the Indian woman' as a foil against which to gauge their own progress.[171] And it is noticeable too that British feminists had almost nothing to say about indigenous women in Africa, Australia, or Canada—although there was considerable concern amongst feminists in those countries about the ways in which imperial practices and white masculine sexual privilege oppressed both white and indigenous women.

The unquestioned assumptions of British imperial predominance were also evident in the moves towards internationalism that were so widespread at the turn of the century. The emergence of women's movements in many parts of Europe as well as North America and in the British Empire led to the formation of a series of international women's organizations. After the establishment of the International Council of Women and of the Women's Christian Temperance Union in the 1890s, an International Woman Suffrage Alliance was set up in 1904. The stated aims of the IWSA suggested that it was an egalitarian association as it was formed 'to secure the enfranchisement of the women of all nations, and to unite the friends of woman suffrage throughout the world in organised cooperation and fraternal [sic] helpfulness'.[172] But in fact, it was an extremely hierarchical organization, which described itself and worked very largely through imperial forms and rhetoric—with a central imperial body and a number of local 'colonial' ones. One popular metaphor which was used by feminists in relation to the International Woman Suffrage Alliance involved the IWSA as a distinct and separate empire of women, with its president, the American feminist Carrie Chapman Catt, depicted as an uncrowned queen, surrounded by ladies-in-waiting, ambassadors, and subjects of many nations.[173]

British women participated enthusiastically in some of the activities of the IWSA, notably its campaign to obtain government support to end the white slave traffic. They endorsed the resolution adopted at the special session on the white slave traffic in Budapest in 1913, 'to send from this Congress of the IWSA a request to the Governments of all countries here represented that they should institute an international inquiry into the extent and causes of commercialized vice'.[174] But few British feminists were keenly interested in the pacifism which was an integral part of the feminism of some other members.[175] Charlotte Perkins Gilman's *Man-Made World*, with its discussion of the appalling impact of militarism on women and its belief that through eugenics and the power of love women would create a new world without war, had little impact.[176] Olive Schreiner's essay on 'Women and War', taken from her *Woman and Labour* but published as a separate essay, was rarely discussed, although it was widely read in England. Britain and British developments dominated the IWSA. By 1909, twenty-one countries were affiliated with it—but British news received most coverage at annual congresses and in the pages of *Jus Suffragii*, the monthly journal of the alliance. The mass marches and demonstrations which began in England in 1907 were reported in great detail because again their significance for other women was taken for granted. Even meetings of the international bodies, including the International Women's Suffrage Association, served for some to re-enforce a sense of British pre-eminence. Thus the main impact of the conference of the IWSA, held in London in 1909, was to make members of the Women's Freedom League realize that 'the victory of British women in this [suffrage] question is one that is going to set the pace for the other countries all the world over'.[177]

# five
# FEMINISM AND THE WOMAN CITIZEN IN THE INTERWAR YEARS

The importance of feminist developments in the 1920s, and indeed, in the whole interwar period, have only recently come to be recognized. Dale Spender's book, *There's Always Been a Women's Movement in this Century*, indicates in its very title the surprise—and delight—which Spender herself felt when, after years of accepting the view that feminist activity and the women's movement somehow came to an end after the First World War, she discovered how much feminist debate and activity had continued into the 1920s and 1930s, and indeed beyond.[1] The last five or ten years, however, have seen a considerable amount of research on interwar feminism and Spender's own work, alongside that of Brian Harrison, Harold Smith, and Martin Pugh, and, more particularly, Jane Lewis, Carole Dyhouse, Johanna Alberti, and Susan Kingsley Kent, have made us very aware of its extent, its complexity, and its relevance for contemporary feminism.[2]

None the less, the fact that this period of the very recent past should have required such comprehensive rediscovery remains significant. That feminist activities and debates should have disappeared so completely even in the immediate aftermath of the momentous suffrage campaign shows clearly how tenuous a hold women have both on history and on popular traditions. Dramatic confrontations or demonstrations, such as those waged by the militant suffragettes, have emblazoned themselves on the popular historical imagination as well as on the academic historical tradition. By contrast, the quieter work of non-militant women before the war or of the many feminist groups which operated after it have been forgotten.[3]

Some historians would argue that the tenor of interwar feminism contributed substantially to its historical neglect. The caution of interwar feminist writers and organizations, evident as much in their constant repudiation of being 'anti-man' as in their wholesale endorsement of the importance of motherhood, ensured that they were not seen as threatening the prevailing sexual order. In 1918, as Harold Smith has suggested, feminists seemed poised for a significant reformation of society; by 1930, however, feminism had become so concerned with issues of welfare, which re-enforced traditional family life, that it offered very little in the way of a threat to traditional structures.[4] Moreover, the techniques and methods of interwar feminists, the continuous rounds of meetings, the persistent but always polite lobbying of MPs, and the confinement of debates and discussion of their work to the pages of a few select periodicals, made their work much less visible than that of any of their predecessors. Mid-Victorian feminists present a striking contrast. Despite their concern about propriety, their many public meetings, their intervention in by-elections, their extensive discussion of their views in all the major Victorian periodicals, and their engagement in debates about issues like prostitution meant that they were considerably more visible and more controversial than their interwar counterparts. Indeed, what is significant here is that the work and the struggles of interwar feminists were largely unknown, not only to the generation of women who burst on to the stage in the Women's Liberation Movement of the late 1960s and early 1970s, but even to their own contemporaries.

Feminist leaders were well aware that they had a very low profile. In 1926, Eleanor Rathbone, the president of the National Union of Societies for Equal Citizenship, commented in her annual address on the criticism sometimes levelled against the society that its methods were too tame and that it failed to attract any publicity. Rathbone herself argued that such methods were necessary because of the task at hand: what feminists were seeking was not 'a big, elemental, simple reform', but rather the 'difficult re-adjustments of a complicated, antiquated structure of case law and statute law' which required the careful drafting of bills and tricky negotiations. There are, she argued, 'thousands and soon will be tens of thousands of women—unhappy wives, widows, tired old working spinsters—who have cause to bless the name of the National Union of Societies for Equal Citizenship (NUSEC). What does it matter that most of them have never heard that unwieldy name and would not understand it if they heard it?'[5] Rathbone recognized that there were some disadvantages in this 'unspectacular method'— not least, its failures to win recruits to the women's movement. But she could not see any alternative.

In this very statement, however, Rathbone was presenting one very particular view of interwar feminism, and ignoring the many conflicts which beset it. For one might just as easily argue that the conflicts which divided interwar feminists were immensely important ones which remain of central significance in our own day. Once the first measure of women's suffrage had been gained, feminists faced crucial questions, not only about where to go next, but also about what women's emancipation and women's citizenship actually meant. The suffragettes, like Josephine Butler some decades before, had believed that the political and legal changes which they sought would almost of themselves bring about a social and moral transformation. By 1918 it was clear that this was not the case. Thus feminists had to ask what it was that they had gained and what it could do for them. The shift away from the suffrage as a central and unifying concern also brought to the fore the question which has proved so explosive in recent years: how to construct a feminist programme which could encompass the diverse interests and needs of all women. This, in turn, led to discussions about the meaning of sexuality and of sexual difference in terms of women's daily lives and in terms of their politics and their aspirations, and about the nature of women's citizenship.

Far more than their Victorian and Edwardian predecessors, interwar feminists had to negotiate a careful relationship between 'feminism' and a range of other 'progressive' social developments. Feminists frequently referred to their opponents as 'old-fashioned', depicting the women who opposed them as so 'deeply imbued subconsciously with the tradition of women's inferiority' that they could not understand modern conditions or needs.[6] In the same way, they tended to represent feminists as 'modern women': educated, rational, and independent. But while many women in the 1920s undoubtedly felt themselves to be considerably freer than their mothers, some recent feminist theorists and historians would argue that many of the developments which were seen as marking this freedom did little to undermine prevailing sexual hierarchies. In particular, the emphasis on proper mothering and the new and apparently freer sexuality which was offered to women after the war, were integrally related to a new form of compulsory heterosexuality, which locked women into family life by stressing that it was only through heterosexual relations and motherhood that women could be healthy, happy, and fulfilled.[7] Moreover, the emphasis on women's sexuality and need for sexual pleasure in marriage, amongst some feminists as well as amongst sexologists, served to undermine the status of single women and to render problematical women's relationships with each other.[8]

There was much debate amongst feminists as to whether some of the new social and medical developments, including birth control, should be regarded as 'feminist' or whether they should rather be seen as valuable social reforms but ones which were not intrinsically feminist.[9] These debates brought into question the meaning of feminism itself: whether it involved personal, sexual, and domestic life, or only public and political ones; whether it should concentrate on achieving equality between men and women, or on asserting a 'woman's point of view' on all matters.[10]

The interwar period also saw new developments in regard to feminist theory. The attainment of at least a measure of enfranchisement for women meant that legal and political rights ceased to be the dominating issue and were replaced by economic and cultural questions. For some, like Virginia Woolf, the most important freedom for women was economic freedom, and the most important right that of earning a living.[11] For others, the stress fell rather on women having their needs met by the state. Thus the relationship between feminism and social welfare was heavily stressed by Eleanor Rathbone and her many followers in developments which clearly moved beyond the liberal and equal-rights ideas of the nineteenth and early twentieth centuries.[12] At the same time, feminist analysis was being extended into areas of cultural critique as Virginia Woolf and Winnifred Holtby explored how educational and professional institutions constructed both femininity and masculinity in ways which aggrandized the masculine while constraining and diminishing the feminine.[13] Questions about sexual difference also came to be asked and formulated in new ways, as psychology added a new language to the discussion of an old problem.

In all areas there was an unprecedented diversity of opinion, reflecting a growing recognition of the differences amongst women, which came to the fore once the vote was won. 'Unenfranchised', as Cicely Hamilton argued, 'we had our common grievance of exclusion, whereon, whatever our views or interests, it was easy to concentrate and hammer; enfranchised, we must needs be class and sectional, divided by our varying interests.'[14] Even accepting that 'the mother-interest' would predominate, there would inevitably be tensions and differences of interest amongst middle-class mothers and their working-class counterparts, or amongst impoverished working mothers and their professional sisters. 'With time and political experience,' she argued presciently, 'these lines of cleavage will be more clearly defined than at present.'

Nowhere are the implications of this recognition of difference amongst women made clearer than in regard to the question of women's sexuality. Sexual campaigns—against the Contagious Diseases legislation or in favour of sexual purity—were distinctive features of nineteenth-century feminism, but there were no sexual campaigns of an equivalent size or scope in the interwar period. This was largely because there was no longer any generally accepted idea about the nature of womanhood or about women's sexuality, even amongst middle-class women.[15] Much mid-nineteenth-century feminism was based on a widely accepted assumption about women's innate sexual purity and chastity.[16] This ideal began to break down in the 1890s when some feminism became associated with the sexual demands of the 'new woman', and when some feminists began to demand a recognition of women's active sexuality. By the interwar period, it was no longer possible to put forward any single idea of women's sexuality. On the contrary, interwar feminists stressed that very little was known about women's sexuality and that individual women exhibited marked differences in sexual temperament. Some women, Margaret Cole suggested, were sexually colder than most men while there were others 'whose sexuality runs so high that no ordinary man is likely to satisfy it'.[17]

Sexual questions in the 1920s thus took a number of different forms. Feminists demanded more adequate protection of female children against sexual abuse at the same time as they fought for reform of the legal status of illegitimate children. They campaigned hard to have the term 'common prostitute' removed from the legal code to ensure that disorderly behaviour and solicitation were dealt with in the same way, whether involving men or women, and that no group of women could be singled out by law for particular treatment based on sexual and moral assumptions.[18] Some of them demanded free access to contraception and even to abortion.[19] But none of these issues served to symbolize or dramatize women's sexual oppression in the ways that the battle against the Contagious Diseases had. At the same time, there was strong disagreement amongst feminists over questions such as divorce reform, the meaning of a single sexual standard, and the relationship between feminism and social purity. Once feminists as diverse as Dora Russell and Maude Royden were beginning to argue that sexual pleasure and fulfilment for women was a feminist issue, it was clear that the demand for sexual restraint and social purity could never again become a fundamental demand within the women's movement.[20] At the same time, sexual freedom could not be taken as a goal, because of the lingering belief in the virtues of celibacy on the one hand, and the endorsement of family life on the other.

Interwar feminists were very well aware that they faced serious problems in terms of their theoretical framework as well as in their organization and practical direction. But they also relished the range of issues and the freedom of discussion which was possible now that there was no longer one all-consuming object to be fought for. While some people stressed the need to 'recapture the old suffragette spirit', the *Woman's Leader* insisted that 'we must not return to the doctrinaire oblivion of all but our own theory which was our strength in the old days'.[21] The suffrage movement focused and concentrated all enthusiasm on a single narrow front. Now that this was partially won, it was necessary to prepare for 'the second round'. This involved recognizing first of all 'that the women's movement had become in a relatively greater degree a problem of thought rather than a problem of action' and then selecting 'from the present heart-breaking tangle of sex injustices' some points on which to focus. Many feminists recognized the potential for internal division which this situation offered, foreseeing 'the danger that the fighting forces of the women's movement may fail, owing to the vastness and diversity of their front, to see that front as a whole and the danger that a section may become isolated and make a separate peace'.[22]

## The Legacy of War

The whole question of the impact of the war on women and on the prevailing gender order is currently the subject of much discussion.[23] Where once the war was seen as bringing a substantial measure of new freedom, independence, and self-confidence to women through their increasing participation in the paid workforce and their relative freedom from earlier social, sexual, and economic constraints, there is now much more recognition that whatever gains were won by women were small and temporary ones.[24] Some women might have found work in new fields and with wages higher than they had previously known, but their numbers were quite small.

'For women of means', as Sylvia Pankhurst pointed out, the war offered 'undreamt-of activities, opportunities, positions, [and] a great unlocking of their energies'.[25] Women's Emergency Corps, Women's Volunteer Reserves, war societies of every sort sprang up and women threw themselves into the work, finding this work more adventurous than anything they had ever done before. But while undoubtedly offering new and exciting activities, much of this voluntary war work simply involved the adaptation of familiar forms of philanthropy and community work to wartime conditions.[26] This work was by its very nature temporary and centred on the provision of various forms of social and economic support for the war effort.

In a similar way, in the fields of industrial and clerical employment, there was a range of new jobs open to women during the later stages of the war. But the terms of their employment and the conditions of their work both served to emphasize that women were temporarily taking men's jobs—and for rates of pay substantially lower than men had earned.[27] Moreover, while expanding women's range of occupations was always a feminist goal, not all of those engaged in pioneering new occupations for women were feminists or sympathized with the wider aims of the women's movement. Thus, for example, the Women's Land Army, designed to provide female agricultural labourers to replace fighting men, was introduced by Lady Denman. A vocal anti-suffragist before the war, Lady Denman mobilized the Women's Institutes in order to establish the Women's Land Army.[28] The Institutes enabled her to help organize women's contribution to the war effort— but within an essentially traditional set of ideas about the need for women to support or supplement the work of their men, rather than with any idea of expanding the horizons of women.[29] And the Land Army was set up with a similar goal.

While the numbers of women in paid work increased somewhat during the war, the vast majority of women continued to be engaged in unpaid family duties. Indeed, family life, domesticity, and motherhood were all emphasized heavily during the war, as domestic economy came to be seen as a patriotic duty. Even the NUWSS, which gave up its suffrage campaigning to help organize wartime relief work, set up a 'Patriotic Housekeeping Exhibition' and sent lecturers around the country to talk about the need to avoid waste.[30] Hence, while the crisis of war affected the lives of all women, it changed the ways in which they carried out their customary tasks rather than redefining their overall relationship to the family and the wider society.

The outbreak of war brought to many feminists a wave of patriotic enthusiasm, but not all of them translated this into a sense of their own identification with questions of national interest. Some felt a renewed sense of women's exclusion from what was becoming the chief interest of men. Vera Brittain wrote movingly of her own sense of loneliness and desolation as the war engrossed all the attentions of her lover, superseding the interest in university life and in literature which they had shared. 'Women get all the dreariness of war, and none of the exhilaration', she wrote, in response to his letter explaining to her how fascinating, ennobling, and even beautiful the war seemed to him.[31] War, 'which you say is the only thing that counts at present, is the one field in which women have made no progress—perhaps never will'. And Brittain charted with care the emotional estrangement which followed the increasing separation of home and battle fronts.

And yet Brittain was herself an example both of what the war could offer women and of the curious ways in which women seemed to be the chief gainers from it. Despite familial disapproval and official discouragement, in 1915 she left Oxford and joined the Voluntary Aid Detachments as a nurse. In the process, she donned a uniform, became very familiar with male bodies—in their most dependent state as wounded soldiers—and travelled overseas. Ostensibly, her *Testament of Youth* records her experiences of suffering and loss as she battled to find a place for herself in the war, facing always the contrast between the importance accorded to men's performing of their patriotic duty, and the refusal of any general recognition that such duty existed for women. She was involved in a constant battle as she sought to obtain training and to be allowed to leave her family in order to nurse wounded soldiers. She was constantly aware of the relatively demeaning nature of her work and of a growing separation between herself and the men she had cared for most. The story of her wartime experience is one of constant fear and grief, as one after another her lover, her brother and her close male friends were killed. While experiencing immense and painful losses during the war, however, Brittain survived it, gaining immense knowledge and experience, and the strength to set up an independent life once it was over. Overcoming her loss, she married, had children, and established a substantial reputation both as a writer and as a peace campaigner. Hence, despite her suffering, she functions also as an illustration of the ways in which the war, for all its apparent celebration of masculinity and male bonding, led to death and destruction for men while the women for whom they fought became increasingly strong and independent.

The 'gender crisis' brought by the war has been discussed in many recent literary studies, which have pointed to the massive body of literature showing how men felt themselves emasculated by the horrors of their war experience.[32] Many of the men who survived the war ended up maimed and impotent. For the first time, large numbers of men suffered from nervous diseases, especially hysteria—once seen as a specifically female problem.[33] The antagonism from men suffering acute hardships on the battle front to those who seemed to be living quite secure lives on the home front was often given an explicitly sexual form, as women were seen as the ones who sent men off to war, and who benefited from their absence.[34] The very images of women which were used as recruitment propaganda or as advertisements for the Red Cross and for relief work exacerbated this, showing at the same time enlarged female figures dwarfing the men they were either sending off to war or nursing once wounded. Press and publicity photographs of 'land girls' or women as transport workers or as drivers or messengers near the battle front, like all the many women in uniform, all suggested a powerful new sense of freedom, physical strength, and independence for women.[35] These images often belied the truth: both on the home front and on the battle front, women workers were exploited, heavily policed in order to ensure that they behaved appropriately, and more often patronized than recognized or respected.[36] But the images certainly emphasized their new freedoms and added an edge to male hostility. Ironically then, while many women sought, through their paid and voluntary work, to show their sense of responsibility and their capacity to contribute to the war effort, these contributions served as much to increase male hostility as to demonstrate women's entitlement to citizenship.

The postwar period in Britain, as in most other European countries, was one of powerful anti-feminist reaction. Britain did not have the *freikorps* or the paramilitary organizations which were so powerful in Germany in the 1920s, nor did it have as many organizations calling for a return of women to their domestic and familial functions and extolling the virtues of large families. But it did participate in the new celebrations of motherhood involving prize-winning babies, large families—and Mother's Day.[37] For some years, feminists were able to argue that there was 'a new attitude' to 'women's questions', evident both in the House of Commons and in society at large, that was more serious and more attentive than had been the case before the war and which resulted both from the enfranchisement of women and from a profound alteration in values that had made life more valuable than property.[38] But the hostility to women's aspirations evident in the newly introduced and rapidly expanding marriage bars, in the restrictions on women's opportunities in the civil service, in the refusals to introduce any form of maternity support for single mothers, all demonstrated only too clearly the powerful opposition which women faced and which had been strengthened by their apparent gains during and immediately after the war.

The war also brought profound changes in terms of the demographic structure and hence the expectations or possibilities for women in regard to marriage and motherhood on the one hand and waged work or careers on the other. England had long had an imbalance in the numbers of men and women, with the numbers of 'excess' women increasing steadily throughout the nineteenth century. It increased again, and very dramatically of course, as a result of war casualties. In 1911, there were 106.8 women to every hundred men; by 1921, this ratio had increased so that there were 109.6 women to every hundred men. In a similar way, the numbers of women between the ages of 15 and 44 who had never married were 664,000 in 1911, but 1,174,000 in 1921.[39] Marriage of course remained the typical experience of women, but there were very significant numbers who did not marry and for whom employment and financial independence was a major concern.

For the majority of women who did marry, wifedom and motherhood was assumed to be a full-time occupation. However, the continuing decline in fertility meant that by 1921, average family size was two children or less, with only 14.8 per cent of families having more than five children. But the constant emphasis on the importance of maternal care of children and the ever-increasing standards of cooking and of household management meant that, even though most women had many years of married life during which they were neither pregnant nor nursing, there was still immense pressure on them to devote themselves to family and home.[40] The desire of many women for both a family and a career seemed to many writers to involve an impossible conflict during the interwar period.[41] Far from demonstrating the possibilities for women to manage both family life and paid employment, the war suggested rather that this was possible only during an emergency and that once 'normal' life resumed, the family and its welfare should become the chief concern of women. Even those, like Vera Brittain, who managed both, regarded this issue as the next great challenge for feminists.[42]

## A Feminist Programme

For historians looking back on the 1920s, it is perhaps the opposition to feminist aims and objectives which seems most noticeable. Feminists at the time were well aware that they were living in a time of reaction in which there was 'a turning against women and their interests'.[43] Some pointed to the fact that the gains themselves were not as great as they might appear; thus Cicely Hamilton pointed out that the vote itself meant less when it was actually granted to women than it had at the height of the suffrage controversy: women attained their rights in very unfavourable circumstances—'at a moment when enfranchisement—comparatively speaking—was discredited' by war and by a growing hostility amongst many to parliamentary processes. The power of the vote was a very limited one and it was of little help when it came to economic independence, which was 'the ultimate aim of feminism' for Hamilton as it was for Ray Strachey.[44] But many still expressed considerable optimism. Women had 'passed the first great toll-bar on the road which leads to equality,' argued Lady Rhondda, while recognizing that 'it is a far cry yet to the end of the road'.[45]

The granting of limited suffrage to women raised the question of what the new feminist programme should be. All the different organizations which made up the women's movement recognized the need for a programme that would inspire a new generation of women 'to complete the work which their grandmothers began',[46] but no one quite knew how. There were disagreements amongst the leading organizations from the start over whether their programme should be a broad one encompassing as many issues of concern to women as possible, or a narrower one concerned with gaining equality between men and women in certain specific areas. Increasingly, there were also disagreements over new issues which had not been a significant part of feminist programmes before the war at all: birth control and family endowment being the two main ones, but both leading to the wider question of the relationship between feminism and social reform.

The largest of the pre-war suffrage organizations, the NUWSS, was the central group in a number of conflicts throughout the 1920s. In 1917, Eleanor Rathbone, the distinguished philanthropist and welfare worker, followed Millicent Garrett Fawcett as president of the NUWSS. Her approach was suggested by her proposed motto of the society: 'I am a woman, and nothing that concerns the status of women is indifferent to me.'[47] In 1919, the society changed its name to the National Society for Equal Citizenship, defining its general aims in broad terms; it sought 'to obtain all such reforms as are necessary to secure a real equality of liberties, status and opportunities between men and women'. It devised a programme consisting of six points: equal suffrage; an equal moral standard; promotion of the candidature of women for Parliament; equal pay for equal work and equality in industry and the professions; widows' pensions and equal guardianship; and active support for the League of Nations and of the practical application of the principle of equal opportunity within it.[48] This programme was strongly opposed by some long-standing feminists, like Ray Strachey, who sought a much narrower and more concentrated programme. Strachey persuaded the society with which she was most closely involved, the London National Society for Women's Suffrage (which later became the London National Society for Women's Service), to take as its general objectives 'equal suffrage and equal opportunities for women', but 'to concentrate its efforts for the present on obtaining economic equality for women'.[49]

Strachey was but one of the prominent feminists who objected to the breadth of the NUSEC programme and indeed to its whole approach. Where Rathbone and her colleagues saw one of their main tasks to be that of educating women for citizenship and changing prevailing ideas and outlooks so that women's equality could become a reality, others felt that this educational programme was no longer necessary. In 1921, Lady Rhondda argued that the old methods of the suffrage societies, involving 'educating by speech and propaganda', were no longer necessary now that it was possible to achieve what women wanted by political action. She worked with a number of others to set up the Six Point Group, 'a definite practical body with definite simple aims' that it wished to effect by using women's newly gained political power.[50] Lady Rhondda agreed with Rathbone that the feminist programme must be broad, but she also felt strongly that it needed to be limited and to contain clear priorities. In an early article in *Time and Tide* she spelt out very clearly the two classes of reform which seemed to her important: first, 'the readjustment of certain old laws and customs', which needed to take account of the enfranchisement of women and the differences between their views and those of men on matters including bastardy and child assault. Secondly, the programme needed to establish the next steps to be taken towards the elimination of the sex barrier. The programme of the Six Point Group included: satisfactory legislation on child assault; satisfactory legislation for the unmarried mother and her child; an equal standard on sex morals; and equal guardianship of children. Its preoccupation with middle-class and professional women was very evident, however, in its commitment to equal pay for teachers and equal opportunities in the civil service rather than to any broader measure of equal pay and opportunities.

But while these groups set up programmes intended clearly to recognize the connection between pre- and postwar feminists, new issues inevitably arose which involved new approaches and carried feminists in directions which were unthinkable in the pre-war period. Some of these issues also raised profound questions about the meaning and nature of feminism and about its relationship with the overall needs and situation of women. Birth control was one of the most contentious new issues in feminist debates of the 1920s. It was also the one which showed most clearly the difficulties feminists faced in setting up programmes that aimed at reforming the situation of most women—but without, in fact, dealing in any way with the existing sexual order.

Birth control became the subject of quite widespread debate early in the 1920s, following the discussion of it in Marie Stopes's *Married Love* and amongst women in the Co-operative Guilds. It was discussed in a number of different forums: in feminist groups, by sex reformers, and extensively by large numbers of women associated with the Labour Party. Most feminist organizations came to support birth control by the mid-1920s, and to demand that information about it be made freely available to (married) women who sought it. For some, particularly Eleanor Rathbone, Mary Stocks, and NUSEC, birth control was one of the welfare measures which feminism needed to support in order to improve the lot of the vast majority of women. But for others, like Lady Rhondda and many of the Six Point Group, improvements in family life, while desirable, remained questions of social reform rather than of feminism.

And indeed, the implications for feminism of the whole birth-control debate are very complex. While birth controllers sought to give women the autonomy which came from exercising control over their bodies and their own fertility, the emphasis on birth control continued the trend of so much interwar feminism in concentrating on married women at the expense of single ones. Moreover, many birth-controllers accepted the views evident amongst sexologists and many doctors and psychiatrists that marriage and active heterosexual relationships were the only basis for a normal and healthy life. While some advocates of birth control argued that it was essentially a feminist issue, because 'the right of women to control their own bodies is as important as the right to vote',[51] for others, it was associated rather with improving sexual relations and marriage. Dora Russell, one of the leading figures in making birth control an issue in the Labour Party, conceded this quite clearly: 'We were trying to set sex free from the stigma of sin, we saw it as an expression of the union and harmony between two lovers; our adversaries' dogma demanded that sex be indulged in only for the procreation of children.' It was in the process of trying to make this argument that she came to see how 'traditional societies . . . completely neglect the views and needs of women'.[52] But Russell assumed unquestioningly that sexual freedom and feminism were the same, arguing that 'the important task of modern feminism is to accept and proclaim sex; to bury for ever the lie that has too long corrupted our society—the lie that the body is a hindrance to the mind'. For her, feminism did not involve a conflict between men and women—but rather the conflict they shared in regard to Victorian sexual restraint.

Janet Chance, a founding member of the Abortion Law Reform Association went further than Russell, not only arguing that sexual pleasure was necessary in marriage, but insisting that pleasure in heterosexual relations was a requirement for women taking any form of public office. No sexologist was more vehement than Chance in her insistence that lack of sexual enjoyment was a national problem. For the most part, Chance believed, the women who had a public voice were ones who feared and disliked sex, having never enjoyed it themselves. She referred to these women as 'child-women', and saw them as doing great harm as they encouraged those who sought 'to control the behaviour of men and women in sex matters without understanding it. . . . Far too many of our women representatives in public life, and not a few of our doctors are spinster-minded. . . . These people are, in part, not yet alive. They have no perception in sex matters. They are sexually blind, and their disastrously vacant eyes see no light in the questions they dare to handle.'[53] Chance ultimately argued that 'non-orgasmic' women—a category which included frigid women, virgins and spinsters—should be kept out of politics![54] While Chance and Russell sought to stress that they were not 'old-fashioned man-hating feminists', some later writers would question whether they can really be seen as feminist at all. Clearly their views were totally at odds with those seeking women's social, economic, and political autonomy.

Birth control and family limitation also brought up another issue: eugenics and the question of 'racial health'. This issue was one that was discussed at length by various feminist groups, especially by NUSEC. One of its main leaders, Eva Hubback, was greatly concerned about eugenics, becoming a member of the Eugenics Society in 1929 and later serving on its central committee. Hubback frequently raised questions about eugenic goals at NUSEC meetings.[55] In 1931, she attempted to gain support of the annual council for voluntary sterilization 'to reduce the incidence of grave hereditary defects seriously impairing physical and mental heredity and efficiency'.[56] Hubback worked constantly to have eugenic goals adopted by NUSEC, but without success.

The differences amongst the various feminist groups which were evident at the start of the 1920s became more and more marked as the

decade wore on. Thus while the Six Point Group dealt extensive.,
the need to reform the laws and the court procedures pertaining to
sexual assaults on children, stressing the need for widows' pensions,
and for satisfactory legislation for illegitimate children, increasingly by
the mid-1920s, it was concentrating more and more on legal and economic equality, adding equal franchise as its first aim and concentrating heavily on equal pay, on the marriage bar, and on training women
in proper business habits. By contrast, NUSEC was becoming increasingly concerned about the status and welfare of wives and mothers,
concentrating much of its energy on questions of family endowment
and birth control, both of which became part of its formal programme
in the mid-1920s.

NUSEC's initial demand for widows' pensions was replaced by a
broader commitment 'to secure improvements in the status of wives
and mothers'. Specified under this heading were the provision of an
adequate maternity service throughout the country; the provision of
Family Allowances; and the freedom of women who desire it to obtain
Birth-Control at Welfare Centres in receipt of Government grants.[57]

Rathbone's influential book, *The Disinherited Family*, provided the
starting-point for making the status of wives and mothers almost the
central concern of NUSEC. In part this was a reflection of Rathbone's
detailed knowledge of and concern about the extent of poverty in England and its provenance amongst women and children. The fight for
family allowances dominated her life, both in her feminist work in the
1920s and in her parliamentary work in the 1930s and 1940s.[58] But this
emphasis on the need to assist women in the discharge of their 'peculiar
and primary function' led very quickly to an emphasis on the need to
find a definition of feminism which did not emphasize its central concern with establishing equal rights as between women and men. Thus
in 1925, in response to a debate conducted in the *Morning Post* on
whether or not feminism was a failure, *The Woman's Leader* took up
the question 'What is feminism?' Arguing against a definition offered
by Rose Macaulay in which she argued that feminism involved 'the
attempts of women to possess privileges (political, professional,
economic, or other) which have previously been denied to them on account of their sex', the paper argued that feminism was *not* seeking the
mere throwing open to women of all the privileges of men. Rather,
feminism should be defined as 'the demand of women that the whole
structure and movement of society shall reflect in a proportionate degree their experiences, their needs, and their aspirations'. Feminism
was not concerned with securing for women rights such as those which

would allow them access to the boxing ring—but they were concerned to gain an adjustment of social values which would secure due recognition, in deed as well as words, for the occupation of motherhood. What was needed was not just a negative clearing away, but a positive demand for fulfilment.[59]

This sense of the need to offer women fulfilment of their special duties became a central aspect of Rathbone's approach and that of the NUSEC. Although she always emphasized the commitment of NUSEC to equality with men in relation to the franchise, pay, and moral standards, Rathbone insisted that she could not see that 'removing from the Statute Book the remaining traces of legal inequality' was sufficiently engaging or satisfying to inspire a new generation of feminists. In place of this old equal-rights feminism, she promoted a 'new feminism'.

At last we can stop looking at all our problems through men's eyes and discussing them in men's phraseology. We can demand what we want for women, not because it is what men have got, but because it is what women need to fulfil the potentialities of their own nature and to adjust themselves to the circumstances of their own lives. . . . Hitherto we have contented ourselves with demanding that in the economic sphere women shall be free to attempt the same tasks as men and shall be paid at the same rates *when they are doing men's work*. But under what conditions are they to labour and at what rates are they to be paid when they are doing work which only women can do or for which they have a special fitness?[60]

Rathbone's presidential statement of 1926, in which she enunciated her views on 'the new Feminism', established a new set of terms for debating the meaning of feminism. Her position was repeatedly attacked in *Time and Tide* by Lady Rhondda, Winnifred Holtby, and various other members of the Six Point Group.[61] While Rathbone saw herself as revitalizing feminism, Lady Rhondda argued that her position and that of some of her friends on NUSEC were not feminist at all. For Lady Rhondda, feminism meant 'equality of status and opportunity' for women, and the other aspects of the NUSEC programme which Rathbone had added—family endowment and birth control, the acceptance of protective legislation for women under certain conditions, and the support for the League of Nations—were all rather the objectives of philanthropists, sociologists, internationalists, and party politicians rather than of feminists.[62] Lady Rhondda herself had no objections to these points in themselves; *Time and Tide* supported birth control and internationalism, but did not see them as 'feminist'. In her view, feminism and equality were synonymous. 'The achievement of real feminism would mean that society laid the stress, not on the sex of an individual, but on his or her humanity, to an extent which is still unknown today.' Hence family endowment and access to birth-control information 'can only be called feminist reforms in so far as they tend to give women a closer approach to equality of freedom and of opportunity with men'. They may be valuable social reforms, but this of itself does not make them feminist.[63]

This conflict between 'old' and 'new' feminism has usually been seen in terms of classic division between 'equality' and 'difference' feminism, and while these terms certainly come up, the debate itself shows the difficulties in attempting to set up this rather simplistic division within feminism.[64] Lady Rhondda and Winnifred Holtby can be seen as 'equal rights' feminists in their stress on the need for women to be seen as 'human' rather than to be categorized in terms of their sex, while Eleanor Rathbone, by contrast, emphasized that women had different needs and perceptions from men in regard to everything: not only in matters of sexuality and sexual relations, but also in regard to matters of housing or local and community organization, or industrial disputes. But the debate went far beyond this in questioning what equality itself might mean for women and in its discussions of the relationship between feminist goals and the overall economic, domestic, and social situation of women.

This debate served also to bring to the fore, as Cicely Hamilton had foretold, some of the divisions amongst women which were based on class. Thus, while Rathbone argued for family endowment and financial support for working-class women, middle-class feminists like Vera Brittain were far more concerned to insist on the need for married women to be able to work—and on the need for marriage itself to become more flexible so that it ceased to be a synonym for 'our domestic menage' and came instead to symbolize 'the union of two careers and two sets of ideals and aspirations'.[65] Throughout the whole interwar period, the marriage bar and the general problem of how married women might combine paid work with domestic and familial duties, was perhaps the one most deeply felt by middle-class feminists.[66]

The historical dimension of this debate was immediately brought to the fore as both sides claimed that they were the true inheritors of the mantle of Victorian and Edwardian feminism. Eleanor Rathbone and her followers, who were labelled 'social reformers' rather than 'feminists' by Lady Rhondda, argued first that in demanding the emancipation of women, feminism was seeking the outstanding social reform of the twentieth century, and secondly, that in connecting feminism and social reform, they were also following in the footsteps of Josephine Butler who had also stood out against the narrow emphasis on equal rights.

When Josephine Butler . . . led her crusade against the Contagious Diseases Acts, exactly the same hue and cry arose; the pioneer feminists of half a century ago were divided on almost the same lines as today. Josephine Butler had the courage to raise her voice on a subject which shocked the conventions and false reticences of Victorian England, and 'equalitarians' of her day and generation cried hands off any reform which may retard the fight for the vote, just as their lineal descendants to-day cry this or that is a social reform, not feminism, when modern problems bound up with the freedom and status of women are under discussion.[67]

By contrast, the 'Old Feminists' always insisted that they were completing the equality programme established by Victorian feminism and more especially by the suffrage movement.

The debate also had an important strategic function. While Rathbone's approach certainly mirrored her own interests and values, it was also one which she believed would appeal to large numbers of women exercising votes for the first time, offering at the same time appropriate avenues of activity for NUSEC and its members. In her insistence that women had different needs and interests from those of men when it came to many social, urban, and industrial questions as well as to questions about family life, work, and political rights, Rathbone was demanding something which would later be called a 'woman-centred' approach and which recognized and even celebrated sexual difference. But Rathbone also made clear her own sense that the circumstances of the 1920s made it imperative that feminism should find new issues and a new programme if it was to appeal to a new generation. She argued repeatedly that the old watchword of 'equality' was becoming hampering and restrictive, and, moreover, that it 'has lost much of its potency for the younger generation, which has never known the harsher forms of inequality'. She felt that, by contrast, the issue of self-determination, as defined in the 'new feminism' with its emphasis on enabling women to discharge their duties as citizens, provided possible avenues for new energy and new activities. A year after calling for an approach based on the 'new feminism', Rathbone argued that one could already see 'among our societies a growing preoccupation with the new issues, with Family Endowment, Birth Control, Social Insurance, International Peace'.[68]

Rathbone was unquestionably correct in her assertion that a reliance on the 'old ideal of equality' lacked the power to galvanize a movement. Even those who believed most strongly that the completion of the old equal-rights programme was their main task accepted Rathbone's reading of it. Those who opposed her most vociferously, and upheld what they saw as the true feminist goal of equality as against her emphasis on the importance of welfare and on improving the lot of wives and mothers, echoed precisely her emphasis on the tedium involved in constantly reiterating the argument for sex equality. Viscountess Rhondda, for example, who argued vociferously against Rathbone's approach was, she admits, 'a little bored' at feeling the need to fight for equal political freedom for men and women after the war, 'when there was so much else of enthralling interest and urgency that one wanted to do in the world'. Finally, when the Franchise Act of 1928 gave women the vote on the same terms as men, she felt it 'a blessed relief not to have to trouble with things of that sort any more'.[69] Similarly, Winnifred Holtby looked forward to 'an end of the whole business, the demands for equality, the suggestions of sex warfare, the very name of feminist'. Holtby wanted to be free to pursue her real interests, 'the study of inter-race relationships, the writing of novels, and so forth', but she felt unable to do so while injustice is done and opportunity denied to the great majority of women. She was, as she said, a feminist 'because I dislike everything feminism implies', and so she chose the 'Old' and limited version of feminism because it focused on one matter: political equality, 'because it restricts to as small a field as possible the isolated action of women, in order that elsewhere both sexes may work together for the good of the community'.[70]

In connecting the issue of women's citizenship, and the need for them to have the health and welfare services which they needed in order to live reasonably and carry out all their various duties, Rathbone attempted to meet the interests and needs of a new generation and a new era and to show the relevance and importance of feminism for all women. Unfortunately, as Jane Lewis and others have pointed out, the radical possibilities evident in Rathbone's demand for a recognition of women's interests and point of view were ultimately dissipated by the focusing of attention primarily on mothers—with the assumption that maternity and child care were the central and necessary experiences and functions of all women. This, in turn, involved a relegation of working women and of women's work to a secondary place. Moreover, Rathbone's attempt to expand the sway of feminism so that it included working-class women and was in some sense in conformity with the

Labour movement required her to make concessions which very few other feminists could accept and which ultimately split her own organization.

For a number of feminists, the question of women's work was the central issue still needing to be resolved. Although many had hoped that the visibility and the success of women in new trades and occupations during the war, combined with the first measure of their enfranchisement, would signal a new attitude to the whole question of women's employment, this hope was short-lived. As Eleanor Rathbone said, in her first presidential address at the Annual Council of NUSEC in 1920, it was a rude shock to those innocents who had thought that the bad old days had come to an end,

to find that one of the first-fruits of the first parliament elected partly by women voters had been the placing on the Statute Book of an Act which, without once mentioning the word 'woman' or 'female' has the effect of legally excluding women, for the first time in British history, from nearly every department of skilled industry except a few trades traditionally their own. The Pre-War Practices Act was passed in fulfilment of a pledge given in war-time . . . But that such a pledge should have been asked for and its literal fulfilment exacted four years later, in spite of the intervening experience of the industrial capacities of women, is only one of many accumulating proofs that when groups of men . . . accept the formula 'equality of opportunity between men and women', they do so with the mental reservation—'except when it may be inconvenient to ourselves or those we want to please.'[71]

The demand for women's industrial and economic equality involved several related but distinct questions: the opening to women of professions, trades, and occupations hitherto denied them; equal pay and the acceptance that women's work, like men's, should bear no relationship to their marital status. As Ray Strachey pointed out, from the very beginning of the women's movement, 'the right to work' had been recognized as an essential part of real emancipation.[72] It was temporarily overshadowed by the suffrage movement, but it had always been of central importance. Although Strachey maintained a resolutely cheerful outlook, insisting on the increase in the availability of work to women, on the recognition of their merits, and on their increasing level of pay throughout the 1920s, many others saw this area as the most difficult one for women—and the one in which they met with their greatest defeats. The dismissal of women workers immediately after the war, the imposition of marriage bars in teaching and in many of the occupations and employment in local government, the refusal of the civil service to admit women on the same terms as men, the imposition of quotas for women students in medical schools, all added up to a power-ful series of barriers to women seeking work. From the beginning, *Time and Tide* carried articles attacking the marriage bar and demanding equality between husbands and wives in terms of access to work and criticizing the actions of local government bodies, of the civil service and of trade unions in excluding women from work. It was particularly critical of the ways in which the civil service evaded the Sex Disqualifi-cation (Removal) Act by denying women equal opportunity and equal pay.[73]

Many contributors to *Time and Tide* also campaigned through the Six Point Group which listed 'Occupational Equality' as one of its chief aims. In addition to trying to exert pressure on the civil service and on local governments, the Six Point Group sought to open occupations to women in industrial fields, such as the building industry, where they were excluded through trade union restrictions. Like their nineteenth-century counterparts, many feminists attacked unions and the Labour movement for their exclusion of women from training and from work, seeking to find ways to influence both individual unions and the TUC. In 1927, many of these women met to form the Open Door Council, spurred on to do so by their increasing alarm at 'the present tendency to legislate with the ostensible object of improving the lot of the woman worker'. The Council accepted that industrial conditions required im-provement, but insisted 'that it is essential that any improvement should affect conditions both for men and women'.[74] It aimed 'to se-cure for women, irrespective of marriage or childbirth, the right at all times to decide whether or not they should engage in paid work, and to ensure that no legislation or regulations shall deprive them of this right'.[75]

Initially, in the early 1920s, all feminist organizations had been com-mitted to the idea of equality between men and women in terms of the right to work. NUSEC had this as one of its aims and had fought bitterly against the creeping imposition of the marriage bar—in apparent con-tradiction of the Sex Disqualification (Removal) Bill. But the civil serv-ice was not required to comply and nothing could be done to prevent the dismissal of women teachers, doctors, and cleaners on marriage. In 1921, they sought to challenge the dismissal of a married woman doc-tor from St Pancras Borough Council—only to be told that the Sex Dis-qualification (Removal) Bill did nothing to infringe the right of the local authority to dismiss someone for any reason it chose.[76] Feeling about the importance of women's employment was strong in NUSEC. Indeed, a number of the founder members of the Open Door Council were members of NUSEC, including Elizabeth Abbot, Crystal Macmillan, and Helen Fraser.

But this commitment to women's right to work irrespective of any claims of marriage or motherhood did not sit well with the overall approach of the 'new feminism'. At the annual council meeting of NUSEC in 1927, Eleanor Rathbone successfully sought to amend the general resolution on this point to allow the executive committee to take into account in any particular case whether the proposed regulation of women's labour would promote the well-being of the community and of the workers affected, whether it was desired by the workers or their organization, and whether it might in itself aid the securing of equality. Eleven members of the executive committee resigned over this, including all those who had become members of the Open Door Council, arguing that by setting up these additional tests in regard to industrial legislation, the society was abandoning its primary emphasis on equality. They regarded the change as a denial of the fundamental principles of the women's movement.[77]

In the 1920s, as in the 1880s and 1890s, the question of labour legislation brought into sharp focus the fundamental disagreements and differences of outlook between middle-class feminists and those connected more closely with the labour movement. While the Six Point Group and NUSEC sought a removal of protective legislation, the Fabian Women's Group and Standing Joint Committee of Industrial Women's Organizations sought rather an extension of industrial legislation to men. While recognizing the problems faced by working women, and speaking out strongly against the marriage bar, they were 'not prepared to sacrifice any legislative protection for women on the grounds that it cannot immediately be obtained for men also'.[78]

This point of conflict was one of the few which existed between middle-class and labour feminists in the interwar period. Elsewhere, although there were considerable differences in emphasis, there was also much underlying agreement. Labour Women's Conference and the Standing Joint Committee of Industrial Organizations in the early 1920s focused considerable attention on the problems of women's work, seeking better education and training for working-class women rather than entry to the professions, and demanding unemployment benefits for working women as well as family endowment. The question of maternal health and mortality and the need for paid maternity leave were also items of significance.

Amongst Labour women, however, as amongst their middle-class counterparts, the formulation of a feminist programme and the capacity to maintain a high level of feminist commitment was difficult in the interwar years. The Women's Co-op Guild was less active and less vocal than it had been prior to 1919, as was the Fabian Women's Group and, as we shall see, the Labour Women's Conference, although providing a venue for the discussion of issues of concern to women was tightly controlled by Marion Phillips, who made sure that the agenda did not contain too many issues that would bring hostility from the party leadership. Thus while Eleanor Rathbone hoped that her endorsement of legislative protection for working women might bring a closer connection between middle-class and working-class women, it did not bring any concerted feminist action. This conflict over industrial legislation brought fundamental divisions into the middle-class women's movement and created barriers which were hard to overcome. It finally worked to separate those feminists concerned not only with women's need for equality but also with the demand for their economic and social autonomy from those for whom feminism and family welfare were becoming synonymous. But it also signalled the start of a decline in feminist activity which, after the final measure of women's enfranchisement in 1928, became both marked and rapid.

As Rathbone was to discover, the capacity of a 'new feminism' to galvanize a new generation was not in fact realized. NUSEC continued working effectively and strongly until 1928, but the final enfranchisement of women on the same terms as men really brought concentrated feminist activity to an end. Rathbone herself foreshadowed this in an article on the future in *The Woman's Leader* in July 1928. Women had deserted the women's movement in 1918, she argued, seeing many of their gains as won, and even more would do so now in the belief that while there was some work still to do, it did not amount to much. Rathbone insisted, however, that there *was* much still to do: women might nearly have come to equal men in terms of status, but certainly not in terms of opportunities. The financial dependence of women, their exclusion from skilled work, their unequal pay were all issues that needed to be addressed. Rathbone reiterated her sense of the need to drop equality as a measure and to begin asking what it was that women needed, for themselves, their children, or their world. But her very discussion lacks any energy or any sense of direction. Her final comment—that the women's movement, like other movements, was becoming international, and that it needed to tackle the problems of women, especially in the Empire—described her own interest while not setting up any programme for others to follow. Rathbone's own career set a pattern for the shift in feminist activities. She was elected to

**195**

Parliament as an Independent member for the Combined Universities in June of 1929 and resigned from the presidency of NUSEC, to devote herself to parliamentary work. While NUSEC continued after this, working on a smaller programme centring on education for citizenship, increasing the numbers of women in all levels of government, working for an equal moral standard, and securing the status of wives and mothers, it dwindled in numbers and energy. It ceased even to be able to sustain its paper, *The Woman's Leader*, which was taken over by the Townswomen's Guild in 1930.

As many historians have noted, the late 1920s, with the onset of the Depression, brought to an end the spate of reform legislation and any real commitment to feminist issues either within the broad political framework—or even within organizations whose *raison d'être* had once been feminist. The sense of things getting worse and worse for women in the late 1920s is evident in many women's organizations. One can see it, for example, in the Women's Freedom League annual conference of 1929. The aim of the League was still 'full equality for men and women in every branch of our national and international life, and the message of the Conference was to get on with that work at an accelerated speed'. But in fact, the report of the conference suggests that its time was taken up entirely in hearing about the insoluble difficulties faced by many different groups of women: women civil servants and teachers told about the special inequalities which they resented; university women discussed striking inequalities between men and women at different universities; they heard that medical schools outside London were about to follow London's bad example by refusing admission of women to medical school in future; women magistrates talked of the problems they faced—the need for women on every bench, their anxiety about getting more women on education committees and parish councils, their concern that the Stockton Board of guardians had adopted new standing orders which excluded women from important committees.[79]

A similar pattern is evident in regard to the Six Point Group and to the paper for which many of its members wrote, *Time and Tide*. From about 1927, writers like Cicely Hamilton began warning readers of the dangers inherent in 'The Return to Femininity', arguing that, while war had brought women new opportunities, the return to peace was being accompanied by a demand by men that women resume more feminine demeanour, garb, and activities. Ironically, she was particularly insistent that women retain the right to wear short skirts and to show their legs, resisting any attempt to make them return to the inconvenience of long skirts, which made a woman into a 'legless animal . . . reduced to the state of dependence implied by her deformity!'[80] *Time and Tide* continued to insist that equal rights and equal opportunities were the feminist goal—but in fact, its own concerns with feminism became markedly reduced in the early 1930s, as it devoted more and more of its attention to questions about the League of Nations, the rise of fascism, and the threat to world peace.

## Training Women for Citizenship

The question of women's citizenship and of the meaning of a 'woman's vote' has recently been the subject of much discussion. On the one hand, Denise Riley has pointed to the paradoxes for feminism inherent in the very notion of a 'woman's vote', whereby women become en-trapped in the gender categories from which feminism has always sought to escape.[81] By contrast, Carole Patemen, Anne Phillips, and many others have shown how women's interests and questions which arise in relation to gender simply cannot be dealt with adequately within our current systems of representation.[82] These questions inevi-tably came to the fore, with the passage of the Representation of the People Act in 1917, leading to a series of debates both about the nature of women's citizenship and about the relationship between women, political parties, and the whole representative process.

Prior to the gaining of the vote, there was a general sense that the suf-frage would in some way transform the situation of women. Not every-one believed that this transformation would be total or instantaneous, though even the most moderate of constitutional suffragists, like Emily Davies or Millicent Garrett Fawcett, shared some of Mill's sense that the vote would not only prove educative and improve women's domes-tic status, but that it would also over time produce substantial legisla-tive change as women's interests would have to be considered seriously in Parliament.

Once the vote was gained, however, it became clear that large num-bers of women really had little interest in it. Rather than explore why it was that women saw political parties and parliamentary processes as having little to offer them, many feminists set themselves the task of educating the new woman voters and making them aware of the impor-tance of exercising their vote in a responsible manner.

The idea that women should be taught to use their vote effectively immediately raised the further question of whether it was meaningful to talk about sexed citizenship. Feminists in the 1920s were as divided over this question as are their contemporary counterparts. There were broad differences of opinion which followed roughly the same lines as those involved in the debate about 'new' and 'old' feminism, with 'new' feminists arguing that women had specific and shared interests, while 'old' feminists tended to insist that women's interests like men's found their clearest expression in the national political parties.

In some ways, it is tempting to see the assertion that women had specific political needs and interests as more radical than the idea that, once enfranchised, women became as citizens almost indistinguishable from men. But very often, this idea of sexed citizenship went along with a tendency to see women's interests as narrower and as less important than those of men. Eleanor Rathbone, for example, argued that it was necessary to educate women for citizenship to ensure that they would take an active role in both local and national politics in order to express their own particular views on matters of local and national significance, views which she thought would be different from those of men. But this very framework enabled her to belittle women's interests. In her presidential address to NUSEC in March of 1922, she insisted that the society must not fix its mind solely 'on what are called, in the narrower sense, "women's reforms"'.

We meet together as a body of citizens no less than as a body of women, each with our separate share of responsibility for the common weal in this country, and throughout the world. Indeed, ... many of us find our minds so burdened and obsessed by the great problems that are perplexing our own and other countries, that we find it difficult to give ourselves wholeheartedly to the tasks that are more especially our own.[83]

Trade depression, unemployment, and world peace were amongst the major issues which she addressed, seeing them as more important than domestic issues. Women had a specific contribution to make even here: their 'practical minds' she argued, 'incline them to interest themselves less in lofty generalisations than in the practical application of those generalisations to existing facts'. Thus while she believed that vital national and international problems far outweighed the importance of attempting to secure better salaries and wages, or better industrial opportunities for women, she also believed that the political influence of women should be made evident in the community 'as a force that entirely refuses to be satisfied with platitudes about a better England, peace, stability, and international independency, but means to insist on having these principles translated into working maxims of statesmanship'.[84]

Lady Rhondda and Winnifred Holtby, the two leading 'old' feminists who opposed Rathbone, commented in *Time and Tide* on her 'dangerous insistence on "women's natures and women's lives"', feeling it more important to stress 'the common humanity of men and women', rather than their differences.[85] For them, as for most contributors to *Time and Tide*, citizenship was a gender-neutral term, which allowed women access to the political world formerly monopolized by men. Thus in 1921, for example, Cicely Hamilton wrote a series of articles on 'The Common-Sense Citizen', intended to offer advice and information to electors about processes of government and their own duties and responsibilities in regard to them. While seeking to explain various views about the nature of the social contract and to combine political theory with discussion of contemporary problems, at no point did she ever suggest that sexual difference was an issue or that gender had any place in thinking about citizenship.[86] In a similar way, Winnifred Holtby believed that once political and legal equality between men and women was achieved, all other questions about social welfare were ones which would affect men and women equally.[87]

And yet, as these women were very well aware, there were many questions and concerns affecting women that men and the existing male-dominated political parties constantly ignored. *Time and Tide* provided frequent discussions about the 'Women's Programme' and about the interests of the 'Woman Voter'. All women's organizations, one leading article argued in 1923, whether they were affiliated with political parties, like the Women's Liberal Federation, or non-party bodies, such as the Federation of Women's Institutes or the Women's Co-operative Guild, were preoccupied with the same issues: peace, children, homes, temperance, and equality. Lady Rhondda was very critical of the extensive press discussion of 'the woman voter' and her interests and behaviour in the lead-up to the 1924 election, arguing that much of it reflected the false assumption 'that women voters all belong to a peculiar and slightly sub-human class which must be treated specially apart, and every member of which can be trusted to exhibit the same characteristics as all others'. But she none the less accepted that 'women voters, like all newly enfranchised classes, have their special demands'—and insisted that the objectives of the Six Point Group were ones endorsed by all women's organizations.[88]

The whole issue of women's citizenship shows up some of the central dilemmas and problems faced by feminists in the 1920s. Those who concentrated their attention on the question of citizenship were certainly aware that enfranchisement raised new questions. But they tended to be concerned primarily with educating women to take a larger part in local and national government rather than to offer critiques of the inadequate ways in which parties or the whole representative process responded to women. They directed themselves towards educating women about their new duties—ultimately making women themselves in some sense the problem that needed to be remedied, rather than the institutions and structures which excluded or marginalized them. Hence one begins to detect a tutelary tone, and sometimes one of some impatience in regard to ordinary women, enter into feminists' discussions.

In the process of celebrating the final victory of women's suffrage in 1929, for example, *The Vote*, the organ of the Women's Freedom League, set out what it saw as the remaining work to be done to establish equality between men and women. It saw as one important question the issue of economic equality, which was still in its infancy. To gain acceptance of the principle of equal work for equal pay would involve almost as great a struggle as that for the suffrage. Governments, municipal authorities, banks, and every kind of business still paid men more for doing the same work as women—and woman themselves did not do anything about this.

We have to face the truth that the great mass of women voters are not really alive to the question in any greater way than they were alive to the question of the vote at the beginning of the century. They regard their low wages as something inevitable. Their idea of life is fatalistic, and we shall have to preach the gospel of equal conditions and equal pay as widely as we preached the equal vote. The attainment of the vote has removed the material obstacle to freedom, but the moral and spiritual obstacles that lie within ourselves are great. More than ever is it true that everything depends upon ourselves, upon our loyalty to the principles of justice, upon our self-surrender to our ideal of freedom, upon our courage and self-respect.[89]

The process of attempting to educate women for citizenship ultimately seemed to submerge any specific feminist ideas or demands for change under the weight of women's duty to understand how to carry out their local and national responsibilities in ways that would keep the existing social and political order functioning smoothly.

This shift, whereby discussions of citizenship lost any connection with feminist demands, can be seen in the various organizations which attempted to educate or mobilize women as citizens. In the years just before the franchise was gained, a number of Women's Citizenship Associations were set up. Eleanor Rathbone pioneered this move by establishing one such association in Liverpool in 1913 with a view to increasing the political awareness of women who had not been associated with the suffrage movement, and similar organizations were set up in a number of other cities.[90] In 1917, a National Council of Women's Citizens' Associations was set up, under the presidency of Mrs Ogilvie Gordon aiming particularly at getting more women to take an active part in local government. This was a long-standing feminist demand and the NWCA eventually took over the work of the earlier Local Government Society.

In terms of their appeal, Women's Citizens' Associations had but limited success: they worked in middle-class urban areas, but could not sustain membership in working-class ones. Their main concern remained that of encouraging women to take an active role in the local community and to add their voice particularly to questions about education, health, child welfare, and the proper use of public space in the interests of women and their families. But as it increasingly came to recognize its lack of success in recruiting younger women to the women's movement, NUSEC itself took up the question of Women's Citizens Associations by setting up Townswomen's Guilds. Although the Guilds were intended to carry out the NUSEC programme, they demonstrated the extent to which that programme was changing. The aims of NUSEC, even when its programme was amended slightly in 1927, remained twofold: the establishment of real equality between men and women and the need to ensure that women were able to carry out their duties as citizens. But when NUSEC began forming Townswomen's Guilds in 1928, this was done explicitly in connection with the second half of that programme—as a way of directing attention to the woman voter to 'enable women as citizens to make their best contribution to the common good'.[91] The Guilds, like the Women's Institutes, believed that while women had the vote, many thousands 'have never fully realized themselves as citizens, and, one might say, as fully developed human beings'.[92] They aimed to appeal to as wide a female population as possible: nothing that affects the well-being and happiness of its citizens will be beneath their notice—local features of beauty or interest, home life, and the simplification of domestic labour, the local social services, the opportunities for music and drama, and all forms of education would be dealt with and discussed.[93] But by 1929, as this programme makes clear, there was almost no suggestion that the Guilds should be political lobby groups actively engaged in seeking real equality between women and men.

Increasingly, the Townswomen's Guilds became the dominant body within NUSEC, taking over *The Woman's Leader*, which, by 1930, was called *The Townswoman*. Its contents dealt more and more extensively with questions of home-making and motherhood, with these matters taking precedence over even local community interests. Hence the woman citizen was increasingly becoming defined as a home-maker, eager to raise her standards of domestic care but not seriously involved in attempting to change the political and social framework in which she lived. Obviously this development was closely connected with the broader political and social trends of the 1930s, but it also reflects the impossibility of combining feminist aims and critiques with a desire to establish groups which could appeal to all women.

## Feminist Questions and Party Politics

While feminists battled in the course of the 1920s over strategies, tactics, and aims in regard to their own organizations, they were also involved in attempting to work with and to exert pressure on the existing political parties and to insert themselves in new ways into parliamentary and political structures. Their success in doing so remains a matter of dispute and disagreement: there was unquestionably a large spate of legislative reform on issues which had been of great concern to women, including child protection and guardianship, widows' pensions, and divorce reform. Moreover, both the tenor of political discussion and debate changed in the course of the 1920s, involving, on the one hand, reforms in elections and political behaviour generally, and on the other, an increasing concern with matters of health, welfare, and domestic life—the issues of most concern to women.[94] But for all this, the impact of women on the political parties and on the whole political framework was quite limited.

The legal and political situation of women in the 1920s, while clearly an advance on what had existed before, was in no way either clear in itself nor was it in conformity with what suffragists had sought. Thus, while propertied women over the age of 30 had been enfranchised, women certainly did not have political equality with men. Moreover, the framework in which women could exercise their vote remained unclear. The legislation promised as a recognition of the 'duty of the new government to remove all existing inequities in the law as between men and women'—the Sex Disqualification (Removal) Act of 1919 did not offer anything approaching all that feminists themselves had sought as a way of removing existing legal inequalities between men and women. The first clause of the bill contained the sweeping statement that 'a person shall not be disqualified by sex or marriage from the exercise of any public function, or from being appointed to or holding any civil or judicial office or post, or from entering or assuming or carrying on any civil profession or vocation'.[95] But in fact the bill was very restricted in scope and was permissive rather than compelling, so that on many crucial issues, particularly those pertaining to married women's work and to the terms of women's employment in the civil service, it could simply be ignored. The Act, as *Time and Tide* commented somewhat bitterly in 1922, was a short one consisting of only four clauses. Although women were led to believe that it was a great measure, what it actually did was allow them to become barristers, solicitors, and magistrates; grant power to Oxford and Cambridge Universities to admit women to degrees if they chose; and admit women to jury service, although not on the same terms as men—since women could apply to be exempted from serving on the grounds of the 'nature of the evidence to be given or of the issues to be tried'.[96]

This Act was, none the less, the first in an impressive programme of legislation dealing with some long-standing feminist demands. It was followed by the Criminal Law Amendment Act of 1922, which raised the age of consent for girls to 16; the Married Women (Maintenance) Act which allowed women some maintenance under separation orders; the Matrimonial Causes Act of 1923, which enabled wives to sue for divorce on the basis of adultery—as men had been able to do since 1857; the Guardianship of Infants Act; the Widows', Orphans' and Old Age Contributory Pensions Act of 1925; and the Equal Franchise Act of 1928. While it is hard not to see the passage of so much legislation on matters of concern to feminist and other women's groups as reflecting a new sense of the importance of women's issues, the ease with which the legislation was passed served also to demonstrate that the need for reform of many aspects of the situation of women and children had come to be recognized by almost the whole of the political spectrum. Feminists tended to be highly self-congratulatory about the legislative achievement of the 1920s. Recently, however, historians like Harold Smith have questioned not only the extent to which feminists can be seen as responsible for this legislation, but also whether in fact it brought about feminist goals.

Some of the legislation, Smith argues, was a substitute for the real changes feminists sought and was phrased in ways which impeded substantial change. Feminists at the time offered very acute comments on the legislation, recognizing both its limitations and its importance. *Time and Tide*, for example, constantly pointed to the demerits in the Widows' Pensions Bill, but still welcomed it as offering real support to many women and hence as taking a 'step towards a finer civilisation'. In a similar way, they recognized that the Guardianship of Infants Act did not meet the feminist demand for equal guardianship—although they accepted that it met the election pledge Baldwin had made.[97] The Act gave mothers equal parental rights to their children once a custodial dispute was taken to court, but left mothers in a subordinate legal position to fathers in all other respects. Most of this legislation enhanced motherhood, thus re-enforcing the view that this was women's primary role. Hence legislative change in the 1920s, while it might have benefited women in some ways, was directed towards the preservation of traditional familial ideas and traditional notions of sexual difference rather than challenging them.[98] By contrast with this apparent success in areas of sexual and family life, some of the changes most important to feminists in the area of employment were simply ignored. Thus although the Sex Disqualification (Removal) Act of 1920 made it illegal to deny employment to anyone on the ground of marital status, a marriage bar was introduced into professions like teaching in the early 1920s and, despite legal challenges, remained in force for several decades. Equal pay made no headway at all. Hence even the successful legislation served to emphasize the primacy of women's familial role and the incompatibility seen to exist in society at large between independence for women and maternity.

Feminists were well aware of how intractable the existing political parties were in relation to women and women's issues. None the less, apart from a brief and abortive attempt by the Pankhursts, there was no thought about establishing a Women's Party in England—and the frequent reporting on the problems and the lack of vitality of its American counterpart in papers like *Time and Tide* certainly did not suggest that such an approach was a viable one. On the other hand, there was considerable interest in the possibility of cross-party alliances amongst women during the 1920s, and, at least in the early years of the 1920s, valiant efforts were made to ensure women's co-operation on measures of joint interest across party lines.

The central figure in these attempts to co-ordinate women's political efforts was Nancy Astor, the first woman to be elected to the House of Commons. Her election in 1919 had been met with dismay amongst feminists who had hoped that the first woman elected would be 'one of ourselves',[99] rather than an American millionairess with no previous connection with organized feminism! None the less, in a spirit of sisterhood, her election was warmly welcomed in the *Common Cause*—and their feelings changed when it became evident that Astor saw herself as having been elected to represent women and their interests.[100] Ray Strachey was so favourably impressed—and so concerned at Astor's absolute lack of parliamentary knowledge—that she acted as her parliamentary secretary while Astor found her feet.

Astor clearly had some dormant feminist sympathies, feeling particularly strongly on questions about maternal welfare, child protection, and an equal moral standard. She was both amenable to becoming a spokeswoman for feminist interests and accessible to the various feminist organizations, being concerned mainly with the relative ineffectiveness of women's groups in making their views known. In March 1921, she called representatives of a wide range of women's organizations to a conference which agreed to establish a consultative committee of representatives of nationally organized women's groups. It included many groups with diverse goals and loyalties: not only non-party feminist ones like NUSEC, the Six Point Group, and Ray Strachey's London Society for Women's Service, but also the more conservative National Council of Women and the more specifically party political groups: the Conservative Women's Reform Association, the Fabian Women's Group and the Women's Co-operative Guild. The consultative committee continued to function until 1928. It worked both formally, through meetings at which women's groups were able to put their views directly to sympathetic MPs, and informally through social occasions, especially Lady Astor's 'At homes'. It is hard to gauge the success of the Committee, but it certainly provided an excellent political education for many women while at the same time working very closely with some of the sympathetic male MPs who promoted the legislation sought by all the various women's groups. It also served to show both the extent and the limitation of common ground amongst women: while there was extensive support for issues such as widows' pensions and equal guardianship, there was division and dissent over issues such as divorce law reform, free access to birth control, and hence also over the deal of a single moral standard. While some, like Lady Astor herself, took this to mean that older ideals of premarital chastity and monogamy should be required of both men and women, others believed rather that sexual and moral standards for all were changing and that new freedoms should be available to women as well as to men.

The idea of cross-party allegiances inevitably led to conflicts with the existing political parties while at the same time showing ever more clearly the limitations of the parties when it came to dealing with women's interests. As Martin Pugh has argued, all political parties made some kind of attempt to address both women electors and 'women's issues' in the 1920s, but their ideas centred on reforms compatible with a domestic ideal of womanhood—and their interest in addressing even these issues became less and less as the 1920s wore on and the problems of the Depression became overwhelming. Tensions were evident amongst different women's groups in all parties, essentially revolving around the question whether women should place their loyalty to party first, or their loyalty to women's groups and a women's programme. For some years, the women's programme won, and a few women, including Ethel Snowden and Edith Picton-Turbervill, refused to stand as party candidates against other women like Nancy Astor, whose feminist views they shared.[101] But this valiant attempt to find a common voice for women foundered both through lack of organizational support and because of the lack of unanimity over how best to approach 'women's issues'.

Both the Conservative and Labour Parties made extensive efforts to become mass organizations after the war, engaging in substantial membership drives which were explicitly directed towards women as well as men. The Conservative Party had long had substantial organized support from women through the Primrose League—many habitations of which quickly became Women's Unionist Associations. Throughout the 1920s, there were approximately one million women members of the organization, many of whom were closely involved in party work. Like Lady Astor, many Conservative women were able to exercise a personal influence through their wealth, social standing, and friendship with male leaders. But the prominence of women within the party did not equate with any pronounced capacity to influence its programme.[102] In 1923, Lady Rhondda herself conceded that the Conservative Party was the least satisfactory of the three when it came to dealing with the demands of women's organizations. Mr Chamberlain's insistence that the record of the party spoke for itself on matters of social reform was no comfort: if he was referring to the last parliament, its record on women's questions was completely blank![103] But while the party did in fact recognize the need to develop new policies in regard to women, and came to support widows' pensions, reform of guardianship laws, and even equal franchise, it faced opposition within its own female ranks to some feminist demands. Thus, while feminists within the party like Lady Rhondda attempted to extend its commitment to social welfare and to equality for women, other Conservative women were hostile both to social welfare measures and to feminists. They objected to attempting to expand the range of employments open to women—feeling aggrieved at the lack of women prepared to go into domestic service; they had no sympathy for raising the school-leaving age; they voted overwhelmingly against family allowances. At the same time, they sought to maintain a more traditional view whereby women acted as party auxiliaries, leaving policy and politics to men.[104] That not all women were or sought in any way to be connected with feminist issues was thus made only too clear, as was the problem of seeing feminism as inseparable from social welfare.

The Labour Party too worked hard to increase its female membership during the 1920s. It never came close to the Conservative Party in terms of numbers, but membership of women's sections in the party did grow to 300,000 by 1927. While lagging behind the Tories in numbers, Labour certainly had the edge in terms of the abilities and reputations of its leading women with Marion Phillips, as Chief Woman Officer, and Ethel Snowden, Ethel Bentham, Mary Macarthur, and Susan Lawrence on the party's National Executive Committee in 1919.[105] The importance of women in the party, and the ways in which the Labour Party took up some issues of concern to women, especially concerning better methods for food distribution and housing design, has recently been commented on. But it is none the less clear that here too there were conflicts over women's interests and particularly over feminist goals. The question of women's paid work remained a very vexed one within a labour movement committed to a family wage, family values, and trade unions. Members of the Labour Party followed the familiar pattern of socialist and labour organizations of the late nineteenth century in their hostility to feminism as something which produced division amongst working-class men and women. Marion Phillips and the prominent women in the party felt, as Mary Macarthur had done earlier, that women needed to be educated and encouraged to support the working-class movement and that the views and policies of any women's groups must accord with broader party policy. They accepted regulation of women's labour and attempted to limit the range of discussion undertaken by Labour women. But there was powerful opposition to this view from some of the feminists within the party who urged the Labour Party to endorse more strongly the cause of women and to fight for their emancipation.

This issue came to a head over the question of birth control. Dora Russell and Freda Laski led the fight to make the party endorse a policy of allowing doctors in publicly funded clinics to offer birth-control information to working-class women who needed it. They were strongly supported by the Labour Women's Conference, but opposed by Marion Phillips, who felt the issue to be one that was too divisive even to be discussed. This conflict led Russell to the realization 'that the Labour Woman Organiser existed, not so much to support the demands of the women, as to keep them in order from the point of view of the male politicians'.[106] The opposition to birth control, both from Catholics within the party and from those who felt that it was a private and not a political matter, ensured that the party did not take the question up. Therefore, in the Labour Party too, there was support for welfare measures which assisted women as wives and mothers, but little support for, and even hostility towards, questions about women's right to work, about equal pay, and about the need for women to be able to control their own bodies and their own fertility.

The lack of support for feminist aims and goals within the political parties was the subject of running commentary in *Time and Tide* throughout the 1920s. While accepting that the Conservatives had the worst record as regards women's issues, *Time and Tide* was also scathing about the Labour Party, arguing that women's interests were completely subsumed within it under trade union demands and male interests. They were particularly hostile to the insistence by the Labour Party on the need for protective legislation for women, seeing it as a means to restrict women's work. None of the parties, nor even the women's groups associated with them, in their view seriously addressed the needs of new women voters: while both the Labour and Liberal parties dealt with questions about birth control and family endowment, none of the parties dealt seriously with the question of equal pay or equal opportunities for work for women.[107]

The passing of the Equal Franchise Act marked the end of any semblance of commitment to women's issues within the national political parties. As Martin Pugh has shown, it was followed by a decline in the extent to which candidates and party programmes specifically addressed women voters or their interests.[108] In the course of the 1920s, all political parties had supported those feminist aims which addressed married women, motherhood, and family life. In the course of the

1930s, while welfare remained an issue, it was supported in ways which emphasized more and more the importance of women's maternal and domestic role. In the Labour Party, women's questions as distinct from social welfare policies were slipping off the agenda; in the Conservative Party too, there was a recognition of the need to address policies to 'the home-maker' as well as the 'breadwinner'. But nowhere was there any attempt to improve the status or the opportunities of women. The women's sections of all parties declined in numbers in the 1930s as their distinctive contribution diminished.

## From Politics to Culture: Feminist Theory in the 1920s and 1930s

Although feminist activities declined in the course of the 1930s, developments in regard to feminist theory did not: both Winnifred Holtby and Virginia Woolf produced influential feminist works in that decade. And the interwar period saw an enormous proliferation in the range of issues included in feminist debates, with analyses of the cultural, psychological, and broad institutional bases of women's oppression being explored with a degree of insight and detail previously applied largely to political and legal frameworks.

Feminist theory paralleled developments in other areas of the women's movement by becoming more and more diverse, so that a number of very different kinds of work with very different interests and concerns were all regarded as significant feminist texts. For large numbers of feminist activists in the 1920s, especially those in NUSEC, Eleanor Rathbone's *The Disinherited Family* was 'the most important feminist work since J. S. Mill's *Subjection of Women*'.[109] But Rathbone was replaced a few years later by Virginia Woolf, whose *A Room of One's Own* was regarded by *The Woman's Leader* 'as the finest and most significant feminist tract of our contemporary age'.[110] For many women, both in the United States and in England, *A Room of One's Own* belonged 'beside Mary Wollstonecraft's *Vindication of the Rights of Woman* and John Stuart Mill's grave and cogent *Subjection of Women*'.[111] In the course of the 1930s, Winnifred Holtby's *Women in a Changing Civilisation* and Woolf's *Three Guineas* were also seen as important feminist works.[112]

That Woolf was accorded this rank of pre-eminent feminist writer and theorist is a further indication of the increasing complexity of feminism during this period, for, while certainly addressing questions about education, employment, and the general impoverishment of women, she was equally concerned with questions about women's place in cultural production and literary traditions and with the ways in which masculinity and femininity were represented both institutionally and culturally. In so far as it offers any kind of programme, *A Room of One's Own* sets up a framework for women's studies rather than for anything involving immediate legislative or social reform. In a similar way, *Three Guineas* appeals to many feminists of the 1980s and 1990s precisely because of the ways in which it rewrites history and redefines politics, and hence because of its refusal to participate in those very organizations which so many feminists were seeking to penetrate.[113]

Following on from the arguments in *A Room of One's Own* concerning women's exclusion from educational and cultural institutions, from material prosperity, and from cultural and historical traditions, in *Three Guineas* Woolf elaborated her idea of women as constituting a 'society of outsiders' who can neither understand not participate in political and professional institutions in the ways that men do. While recognizing the social, political, and economic changes in regard to women which have occurred, Woolf also insists on recognition of the ways in which women remain marginalized, excluded constantly and deliberately by masculinist beliefs and institutions.[114] Where earlier feminists had complained about the ways in which legal and political structures perpetuated the oppression and subordination of women, Woolf looked rather at the ways in which professional bodies, language and dress codes, and cultural institutions celebrate and protect masculine values—thus diminishing and excluding women. But Woolf emphasized her sense of the power and the threat to women involved in masculine rituals and behaviours by suggesting the inherent connection between professional costumes and processions, such as those evident in the law, and the rituals and the uniforms integral to armies—and fascist organizations. These rituals excluded and threatened women, and could not be entered into by them. At the same time, Woolf insisted on the value of the marginal position of women, of the 'society of outsiders', because of the way it allowed them 'freedom from unreal loyalties'.

While Woolf's current status as feminist theorist is unquestioned, her relationship to feminism and the women's movement in the 1920s has been the subject of much discussion and debate, largely because, both in her texts and in the advertising of her work, she carefully disassociated her work from 'feminism'. It is, however, clear that she wrote with a detailed knowledge of the history of feminism and of the women's movement.[115] Moreover, as Naomi Black has recently argued, Woolf had extensive feminist connections. She was associated particularly with the Women's Co-operative Guild and, more particularly, with the Women's Service Library (now the Fawcett Library), which she used extensively in researching *Three Guineas*. Her friendships and personal connections with feminist activists were probably even more significant: she numbered amongst her close friends Margaret Llewellyn Davies, long-time secretary of the Women's Co-operative Guild, and was a very close friend of the Strachey family, knowing both Pippa and Ray Strachey well.[116] After *Three Guineas* was published, Woolf waited anxiously for the response of her close feminist friends to the work. When Philippa Strachey wrote to say 'I have read it with rapture—It is what we have panted for for years and years,' Woolf noted in her diary that Pippa's enthusiasm lifted,

the last load off my mind—which weighed it rather heavy, for I felt if I had written all that and it was not to her liking I should have to brace myself pretty severely in my own private esteem. But she says it is the very thing for which they have panted; & the poison is now drawn. Now I can face the music, or donkey's bray or geese's cackle by the Reviews so indifferently that (truthfully) I find myself forgetting they'll also be out this week end. Never have I faced review day so composedly.[117]

While not very active in feminist organizations in the 1920s, Woolf both read other feminists and wrote for feminist periodicals like *Time and Tide*. Her work drew significantly on the work of contemporary feminists, and most noticeably on another contributor to *Time and Tide*, Rebecca West. West wrote many articles on feminism and on sexual antagonism in the 1920s and some of her ideas seem to have been taken up and elaborated by Woolf in *A Room of One's Own*. Thus, for example, in an article attempting to explain why male teachers opposed equal pay for their female colleagues in the early 1920s, West referred to 'the desire felt by the mass of men that women in general should be subjected to every possible disadvantage'. Men, she argued,

like women in particular; . . . But all save the few who have cut down the primitive juggle in their souls want women in general to be handicapped as heavily as possible in every conceivable way. They want this not out of malignity, but out of a craving to be reassured concerning themselves and the part they are playing in a difficult universe. They fear that they are not doing well enough. . . . It would help them to have faith in themselves if they could see others doing much worse. So, hiding their purpose from themselves by a screen of argument they set about contriving that women shall furnish them with this welcome sight. They exclude women from as many occupations as possible, debase the specific work of women as wives and mothers and wherever possible arrange that women shall face life in unequipped condition that comes of having too little money.[118]

Woolf later elaborated and refined this comment to provide her own wonderful image concerning the ways women function as the reflectors through whom men see themselves as they wish to be. Women, Woolf argued, protected men from seeing themselves as they were, serving 'as looking glasses possessing the magic and delicious power of reflecting the figure of man at twice its natural size'. Without that power, Woolf argued, 'probably the earth would still be swamp and jungle'.[119] If women told the truth and reflected men as they are, 'the figure in the looking-glass shrinks; his fitness for life is diminished. How is he to go on giving judgement, civilizing natives, making laws, . . . unless he can see himself at breakfast and dinner as twice the size he really is.'[120]

Woolf's indebtedness to and fascination with Rebecca West is evident both in her diaries and in the discussion of West in *A Room of One's Own*.[121] Indeed, Woolf incorporated West directly into her discussion of the violence of masculine reaction to the term 'feminism' and to any critical comments made about them by women.[122] West, who was considerably more outspoken and aggressive than many of her contemporaries in asserting that she was 'an old fashioned anti-man feminist', was the subject of virulent masculine attack, and Woolf described ironically the way that West was referred to as a snob and a feminist by men who found her views intolerable.

While Woolf certainly extended beyond other contemporary feminist writings in her concerns with questions of culture and representation, in many ways she shared with Rathbone, Holtby, Brittain, West, and other contemporaries, approaches and assumptions which distinguish them all from earlier feminist writings. All feminists writing in the 1920s and 1930s show the impact of the enfranchisement of women in the way that economic questions had come to replace the concern of pre-war feminists with legal and political ones. Woolf's concern with the impoverishment of women's institutions and with women's lack of the kind of economic independence which allowed for creative work reflected the immediate issues of her own privileged social and intellectual milieu. Others took the question up in other ways: West and Holtby were concerned primarily with equal pay; Vera Brittain with the need for women to be able to combine marriage and family life with the pursuit of a profession or career; and Eleanor Rathbone, with the ways in which existing wage structures, which assumed that men were providers for their wives and children, increased women's dependence and neglect.

The treatment of women's economic problems by all of these writers shared another common feature which was widely characteristic of the time: all were concerned as much to explore the psychological basis and consequences of women's financial and economic dependence as with their actual material deprivation. Thus, while Rathbone detailed the housing, dietary, and health problems faced by poor women, she was even more concerned about the exhaustion, depression, and hopelessness which resulted from constant confinement, inadequate support, and limited opportunities. At their worst, these physical and mental conditions produced 'hysteria and loss of mental balance' in women, depriving them even of the capacity to carry out the most menial domestic tasks.[123] Woolf too used psychological concepts and language in many ways: in comparing the relative effects of the affluence of male college life and the poverty of female colleges on the self-esteem and the creative capacities of their inmates, and in all her fanciful discussions of aspiring but thwarted women. In the 1930s, Winnifred Holtby related women's low pay with low self-esteem and with the widespread existence of an 'inferiority complex' amongst them.

The use of psychological terms and explanations was widespread amongst feminists in the 1920s when it came to looking at men and, more especially, at male power and resistance to change. Where Mary Wollstonecraft and Mill had discussed the difficulties faced by those seeking to make a case which went against custom, habit, and prejudice, Rathbone pointed to the need 'to look beneath the surface for the hidden motive, unacknowledged and probably unconscious', which explained why it was so difficult to make people look beyond men and to demonstrate the individual needs of women and children. She was particularly concerned to explore the 'instinct of domination' and to show why men fought so hard to preserve a view of themselves as the supporters of dependent families. In a similar way, Virginia Woolf paid close attention to the reasons why men spent so much time discussing and defining women, and more particularly, why any suggestion of women's equality with them should make men so angry. She used popular psychology, suggesting both that men who failed to attract women might be particularly antagonistic towards them, and even that some of the better-known opponents of women's intellectual ambitions were homosexual.

The use of psychology was definitely a double-edged sword in feminist writing, for while it opened some new possibilities for thinking about women's oppression, it moved all too quickly to the conclusion that women were themselves responsible for their situation. For much of this period, women were frequently discussed in terms of the various psychological 'complexes' which circumscribed their potential and limited their range of possibilities. 'Woman's inferiority complex' was a particularly common theme in the 1920s and 1930s, replacing the nineteenth-century concern about the extent to which women were *really* equal to men in ability with an argument about the effects on women of centuries of discrimination, injustice, and insistence on traditional beliefs about their innate domesticity and ignorance. This complex was seen by many to derive from the fact that 'through the ages we [women] have been shaped by man's conception of what we should be', and hence that women had never had the opportunity to develop freely. But now, as several feminists argued,

the chief obstacle to winning political, social and economic equality was 'the humbleness, the timidity, the fear in the hearts and minds of women themselves, planted there by centuries of teaching that woman is the inferior sex. If we could only change our opinion of ourselves . . . our shackles would drop off instantly. But in our man-made world we still permit the highest praise of a woman to be, 'She has a masculine mind'.[124]

Thus the notion of women suffering from an inferiority complex could be used in order to argue that women were now their own worst enemies, and that they needed to change before any further progress could be made. The dangers in the use of psychology, only too evident when one looks at the comments on feminists made by many doctors and psychiatrists, are thus evident also in feminists themselves. Sometimes, the language of inferiority complexes served to undermine specific opponents: for example, Eleanor Rathbone argued that those who concerned themselves only with removing the barriers which denied women equality with men—and who opposed her 'new feminist' programme—'are suffering from a sort of "inferiority complex" bred in them by generations of sex subjection, which prevents them from thinking except in "terms of men." '[125] Her sense of the nature of sexual difference was, or so she assumed, immune to this kind of criticism.

The interest in psychology, in conditioning, and in the effects of particular beliefs, behaviours, and institutions was also brought to bear on the question of women's sexuality, for psychology, psychiatry, and sexology were all involved in the extensive discursive elaboration of the importance of recognizing women's heterosexuality—and their need for a stable and fulfilling heterosexual relationship if they were to be balanced and mature. This discussion carried implicitly, and often explicitly, the argument that unmarried women—of whom there were always substantial numbers in the women's movement—were at best frustrated and unfulfilled, and at worst deviant and unnatural. As we have seen, even some feminists in their advocacy of birth control made derogatory comments about unmarried women. But as Alison Oram has recently shown, while marriage was not under attack in the interwar period as it was in the late nineteenth century, none the less many feminists, including feminist doctors and psychiatrists, mounted a defence of spinsters and of celibacy in terms of the very disciplines in which they had been attacked.[126] In some cases, these women openly acknowledged that many women would find more emotional and even sexual satisfaction in relationships with other women, insisting that such relationships 'cannot be considered perverted if their actions are motivated by love'.[127] Both Maude Royden and Winnifred Holtby also entered into this defence, with Royden insisting on the beneficial ways in which love and sexual desire could be sublimated and transformed into religious, social, and philanthropic work, while Holtby, following rather more in the tradition of Frances Cobbe, insisted that single women could have busy, active, and fulfilled lives.[128]

In all of these discussions, the question of the sexual differences between women and men was obviously central. The extent and the meaning of sexual difference was always, necessarily, a central preoccupation of feminism. The emphasis on heterosexuality evident in so much medical and scientific literature brought with it a sense of the contrasts and differences between men and women—contrasts which were evident in sexual behaviour, in childbirth, and in familial and child-care responsibilities.

The question of sexual difference was strongly debated amongst feminists. Some, like Eleanor Rathbone, accepted without question that biological differences and different familial roles led to different interests, needs, and outlooks for men and women. This indeed was the basis of her 'new' feminism. Those who opposed her, the most articulate of the 'old' feminists, strongly disagreed. Winnifred Holtby echoed earlier figures like Emily Davies in her insistence that, while sex differentiation was important, its influence was overestimated. 'It belongs to the irrational, physical, and emotional part of a man's nature, where it holds almost undivided sway', but has little impact on intellectual, social, or political behaviour.[129] When it came to political beliefs, as to interests and inclinations, Holtby insisted that men and women were fundamentally similar. It was for this reason that she was an 'old' feminist, seeking to restrict 'to as small a field as possible the isolated action of women, in order that elsewhere both sexes may work together for the good of the community'.[130]

There was a strategic question involved here, with some feminists arguing that difference 'has been so stressed in the past and been made such a weapon of destruction against women that it is safer to refuse to recognise it even where it indubitably seems to exist'.[131] But others felt that much of the difference evident between the sexes was socially constructed and temporary. Thus I. B. O'Malley, while arguing that 'we feminists are trying to get the world so arranged that the view of life "characteristic of, peculiar or proper to women" shall have as free expression as that "characteristic of, peculiar or proper to men"', felt unhappy with her own definition, because 'I am not convinced that in the ultimate scheme of things there are points of view "characteristic of, peculiar or proper" to each sex respectively'.[132] But it was also an issue in much discussion about women's writing and creative capacity. Winnifred Holtby had to argue out this issue constantly—not just in battles in the women's movement, but also in her major literary and intellectual work, her study of Virginia Woolf. For Woolf shared something of Eleanor Rathbone's belief that women had a different perspective from men, extending it into her discussions of literary styles and traditions and arguing that women learnt fundamentally from each other and could do little with the male sentence. Woolf's sense of the importance for women of earlier women writers and of the current need for a new and different style to describe new female experiences—such as that of the kinds of work-based friendships now open to women, or the new psychology of sex—all raised questions about the extent to which sexual difference resulted in intellectual and imaginative differences that undermined Holtby's sense of a universal human mind. Woolf's own position, both in her emphasis on women's differences in style and outlook and in her advocacy of an androgynous creative mind, has been the subject of extensive discussion and debate. But for Holtby, her position was unacceptable because it served, as earlier conventions had done, to emphasize the sway of sexual difference at the expense of recognizing common humanity.[133]

## Feminism and Internationalism

The concern with international and imperial questions which was becoming so important for English feminists in the later nineteenth century continued and expanded in the interwar period. As we have seen, the First World War, like the Boer War earlier, had suggested to many the direct connection which existed between feminist concerns and peace. Militarism, as many feminists argued, required the subordination of women—hence women's emancipation depended on the discrediting of militarism.[134] Thus for both Labour women and for middle-class women, one of the main concerns was to ensure peace. But even those feminists not committed to pacifism turned increasingly to internationalism, stressing the importance of international arbitration of national disputes on the one hand, and the need for international bodies committed to women's emancipation on the other.

Millicent Garrett Fawcett, who ranked second to none as a patriot and a supporter of England in the Boer and First World Wars, urged both of these points. In 1919, when it became clear that women's rights had been omitted entirely from the first draft of the League of Nations Covenant, Fawcett led a deputation, organized under the auspices of the international Woman Suffrage Alliance and the international Council of Women, to wait on President Wilson in Paris to urge that women's interests should not be overlooked in the treaties that were being drawn up. The League of Nations covenant itself declared that all positions in the League would be open equally to men and women—a declaration, which, as *Time and Tide* constantly pointed out, was honoured only in the breach.[135]

Their stress on internationalism, as Carol Miller has recently argued, pointed clearly to the sense of their own vulnerability evident amongst many feminists and to the difficulties they faced in gaining reforms at home. For many of them, as for their American counterparts, there seemed little likelihood of gaining equal rights within their own national frontiers, and their support for the League of Nations and for some of the conventions of the ILO, far from diverting their attention from feminist concerns at home, seemed the only way to affect them.[136] This was most particularly the case in regard to the question of the nationality of married women, as British women sought international treaties to override the legislation which deprived a British woman who married a foreigner of her British nationality.

Here too, it seemed to be international action that was the key. Thus the setting up by the League of Nations of a Special Body of Experts on child prostitution and the white slave traffic was greatly welcomed, and the various reports of this body were constantly featured in *Time and Tide* and in *The Woman's Leader*, both journals making clear their sense of relief when there was evidence that licensed brothels were being closed down or made illegal as a result of the League's investigations.[137] The extent of the apparent traffic in women and young girls was regarded as horrifying—and feminists pointed constantly to the fact that this traffic was not the result of sinister organizations, but rather because 'all over the world there are thousands of otherwise decent and kindly men who are willing to pay 5s., 10s., or 20s. for casual sexual gratification'.[138] That prostitution and the traffic in women were rife in the countries in which the status of women was lowest provided powerful evidence for feminists like Vera Brittain to insist on recognition of the connection between unequal pay and economic opportunities for women and their degradation. But ultimately the international scene closely paralleled the national one, with the widespread concern about women's welfare and the considerable feminist activity of the 1920s declining markedly in 1929. Just as ideas about the need for progressive reform in regard to women gave way to an emphasis on domesticity and femininity in England, so too by 1929 Vera Brittain accepted that feminism had made very little progress at the League headquarters in Geneva and that concern about women was almost negligible. Representation of women on the various League committees had fallen steadily from a high point in 1920, while discrimination against women in terms of pay, conditions, and promotion was evident throughout the League—and even more marked at the International Labour Organization, 'which has tended from the first to treat women as a class apart, and to maintain the tradition that regards them as a "controlled annex to industry"'.[139]

In the course of the 1930s, for those feminists whose primary focus was an international one, questions about women's well-being gave way completely to concern with armaments control, the rise of Nazism, and then the growing concern about imminent war. The feminist papers themselves reflect this: *Time and Tide*, while continuing and even extending its coverage of international events, published almost nothing which dealt with feminist issues or women's welfare after 1929. The foremost issue on which there was complete agreement 'among thinking women', argued *The Woman's Leader* in that year, was 'the usual demand for the peaceful settlement of disputes by means of international arbitration'.[140]

Interest in peace and arbitration and in the League of Nations necessarily focused the attention of interwar feminists on European developments. Interest in American developments continued, but declined relative to interest in specific European countries, especially Germany, France, and Spain. This growing interest in Europe did not, however, mean that feminism ceased to have an imperial dimension.

At the same time, this sense of vulnerability did not seriously undermine the imperialist consciousness of interwar feminists, many of whom continued their sense of having a special burden in the plight of Indian women. Eleanor Rathbone, as Antoinette Burton and Barbara Ramusack have shown, was a particularly important figure here. Indian women were the particular imperial burden of white women. In the course of the discussions about Indian self-government in the 1920s, Rathbone insisted that,

it must be the task of British women whatever their views as to India's future, to recognize that what *has* been and what *is still* in itself constitutes an imperial responsibility, to watch over the interests of their far-off, unseen, unheard Indian sisters. Their claim is not merely the claim of all women on all women, not merely that of those who have not yet achieved on those who have achieved full citizenship. It is something much closer and more poignant than that, the claim of those who have a right to say to us 'What have you been doing, . . . during the hundred and fifty years of British rule, while Great Britain was as yet the unchallenged dominant power, that you find us still so weak, so helpless, so illiterate, so ravaged with disease, so frequently the victims of premature and cruel death? What are you doing now to safeguard our future?'[141]

The importance of the British imperial context for the development of middle-class feminism, which Antoinette Burton has stressed in regard to the late nineteenth and early twentieth centuries, needs to be underlined also in regard to the interwar period.[142] Then, as earlier, concern about Indian women focused particularly on the savagery of Indian customs and on the need for English women to assist Indian women to attain the status and rights shared by their English sisters.

The tenor of English feminist concern, and its fundamentally imperialist assumptions, is made clearly evident in the work which set it off, Katherine Mayo's widely read *Mother India*, published in 1927. The central concern for Mayo was the institution of child marriage, which she saw as both indicating the low status of Indian women and as bringing the physical and mental destruction of vast numbers of young Indian girls. While the issue of child marriage was one of great concern to many Indian educationalists and nationalists at the time, Mayo ignored this. Her illustrations of child marriage and its consequences drew rather on traditional English feminist preoccupations, by insisting on the connection between the sexual exploitation of child brides and venereal disease. Mayo gave graphic illustrations of young Indian girls married to older men who were known to be suffering from venereal diseases, and who thus inflicted on their wives not only painful illness and sometimes death, but also the tragedy of stillborn children. Mayo's text constantly contrasts the sympathetic British doctors and philanthropists with the uncaring Indian parents of the girls and with the whole Indian community which accepts this institution.[143]

Mayo's book had its most profound impact on Eleanor Rathbone, who became intensely involved with Indian questions after reading it in 1927.[144] Both her educational and political interests and her philanthropic background came into play on this issue. Rathbone first sought to determine the accuracy of Mayo's data, organizing a small conference to discuss the book and then setting up a survey on women in India. Rathbone's efforts evoked a mixed response from Indian women and organizations, some of whom shared her concerns but were very critical of the fact that she was seeking to carry out a survey without Indian associates. Once elected to Parliament in 1929, Rathbone was able to extend her efforts in this direction, working on two fronts at once.[145] She lobbied to raise the minimum age for women at marriage, seeking primarily to ensure that British and Indian officials implemented existing legislation regulating the age of marriage more vigorously. But as the whole question of India's government was under discussion, with the push for self-government being made more and more strongly by Indian nationalists, Rathbone also worked to ensure greater involvement of Indian women in the constitutional process. Rathbone and her supporters sought particularly to have Indian women appointed as delegates to numerous conferences and commissions that were formulating constitutional reforms for India from 1927–35. She also pressed for the extension of the franchise to Indian women and sought mechanisms to ensure that women would be members of reformed central and provincial legislatures. Despite her efforts, Rathbone was not well received either by colonial officials or by Indian women when she visited India in 1932.

Like her nineteenth-century predecessors, including Mary Carpenter, Rathbone was regarded by colonial officials as a busybody and a do-gooder who lacked any understanding of the constraints under which they worked. In a similar way, Indian women, like Indian men, resented her attempts to tell them what they needed—evident particularly in her assumption that colonial government was a civilizing force which would assist in raising the status of Indian women. Rathbone, Barbara Ramusack has argued, assumed a 'mother-knows-best' tone when she lectured Indian women on lessons to be learned from the British suffrage movement, a tone not well received by her audience.[146]

But while India remained a predominant concern, the imperial interests of British feminists expanded during this period. In the 1930s, NUSEC expanded its programme to include as a sixth point its aim 'to assist women throughout the British Empire to achieve rights of equal citizenship and equality of status and opportunity with men'.[147] This heralded a slight shift in focus as the concern about the 'problems' of Indian women was extended to include concern about organized prostitution in Hong Kong and Malaya. Interwar feminists had been greatly concerned about the plight of prostitutes in England and had also fought to end systematic prostitution in the Empire, particularly targeting the system of *mui tsai* in Hong Kong.[148]

Overall, the international interests and concerns of interwar feminism serve to re-enforce the general pattern of feminist developments. In some ways, these concerns show strong continuity with earlier periods of feminist thought and activity. This is so particularly in regard to India, which remained the privileged centre of imperial concern—and hence showed how important imperialist assumptions were in determining the targets and setting the agendas for the ways English women took up the question of sexual exploitation in the empire. But there were also new issues, as feminists took to international politics and political organizations, seeing the League of Nations as much more significant than any international feminist body. But here, one can see also the ways in which involvement in international politics—which was originally seen as connected with feminism, as it was something that was only possible because women were enfranchised—became less and less focused on women's issues as other international questions assumed greater prominence.

# six
# THE POSTWAR WORLD

The postwar period is a particularly difficult one to deal with when writing a history of modern feminism. Just as the drama of the militant suffrage campaign made the quieter activities of interwar feminists almost invisible, so too the sudden and dramatic rise of the Women's Liberation movement in the early 1970s has made it very hard to see or understand the feminist activity or debates about women of the preceding decades. The Women's Liberation movement itself has made this task more difficult: in its concern to safeguard and record its own history it has collected and published a number of accounts which have served to re-enforce a strong sense that the 'second wave' of feminism created itself from conflicts experienced by women within left-wing political and youth movements of the 1960s, and that it was almost *sui generis* in relation to feminist organizations and activities.[1] Seeking to emphasize the novelty and the politically and sexually radical character of the Women's Liberation movement, its spokeswomen have emphasized the discontinuities between it and prior feminist agitation, barely deigning to recognize the campaigns for legal reform, for equal pay, and for an end to discrimination in the workforce which had continued for decades.[2]

The first move in a revisionist history might then be to establish whether or not it was actually the case that feminism, either as a form of political and social thought, in terms of specific campaigns, or as a social movement, was more or less moribund during this period, and some work in this direction has already been done. Olive Banks has recently stressed the need to recognize that the final years of the war and those that followed brought some quite significant feminist developments. It was during these years that some of the issues which had been of most concern to feminists in the 1920s and 1930s were satisfactorily resolved.[3] The marriage bar, which had been so bitterly fought against by feminist groups in the interwar period, began to disappear; it was suspended for teachers during the war and abolished by an amendment to the Education Act of 1944. The civil service followed suit, abolishing the marriage bar in 1946. The campaign to have women police recognized as a permanent part of the police force was successfully completed in 1945 and the 1948 British Nationality Act allowed British women to retain their nationality on marriage. Women were also now admitted to the Diplomatic and Foreign Service. Much had thus been done. Some issues from the agenda of the 1920s were still outstanding, most notably equal pay, which was regarded by the Six Point Group and others as 'beyond all doubt the major issue facing us today'.[4] But the first measure of equal pay was introduced in the early 1950s. Ironically here, as with the vote, success was sometimes the worst enemy of organized feminism, as the achievement of each goal brought to an end the campaign which had been organized around it, leaving nothing in its place. Thus in 1945, the Women's Police Committee was disbanded, while government support for a measure of equal pay in 1956 saw the end of the Equal Pay Campaign Committee.[5]

Moving beyond the question of specific campaigns and into the area of feminist theory, there has also been some re-evaluation of the period. Many of the new feminists of the 1970s combined a sense of their own radical departure from the past with a strong interest in women's history and a belief that if women were ever to gain a voice in political debate, they needed a clearer sense of their own past. This brought some re-evaluation of the immediate past: in 1979, the Birmingham Feminist History Group began the rehabilitation of the feminist activities of the 1959s by stressing the need to place the feminism of any period within the dominant construction of 'femininity' in which it developed. The Women's Liberation Movement of the 1970s, they explained, saw feminism as transforming femininity in a fundamental way. By contrast, 'the feminism of the fifties seemed to be more concerned with the integration and foregrounding of femininity in a masculine world'. Their aims required a modification rather than a complete reappraisal of prevailing notions of femininity, and hence their feminism 'was bound by femininity in such a manner that we as feminists today do not easily recognize its activities'.[6] Shortly afterwards, Dale Spender interviewed a number of feminists who were active during this period, including Dora Russell and Hazel Hunkins-Hallinan, to demonstrate the continuity of feminist actions and concerns throughout the twentieth century.[7]

This argument, that feminism was not completely dead in the postwar years, is becoming more or less accepted, although the period still remains a troubling one. Thus, for example, in his recent history of *Women and the Women's Movement in Britain*, Martin Pugh repeats the familiar idea that the period 1945–59 saw 'The Nadir of British feminism . . .', but adds a significant question mark to the term. Pugh's own unease is demonstrated by his somewhat equivocal conclusion that the idea that feminism was a spent force during that period, while 'not without empirical foundation, is a considerable exaggeration'.[8]

While Banks deals with the long-standing feminist concerns and Pugh charts the continuing existence of a few organizations and campaigns throughout this period, neither historian examines what seems to be a key interpretive question here: namely, the relationship between the feminist discussions and debates of the 1950s and 1960s and those of the Women's Liberation Movement in the 1970s. Nor is this question really answered by the Birmingham Feminist History Group. Their extremely sympathetic reading of the feminist activity of the 1950s testifies to a more conciliatory move within contemporary feminism towards the immediate past and a desire to encompass past generations of women within a comprehensive feminist framework. But what still remains at issue is the complex task of attempting to establish the precise connection between the feminism of the 1950s, with its acceptance of the postwar emphasis on marriage, motherhood, and the pursuit of family life, and the emergence of a form of feminism in the late 1960s and early 1970s which rejected and challenged all these things.

The continued use of the term 'feminism' during the interwar period is itself an issue here. In some earlier periods there is a sense that the lack of a common language, or of a readily grasped term like 'feminism', to describe women's ideas and activities serves to inhibit any sense of continuity, in the postwar period it is the persistent use of the term which creates the problem. Although often greeted with scorn and opprobrium, the term 'feminist' was used openly by a number of groups and individual women to refer to their beliefs, their writing, and their activities. But while frequently used, the term was often defined in ways which emphasized moderation and acceptance of prevailing social and sexual norms. Thus many feminist activists went to great lengths to stress that their position was that of 'reasonable modern feminism', which accepted sexual diversity and sought to establish what women's social contribution was rather than emphasizing equality or the similarity of the sexes.[9] The question that faces a historian attempting to understand this period then becomes one that centres on the value to be attributed to continuity as compared with change. In emphasizing that feminist activity never ceased at any point in the twentieth century, might one not be constructing a rather spurious sense of continuity and ignoring the more significant discontinuities and changes between the 1950s and the 1970s? Even though the term 'feminism' never lost adherents, is it not still more important to recognize that the aims, objectives, strategy, rhetoric, and style of the feminism of Women's Liberation in the 1970s bore almost no relationship to that feminist activity which continued during and after the war through organizations like the Six Point Group or the Open Door Council? The key point, one might argue, is that feminism ceased to be defined in terms of women's political and legal 'emancipation' and became concerned with their personal 'liberation', and that this was a point of very significant change.

Feminism within the postwar period needs of course also to be seen in relation to the still complex and contradictory interpretations which histories of this period offer in relation to the situation of women. The once widely propounded view that the war brought women new opportunities, not only in regard to paid employment, but also in terms of personal independence, sexual freedom, and a whole range of new experiences, has come to be almost completely discarded, as more and more historians stress the emphasis on femininity, domesticity, and maternity which came with the advent of peace. Once the war was over, sociologists, psychoanalysts and welfare workers joined forces with the popular press to stress the imperative of domesticity, family life, and an acceptance of their 'natural' femininity for women, not only for their own happiness, but also for the well-being of children and society at large.

At the same time, however, the pattern of women's lives underwent certain marked changes, with higher rates of marriage, a decreasing birth rate, and with an increase in the numbers of married women in paid employment. Standards of health and of living increased markedly for many women, with the expansion of the welfare state and the introduction of the National Health Service. None the less, as Jane Lewis has recently argued, it is hard to ascertain the precise meanings and the impact of these changes on the lives of women, or to establish whether changing work, marital, and fertility patterns reflect a greater power for women to make choices that follow their own wishes and desires.[10]

Any analysis of post-war feminism needs also to come to terms with the changes evident between the 1950s and 1960s. Writing of the history of feminism and of the political discussion of women's issues in the United States, Cynthia Harrison argues that one has to see a break

occurring in 1960. There was a decade and a half of 'post-war consoli-
dation' after 1945 in which the longing for social stability and for a return to the pre-war world with its 'traditional family arrangements'
meant that there was an inhospitable environment for policy initiatives
on women's issues. By 1960, however, there was a marked change, as
concern about Russian domination brought some rethinking of the
values placed on traditional values, including family ones. Even without strong external pressures from women or women's organizations,
new policy initiatives intended to expand civil rights and reduce discrimination brought the start of a new climate for women.[11] And similar developments were evident in England as the immediate concerns
of the postwar period gave way to new social and cultural concerns by
the late 1950s and the 1960s.

The preoccupation with family life and with women's work in the
late 1940s and 1950s continued, but by the late 1950s and increasingly
throughout the 1960s, concern about family life was giving way to an
immensely widespread discussion of the 'woman question'. The col-
umns and correspondence sections of *New Society*, the *New Statesman*,
the *Listener*, and even *The Economist*, together with the 'Woman's
Page' of the *Guardian*, and a whole host of academic and popular journals were filled with letters and articles discussing the 'problem' of
women's work: of why married women sought or needed it; of how
their families fared when they undertook it; of why they did certain
kinds of work; and of calls for a 'womanpower policy'. Clearly the question of women's paid work was a major source of concern. But alongside it, there was also considerable discussion of the current status of
women and the meaning and nature of women's emancipation, particularly whether emancipation had brought women equality, whether
or not the vote had been worth the struggle, and whether or not women
had made adequate use of the powers and privileges that suffrage gave
them.

British discussion and debate during this period was of course
closely informed by and connected to developments in other countries. Indeed, it cannot be understood without recognizing the significance of Simone de Beauvoir's *The Second Sex*, which was translated
into English in 1954, or of Betty Friedan's widely read *The Feminine
Mystique*, published in 1963. Both of these texts made it clear that there
were systemic problems facing women that could not be solved simply
by individual women 'taking a grip on their lives' and reaching out for
existing opportunities. This continued discussion of the 'problem' of
women's work, along with the debates and discussions about marriage

and family life, and about women's discontents and demand for change, did not provide any coherent feminist analysis. But it did make clear the sense of crisis and of need for dramatic change in the situation of women, which provided the immediate backdrop for the women's liberation movement—and merged imperceptibly with it.

## The Impact of War

The question of women's participation in the Second World War defines the necessary starting-point for any consideration of the immediate postwar period. And indeed, the general question of the impact of war on women's lives, participation, and overall status and situation has been and continues to be subject to extensive debate. For the Second World War, even more than the First, was so drastic in its impact on the daily lives of masses of civilians as to make it seem likely, even inevitable, that it would be accompanied and followed by extensive social change. The optimistic if somewhat simplistic idea propounded in the 1970s, that the Second World War, like its predecessor, played a significant role in the emancipation of women has had to be revised.[12] Although some would argue that the war unsettled marital and sexual mores, while bringing a range of new work and social experience to those women who entered the paid workforce and the auxiliary services, more careful study of women during the war has shown both the limitations in opportunity available to them and the extent to which wartime experience was seen as temporary and exceptional.[13] While women certainly worked in some non-traditional areas during the war, especially in engineering industries and munitions, their training, pay, and status were all emphatically designed to ensure that the prevailing sexual division of labour was not upset. Women received less training and less payment during their apprenticeship than men and were shunted back into lower-paid female occupations even before the war ended. The Second World War, like the First conflict, therefore brought quite large numbers of women a range of new experiences, including a higher income than they had earned previously, a range of new social experiences, and some new knowledge. Yet while many individuals may well have found the experience rewarding and enriching, it did not provide a basis for altering the gender order or for transforming social, sexual, and familial expectations once the war was over.[14] On the contrary, as Denise Riley has argued, war work, far from revolutionizing women's employment, 'was characterized as an exceptional and valiant effort from which women would thankfully sink away in peacetime'.[15] And the war was followed by a powerful evocation of a traditional family, which ascribed to women a more domesticated role than they had ever actually undertaken.[16]

Those who have examined closely the ways in which women were recruited for industrial work or for the auxiliary services, point to the fact that the very terms on which women worked or were engaged served to re-enforce traditional ideas about women's basic responsibilities and duties. The 'manpower' shortages in England in 1941 forced the government to introduce compulsory registration of all women aged between 19 and 40 so that they could be allocated by Labour Exchanges to essential war work. But 'household duties' were sufficient to prevent a woman being sent away from her own home to work—even if the household contained no children, but consisted only of a woman and one other adult.[17] Thus the primacy of women's domestic duties was never challenged, but was even enhanced during the war as part-time work was introduced to enable women more efficiently to combine work with housekeeping. Moreover, the emphasis placed on women's sex in the workplace and in the auxiliary services—an emphasis evident as much in almost systematic sexual harassment as in the restrictions on their labour and promotion—served also to underline the significance of sexual difference and to confine and limit women's opportunities.[18]

Britain was unique in its introduction of registration and a form of conscription of women for labour and national service during the war.[19] Even Germany, although desperately short of labour, refrained from conscripting women, relying rather on propaganda as a means to entice more women into the industrial workforce.[20] The unemployment amongst women in the early stages of the war was largely over by the end of 1942, and by 1943, some 46 per cent of women aged between 18 and 40 were engaged in some form of national service. Over 80 per cent of single or childless women were so employed, but there were also very considerable numbers of women with young children employed.[21]

In some ways, women workers were better provided for during the Second World War than they had been in the First. There was, for example, considerably more provision of child-care facilities for working women: by 1944 some 1,500 nurseries had been set up, offering something in excess of 70,000 places. This contrasted dramatically with the 105 nurseries set up in the First World War, which had offered only about 4,000 places. Recent studies, however, suggest that there was still only provision for about 25 per cent of the children needing care, and that women were still mainly forced to make expensive and often unsuitable private arrangements. Moreover, child-care provisions were but one of many social programmes which aimed to assist women in carrying out their domestic tasks, without ever questioning the sexual division of labour or the sexual hierarchy which designated those tasks as female ones. Besides, in regard to child care as in regard to work, the wartime situation was 'for the duration only', and the end of the war brought a closure of nurseries and a renewed stress on the importance of close and continuous contact between children and their mothers.[22]

Nevertheless, the Second World War provides a marked contrast to the First in terms of its obvious and immediate impact on feminist organizations and on feminist developments and debates. The First World War brought to a sudden and immediate halt the most energetic and widely publicized period of political agitation for women's rights ever known. By contrast, the Second World War came after almost a decade of relative feminist quiescence, and has seemed to many to have provided a stimulus to new activity and agitation. Differences amongst the various feminist organizations were submerged as long-standing feminist groups worked closely with women Members of Parliament both to publicize women's grievances and to seek a number of specific reforms.[23]

The outbreak of war highlighted a range of long-standing grievances, particularly in terms of discrimination against women in employment and in pay. It also brought new grievances and new forms of discrimination in training, in insurance, and in disability payments. Two central questions were of great concern to feminists of all shades of opinion: how to ensure that women were allowed to contribute adequately to the war effort; and how to ensure that they were adequately remunerated and acknowledged once they had done so.[24] Throughout the war most of the existing feminist organizations, including the Six Point Group, the Open Door Council, the Women's Freedom League, and the Fabian Women's Group worked towards both of these aims in a concerted and collaborative way.[25]

This unity of action amongst feminists was greatly facilitated, indeed it was probably made possible, largely because they worked alongside the women MPs. For the first time since the early 1920s, the war brought concerted action from women MPs working across party lines. The establishment of a coalition government in 1940 made it much easier than it had been for women to collaborate in this way, and early in 1940, a Woman Power Committee was established which included the Conservatives Lady Astor, Irene Ward, Mavis Tate, and Thelma Cazalet-Keir, the Labour women Edith Summerskill, Agnes Hardie, and Jennie Adamson, the Liberal Megan Lloyd-George, and the Independent Eleanor Rathbone. Along with a number of representatives from the Trade Union Congress and from a number of women's groups, this committee worked to expand the range of opportunities open to women and then, a few years later, in a concerted campaign for equal pay.[26]

Ironically, while feminist groups and women Members of Parliament worked easily together, their first big project served only to show how hard it was to campaign simply on behalf of 'women', assuming that their sex alone determined their interests and needs. In the early stages of the war, some feminist groups and most women MPs were appalled by the widespread unemployment amongst women that existed alongside labour shortages in essential industries. It was this that provided the stimulus for the establishment of the Woman Power Committee. They held meetings to discuss the best way to address this issue and to attack the government and end its reluctance to make use of women's labour. Working alongside the British Federation of Professional and Business Women, women backbenchers organized deputations to ministers and finally forced the government to accept the need for a debate on 'womanpower' and to set up a Woman Power Committee as an advisory body to the minister for labour. Soon, however, it was clear that there was a serious conflict between the views and ideas of different groups of women. The Woman Power Committee and its close ally, the British Federation of Business and Professional Women, were largely composed of upper-middle and upper-class women to whom it seemed only too obvious that educated women needed to be placed in positions of authority, not only in government services, but also in all large workplaces and factories. But, as the Labour MP Ellen Wilkinson pointed out, this was completely unacceptable to working-class women and to the Labour movement.[27] To have educated women as forewomen in factories and workshops as advocated by the British Federation of Business and Professional Women would immediately eliminate the only possible promotional avenue for women workers. Hence she and a number of other Labour women opposed any suggestion that the Woman Power Committee should have a say in factory and industrial organizations. Eventually, although one woman MP was given advisory status on the Labour Supply Board, the status of the Woman Power Committee was seriously undermined.

But the issue of difference, in terms both of class differences and of the differing needs of married as compared with single women, was a difficult and divisive issue even within the Woman Power Committee itself. While advocating a better and more extensive employment policy in regard to women, and demanding that women be allowed and even required to contribute to the war effort, its members shared the ambivalence of many feminist groups over the question of exactly what sort of service was appropriate for different groups of women. Thus, even while demanding a better utilization of women's skills and labour, many members of the Woman Power Committee opposed the idea of compulsory registration or conscription of women for national service, believing that married women's familial and domestic duties ought to preclude them from such measures, and being prepared to support registration only once assured that there were adequate measures to safeguard women's traditional duties.[28]

Although the women Members of Parliament remained a little undecided over exactly how women should prioritize their responsibilities in wartime, they played a notable role in their attempts to ensure that during the war women were protected and remunerated equally with men. The concern which the various women's groups had expressed at the outbreak of war about the ways in which women's general social and economic inequality would be compounded in wartime was early shown to have been well-founded. Just as the Government accepted that women should be paid less than men, so too it assumed that women required less compensation than men for war injuries, setting the rate of payment for women at two-thirds that of men. Women MPs led a successful parliamentary battle to defeat the government when the compensation issue was voted on, and succeeded in having women who suffered war injuries paid equal compensation with men.[29]

The long-standing feminist groups, including the WFL and the Six Point Group, worked alongside the Woman Power Committee on the general question of women's employment, on the question of accident compensation, and in the campaign to ensure that the family allowances paid to soldiers went to women and not to men. This concerted action appeared in some ways to be markedly successful and it provided the framework for the campaign for equal pay which began in the final years of the war. The demand for equal pay, especially for teachers, professional women, and civil servants, had been a powerful rallying cry for feminist groups, especially the Six Point Group, the Open Door Council, and the London Society for Women's Service in the 1920s.[30]

The campaign had continued in a small way through the 1930s, but it sprang to life with greatly renewed vigour during the war. When the issue of women's registration had been raised, the Woman Power Committee had sought equal pay for women as one of the main safeguards. But in fact, equal pay was not offered to women in any sphere. There was the Extended Employment of Women Agreement of 1940, which specified that after a probationary period women employed in men's jobs would receive the same wages. But this applied to only a very small minority of women, even in the engineering trades.[31] For the most part, even in industry, women were confined to tasks designated as female and the government refused to interfere to regulate or raise their wages.[32]

An Equal Pay Campaign Committee was set up with some one hundred affiliated women's organizations in 1943. Headed by two MPs, Edith Summerskill and Mavis Tate, and the long-serving feminist activist and organizer, Pippa Strachey, it included a wide spectrum of feminist opinion and immediately began a lobbying campaign.[33] It serves very well to illustrate both the methods and the problems faced by feminist campaigns that were centred on Parliament. Early on, it was clear that when the women MPs were actually forced to choose between party loyalties and feminist sympathies, party came first. When an amendment on equal pay for women teachers seemed likely to be passed as part of the 1944 Education Bill, Ernest Bevin as Minister for Labour and Churchill as Prime Minister ran a concerted campaign to prevent it, with Churchill insisting that support for the bill in its unamended form amounted to a vote of no confidence in his government. Faced with this blackmail, Thelma Cazalet-Keir, who had been a moving force within the EPCC, deserted it and voted for the Government.[34] A Royal Commission into Equal Pay was set up in that year, but its terms of reference were not such as to allow for a conclusive report. It was not asked for recommendations, but only to 'examine the existing relationship between the remuneration of men and women in the public services, in industry, and in other fields of employment', to consider the social, economic, and financial implications of the claim for 'equal pay for equal work', and to report. In the view of the Six Point Group, the commission's report served to 'confuse a perfectly clear issue in a fog of words', since it seemed to argue that no catastrophic consequences would follow from the introduction of equal pay for women in teaching, in government services, and in the professions—but that equal pay in private industry and commerce would be 'impractical, uneconomic for employers, disastrous for women in particular and dangerous to the country in general'.[35] Ultimately, it offered as a firm recommendation that equal pay should apply only in those very few occupations where men and women did exactly the same work.[36]

Although the EPCC did not meet while the Royal Commission was sitting, it re-emerged at the end of the war, continuing its persistent and careful lobbying campaign until 1956. The committee worked carefully, in close co-operation with feminist organizations, but proceeded cautiously and doggedly, eschewing radical or confrontationist steps, such as any form of strike, and relying on deputations, lobbying MPs, and writing letters to newspapers. In these years, public sentiment and shifts in local and national government policy brought the first slow measures of equal pay, particularly for middle-class and professional women. The London County Council introduced equal pay for men and women teachers in 1952, and finally equal pay was introduced gradually for the civil service by the Conservative Government in 1954. After this, the EPCC dissolved itself, taking comfort in small measures and perhaps aware that it lacked the financial or popular support needed to extend the equal pay campaign to cover commerce and industry.[37]

But while the war did see the acceptance of some measures advocated by feminists and some concerted action by women's groups both within and outside Parliament, it did not really bring any wider recognition of the need to consider women's views or to include women in the chief national decision-making bodies or processes. The government's capacity to ignore women's voices and concerns was shown at its most obvious when, in 1942, it appointed an all-male committee to investigate the alleged sexual immorality amongst women within the auxiliary services! Women MPs protested so vehemently that the constitution of the committee was changed to include three women alongside the five men. But its original composition is symptomatic of government attitudes and approaches.[38] The prevailing view of women, as dependents rather than as independent workers, was made very clear in the Beveridge Report of 1943, which became the basis for the introduction of the postwar welfare state. The Women's Freedom League led a campaign against the report, arguing that women should pay the same contributory insurance as men and be able to recover the same sickness, unemployment, or old age benefits—but to no avail.[39] While women's voices were raised loudly on issues of women's pay, welfare, and conditions during the war, the idea that women might be consulted or included on other questions was not accepted. Thus, although there had been some discussion of the need to include women

.n planning the peace, there were no women involved in the peace conference, nor were there any women in the British delegation to the United Nations Assembly. Indeed, to all intents and purposes, it appeared that women's political agitation for a better deal during the war was, like their expanded range of employments, recognized as being only for the duration of the war.

## Feminist Organizations and the Feminist Agenda

Despite the resurgence of activity on behalf of women during the war, most organized feminist groups greeted the postwar period with anxiety and with a strong sense of their own inadequacy for the tasks at hand. The Six Point Group report for 1945–6, for example, began in this lugubrious and even defeatist manner:

The year under review has been a difficult and busy one. The work accomplished has been appallingly inadequate in comparison with the opportunities and the demands of the socio-political situation; it has however been considerable when the difficulties under which it has been carried out are taken into account.[40]

The difficulties it faced were immense: lack of funds to allow for paid staff, no office space, and declining membership. It would not have been able to carry on at all 'had it not been for a legacy unexpectedly received under the will of a member long since dead'.[41] Like all feminist groups at the time, the Six Point Group worried particularly about its ageing membership and inability to recruit younger women. But looking back at its records and papers, what seems equally noticeable is its lack of any clear or cogent feminist agenda, or indeed of any sense of the need to rethink and reformulate feminist demands in a new period. Where the 1920s saw a concerted attempt to explore what the vote meant and how feminists might address questions about women's citizenship, the late 1940s saw no new questions, but rather a concern to find sufficient energy to deal with what were regarded as the remaining items on an agenda set decades before. Equal pay, equality in terms of national insurance, and better access for women to employment, seemed to be the main issues for feminists to address and none of these went along with any new analysis of the meaning of women's oppression or indeed of feminism.

The years immediately after the war none the less saw a flurry of activity. Dora Russell certainly recalled it as a busy and active period in which groups and societies that had little scope for activity during the war gained new energy through Labour's accession to power in 1945. For her, the government's preparedness to set up Royal Commissions on marital property and divorce as well as on equal pay signalled the start of a new era. Russell herself was closely involved with both the Six Point Group and with the Married Women's Association, which was concerned primarily to ensure that women who devoted themselves to the welfare of the family received an equal share of family income, a recognized entitlement to the family home, and equal guardianship rights with men.[42]

While Russell attempted to stress the activity and vitality of the Six Point Group and the Married Women's Association in the late 1940s and 1950s—as indeed of other groups including the WFL, the International Women's Day Committee, the Status of Women Committee and the Women's Peace Movement—her account lacks conviction. Her main concern is to chart her own growing preoccupation with the peace movement, and her shift away from those feminist organizations which decided to concentrate on national and domestic rather than on international questions. As a result, she does not address what all their own reports show as the central problem for many of those groups: their inability to recruit or gain adherents among younger women. The reports of the Six Point Group refer repeatedly to their declining membership, their lack of funds, and hence of any capacity to have paid organizers and their increasing lack of energy. At various stages, the Six Point Group thought of merging with the Married Women's Association or the Women for Westminster Group, which had as its main aim increasing the number of women MPs. But the commitment of the small numbers of active women to their own specific aims, and the fact that no group was really able to offer financial or administrative support to another, meant that none of the proposed mergers was really helpful or practicable.[43]

Postwar feminist organizations had difficulty not only in recruiting members and raising money, but also in establishing agendas and finding goals and objectives for which to fight. The lethargy that pervades these organizations was as much intellectual as political and financial, as feminism offered them nothing new. The lack of a new programme had much to do with the caution and timidity of those who still connected themselves with feminist organizations. Even those individuals and organizations who labelled themselves 'feminist' had profound unease about the term and went to great pains to define it in ways that accorded with prevailing familial and maternal ideas. This unease with the term 'feminism' was not unprecedented. As we have seen, some feminist groups in the 1920s attempted to reformulate feminism in ways which were distinctive and 'new' and which stressed a recognition of 'difference' in order to distinguish themselves from what they saw as the excessive concern with equality in late nineteenth- and early twentieth-century feminism. But while interwar feminists like Eleanor Rathbone sought to articulate a feminism suited to a new age, postwar feminists seemed mainly concerned to show how moderate their feminism was. Judith Hubback, for example, while labelling herself a feminist, explained at length that hers was a 'reasonable modern feminism' which accepted contemporary ideas about sexual difference and maternity. 'Reasonable' feminism was not 'crudely egalitarian', Hubback insisted. It took sexual difference into account, not with the aim of overemphasizing it, but with the sole purpose of seeing what contribution each sex can make to the common good.[44]

Hubback's study of educated married women illustrates the tenor of the feminism of the mid-1950s quite well. Its focus is entirely on middle-class women and it was carried out with a double purpose: to see if society was using all available talent as fruitfully as possible and 'to help individual women to work out their own adjustments to certain problems by clarifying the issues involved and by describing different ways of tackling these problems'.[45] The idea that 'feminism' involved opposition to prevailing ideas about sexuality and sexual difference or to the existing sexual hierarchy, or that feminists might have a particular concern about the situation and sufferings of women, seemed to have little place in her, or indeed in much other, 'feminist' thinking. That feminism should have as its primary concern the well-being of society as a whole, even if that well-being involves strain and sacrifice for women—rather than the needs and problems of women—unquestionably serves to distinguish the feminist writings of the 1950s and early 1960s from that of preceding decades. It was precisely the refusal to subordinate the interests of women to any notional social good—arrived at somehow without taking women into account—which was the distinguishing mark for feminists prior to this time. In the 1950s and 1960s, however, those who labelled themselves 'feminist' so strongly endorsed prevailing ideas about the primacy of children's needs and of social stability as to accept that these things had priority over the needs of women. Hence they sought, as Hubback did, not so much to change structures or to remove widespread economic and social injustices as to assist individual women to come to terms with their own dilemmas.

Hubback, like Dora Russell, saw the finest statement of postwar feminism as that embodied in the report of the Six Point Group Conference of 1952. But within the broader context of the history of feminism, the report of this conference makes for unusual reading. The conference was held in the light of a growing sense of social tension and crisis and amidst continual demands that women become more involved and use their own specific abilities and approaches to resolve social issues. The conference itself sought to address the following questions: 'Is there a feminine point of view? if so what are its characteristics and their relevance to contemporary problems? What defects in society and in women themselves are preventing it from being more effective? What can be done to increase its influence?'[46] The discussion and the report scrutinized literature, history, and contemporary sociology to establish what was generally accepted as the distinctive nature of women and their outlook and approach. There was no suggestion at any point in the discussion that 'feminism' might be distinct from and critical of what was accepted as 'the feminine'. Attention focused rather on the sense of inferiority and the lack of self-confidence amongst women and on the ways in which their lack of opportunities prevented the adequate development of their powers or of their capacity to express their distinctive feminine viewpoint. Thus the conference ended up by suggesting ways whereby women's sense of inferiority might be addressed, in order to enhance their contribution to social life.[47]

That the approach taken in this conference was at odds with earlier feminist activity was accepted from the start, as conference participants recognized that previously 'those dissatisfied with women's position in society have emphasized the need for "equality", meaning by this women's right to do, experience and express the same kind of things as men.' By contrast, we 'have focused our attention on the ways in which women seem to differ from men'. The conference spent much time debating the difference between the sexes, referring to literature, history, and contemporary social research for their material. But throughout, it is striking that there was no sense that feminism might come into conflict with prevailing ideas about what constituted 'femininity' or that women themselves might actually have some interest in or concern about how this definitional question was approached. This widespread acceptance of prevailing ideals on femininity amongst those who labelled themselves 'feminist', their unquestioned assumption of the primacy of family life for women, and their reliance on individual causes and individual solutions which accepted that the well-being of the family and of society took precedence over the needs of women themselves, make it almost impossible to differentiate 'feminist' from non-feminist concerns about the status of women during this period, and make it necessary to see the few books and articles written by those who labelled themselves as 'feminist' as significant not in themselves, but rather as part of the increasingly widely debated woman question of the period.

While feminist organizations bewailed the lack of interest or concern in their activities amongst the young, they devoted a great deal of energy and attention to providing an ongoing recognition of the earlier and the continued contributions of elderly and ageing women. From the late nineteenth century onwards, feminist groups had self-consciously and explicitly engaged in the public veneration of women activists of a previous generation, often quite clearly seeking to provide women with the public tribute and recognition available to men who had public lives or careers, but denied to women. And ironically, while feminist groups or societies like the Six Point Group bemoaned their ageing membership, it does seem to be the case that their principal *raison d'être* was that of honouring ageing suffragists. From the start, the Six Point Group had instituted a system of honouring men and women who had made a significant contribution to the cause of women by making them vice-presidents. During and after the war, as their active membership and energy declined, their lists of vice-presidents increased. In 1940, for example, the Six Point Group had twenty-one vice-presidents, including Dame Ethel Smythe, Lady Astor, Margaret Wintringham, Vera Brittain, and Viscountess Rhondda. At that point, their national president was the militant, Emmeline Pethick-Lawrence. When Lady Pethick-Lawrence resigned from that position in 1952, the Six Point Group created the office *President of Honour*, explaining to their members that it 'is the highest title we could think of to bestow on Lady Pethick-Lawrence, who has been one of our ablest supporters during most of the life of the organisation'. On her death in 1955, she was replaced by Viscountess Rhondda, the original founder of the Group and the first owner of the journal *Time and Tide*.

The honouring of long-standing activists was not confined to women; it was extended also to the men who had made significant contributions to the cause. Thus in the year that Lady Pethick-Lawrence was honoured, the Six Point Group added to their list of vice-presidents Mr H. N. Brailsford, 'known to everyone but especially endeared to us as one who stood with Lord Pethick-Lawrence in the early days of the militant suffrage campaign, one of the few pro-militant men to espouse the cause'. They were pleased that they had also been able to 'add Mrs Billington-Greig to our list—one of the most devoted and ablest among the early feminists'.[48]

But this emphasis on honouring older feminists made recruiting the young even more difficult. Thus in the 1970s, when three younger women were found who were willing to be members of the Six Point Group executive, they were unknown to most of the group and there was much negotiating to find existing members who were prepared to propose and second their nominations.[49] Ultimately, it was this inability to recruit that finally brought their demise, as one after another, feminist groups ceased to exist when their last active members became too old to carry on the work. The Women's Freedom League came to an end in 1961, followed shortly after by Women for Westminster, the Suffragette Fellowship, and finally the Six Point Group in 1980.

The issue of age and of generational conflict was a central one in the postwar period, but it is one that needs to be seen from a range of different perspectives. It is clear that the advent of the Women's Liberation movement confirmed and exacerbated the problem felt by older societies concerning their inability to attract new or younger members. The late 1960s and early 1970s saw the emergence of new feminist groups, and of feminist conferences, marches, and demonstrations, but little of it served to revitalize older societies or indeed to arouse their enthusiasm and support. What was most evident was the complete disjunction and contrast between the aims, goals, and methods of the older feminists and those of the new Women's Liberation movement. While the older societies continued to concern themselves with questions about equal pay and legal status for men and women, about discrimination in regard to criminal law, and with the question of getting more women into Parliament, the new generation of women's liberationists were concerned much more with abortion rights and sexual freedom, on the one hand, and with the need for sweeping social and economic transformation on the other. Far from accepting any idea that they were connected with the surviving activists of earlier decades, the new generation did everything they could to differentiate themselves from the careful and modest existing societies. The older women, in turn, were often appalled by the young, and while many of them adopted the title 'Ms', they felt very little enthusiasm for the new developments. Mary Stott, editor of the *Guardian*'s woman's page, addressed the AGM of the Six Point Group in 1972, stressing the need for greater tolerance and co-operation between old and new societies, but to no avail. Throughout the 1970s—a period of furious debate and discussion at Women's Liberation meetings and conferences—members of the Six Point Group could not find enough issues of concern to engage the attention of their members or to make their newsletters worth reading. It limped on, with more and more frequent comments in its reports of meetings about its lack of a programme or of any sense of the issues which it should pursue. Finally its president, Hazel Hunkins-Hallinan, was forced to recognize that her own ill health made it impossible for her to run the organization, and the Six Point Group therefore went 'into abeyance for an indefinite period to allow the rejuvenation of the group'. Of course this did not happen, and Hunkins-Hallinan's death brought the Six Point Group to an end.[50]

## The Woman Question in the 1950s and 1960s

In the period after the war, and more particularly in the late 1950s and 1960s, there was much attention paid to the woman question, on radio, in fiction, and in social, psychological, and sociological research. Indeed, by 1964, conservative weeklies like *The Spectator* were expressing fear at the signs 'that we may be in for an orgy of "The Condition of Women" discussions'.[51] The woman question was not confined to England. 'The feminine sex', argued the international expert on population and family policy, Alva Myrdal, 'is a social problem. Whether a woman is young or old, whether she is married or not, whether a wife works or not, she is likely to be a problem. This problem is largely economic in origin as marriage and family are as yet poorly adjusted to the new social order.'[52]

While the woman question had existed for nearly two centuries in various forms, it had a particular cast and focus in the postwar period, the 'problem' of women and especially married women when seeking paid employment came to the fore.[53] There was particular concern about this question because of the small but marked increase in paid employment amongst married women during the late 1940s and the 1950s. But its tone was set by the fact that this trend to increased employment came at a time when there was a widespread sense of the need to restore 'traditional' or 'normal' family life after the disruptions of a long war.[54]

The massive wartime disruption of family life heightened already existing fears about the future of the family. The falling birth rate had been a cause for concern in Britain, as elsewhere in Europe, for at least half a century. It suggested both national decline and a flight from parenthood by those who ought to recognize the importance of having children. Ironically, although the birth rate in fact began to rise after the war, the debate about women and family life took place against a backdrop of concern about population which was the subject of a Royal Commission set up in 1945. The commission saw its task as that of recommending ways to encourage parenthood, but to do so by reconciling 'modern' marriage, in which contraception was used to space births, with the ideal of a three- or four-child family. By the time the commission reported in 1949, the postwar 'baby-boom' had reduced the worst fears of a decline in the birth rate. But it none the less provided a focal point for widespread concern within the government, the welfare community, and the medical profession about the need to 'rebuild' the family and to overcome the stresses on it which had accompanied war, evacuation, and long-term separations of parents from each other and sometimes from their children.[55]

The evils of 'feminism' were clearly addressed in the Commission report, where it was presented not as a movement to assist women, but as a considerable and significant social threat. In the eyes of the commissioners, feminist concerns with women's paid employment and their challenge to masculine and paternal authority had been both a prime cause of fertility decline and a threat to the traditional family.[56] The commission's report thus harmonized well with the increasing concern amongst psychologists, social workers, and doctors to reaffirm the importance of the family and to stress the centrality of women's familial role for the stability of the family and for the proper care of children.

While concern to stress the importance of women's maternal role was not new in the 1940s, its precise focus in those decades changed. Early nineteenth-century concerns with the importance of mothers in terms of the moral and religious well-being of their children were replaced at the end of the century by eugenic concerns about the physical well-being of children and the health and efficiency of the race.[57] In the postwar period, this concern in turn was replaced by one which centred on the mental and emotional health of children, reflecting the growing dominance of the new discipline of child psychology.

The war provided an immense amount of data and a huge experimental field for those interested in child psychology. The massive and long-term disruption to the lives of many children, along with new forms of testing and assessment, gave psychologists great scope to explore many forms of disturbance and to establish a range of measures by which they felt they could define a 'normal' child. The difficulties faced by children who had been separated from parents and placed in institutions led to an immense concern with the mental and emotional health of children and the need to ensure that children had the appropriate nurturance to develop into 'normal' effective adolescents and adults. The concerns of specialists and professionals with the restoration of family life harmonized with those in the wider society, so that the ideas of 'experts' were widely disseminated through the press and on radio. The importance of constant nurturing care by a mother if a child was to develop and mature into an adequate and emotionally mature adult, contained in John Bowlby's *Child Care and the Growth of Love* (1953) and D. W. Winnicot's *The Child and the Family* (1957), thus became very widely known. Influential figures, including psychologists, psychiatrists, and pediatricians speaking with the authority of the medical profession, or magistrates speaking with the authority of the law, all joined forces to emphasize the importance for children of a stable family life and of constant maternal care. The closeness of the wartime experience and the social problems which seemed to re-emerge once peace was restored, added a sense of urgency to the discussion of children and of child development. Retardation, delinquency, neuroses, incapacity to form proper relationships, were all constantly cited as the immediate and necessary consequences of maternal deprivation in children.

The apparent increase in street crime after the war and the preoccupation with juvenile offenders meant that discussions of family life and child-rearing practices occurred within a framework which constantly suggested that inadequate maternal care produced delinquency. As a consequence, discussions of the need for women to devote themselves entirely to their children always carried the suggestion that there would be dire and terrible consequences, both for the children and for society at large, should women fail to do so. And while the influential research by Bowlby on maternal deprivation centred on children who had been institutionalized and deprived of any contact with their mothers or families for periods of some years, the term 'maternal deprivation' came to be used to describe children who were not constantly with their mothers. One researcher even went so far as to argue that maladjusted behaviour in a large group of children was a consequence of the length of time it took them to walk or travel home from school—

a period in which their mothers were inaccessible! Similarly, Hannah Gavron's working-class captive wives assumed that they could never leave their children—not even occasionally for a couple of hours. Hence they saw themselves as unable to have any independent life or time away.

Inevitably, this preoccupation with children and the requirements of appropriate child care extended over into redefinitions of femininity, so that experts in many fields argued that complete devotion to children was necessary not just for the well-being of children, but for that of women themselves. Mature adulthood and satisfaction for women required immersion in family life. 'Natural Motherhood', as Jane Lewis has recently argued, also meant full-time motherhood, and the many specialists and popular authors who addressed these questions emphasized the need for women to give all of their time to family life and to eschew outside concerns which would serve to divert their attention from the things that really mattered.[58] This theme was reiterated not only in psychological literature, but also in medical journals, daily newspapers, and in films and popular magazines. Discussions of current events, such as the increasing numbers of women engaging in paid work, thus occurred within a framework which stressed the problematic nature of this development.[59] The concomitant of this view—the idea that 'the working wife is a bad wife'—was one of the most frequently repeated messages in fiction in women's magazines in the 1950s.[60]

Widespread and frequently repeated though they were, these ideas did not go entirely unchallenged. Professional women in several fields analysed and criticized the influential work of John Bowlby in particular, questioning the widespread and popular acceptance of his research on maternal deprivation and its relevance to stable family life.[61] Bowlby's insistence on constant maternal care to ensure healthy mental and emotional development received no support from the anthropological record, Margaret Mead argued, and she herself tended to see the new emphasis on maternity as a psychological way of tying women to the home that was made necessary because of the freedom open to women with the advent of baby carriages and bottle-feeding.[62] Barbara Wootton poured scorn on the vagueness of the definitions and of the precise measures either of 'maternal deprivation' or of its threatened outcomes evident in the research of Bowlby and of other researchers who supported his views, including Cyril Burt. Surveys of the juvenile delinquents, 'social incompetents', or institutionalized adolescents turned out to be inconclusive and often to rest on data which had not been collected systematically. Bowlby himself recognized this, Wootton argued, claiming that the lack of thoroughness in individual work on maternal deprivation 'is largely made good by the concordance of the whole'. But Wootton rather queried whether all the research on the subject done in the 1940s and 1950s ultimately served to do more than suggest 'that children (like their elders) need to be dependably loved, and that without such dependable love, they are likely to become frightened, unhappy or mentally retarded?' It was, she said, 'a melancholy conclusion that it had been thought necessary to employ so much costly research, with so pretentious a scientific facade, in order to demonstrate these homely truths'.[63]

Moreover, the emphasis on domesticity contained internal stresses and contradictions. Alan Sinfield has pointed to the rhetorical strains and awkwardness in the work of Bowlby and Winnicot, who have to tell mothers what they naturally 'know' about themselves and their children.[64] But this very stress on the importance of family life and of women's pivotal role within it contained other problems as well. There was almost no discussion in the postwar psychological or scientific literature of the role or importance of fathers, for example. Their absence seemed to be assumed and hence not to be discussed as a problem either for women or for children. When they were addressed, they were given a largely economic role within the family. Thus, while some psychiatrists and psychologists criticized 'feminism' for challenging the authority of fathers within families, they themselves seemed unable to restore it in any meaningful or functional way.[65] Furthermore, the question of how women could best contribute to their families' well-being was amenable to a range of different answers at this time: an alternative to constant care and attention being provided by the possibility of paid work, which would materially improve the well-being of their families.

While both the burgeoning professions of psychology and psychiatry and the popular press demanded the complete absorption of women in family life, women did not immediately comply with this *en masse*. Alongside the demand for a return to family life, there was a constant and increasing demand for married women in the paid workforce because of the labour shortages which accompanied the postwar boom. Although there had been much fear amongst women's groups that the end of the Second World War would parallel the First, in fact there was not an immediate or total withdrawal of women from paid labour, but rather a slow trend towards an increasing participation rate of married women in the workforce. Some women sought paid work because of the companionship it offered, but many also undertook it because they saw their financial contribution as essential for their families. Women were thus subjected to contradictory pressures and demands at this time: they were supposed to devote themselves to families in ways which were both filled with self-sacrifice and yet provided them with complete fulfilment; required to attend to marriages in which the role of their husbands was never stated; expected to engage in paid work when necessary, but always to subordinate this to family.

All of these new trends and developments led to immense debate on many questions: why women worked; whether or not they should do so; how their work related to family care and responsibilities. Throughout the postwar period, there was a series of investigations into women's paid work, accompanied by extensive discussion of why women should choose to work and of the consequences of this choice. Although the patterns of increase in paid work amongst married women was not confined to the middle class, there was probably more discussion of middle-class working women than there was of any other group. In part this reflected the fact that many middle-class women were themselves interested in this phenomenon and belonged to groups and organizations which could sponsor or initiate research. Thus, for example, Alva Myrdal and Viola Klein's book, *Women's Two Roles: Home and Work*, which is often seen as a central text of the period, originated in the suggestion made to Myrdal by the International Federation of University Women that she make an international survey of the social reforms necessary if women were to be able to reconcile family and professional life.[66] Members of the federation were concerned primarily with the contradictory situation in which educated middle-class women found themselves. Having been educated along lines similar to men, they found once married, that their early assumptions about sexual equality and about their own status were incorrect, and that every ability or skill or habit which their education had provided had to give way in the interests of family life.

Myrdal and Klein's text is an interesting and significant one, the first, Jane Lewis argues, 'to suggest, albeit with extreme caution, that there was a case for women "having it all", sequentially, becoming first workers, then wives and mothers, and finally re-entering the labour market again'.[67] But it is also a text which shares the predominant tone in which the 'woman question' was discussed in this period. While recognizing that there was a social problem concerning the situation of women, the book made clear right from the beginning that ultimately women

**245**

themselves *were* the problem. For one thing, they failed to recognize their true circumstances and opportunities. Women, Myrdal and Klein argued, saw themselves as guided by apparently conflicting aims in that they sought like men to develop their personalities to the full—while at the same time wanting a home and a family. These desires had not been in conflict when home and workplace were the same, but industrialization set them up in opposition. The technological and social developments of the current and previous decade, however, meant that the conflict was now over. No longer, Myrdal and Klein insisted, need women forgo the pleasures of one sphere in order to enjoy the satisfactions of the other. 'The best of both worlds has come within their grasp, if only they reach out for it.'[68]

While Klein was only too aware of the ways in which femininity and the 'feminine character' was socially constructed—sometimes by significant male intellectuals—and then imposed on women through social and educational policy, medical practice, and psychological beliefs, when she wrote as the subordinate working with the forthright Myrdal, none of this came to the fore. Myrdal and Klein refused to countenance the notion that women were oppressed or shackled by male dominance.[69] Where Eleanor Rathbone, herself a powerful advocate of the family, none the less wrote critically about the 'Turk complex' in men, Alva Myrdal refused to accept that women's emancipation had anything to do with a revolt of the weaker sex against 'the shackles imposed on it throughout the centuries by the strong, free male—effective though the emotional appeal of this image may be'![70] Instead, they argued rather more along the lines of nineteenth-century Social Darwinists that 'women lagged one step behind in the process of social evolution' and thus that it took them longer than it did men to gain economic and political rights or a full education. Myrdal and Klein did not deny the existence of prejudice amongst men as husbands and employers or some of the structural problems which women faced. They recognized, for example, that the idea that it is possible to combine home, family, and a career was one held only by middle-class women, as 'men have, for a variety of reasons, found it difficult to adjust themselves to the idea of a wife who so radically differs from their mothers'.[71] But they neither suggested any ways to deal with male prejudice, nor did they recognize it as a significant factor in preventing women working. Their emphasis was rather on the need for women to come to terms with the issues and problems that faced them. Far from suggesting that the whole question of domestic labour required analysis, Myrdal and Klein took for granted the centrality, both for women and for society, of women's child-bearing role, seeing maternity as the main reason for their retardation in terms of gaining independence and political power. Similarly, they accepted without question the need for close maternal care of children during infancy, arguing that it was the small size of families and the limited duration of active child care which made it imperative that women also have outside work.[72]

While Myrdal and Klein held a somewhat different position from that of psychologists like Bowlby and Winnicot, they adopted a strikingly similar tone, and one which made very clear that inadequate understanding and incorrect choices made by women could have severe and deleterious social and psychological consequences. Where Bowlby and his followers argued that it was imperative that women devote themselves entirely to family life, Myrdal and Klein insisted that women should not do this. 'Modern mothers who make no plans outside the family for their future will not only play havoc with their own lives,' they argued, 'but will make nervous wrecks of their over-protected children and their husbands'.[73] It was antisocial and irresponsible for women to live without paid work, for our 'modern economy cannot afford, nor can our democratic ideology tolerate the existence of a large section of the population living by the efforts of others'.[74] But women must bear the consequences of the dual demands on their time. They must recognize that their employment and their earning capacity were necessarily limited by the fact that they took time off to bear children, and that for substantial periods their energy was largely absorbed in domestic life. They could not demand equal pay if they also complained of the housewife's load.[75]

Myrdal and Klein were certainly unusual in their insistence on the importance of women working and combining family life with a career. However, they adopted what became a familiar tone in their assumption that women themselves were the problem, because they were now emancipated and hence could choose their own path. This was so, not only because of a half-century of legal change, but also because of the changes that had come with war. After the war, and especially after the mobilization of women in Britain, they declared 'sex discrimination in matters of employment almost disappeared'. They held this position, even while recognizing that after the war, many women returned home, and that those who remained tended to be confined to a relatively small group of occupations, so that 'the effect of emancipation has been . . . to replace amateurs by professionals in the "feminine" occupations', insisting still that the movement bringing married women into the workforce amounted to a silent revolution.[76] Within their reading of the situation, the opposition of husbands or employers to women working or having careers or opportunities equal to those of men, while recognized, was rendered unimportant as compared with the need for women to sort out their own dilemmas.

Myrdal and Klein's work, and the many reviews it elicited, inaugurated a new phase in the discussion of women. While there was unquestionably a great deal of discussion of 'the feminine paradox' in the immediate postwar period, both the extent and the nature of this discussion changed towards the end of the 1950s.[77] Where the earlier discussion had focused on the demands of maternity and of family life, the late 1950s and the early 1960s also brought discussion of the need for social change and reform. The history of feminism and of the women's movement played a large part in this discussion. The appearance of Roger Fulford's *Votes for Women* a year after *Women's Two Roles* both reflected and extended the increasing interest in the woman question. Fulford's concentration on the militant campaign of the WSPU led to considerable discussion of militancy, accompanied inevitably by a certain amount of humorous scoffing at what was deemed to be its excesses.[78] At the same time, it brought a basic reconsideration of the suffrage campaign, in which those who disagreed with Fulford's reading stressed their sense of the need to show the contrast between militants and constitutionalists. Mary Stocks used this publication as an occasion to emphasize her sense of the continuity which existed between the constitutionalist NUWSS and the Women's Institutes and Townswomen's Guilds which continued to function.[79] The renewal of the discussion on the suffrage allowed for a large-scale disavowal of militancy, with a number of writers asserting that it was not militancy that had gained the suffrage for women and that, dramatic as she had been, Emmeline Pankhurst 'does not rank among the illustrious leaders of successful rebellion'.[80] But this very discussion served to focus attention on the history of feminist agitation and to link debate about the contemporary situation and dilemmas faced by women with the feminist analyses and struggles of the past.

Much discussion about women and their situation in the 1950s and 1960s was based on a central paradox. On the one hand, there was the constant insistence on the need for women to devote themselves to family and home and to subordinate any wishes for independence or a career or a public life to the requirements of a family—and all of this was somehow seen as fulfilling their own needs and requirements as it followed from their own feminine nature. At the same time, women were seen as being completely emancipated—and hence as having open to them all the educational and career opportunities and the scope for public action available to men. This, in turn, led some to argue that the lack of representation of women in the higher reaches of the professions, the civil service, and the government was a result of women not properly 'pulling their weight', and to ask whether women were 'justifying their claim to the privileges they are now accorded'.[81]

This focus on the narrow range of positions and occupations actually open to women, and the constant reiteration of the small numbers of women to be found in senior positions in any sphere of government, business, or society inevitably led into a broader discussion of what the vote had achieved. Postwar women who felt some sympathy with feminism had enormous difficulties in dealing with this question. Margaret Cole addressed it directly in 1962, pointing to the fact that suffragists and suffragettes had followed earlier nineteenth-century political reformers in assuming that the suffrage was a complete panacea to women's ills. Both militants and constitutionalists, she insisted, had 'claimed that the enfranchisement of women would not merely remove the stigma of equating them with infants, felons and idiots . . . but would also raise up women to positions of high authority in Parliament and the professions, would lift the status of the downtrodden, and generally humanise and improve all round the condition of society'.[82] Cole pointed implicitly to the erroneousness of this assumption as she showed how little headway women had made in terms of their direct presence in Parliament, in the universities, and in higher education.

Cole clearly felt some ambivalence on this question and had great difficulty in presenting a coherent and clear argument—difficulties which were exacerbated by her desire to emphasize the importance of recognizing the 'natural' differences between men and women. Cole also adopted the dominant tone of the mainstream press in her suggestion that women did not quite take advantage of the opportunities offered to them—while at the same time showing quite clearly the obstacles which they faced in terms of the continuing hostility to women's claims within the political parties, the civil service, and the professions. She refrained from stating any conclusion about the figures she provided for women's participation rates, preferring to emphasize the changes in public opinion which suggested that 'in ordinary life there is hardly any obstacle to a woman doing what she likes, provided she wants to do it, and can'. None the less, her whole article served to demonstrate the fact that formal emancipation had not brought women anything like actual equality economically, politically, socially, or educationally.

Cole's article thus encompasses in embryo the framework for the critical step that was taken in the woman question in the late 1950s and 1960s: its recognition of the need to rethink and reformulate the whole project of women's emancipation. This step was not one taken quickly or easily. On the contrary, it was rather an undercurrent both to the predominant arguments and to the dominant tone in which discussions about women were conducted. But, as a number of women recognized, it was a necessary and logical conclusion to most of the debate of this decade. The sense of the need to rethink the project of women's emancipation was felt by many women themselves in reaction against the dominant tone of discussion about women, evident particularly in the press. Barbara Wootton, for example, wrote at length in her autobiography of the impact on her of a lead article in *The Times* in 1960, which argued that women did not adequately pull their weight. The very language being used, Wootton pointed out, revealed the widespread assumption that the rights which men took for granted suddenly became privileges that had constantly to be earned by women. The suggestion that women themselves were responsible for their lack of status and for their poor showing in the upper echelons of business and government provoked not only her ire, but also served as the stimulus to a general discussion of the reasons why formal emancipation had not brought women all that had been expected. She pointed to the social conventions and attitudes within the field of higher education, for example, where 'promising younger men' were always being sought for appointments while no one was ever asked to name 'promising younger women'. Wootton too showed considerable ambivalence on this matter, insisting on the need to recognize that 'when all is said, men are men and women are women'. For reasons all too easily understood, she argued, earlier feminists regarded feminism and femininity as mutually exclusive—an error no longer being made! But she also emphasized in the way that Cole had done, and that Lena Jaeger and many other women MPs were also to do,[83] the need to recognize the exhaustion of 'emancipated' women who 'often weep from the sheer strain of having always to cope with two jobs at once'.[84]

Just as one can see a notable increase in the volume of work on the woman question and a shift in focus in 1957 and 1958, so too there seems to be a further shift in the mid-1960s and late 1960s. This shift in part was reflected in broad and general discussions about women and their situation in the press and can be charted in terms of the new issues which came to the fore and which were the focus of debate for the following decades: in place of the constantly repeated question as to why married women worked came a new emphasis on the need for and the meaning of equal pay and on the reasons why women seemed to have such limited job opportunities. In place of the stress on maternity as necessary for women came a new concern with abortion and with a woman's right to determine her own reproductive pattern. Alongside the stress on the importance of maternity for society and for women's own health and well-being came an increasing concern about the inequities of property arrangements in marriage, the problems of widows seeking to retain leases, and the many problems faced by married women. These matters had long been of concern to the small feminist groups, but they now became matters of wider debate in the press and on the radio. Dora Russell had commented on how, in the early 1950s, the idea of there being a woman's point of view was one that had still to be generally accepted; by the mid-1960s, there was more and more evidence that it was. Thus, for example, the BBC ran a series of programmes in 1964 entitled 'The Second Sex', in which prominent women novelists and writers including Margaret Drabble, Edna O'Brien, Elizabeth Jane Howard, and Brigid Brophy gave their views on men as lovers, husbands, and children.[85]

The need for special facilities for women in the form of women's pages, women's magazines, or special radio programmes was also widely discussed. The main quality papers, and especially *The Times* and the *Guardian*, dealt increasingly with the problems women faced at home, in the work place, and in regard to child care. The question of women's loneliness and isolation was particularly an issue, resulting in the establishment of a Housewife's Register in the *Guardian*. The 'Woman's Hour' on the BBC was talked of 'not just as an entertainment—for many woman a lifeline' because of its discussions of sex and of many of the problems faced by women in daily life.

Although of course the emphasis on women's domestic role remained, alongside many discussions arguing that women lacked the drive or capacity to succeed in careers and professions, there does seem to be a marked shift in the tone of some of the discussion and of the assessment of the needs and demands of women: in place of the earlier assumption that women had been emancipated and now had individually to find ways to adjust their family needs to their own desires for independence came a much stronger sense that women were still oppressed and that, if emancipation had been achieved, then it in itself was inadequate. This shift in tone is made particularly clear if one looks, for example, at the move from Alva Myrdal and Viola Klein's *Women's Two Roles*, published in 1957, to Hannah Gavron's hauntingly titled *Captive Wives*, published a decade later in 1966.[86] Where Myrdal and Klein assumed that women had been emancipated, Gavron made clear her sense that earlier feminism had concentrated so much on winning the vote that no one had cared that not all was resolved when it was finally gained.[87] Her primary concern was with the remaining areas of women's oppression. While *Women's Two Roles* emphasized the social responsibility of women to be economically active and to undertake paid work once their children were old enough, *Captive Wives* concentrated rather on the intolerable fate of married working-class women, imprisoned in their homes and lacking occupation, companionship, and support. Clearly one needs to recognize here the importance of Betty Friedan and her analysis of the unhappiness and sense of malaise amongst middle-class women, although Gavron's main concern was not with this group but rather with working-class women. But her sense of the structural basis of women's unhappiness and of their entrapment within prevailing norms of femininity suggests clearer affinity with Friedan than with Myrdal. Where Myrdal and Klein suggested some social reforms while insisting on the need for women themselves to change and take advantage of what they saw as available opportunities, Gavron suggested rather that their very emotional and even physical survival depended on social reforms that would serve to reduce their isolation and give them more independence and scope for a meaningful life. Myrdal and Klein were concerned about women's social role and responsibility as mothers and workers. Gavron, as her first sentence makes clear, was writing a 'study of women', involving an investigation which was at least as concerned about the ways in which numbers of women experienced their own lives and difficulties as it was about the nature and functions of the family. Writing as she was as an academic sociologist, Gavron necessarily took her framework from the prevailing academic discourse that constituted women as a problem and that looked at women and work still in relation to questions about the family rather than in relation to their own needs. She was, as Anne Oakley has argued, suspended uneasily in the air of prevailing and profoundly sexist debates which took no notice of women's perspectives or concerns.[88] But the book's insistence on the loneliness, the unhappiness, and the confusion of working-class women especially, gives both urgency and poignancy to her demand for social changes that give women greater scope as workers and which 'reintegrate women in all their many roles with the central activities of society'.[89] Gavron's own suicide shortly before the book was published seemed to many to provide the anguished and impassioned plea which the careful and statistical framework of the book denied and to underline her sense of how imperative it was to draw attention to the needs of women.[90]

Gavron's work both reflected and expanded the critical discussion of the meaning and nature of women's emancipation, offering a new exploration of the structures which ensured the continuity of women's oppression and suggesting that social attitudes and values had to change in order for women's second-class status to be removed. The period in which it was published marked perhaps the final stage in the postwar demand for a rethinking of an earlier feminist project which, by concentrating on the formal emancipation of women, had left unaddressed so many aspects of social, sexual, and economic life that enabled their oppression to continue. The final rejection of this project, one might well argue, came in 1968: a year which is remembered mainly because of the massive demonstrations, rioting, and radical activity in a number of Western countries amongst students and workers critical of prevailing political, economic, and social structures and deeply opposed to Western imperial domination, especially as exemplified in the Vietnam War. But 1968 was also the fiftieth anniversary of the first measure of women's suffrage in Britain. While this anniversary was not greeted with massive demonstration or fulsome rejoicing, it was certainly not ignored. In the press, and most particularly on the BBC, it was recorded, acknowledged, and commemorated—with a combination of stories from ageing suffragettes and debates and discussions about the meaning of women's emancipation and the battles still to be fought. The limited gains brought by women's suffrage and the inadequacy of 'emancipation' came to the fore again and again, with the increasingly trenchant demands being made for abortion law reform on the one hand, and for equal pay on the other, neither of which had been encompassed in the struggle for emancipation.[91]

The inadequacy of the goal of women's emancipation was stated most clearly and unequivocally in an essay published in 1966 by Juliet Mitchell, 'Women: The Longest Revolution' in *The New Left Review*. Mitchell's essay moved the debate about women into a completely new direction.[92] It was the first lengthy discussion of women in the 1960s which attempted to explore the nature and meaning of women's oppression in the context of socialist theory. Eschewing any suggestion of a connection with a British feminist past, Mitchell turned her attention to the European socialist tradition, offering a brief review of the ideas on women contained within the writings of the utopian socialists, of Marx and Engels, and of de Beauvoir, and pointing to the lack of theoretical resolution of the 'woman question' evident in the nineteenth century and to the inadequacy of the ways in which both Marx and de Beauvoir gave an 'economist emphasis' that stressed the subordination of women to the institutions of private property. What was necessary, Mitchell argued, was the recognition of the specific structure of women's oppression and of the complex unity which emerged if one examined the different elements and saw how the existing structures of production, reproduction, sexuality, and socialization all intersected and contributed to women's oppression. Taking her cue from the other liberation struggles of the 1960s associated with postcolonial and independent governments, Mitchell did not talk about women's emancipation, but rather about her belief that their 'liberation' could only be achieved if all four of these structures were transformed. The gaining of political rights, she insisted, 'left the socioeconomic status of women virtually unchanged'. The legacy of the suffragettes, in her view, was virtually nil and it was only under socialism that women could be emancipated.

Mitchell's essay heralded the advent of women's liberation, a movement in which she was herself very closely involved. It indicated the importance of left-wing politics, and of international socialism for the feminism of women's liberation. But within the broader history of English feminism, one might well suggest that it offers an end as well as a beginning: namely, that while pointing feminism in new directions it also provided the culmination of an extensive critique of the earlier feminist goal of emancipation.

# afterword
# FROM FEMINISM
# TO FEMINISMS

The quiet, sometimes imperceptible, ebb and flow of feminist activities which continued more or less from the First World War until the late 1960s was dramatically altered by the advent of the Women's Liberation movement in the early 1970s. This movement exploded onto the public and media stage in Britain in 1970 with the staging of a demonstration against a Miss World beauty competition in London.[1] Just as the beauty contestants were lined up on stage in front of Bob Hope, 'a posse of ill-kempt women, who contrasted bizarrely with the gloss and glamour of the occasion, burst onto the stage mooing like cows, blasting whistles, whirring football rattles and bearing placards with the titles "Miss-conception", . . . "Miss-treated", . . . "Miss-placed", . . . and "Miss-judged"'.[2] They threw flour-, smoke-, and stink-bombs, and leaflets at the stage, from which Bob Hope and the judges immediately fled, followed by a crowd of tearful beauty queens. Order was finally restored by the police who arrested five of the miscreants.

The focus of Women's Liberation on Miss World contests or on offensive posters and pictures of women on billboards shows the extent to which Women's Liberation was concerned with ways in which visual and cultural representation and conventional ideas of femininity contributed to the oppression of women. The disruptive and indecorous methods employed by Women's Liberation serve quite as much as the targets and objects of their protests to illustrate the differences between the cautious and moderate feminism of the 1950s and that of the early 1970s.

The term 'women's liberation' served both to differentiate the new movement of the 1970s from the limited programme sought by earlier feminists and to emphasize the connection between the new women's movement and the other liberation movements of the 1960s with which it had a close affinity. For many early participants in Women's Liberation, the movement was closely connected to the black power and student movements, and the postcolonial liberation movements which were transforming political life. It was also clearly connected to the sexual liberation movement of the 1960s. As a result, the women's liberation movement brought a quite new tone to the discussion of women's oppression. It sought to confront existing structures of oppression, to challenge their power, and to demand rapid and radical change. The Women's Liberation journal, *Red Rag*, for example, explained in its first number that it stood,

for revolutionary change in society, for ending capitalism and establishing socialism.

We challenge whatever and whoever denies the right of women to be free— from economic inequality and from the tyranny of the role forced upon them in our society.[3]

Like many journals and collectives at the time, *Red Rag* was socialist in its overall outlook and its tone was quite typical of the movement. The programme of the Women's Liberation movement was articulated in terms of 'four demands'—for equal pay, equal education and opportunity, free contraception and abortion on demand, and 24-hour nurseries—which were agreed to at the first national Women's Conference held at Ruskin College in February of 1970.[4] These demands were not discussed quietly, but were rather emblazoned on banners, printed on badges and shouted in the streets during mass demonstrations.

The initial demands of the movement made clear that those seeking women's liberation had no interest in negotiating or addressing contemporary ideals of womanhood. Women's Liberation did not for a moment accept the idea that women's primary duty was to their family—demanding rather that women be free to choose what kind of sexual relationship they wanted and whether or not to become mothers. Those who were or wished to be mothers demanded that this not be seen as the entire sum of their existence, but that they be able to combine maternity with the pursuit of other professional, personal, and public interests and activities. The later addition of three more demands—for legal and financial independence, for the right to a self-defined sexuality, and for an end to the oppression of lesbians—showed even more clearly the belief within the movement that drastic and dramatic change was possible and that women should be able to live by a wholly new set of rules and expectations.[5]

But even in its earliest days, Women's Liberation was closely connected to the past. The very recognition of the need to coin a new term carries with it a sense of a historic past. Thus while the tenor of Women's Liberation bore little resemblance to the demeanour of the feminism of the 1950s and early 1960s, its reaction against them was a formative influence. Moreover, while Women's Liberation brought to the fore new questions about personal and familial life and about social and cultural practices, it also continued to work on some of the feminist programmes and projects which had been the subject of campaigns since the nineteenth century. Only one of the four demands, that for 24-hour nurseries, was completely new. The others had all been accepted in some form by earlier feminist groups.[6] And the new movement constantly invoked the history of feminism, albeit a selective one.

The importance of history within the British Women's Liberation movement can hardly be overestimated. It is illustrated most clearly by the fact that the first national Women's Liberation conference grew out of an idea for a conference on women's history made at an annual conference of History Workshop at Ruskin College. History Workshop, in turn, was a product of the New Left and of the attempts being made by socialist historians to expand and redefine their discipline so that it could take proper cognizance, not simply of labour history, but of a broader kind of working-class history which explored popular movements and the many various kinds of political struggle.[7] For Rowbotham and Mitchell, as for many of the women who came to women's liberation through socialism and through the Ruskin History Workshop, history was crucial for anyone seeking to understand the predicament of women and for any kind of explanation of the advent and the nature of women's liberation. History, of course, has a privileged place within Marxism, and any other forms of socialism derived from it, both because of its explanatory function and because of the close connection evident since the late nineteenth century between demands for new and appropriate history and the development of political consciousness. Hence what they sought was to provide a coherent historical account of women's liberation which would link it to the broader history of radicalism and socialism.

The approach to history evident within socialism, and even in History Workshop, however, posed problems for those seeking to explore the history of women and of women's liberation. The main texts for many of those concerned either with the 'new social history', or with the New Left and its interest in culture, in the practices and rituals of everyday life, and in the need to explore the relationship between social, cultural, and political history, were E. P. Thompson's *The Making of the English Working Class*, and Raymond Williams's series of works on *Culture and Society*.[8] Thompson's history emphasized the role of popular cultural and religious beliefs and local political developments in the development of class consciousness, and insisted on the role of the working class in establishing the national political framework. Williams, in turn, emphasized the radical literary and intellectual tradition and the ways in which concern with the nature of industrial society and with class oppression had functioned in the work of prominent British literary and intellectual figures since the late eighteenth century. But these works provided a difficult and contradictory framework for those interested in women's history. While offering an approach which centred on social questions and on everyday life, they perpetuated the omission of women as activists or as writers, ignored questions about sexual and family relations, and absolutely privileged questions of class oppression over those of sexual hierarchy.

This difficult inheritance is evident in the work of both Rowbotham and Mitchell. Rowbotham's first and most widely read book, *Hidden from History*, follows the lines of E. P. Thompson, offering a polemical history focused specifically on England and seeing both capitalism and sexual puritanism as central to women's oppression. Adhering very closely to the traditions of labour history, Rowbotham sought to chart the 'resistance' to women's oppression evident within popular radicalism, early socialism, trade unionism, and some aspects of early twentieth-century feminism.[9]

Juliet Mitchell in her early work *Woman's Estate* broadened out from this focus (as Rowbotham too was later to do); following Shulamith Firestone in America, she sought to locate women's liberation within the broader context of European socialism. Mitchell pointed to Charles Fourier, Engels, and Simone de Beauvoir to demonstrate both the concern about women's oppression within the history of socialism, and the inadequacy of previous discussions.[10] The 'economist' analyses which linked the subordination of women to the institutions of private property, she argued, failed to understand the ways in which the organization of production and reproduction, of sexuality and socialization, all combined to determine the status and situation of women. Thus while the liberation of women remained a normative ideal within socialism, it was an adjunct to it rather than an integral part of socialist theory.[11]

This attempt to construct a historical account of women's oppression and of women's liberation contrasted quite strongly with an alternative and more popular approach to the history of feminism which constantly stressed the connection between Women's Liberation and the militant suffrage campaign in its demonstrations, public activities, and rhetoric. The women demonstrating against the Miss World competition and then continuing their protest through pamphlets and in court in 1970, for example, discussed the parallel between themselves and the suffragettes at some length. Their pamphlet, 'Why Miss World?' argued that theirs was the first militant confrontation with the law by feminists since Annie Kenney and Christabel Pankhurst were sentenced to imprisonment in Strangeways for addressing the crowd outside a meeting of liberal candidate Winston Churchill in Manchester.

This first illegal action of the suffragettes was followed three years later in 1908 by the celebrated trial of Mrs Pankhurst, her daughter Christabel and Mrs Flora Drummond. They appeared at Bow Street charged with conduct likely to cause a breach of the peace, and received 2 and 3 month sentences. . . . The Pankhursts conducted their own defence . . . the speeches they made in court amounted to a brilliant exposure of male prejudice and of the legal system. In the course of the trial we re-discovered the political importance of self-defence, both as a means of defending our self-respect and as a means of consciously rejecting the image of female acquiescence. Self-defence is a public demonstration of our refusal to collude in our own repression. It is an expression of the politics of women's liberation.[12]

In a similar way, the marches of the 1970s were hailed as the first great demonstration since those organized by the militants in 1907.[13]

For many of those active in the early stages of the Women's Liberation movement, therefore, the suffragettes and their militant campaign were a central reference point. As many people recognized, even the fashions of the time—the long hair and long velvet coats, even if worn over crocheted mini-dresses—brought to mind in some ways the suffragettes, and the image of the militant campaign hovers constantly over and around the 1970s women's movement.[14] The importance of the suffragettes was emphasized also by the widely read feminist magazine *Spare Rib*. Its first issue contained a lengthy extract from Antonia Raeburn's recently published book on *The Militants*, and it provided a considerable number of discussions and articles about the Pankhursts and their movement.[15] *Spare Rib* played an important role in reviving and popularizing the history of feminism, extending beyond the suffragettes with its articles on nineteenth-century feminists, especially on Josephine Butler and the Contagious Diseases agitation.[16] But it also established direct links between the women's movement of the 1970s and earlier feminist activities and ideas through interviews with women who had been active in earlier decades, such as Mary Stott, Dora

259

Russell, and Hazel Hunkins-Hallinan.[17] *Spare Rib* also developed a women's version of the new social history which was so important at the time, attempting to provide information and insights into the lives of ordinary women and the many different struggles in which working women had been involved. Thus from the start it published interviews with and discussions of the lives of working-class women, detailing their early struggles, their privations, their understanding and aware-ness of their own situation, and their political activities. Its approach to the past was both informal and eclectic, demonstrating the longevity and the variety of women's struggle by introducing to the world both contemporary feminists and the work of many women of previous dec-ades including many different kinds of feminists.

While many of those involved in *Spare Rib* sought to stress the con-nections between contemporary feminism and earlier feminist activi-ties, however, both Mitchell and Rowbotham sought to minimize it, even rejecting the idea that there was a link between Women's Libera-tion and the suffragettes. For them, the militancy of the suffragettes was of less consequence than was their endorsement of a liberal-radical and individualist feminism which, as socialists, they rejected. And of course, the political conservatism, the authoritarianism, and the mili-tarism of Emmeline and Christabel Pankhurst was immensely prob-lematic. Thus while acknowledging the existence of earlier feminists, Rowbotham completely rejected any sense of connection between the current movement and what she saw as a liberal-radical feminist herit-age. This liberal-radical approach, evident in Mary Wollstonecraft, in some nineteenth-century feminism, and in the suffragettes was, in Rowbotham's view, inadequate for contemporary feminism. It pro-vided a framework for demanding equal rights, but it could not come to terms with the issue of social class, nor could it define itself except in terms of the dominant group. Hence it failed to produce any prospect for a real social emancipation which could include all women, or to cre-ate a consciousness through which women could appreciate their own identity. It laid bare one layer of sexual domination, but 'like a snake's skin, as one idea system is peeled off another forms beneath it. Liberal-radical feminism is now only the shrivelled skin of a past reality shed on the ground.' It had ceased to have any connection with the living crea-ture.[18] In a similar vein, Juliet Mitchell, while recognizing that the Women's Liberation movement was assimilated in some ways to ear-lier feminist struggles, argued that while there were resemblances in the characteristics of the movements, there were no similarities in their ori-gins or in their aims.[19]

For Mitchell in particular, it was the connection between women's liberation on the one hand, and the contemporary black power, student, civil rights, and hippy movements on the other, which brought a break with an earlier feminist past.[20] This new context, she argued, established a break with earlier feminism, and made the current women's struggle against oppression 'a revolutionary one—a struggle in which all groups can ultimately be allied'.[21] The exclusivity of the suffragettes—their middle-class membership and concerns; their refusal as a group to encompass the concerns of working-class women or blacks; or to see the situation of women as in any way comparable to that of the oppressed Irish—created a wide chasm between their reformism and the revolutionary demands of Women's Liberation.

This emphasis on history, then, was emphatically not one which included any clear or direct attempt to establish a feminist tradition. On the contrary, what is most notable looking back on it now is the lack of interest accorded those earlier figures, who stood out in the established historical record as leading spokeswomen and radical agitators on behalf of their sex, especially Mary Wollstonecraft. Showing very clearly her interest in people's history and in recording the history of the hitherto unknown, Rowbotham afforded Mary Wollstonecraft little more space than she gave to an obscure washerwoman, Mary Collier, who in 1793 wrote a poem entitled 'The Woman's Labour'.[22] For Rowbotham, Wollstonecraft was far too class-bound and concerned with middle-class issues to be helpful to a radical movement. Moreover, Rowbotham was critical of the fact that Wollstonecraft could not imagine the possibility of women organizing themselves for their own emancipation. Ignoring entirely Wollstonecraft's personal life as a symbol of feminist revolt, Rowbotham concentrated mainly on the text of the *Vindication*, seeing it as 'the important theoretical summation' of the first moral phase of feminism, which involved the emergence of 'the religious and moral idea of the individual worth and dignity of women'.[23] Rowbotham's rejection of past feminism extended to her selective use of the very sparse material available in the early 1970s. She was clearly fascinated by the suffragettes, if critical of them, and traced in some detail the origin of the WSPU in relation to the ILP, showing how it moved further and further away from its labour roots or any sense of itself as a mass movement involving all women as the Pankhursts took ever tighter control of the movement and made it into a small and increasingly elitist militant body.[24] But Rowbotham's discussion concentrated entirely on the struggle amongst the militants between those women who remained in some way affiliated with and sympathetic to labour, such as Sylvia Pankhurst, Hannah Mitchell, Theresa Billington-Grieg, and the WFL, on the one hand, and Emmeline and Christabel Pankhurst on the other. She allowed no place for the largest suffrage organization, the NUWSS, and no mention even of its connection with the Labour Party after 1911. While recognizing the limited sources available, Rowbotham's book does not even list or refer to Ray Strachey's classic account of the movement for women's emancipation in England, *The Cause*.[25] Hers, as she later recognized, is a peculiarly narrow history, privileging socialist and labour movement concerns heavily over feminist commitment.[26] Indeed, it serves in a very complete way to show the problematic nature of the history of feminism to Women's Liberation. It offers at one and the same time a claim and a demand for knowledge of women's past and women's history and a rejection of that history, pointing to the importance of this history for the political consciousness and development of the Women's Liberation movement, while at the same time ignoring and censoring what was already known of that past by its refusal even to acknowledge the existence of important feminist activists or campaigns, and by its emphasis on discontinuity in the struggles of women. It recognizes in a general and theoretical way the continuity and historical origin of contemporary dilemmas, but rejects as part of that history the 'bourgeois feminism' which was so significant in England.

Rowbotham's approach to the history of feminism does serve to express a widespread view within the Women's Liberation of the early 1970s in its determination to connect feminism with the left, to extol its sexual radicalism, and to eschew its bourgeois past. This approach, which was widely endorsed within socialist feminism, involved not only a particular approach to the feminist past, but also to the origins of the Women's Liberation Movement itself. While it is of course too early for a full-scale study of Women's Liberation and its aftermath, to write its history in a way which reflects the diversity now accepted within feminist theory will not be easy to do. For there are already significant problems associated with the recording and documenting of the history of contemporary feminism. Ironically, the very attempt to preserve the record of the Women's Liberation Movement, which has been under way since the early 1970s, simply adds to the problem. The need to do so much groundwork, rescue, and recovery of past feminisms, and of the history of women generally gave many of those involved in the Women's Liberation movement a strong sense of the need to protect and preserve the records of contemporary developments. The plethora of newsletters and pamphlets which the move-

ment created made this only too likely and so from the very start measures were taken to prevent Women's Liberation itself from falling into a
void. Attempts were therefore made at a very early stage to collect and
edit some of these documents. By 1972, Michelene Wandor had edited
*The Body Politic* intended as 'a minimal historical account of the movement'; articles from the first 100 issues of *Spare Rib* were collected and
published separately; *Red Rag* recorded its own history after ten years,
and so on. Hence there are now quite a number of published documents dealing with the history of Women's Liberation as well as extensive numbers of published recollections and memoirs which serve to
record something of the outlook, the ideas, and the changes evident
within contemporary feminism. But inevitably, these collections privilege certain groups and events over others. An extraordinary number
focus on the Ruskin Conference, which has now come to stand for both
the focus and the symbol of how English women came 'to political consciousness as women'.[27]

This story is one which fits very well into the predominant framework of the 1970s, with its emphasis on the connection between sexual
freedom and women's liberation, and with its spontaneity and insistence on the connection between feminism and wider political and social issues. But increasingly, it is a story which excludes others and
which makes the coming to feminist consciousness of women outside
the charmed circle of Ruskin into a peripheral and subsidiary matter
that does not affect or connect with the key points in the development
of Women's Liberation in Britain. Amongst those thus excluded are
provincial women, who were unaware of Ruskin; women not involved
in left politics; black women; and women who were either too young or
too old to be university students or young mothers in places where
there were consciousness-raising groups in 1968. The stories of these
other women and of the women's movement which they created thus
wait to be told.

Ironically, it was only in the late 1970s and the early 1980s—when
the radical and revolutionary hopes and ideals of Women's Liberation
were giving way in the face of the Thatcher revolution in England and
the domination of Republican governments in the United States—that
the serious and detailed investigation of earlier feminist movements
and ideas developed. The seeds of this broader historical approach had
been laid earlier. Rosalind Delmar, for example, in her article 'What is
feminism?', emphasized in 1972 the diversity and heterogeneity of
historical forms of feminism, and the need to recognize abolitionism
and liberalism, as well as Marx, Engels, and Freud, if one wished to un-

derstand the connections between past and present forms of feminism.[28] One of the first theoretical tasks of the women's liberation movement, Delmar argued, was the reclamation of the term 'feminist', a project which involved the reassessment of an earlier women's movement and research into its origins, methods, and significance.[29] But it was not until at least a decade later that the task of rediscovery and analysis really began. This sense of rediscovery is evident in the changing language used by and about the women's movement. While the label 'women's liberation' signalled a moment of revolt in 1969 and 1970, the term 'feminist' had crept back into use by 1972.

It is interesting to note that here, as earlier, while suggesting unity, the term 'feminism' served to denote differences and even conflict: it came into usage when the euphoria and the sense of universal sisterhood which many had felt during 1969 began to disappear as differences in political outlook and sexual orientation became sources of tension and conflict. Although there were already divisions evident within the women's movement in the United States that had emerged in the late 1960s, in England many activists in 1970 still believed that there could be one 'women's liberation'.[30] When that belief proved illusory and it became necessary to recognize the many divisions and tensions amongst different groups concerned wtih women's liberation, the term 'feminist' came back into use—routinely governed by particular adjectives that served to differentiate socialist from radical, or lesbian from heterosexual or black from white feminists.

Recognition of the extent and the diversity of past feminisms, and of the importance of different approaches to the history of feminism began to develop in the 1980s, in the wake of a series of major conflicts which had brought to an end the very idea that there could be a single, unified Women's Liberation movement. Throughout the 1970s, national Women's Liberation conferences had constantly been disrupted by intense and sometimes even violent disagreements as different groups of women demanded primacy for their particular ideas and goals and objectives.[31] These tensions and divisions were hardly surprising. Where the suffrage movement had held together because of a shared commitment to the vote, the very breadth of the claims possible under the term 'women's liberation' made unity impossible. The liberation sought was intended to encompass every aspect of women's lives, and hence constantly brought to the fore the vast differences amongst those women on behalf of whom the movement attempted to speak.[32]

For many of those actively involved in the Ruskin Conference, British Women's Liberation was an outgrowth of left-wing and socialist politics and remained firmly committed to the need to locate women's liberation within a wider goal of social transformation and the end of an exploitive class structure. This was not in any way because of the concern about women's oppression evident within the left generally. Indeed, as Juliet Mitchell, Sheila Rowbotham, and others have pointed out, the growing demand from many women on the left for recognition of their oppression as a sex was greeted in Britain as elsewhere with extreme hostility.[33] Britain was unusual, however, in that women decided to remain within the broad socialist fold. In the United States, by contrast, this aggressive masculinist socialism led to a large-scale walk-out by women who termed themselves radical feminists and rejected Marxism, sometimes reformulating key Marxist ideas in order to stress their belief that women's oppression was the primary oppression, pre-existing and underlying all other forms of economic or racial oppression.[34] Their ideas, especially as formulated by Shulamith Firestone, were widely read and quite influential in Britain. But her demand that the Marxist dialectic be reformulated in terms of sex, and her insistence that women's liberation required not just a change in cultural values, but also a rejection of the biological imperatives of motherhood and the use of technology for reproduction were not seriously taken up. But even amongst feminists who saw themselves belonging to the left, there was often conflict. The left was immensely faction-ridden in Britain at this time, and within the women's movement this factionalism was replicated through the tensions between revolutionary and non-revolutionary groups and between those with a specific affiliation to the Communist Party or the Trotskyists or the International Socialists and those who were not aligned with any specific group.[35]

Perhaps the most significant point on which there was agreement amongst many socialist feminists was their difference from 'radical feminists': that is, from those who saw women's oppression as centring in male domination and particularly in sexual relations. For British radical feminists, as for their American or Australian counterparts, women's oppression was so deep-seated that it deprived them even of understanding their own lives and feelings. Liberation demanded first and foremost that women become conscious of how they were oppressed in every aspect of their daily lives. The best way to do this was seen to be in the form of consciousness-raising, for many the most important activity of the groups which made up Women's Liberation.[36] For 'radical feminists' like Sheila Jeffreys, for example, consciousness-raising was the core of women's liberation. It was the basis of the revolutionary struggle of women. Its purpose is the development of revolutionary anger and strength with others with whom we can take political action. Its method . . . involves the pooling of the collective experiences of women, in small personal groups, in order to analyse the structures of our oppression and the best way to fight them.[37]

But by contrast with this approach, those women who connected their involvement in Women's Liberation with a continued concern with class struggle, it was hard to see 'consciousness-raising' as a political activity, because it could be seen as 'simply talking to other middle-class women'.[38] Thus many British feminists tended rather to set up discussion and study groups which read Marx or Althusser or Lacan, hoping to find there the theoretical apparatus that would enable them properly to understand the nature of women's oppression.

This difference of approach was the cause of much bitterness. For those who sought to combine socialism with their involvement in Women's Liberation, 'radical feminists' appeared disruptive and narrow in their focus and concerns. For them, the path was clear. Radical feminists, by contrast, continue to feel that they were marginalized by those who sought to ensure a complete identity between the British Women's Liberation Movement and socialist feminism.[39] Those British women who saw themselves as 'radical' feminists right from the start, see the early 1970s as a period in which socialist feminists set themselves up as an elite, determining what the issues in feminism would be. While women on the left saw the first phase of developing a feminist consciousness as requiring the reading of *Das Kapital*, radical feminists were more concerned about political independence and personal separatism. Theirs was very much a form of lifestyle politics. As Amanda Sebestyen later recalled,

we wanted to leave men no matter what, we started squatting so we could live with other women, we acquired of necessity new 'male' skills of plumbing, electricity, carpentry and car maintenance, setting up our own discos and then forming bands to dance to. We cut our hair very short and stopped wearing 'women's' clothes, we stopped smiling and being 'nice'.[40]

This initial difference brought continuing and escalating antagonism. It involved conflict over whether men should be admitted to Women's Liberation meetings and increasingly also over questions of sexuality and the place of lesbianism within the women's movement. Even in 1970, the year of Ruskin, when many still believed in one Women's Liberation, there was widespread awareness of the conflict within the American Women's Liberation movement over the issue of lesbianism, on the one hand, and of how feminism analysed and dealt with the question of rape on the other. While Women's Liberation had begun by demanding sexual freedom, it did so in implicitly hetero-sexual terms, couching the demand in terms of access to contraception and abortion. Lesbians argued that they were a particularly oppressed group in a society which did not recognize as legitimate their sexuality, and that they were oppressed within the Women's Liberation move-ment itself.[41] At the most extreme, they demanded recognition that het-erosexuality itself oppressed women. In a particularly vitriolic set of articles, some lesbians argued that 'straight women' were not really women at all. The tone and intense bitterness of this conflict can be seen in the 'CLIT Statement', a series of letters which originated amongst American radical feminists and were reprinted in *Shrew*, the newsletter of the Women's Liberation Workshop in 1974. Straight women, it argued,

look like women. And sometimes remnants of the infant women they once were cut loose for a fleeting instant. But that passes and they quickly become again what daddy programmed them to be, . . . that is . . . dependent, passive, domestic, animalistic, nice, insecure, approval and security seekers, cowardly, humble; 'respectful' of authorities and men, closed, not fully responsive, half dead, trivial, dull, conventional, flattened out and thoroughly contemptible. They are males in disguise.[42]

Different views about women's sexuality and about how to deal with sexual questions had always been a complex and divisive issue within feminism. But this time the divisions ran deeper, because what was at issue was not a specific feminist campaign, but rather whether femi-nism itself required a particular form of sexual orientation and prac-tice. In 1978, at the Birmingham Conference, the divisions came finally to the surface with an intensity and violence which shattered any illu-sion of feminist unity and brought to an end any attempt to provide a national framework or focus for the women's movement.[43]

The bitter differences and divisions of the 1970s, as much amongst different groups of socialist feminists as between socialist and radical feminists, had occurred within a movement that assumed that sexual difference was more significant than ethnicity. In the late 1970s, this is-sue too became a subject of discussion and concern as black women began to demand recognition of their place within the women's move-ment, and to point to the implicit and explicit racism of a movement which assumed that the experiences and ideas of white women could be applied to all women. Hazel Carby's powerful article, 'White Woman

Listen! Black Feminism and the Boundaries of Sisterhood', demanded recognition of the very different ways in which white and black women saw and understood their oppression.[44] The issue was not simply one of omission, she argued, for black women couldn't simply be included within contemporary feminist theory. Racism and the various ways in which white domination had spread meant that any attempt to understand the oppression of black women questioned and undermined key concepts within white feminist theory.[45] Where white women saw the family as the main site of women's oppression, black women saw it often as the site of resistance; where white women demanded access to employment, black women were brought into Britain as labourers; where white women demanded abortion on demand, black women sought the freedom to have and keep families.[46] The very meaning of 'womanhood' and cultural constructions of black femininity in themselves raised issues and problems which had never been faced by white feminists.

Carby's article not only demanded recognition of the very different experiences, situations, and needs of different groups of women, it also pointed to the implicit assumptions of superiority evident within Western feminism—and the ways in which white women, even feminists, had been and were still involved in the oppression and exploitation of black women. Contact with the West had not brought 'progressive' change for African and Asian women or produced more enlightened systems of marriage and sexual relations. At the same time, even histories of women tended to underplay or misunderstand the nature of black feminism and the involvement of women in fighting against imperial domination. For Carby, the central demand of black feminism was that white feminists begin to hear and understand the different concrete historical experiences of different groups of women—not so that African or Asian or South American women could be encompassed within Anglo-British white feminism, but so that feminism itself could be transformed to encompass ethnic diversity.[47]

For a women's movement which had begun with a sense of its affinity with the black liberation and the postcolonial liberation movements, the charge of racism was one that was profoundly disturbing. And all the more so as black feminists argued that white feminists endorsed a loose 'Third Worldism', which lumped all non-whites into a single category and thereby managed to avoid dealing either with the racial issues that occurred at home or with their own racism.[48] Many attempts were made in the course of the 1980s to deal with this issue.

*Feminist Review* took up the criticisms that had been levelled against its practices, organizing a special issue in 1984 entitled 'Many Voices, One Chant: Black Feminist Issues and Perspectives', bringing black feminists into its collective, and attempting to reformulate socialist-feminism in ways that took up the question of racism.[49] *Spare Rib* had begun to attempt this process both of self-reflection and of breaking down its own ethnic barriers and developing a more diverse collective a couple of years earlier.[50] In the very act of attempting to overcome perceived racism, these early attempts demonstrated how exclusive the women's movement had been in political, ethnic, and class terms—and overcoming this was not easy. There were tense battles and conflicts within the new collectives, and new conflicts inevitably came to the fore. Thus, for example, the critique of imperialism in general and support for Palestinian women in particular brought attacks on Zionism—which in turn raised questions and bitter arguments about anti-Semitism.[51] At the same time, recognition of the complete omission of analysis or understanding of racism within feminism both brought to the fore questions about conflicting personal and political identities, and served to make feminism more reflective and to raise questions about the many different ways in which different peoples experienced or understood the very process of being a woman.[52]

By the 1980s, the very suggestion that there could be one unified feminism was deemed prescriptive and exclusionary and there was an increasing tendency to recognize, and even endorse, diversity through the use of the plural 'feminisms' rather than of any singular 'feminism'.[53] This emphasis on diversity and on pluralism reflected the increasing numbers of different groups of women who demanded a say in defining feminism and in articulating their own sense of oppression and their own needs. But this in turn provided an empirical and immediate political illustration of an issue which was becoming a source of debate and discussion within feminist theory: that is, concerning the ways in which feminism assumed or constructed a particular idea of womanhood which was both restrictive and exclusionary.[54] The early assumption within Women's Liberation that feminism took as its subject the group that was biologically defined as 'women' was increasingly challenged by many feminists who sought to relate the new approaches to psychoanalysis and language associated with Lacan, and, more generally, to relate poststructuralism to feminism and to question how the category 'women' was established. The journal *m/f*, which was established in 1978 with the specific aim of expanding the theoretical framework of feminism, insisted on the need for more extensive analysis of the basis and meaning of sexual difference and of the construction of the category of 'women'. The idea that women were a biological group and not a social category was, its first editorial insisted, part of the naturalizing ideology which perpetuated women's oppression. What was needed now was rather recognition of the need to consider how specific practices have produced both the category of 'women' and our understanding of sexual difference.[55]

Where Marx and Marxism had dominated the theoretical discussion of the 1970s, by the 1980s it was the poststructuralists, Lacan, Foucault, and Derrida who were becoming most influential, as ideas centring on psychoanalysis and on the importance of language in constructing rather than reflecting subjectivity and experience came to dominate the intellectual and theoretical reaches of feminism. These approaches helped also to explain why the earlier goals both of emancipation and of liberation had proved so elusive. The acceptance of psychoanalysis, of the importance of unconscious desires, and of the psychic dramas that underlay or meshed with political and economic structures all suggested that the oppression of women was far too deepseated to end simply with the changing of particular laws.[56] In a similar way, concern with the ways in which language itself served to construct meanings and to re-enforce male dominance and female oppression made the complexity of women's subordination more apparent. While these theoretical debates have brought a new sophistication to feminist theory and have suggested new objects for feminist action and new kinds of feminist approaches, they have also served to make it much more difficult to imagine or even contemplate what 'liberation' might mean for women.

While there is still very considerable disagreement amongst feminists, both the theoretical developments of the late 1970s and 1980s and the political concern to deal adequately with questions of difference, especially ethnic difference, have brought a new sense of the importance of acceptance and of negotiation amongst different groups of women with different ideas. It is not surprising that this new accommodation occurred mainly in the 1980s—after the peak period of women's liberation was over and when, in the eyes of many, it was on the defensive. By contrast, the period of most intense conflict between different socialist feminist groups or between socialist and radical feminists, which saw the splintering of the movement and the proliferation of new groups, occurred during the 1970s when the women's movement was undergoing rapid expansion and development. These years saw the proliferation of local groups and organizations and the establishment of important national campaigns, such as the National Abortion Action Campaign, which began in 1975, and the campaigns to establish rape crisis centres, refuges, and housing programmes. The high point of feminist activism was reached in the mid-1970s. After this the government cutbacks which followed the election of Margaret Thatcher made many earlier projects impossible. In the early 1980s, activism still continued, focused largely on Labour local councils and boroughs—until they too were destroyed. But by the end of the 1980s, changes in government policy and the apparent decline in feminist activism brought much discussion as to whether or not one could talk about a 'women's movement' any longer.

None the less, it is still too early to assess the developments and changes of the last few years, or indeed the whole question of the women's movement since the 1970s. The political and theoretical developments of the last two decades can be and have been represented as a period of immense hopefulness and growth, followed by one of contraction and decline as the ideal of rapid social and sexual transformation of the 1970s gave way to a grim recognition of the limited possibilities for change in the face of economic recession, conservative government, and social stagnation. Equally, however, one can point to the extraordinary number of feminist initiatives which developed outside government circles, based on voluntary groups and collective action and intended to offer support and assistance to homeless women or women who were victims of many forms of sexual and physical violence. It is necessary also to recognize the immense and fundamental challenge that the feminism of the 1970s and 1980s has posed to prevailing ideals of femininity and womanhood and of the meaning of sexual difference. The shift from 'feminism' to 'feminisms' in itself recognizes this challenge through its insistence on diversity, both amongst women and amongst their many and different emancipatory projects.

# Notes

## Introduction

1. See for example Olive Banks, *Faces of Feminism: A Study of Feminism as a Social Movement* (Oxford, 1986); Moira Ferguson, *First Feminists: British Women Writers, 1578–1799* (Bloomington, Ind., 1975); Ruth Perry, *The Celebrated Mary Astell: An Early English Feminist* (Chicago, 1986); Alice Browne, *The Eighteenth-Century Feminist Mind* (Brighton, 1987).

2. See for example Marilyn Butler, *Romantics, Rebels and Reactionaries: English Literature and its Background, 1760–1830* (Oxford, 1981); Rose Marie Cutting, 'Defiant Women: The Growth of Feminism in Fanny Burney's Novels' *SEL* 17 (1977), 515–30; Anne Doody, *Frances Burney: The Life in the Works* (New Brunswick, NJ, 1988); Julia Epstein, *The Iron Pen: Frances Burney and the Politics of Women's Writing* (Madison, 1989).

3. Joan Landes, *Women and the Public Sphere in the Age of the French Revolution* (Ithaca, NY, 1987).

4. Antoinette Burton, *Burdens of History: British Feminists, Indian Women and Imperial Culture, 1865–1915* (Chapel Hill, NC, 1994); Vron Ware, *Beyond the Pale: White Women, Racism and History* (London, 1992).

5. See Sally Alexander, *Becoming a Woman and Other Essays in the 19th and 20th Century* (London, 1994).

6. See e.g. Sheila Jeffreys, *The Spinster and her Enemies: Feminism and Sexuality, 1880–1930* (London, 1985); Susan Kingsley Kent, *Sex and Suffrage in Britain, 1860–1914* (Princeton, 1987); Lucy Bland, 'The Married Woman, the "New Woman" and the Feminist: Sexual Politics of the 1890s', in Jane Rendall (ed.), *Equal or Different: Women's Politics, 1800–1914* (Oxford, 1987).

7. See Elizabeth Grosz, 'Feminist Theory', in Barbara Caine, Elizabeth Grosz and Marie de Lepervanche (eds.), *Crossing Boundaries: Feminism and the Critique of Knowledges* (Sydney, 1987).

8. Anna Yeatman, 'Interlocking Oppressions' and Ien Ang, 'I'm a feminist but . . . : "Other" women and postnational feminism', in Barbara Caine and Rosemary Pringle (eds.), *Transitions: New Australian Feminisms* (Sydney, 1995).

9. Denise Riley, 'Does a Sex Have a History?', in id., *Am I that Name· Feminism and the Category of 'Women' in History* (Basingstoke, 1988) 1–17.

10. Barbara Caine, *Victorian Feminists* (Oxford, 1992), 28–30; Susan Sheridan, 'Feminist Readings: The Case of Christina Stead', in Barbara Caine, E. A. Grosz, Marie de Lepervanche, *Crossing Boundaries: Feminism and the Critique of Knowledges* (Sydney, 1988).
11. See e.g. Ray Strachey, *The Cause: A Short History of the Women's Movement in Great Britain* (London, 1928; repr. London, 1978), 13, 18–23.
12. See e.g. Jane Rendall, *The Origins of Modern Feminism: Women in Britain, France and the United States, 1780–1860* (London, 1985), 1–6.
13. Christine de Pizan, *The Book of the City of Ladies*, trans. Earl Jeffrey Richards (New York, 1982); Constance Jordan, *Renaissance Feminism Literary Texts and Political Models* (Ithaca, NY, 1990), 104–16; Mary Astell, *A Serious Proposal for the Ladies, for the Advancement of their True and Greatest Interest* (London, 1696); Ruth Perry, *The Celebrated Mary Astell: An Early English Feminist* (Chicago, 1986).
14. See e.g. Elisabeth G. Sledziewski, 'The French Revolution as the Turning Point', in Genevieve Fraisse and Michelle Perot (eds.), *A History of Women: Emerging Feminism from Revolution to World War* (Cambridge, Mass., 1993), 15–32; Barbara Caine, 'The Rights of Woman', in Ian McCalman (ed.), *The Oxford Companion to the Age of Romanticism and Revolution* (Oxford, forthcoming).
15. Genevieve Fraisse, *Muse de la raison: La democratie exclusive et la differences des sexes* (Aix-en-Provence, 1989), 14; see also Landes, *Women and the Public Sphere*; Christine Faure, *Democracy without Women: Feminism and the Rise of Liberal Individualism in France*, trans. Claudia Gorbman and John Berks (Bloomington, Ind., 1991).
16. See e.g. E. K. Bramsted and J. K. Melhuish (eds.) *Western Liberalism, a History in Documents from Locke to Croce* (London, 1978) and Carl Bogg, *The Socialist Tradition* (London, 1995).
17. See Barbara Caine, 'Feminism and Political Economy in Victorian England', in Peter Groenewegen (ed.), *Feminism and Political Economy in Victorian England* (Aldershot, 1992).
18. See Fraisse, *Muse de la raison*.
19. Sylvia Harcstark Myers, *The Bluestocking Circle: Women, Friendship and the Life of the Mind in Eighteenth-Century England* (Oxford, 1990), 256–7; Bridget Hill, *The Republican Virago: The Life and Times of Catherine Macaulay, Historian* (Oxford, 1992), 105–29.
20. Karen Offen, 'Defining Feminism: A Comparative Historical Approach', *Signs*, 14 (1988), 119–57; Nancy Cott, *The Grounding of Modern Feminism* (New Haven, 1987), 10–13.
21. Barbara Caine, 'Women's Studies: Feminist Traditions and the Problem of History', in Barbara Caine and Rosemary Pringle (eds.), *Transitions: New Australian Feminisms* (Sydney, 1995).
22. Ibid.

## Chapter 1

1. See Joan Wallach Scott, 'French Feminists and the Rights of "Man": Olympe de Gouges's Declarations', *History Workshop Journal*, 28 (1989), 17–24; Alice Browne, *The Eighteenth-Century Feminist Mind* (Brighton, 1987); and Jane Rendall, *The Origins of Modern Feminism: Women in Britain, France and the United States, 1780–1860* (London, 1985).
2. Genevieve Fraisse, *Muse de la raison: La democratie exclusive et la differences des sexes*, (Aix-en-Provence, 1989), 14; see also Joan Landes, *Women and the Public Sphere in the Age of the French Revolution* (Ithaca, NY, 1987), 1.
3. Landes, *Women and the Public Sphere*, 1–3.
4. See e.g. Elisabeth G. Sledziewski, 'The French Revolution as the Turning Point', in Genevieve Fraisse and Michelle Perrot (eds.), *A History of Women: Emerging Feminism from Revolution to World War* (Cambridge, Mass., 1993), 15–32.
5. See e.g. extensive republication of late-18th-cent. texts on and by women in series the Feminist Controversy in England, 1780–1830, Garland Press, New York.
6. Janet Todd, *The Sign of Angelica Women: Writing and Fiction, 1660–1800* (London, 1989), 236–521; Margaret Anne Doody, *Frances Burney: The Life in the Works* (New Brunswick, NJ, 1988), 300–65; Martha G. Brown, 'Fanny Burney's "Feminism": Gender or Genre?', in Mary Anne Schofield and Cecilia Macheski, *Fetter'd or Free? British Women Novelists, 1670–1815* (Athens, Oh., 1986), 29–36.
7. See e.g. Ray Strachey, *The Cause: A Short History of the Women's Movement in Great Britain* (London, 1928; repr. 1978), 13.
8. See Ivy Pinchbeck, *Women Workers and the Industrial Revolution*, (1930; repr. London, 1981); Louise Tilly and Joan Scott, *Women, Work and Family* (New York, 1978); Laura Levine Frader, 'Women in the Industrial Economy', in R. Bridenthal *et al.* (eds.), *Becoming Visible: Women in European History*, 2nd edn. (Boston, 1987), 309–33; and Maxine Berg, *The Age of Manufactures, 1700–1820* (London, 1980).
9. See Angela V. John (ed.), *Unequal Opportunities: Women's Employment in England, 1800–1918* (Oxford, 1986), pts. I and II; and Sally Alexander, *Women's Work in Nineteenth-Century London: A Study of the Years 1820–1850* (London, 1983).
10. Rendall, *Origins of Modern Feminism*, 124, 262–300.
11. See Leonore Davidoff and Catherine Hall, *Family Fortunes: Men and Women of the English Middle class 1780–1850* (London, 1987).
12. Joan Scott and Louise Tilly, 'Women's Work and the Family in Nineteenth-Century Europe', *Comparative Studies in Society and History*, 17 (1975), 36–64.

13. Davidoff and Hall, *Family Fortunes*; Theresa McBride, *The Moderniza-tion of Household Service in England and France, 1820–1920* (New York, 1976).
14. Edward Shorter, *The Making of the Modern Family* (London, 1976), 62–75.
15. See e.g. Michael Mitterauer and Reinhard Sieder, *The European Family* (Oxford 1982), 1–23.
16. Barbara Corrado Pope, 'The Influence of Rousseau's Ideology of Do-mesticity', in Jean Quataert and Marilyn Boxer (eds.), *Connecting Spheres: Women in the Western World, 1500 to the Present* (New York, 1987), 136–45.
17. Lawrence Stone, *The Family, Sex and Marriage in England, 1500–1800* (London, 1977).
18. Fraisse, *Muse de la raison*, 30–6; Landes, *Women and the Public Sphere*; Candice E. Proctor, *Women, Equality, and the French Revolution* (New York, 1990), 5–17.
19. Catherine Hall, 'Early Formation of Victorian Domestic Ideology', in Sandra Burman (ed.), *Fit Work for Women* (London, 1979).
20. Hall, 'Victorian Domestic Ideology'; Mary Poovey, *The Proper Lady and the Woman Writer: Ideology as Style in the Works of Mary Wollstonecraft, Mary Shelley and Jane Austen* (Chicago, 1985).
21. Mitzi Myers, 'Reform or Ruin: "A Revolution in Female Manners"', in Harry C. Payne (ed.), *Studies in Eighteenth Century Culture* (Wisconsin, 1982), 205.
22. Jurgen Habermas, *The Structural Transformation of the Public Sphere* (Oxford, 1984), 20.
23. Linda Colley, *Britons: Forging the Nation, 1707–1837* (New Haven, 1992), 244–5.
24. Landes, *Women and the Public Sphere*, 25.
25. See Moira Gatens, *Feminism and Philosophy* (Oxford, 1991) and Carole Pateman, *The Disorder of Women* (London, 1989), 17–32.
26. See David Williams, 'The Politics of Feminism in the French Enlighten-ment', in Peter Hughes and David Williams (eds.), *The Varied Pattern: Studies in the Eighteenth Century* (Toronto, 1971); Elizabeth Fox-Genovese, 'Women and the Enlightenment', in R. Bridenthal *et al.* (eds.), *Becoming Visible: Women in European History*, 2nd edn. (Boston, 1987), 251–77; and Rendall, *Origins*, 7–32.
27. See Lynn Hunt, *The Family Romance of the French Revolution* (London, 1992); Olwen Hufton, *Women and the Limits of Citizenship in the French Revolution* (Toronto, 1992); and Landes, *Women and the Public Sphere*, 129–38.
28. Quoted in Hunt, *The Family Romance*, 123.
29. Ludmilla Jordanova, *Sexual Visions* (London, 1990); Thomas Laqueur, *Making Sex, Body and Gender from the Greeks to Freud* (Cambridge Mass., 1990).

30. Stone, *Family, Sex and Marriage*; Shorter, *Making of the Modern Family*.

31. Jay Fliegelman, *Prodigals and Pilgrims: The American Revolution against Patriarchal Authority, 1750–1800* (Cambridge, 1982), 15–35.

32. Mary Wollstonecraft, *A Vindication of the Rights of Woman*, in Janet Todd and Marilyn Butler (eds.), *The Works of Mary Wollstonecraft*, vol. v (London, 1989), 232.

33. Elizabeth Kowaleski-Wallace, *Their Fathers' Daughters: Hannah More, Maria Edgeworth and Patriarchal Complicity* (New York, 1991); and Margaret Anne Doody, *Frances Burney: The Life in the Works* (New Brunswick, NJ, 1988).

34. See also Poovey, *The Proper Lady*, 18–25.

35. Habermas, *The Public Sphere*, 20.

36. Jane Rendall, 'Virtue and Commerce: Women in the Making of Adam Smith's Political Economy', in Ellen Kennedy and Susan Mendus (eds.), *Women in Western Political Philosophy: Kant to Nietzsche* (Brighton, 1988), 44–73; and Genevieve Pujol, *Feminism and Antifeminism in Political Economy* (Toronto, 1992).

37. Alexander, *Women's Work*.

38. See e.g. Berg, *The Age of Manufactures*.

39. John Stuart Mill, *Essays on Some Unsettled Questions of Political Economy* (London, 1874), 75–87; and Barbara Caine, 'Feminism and Political Economy in Victorian England—or John Stuart Mill, Henry Fawcett and Henry Sidgwick Ponder the "Woman Question"', in Peter Groenewegen (ed.), *Feminism and Political Economy in Victorian England* (Aldershot, 1994), 25–47.

40. Christine Battersby, *Gender and Genius* (London, 1990), 103.

41. Dorothy Thompson, 'Woman, Work and Politics in Nineteenth-Century England: The Problem of Authority', in Jane Rendall (ed.), *Equal or Different: Women's Politics 1800–1914* (Oxford, 1987), 57–81.

42. Virginia Sapiro, *A Vindication of Political Virtue: The Political Theory of Mary Wollstonecraft* (Chicago, 1972), pp. xiv, 61–3.

43. Barbara Taylor, 'Mary Wollstonecraft and the Wild Wish of Early Feminism', *History Workshop Journal*, 33 (1992), 199.

44. Margaret George, *One Woman's 'Situation': A Study of Mary Wollstonecraft* (Urbana, Ill., 1970), 84–95; see also Richard Holmes, *Footsteps: Adventures of a Romantic Biographer* (London, 1985), 133–98.

45. Wollstonecraft's early enthusiasm for the revolution changed during and after the 'terror'.

46. See Sapiro, *A Vindication*, 1–24.

47. Mary Wollstonecraft, 'A Vindication of the Rights of Men', in Janet Todd and Marilyn Butler (eds.), *The Works of Mary Wollstonecraft*, vol. v (London, 1989), 8.

48. Wollstonecraft, 'Rights of Men', 17.

49. Ibid. 10.

50. Ibid., *Vindication*, 86.
51. 'Rights of Men', 30–1.
52. Ibid., *Vindication*, 13.
53. Ibid. 185–6.
54. Ibid. 91.
55. Ibid. 218.
56. Ibid. 220.
57. Ibid. 223.
58. Myers. 'Reform or Ruin', 200–15.
59. Wollstonecraft, *Vindication*, 223.
60. Ibid. 57.
61. Battersby, *Gender and Genius*, 93.
62. Ibid. 95.
63. Wollstonecraft, *Vindication*, 151.
64. Ibid. 100; on this point, see Taylor, 'Mary Wollstonecraft', 213.
65. Wollstonecraft, *Vindication*, 231.
66. Gatens, *Feminism and Philosophy*.
67. Wollstonecraft, *Vindication*, 220.
68. Carole Pateman and Teresa Brennan, ' "Mere Auxiliaries to the Commonwealth": Women and the Origins of Liberalism', *Political Studies*, 27 (1979); and Carole Pateman, *The Sexual Contract* (Oxford, 1988), esp. ch. 4; see also Zillah Eisenstein, *The Radical Future of Liberal Feminism* (Boston, 1986), 140–3.
69. Wollstonecraft, *Vindication*, 219.
70. Ibid., 'Rights of Men', 28.
71. Catherine Macaulay (1731–91); see id., *Letters on Education with Observations on Religious and Metaphysical Subjects* (London, 1790); and Bridget Hill, *The Republican Virago: The Life and Times of Catherine Macaulay, Historian* (Oxford, 1992).
72. Mary Wollstonecraft, 'Review of *Letters on Education: With Observations on Religious and Metaphysical Subjects*, by Catherine Macaulay Graham', *Analytical Review*, 8 (November 1790), repr. in Todd and Butler (eds.), *Works of Mary Wollstonecraft*, vii. 322–3.
73. Wollstonecraft, *Vindication*, 175.
74. Taylor, 'Mary Wollstonecraft', 198.
75. Wollstonecraft, *Vindication*, 267.
76. Joyce Zonana, 'The Sultan and the Sultan and the Slave: Feminist Orientalism and the Structure of *Jane Eyre*', *Signs* 18 (1993), 601–2.
77. Wollstonecraft, *Vindication*, 267.
78. Mary D. Stocks, 'The Spirit of Feminism', *The Woman's Leader*, 13 Sept. 1929, p. 239.
79. Wollstonecraft, *Vindication*, 84.
80. Cora Kaplan, *Sea Changes: Essays on Culture and Feminism* (London, 1986), 34–50; see also Barbara Taylor, *Eve and the New Jerusalem: Socialism and Feminism in the Nineteenth Century* (London, 1983), 47; and

Landes, *Women and the Public Sphere*, 134–7.

81. Poovey, *The Proper Lady and the Woman Writer*.

82. Patricia Meyer Spacks, *Imagining a Self: Autobiography and the Novel in Eighteenth-Century England* (Cambridge, Mass., 1976), 71–3.

83. Claudia Johnson, *Equivocal Beings: Politics, Gender, and Sentimentality in the 1790s: Wollstonecraft, Radcliffe, Burney, Austen* (Chicago, 1995), 49–58.

84. Mary Wollstonecraft, *Maria or the Wrongs of Woman* (London, 1798; reprinted, London, 1979), ii.

85. See also Johnson, *Equivocal Beings*, 58–69.

86. William Godwin, *Memoirs of the Author of The Rights of Woman* (London, 1796), repr. in Mary Wollstonecraft and William Godwin, *A Short Residence in Sweden* and *Memoirs of the Author of The Rights of Woman*, ed. Richard Holmes (Harmondsworth, 1987), 276–7. Johnson, *Equivocal Beings*, 11–19 and Claire Tomalin (1974), *Life and death of Mary Wollstonecraft* (London, Weidenfeld and Nicolson) 228–54.

87. Godwin, *Memoirs*, 276–7.

88. William Godwin (ed.), *The Posthumous Works of Mary Wollstonecraft Godwin* (London, 1798; repr. Clifton, 1972), vol. iii, Preface.

89. Godwin, *Memoirs*, 238.

90. See, by contrast, Holmes, *Footsteps*, 97–123 and 133–98, which offers extensive discussion of her life in France prior to this, looking particularly at her political interests and at the dangers of her situation.

91. Godwin, *Memoirs*, 233.

92. Ibid. 231–2.

93. Mary Wollstonecraft, *A Vindication of the Rights of Woman: With Strictures on Political and Moral Subjects*, 3rd ed. (London, 1844), p. vi.

94. See Katharine Rogers, 'Sensitive Feminism vs. Conventional Sympathy: Richardson and Fielding on Women', *Novel*, 9 (1976), 256–69.

95. Jane Spencer, *The Rise of the Woman Novelist from Aphra Behn to Jane Austen* (Oxford, 1986), pp. ix–xi, 98.

96. Browne, *The Eighteenth-Century Feminist Mind*.

97. Marilyn Butler, *Romantics, Rebels and Reactionaries: English Literature and its Background, 1760–1830* (Oxford, 1981), 94.

98. Spacks, *Imagining a Self*, 57–63.

99. Poovey, *The Proper Lady*, p. x.

100. Ibid. p. xv.

101. Catherine R. Stimpson, 'Foreword' to Johnson, *Equivocal Beings*, p. xl.

102. Mary Wollstonecraft, 'Article VI' (review of *Camilla or a Picture of Youth*), *Analytical Review*, 24 (1796), repr. in Todd and Butler (eds.), *Works of Mary Wollstonecraft*, vii. 465.

103. Mary Wollstonecraft, 'Article XXII' (review of Ann Radcliffe, *The Italian, or the Confessional of the Black Penitents*), *Analytical Review*, 25 (1797), repr. in Todd and Butler (eds.), *Works of Mary Wollstonecraft*, viii. 484.

104. See e.g. Janet Todd, *A Dictionary of British and American Women Writers, 1600–1800* (London, 1984).
105. Anne K. Mellor, *Romanticism and Gender* (New York, 1993), 49.
106. Mary Hays, *Emma Courtney* (London, 1796; repr. London, 1987), 25.
107. Fanny Burney, *The Wanderer* (London, 1988), 161. For discussion about Burney and feminism, see Kristina Straub, *Divided Fictions: Fanny Burney and Feminine Strategy* (Lexington, 1987); Julia Epstein, *The Iron Pen: Frances Burney and the Politics of Women's Writing* (Madison, 1989); Margaret Anne Doody, *Frances Burney*; Martha G. Brown, 'Fanny Burney's "Feminism" Gender or Genre?'
108. Ibid. 163.
109. See Margaret Kirkham, *Jane Austen, Feminism and Fiction* (Brighton, 1983); Lloyd Brown, 'Jane Austen and the Feminist Tradition', *Nineteenth Century Studies*, 28 (1973), 321–38; Johnson, *Equivocal Beings*, 191–204.
110. For a very different reading of Austen, see Patricia S. Yaeger and Beth Kowalski-Wallace, *Refiguring the Father: New Feminist Readings of Patriarchy* (Carbondale, Ill., 1990).
111. Hannah More (1745–1833); see Hannah More, *Strictures on the Modern System of Female Education* (London, 1799), 105–6; M. G. Jones, *Hannah More* (London, 1952); Kowaleski-Wallace, *Their Father's Daughters*.
112. Strachey, *The Cause*, 13.
113. Kowaleski-Wallace, *Their Father's Daughters*, 15.
114. Hannah More, *Strictures on the modern System of female Education* (London, 1799) and *Colby in Search of Wife* (London, 1808).
115. Mitzi Myers, 'Reform or Ruin'; Marilyn Butler, *Maria Edgeworth* (Oxford, 1978).

# Chapter 2

1. Linda Colley, *Britons: Forging the Nation, 1707–1837* (New Haven, 1992), 250–2.
2. See Claire Tomalin, *The Life and Death of Mary Wollstonecraft* (London, 1974), 228–54; Claudia Johnson, *Equivocal Beings: Politics, Gender and Sentimentality in the 1790s: Wollstonecraft, Radcliffe, Burney, Austen* (Chicago, 1995), 1–19.
3. Johnson, *Equivocal Beings*, 196–203; Nancy Armstrong, *Desire and Domestic Fiction: A Political History of the Novel* (New York, 1987).
4. Barbara Caine, *Victorian Feminists* (Oxford, 1992), 18–27; Nancy Cott, *The Bonds of Womanhood. 'Woman's Sphere' in New England, 1780–1835* (New Haven, 1977).
5. Colley, *Britons*, 256–62.

6. F. K. Prochaska, *Women and Philanthropy in Nineteenth Century England* (Oxford, 1980).

7. Claire Midgley, *Women against Slavery: The British Campaigns, 1780–1870* (London, 1992), 155.

8. John Kilham, *Tennyson and The Princess: Reflections of an Age* (London, 1958); Barbara Taylor, *Eve and the New Jerusalem; Socialism and Feminism in the Nineteenth Century* (London, 1983), 15–19.

9. Louis Billington and Rosamund Billington, '"A Burning Zeal for Righteousness": Women in the British Anti-Slavery Movement', in *Equal or Different: Women's Politics 1800–1914* (Oxford, 1987), 83; Blanche Glassman Hersch, *The Slavery of Sex: Feminist-Abolitionists in America* (Urbana, Ill., 1978); Jean Fagin Yellin, *Women and Sisters: The Anti-slavery Feminists in American Culture* (New Haven, 1989).

10. Helen Maria Williams (1762–1827), see Gary Kelly, *Women, Writing and Revolution* (London, 1994).

11. (Anna) Letitia Barbauld (1743–1825), see Betsy Rogers, *Mrs Barbauld and her Contemporaries* (London, 1958).

12. Moira Ferguson, *Subject to Others: British Women Writers and Colonial Slavery, 1670–1834* (New York, 1992).

13. Midgley, *Women against Slavery*, 24.

14. Ibid. 43–62.

15. Ibid. 44.

16. Jane Rendall, *The Origins of Modern Feminism: Women in Britain, France and the United States, 1760–1860* (London, 1985), 217–24, 307–9, Olive Banks, *Faces of Feminism: A Study of Feminism as a Social Movement* (Oxford, 1981), 48–55.

17. Taylor, *Eve and the New Jerusalem*.

18. Anna Wheeler (1785–1848), see Richard Pankhurst, 'Anna Wheeler: A Pioneer Socialist and Feminist', *Political Quarterly*, 25 (1954).

19. Its full title was William Thompson, *Appeal of One-Half of the Human Race, Women, against the Pretensions of the other Half, Men, to retain them in political and thence in civil and domestic Slavery; in Reply to a paragraph of Mr Mill's celebrated 'Article on Government'* (London, 1825; repr. London, 1983).

20. See Frances E. Mineka, *The Dissidence of Dissent: The Monthly Repository, 1806–1838* (New York, 1972), 195–200.

21. See Deirdre David, *Intellectual Women and Victorian Patriarchy: Harriet Martineau, Elizabeth Barrett Browning, George Eliot* (London, 1987), 30–45. This aspect of Martineau's work was noted by later Victorian feminists; see Florence Fenwick Miller, *Harriet Martineau* (Boston, 1885), 50.

22. Caroline Norton (1808–1877), in id., *English Laws for Women in the Nineteenth Century*, privately printed (London, 1854); see also Alicia Acland, *Caroline Norton* (London, 1948); Margaret Forster, *Significant*

*Sisters: The Grassroots of Active Feminism, 1830–1930* (Harmondsworth, 1986); Mary Poovey, 'Covered but Not Bound: Caroline Norton and the 1857 Matrimonial Causes Act', in id., *Uneven Developments: The Ideological Work of Gender in Mid-Victorian England* (London, 1989), 51–88.

23. Norton, *English Laws*, 165.
24. See Rendall, *Origins of Modern Feminism*, 73–108; Caine, *Victorian Feminists*, 18–53.
25. Taylor, *Eve and the New Jerusalem*, 16.
26. James Mill, 'An Essay on Government', published in the Supplement to the Encyclopaedia Britannica (London, 1821; repr. Cambridge, 1937); see also Thompson, *Appeal*, 9.
27. Taylor, *Eve and the New Jerusalem*, 16.
28. Thompson, *Appeal*, 7.
29. Ibid. 34–9.
30. Ibid. 57.
31. Ibid. 86–102; cf. John Stuart Mill, *The Subjection of Women* (London, 1869), repr. in John Stuart Mill and Harriet Taylor Mill, *Essays on Sex Equality*, ed. Alice S. Rossi (Chicago, 1970).
32. Thompson, *Appeal*, 107.
33. Ibid., p. xxvi.
34. Ibid. 200–1.
35. Ibid. 80.
36. Ibid. 64.
37. The fullest study of feminism and feminist struggles within the Owenite movement is Taylor's *Eve and the New Jerusalem*, but see also Sally Alexander, 'Women, Class and Sexual Difference in the 1830s and '40s: Some Reflections on the Writing of a Feminist History', in id., *Becoming a Woman and Other Essays in 19th and 20th-Century Feminist History* (London, 1994).
38. Thompson, *Appeal*, p. xxii.
39. Ibid., p. xxiii.
40. There is as yet no detailed study of Wheeler. See Taylor, *Eve and the New Jerusalem*, 22–48, 59–60; Richard Pankhurst, 'Anna Wheeler: A Pioneer Socialist and Feminist', *Political Quarterly*, 25 (1954).
41. W. J. Fox, 'A Victim', *The Monthly Repository*, ns 7 (1833), 165–80. The article is a lengthy review of John Dove, *A Biographical History of the Wesley Family* (London, 1833). It is attributed to Fox by Mineka, *Dissidence of Dissent*, 104.
42. Fox, 'A Victim', 171–2.
43. Junius Redivivius, 'On the Condition of Women in England', *The Monthly Repository*, ns 7 (1833), 225.
44. Ibid. 228.
45. Ibid. 219.

46. Ibid. 217.
47. Mary Leman Grimstone (*c.*1790); see Mineka, *Dissidence of Dissent*; Kilham, *Tennyson and the Princess*; Mrs Leman Grimstone, 'Quaker Women', *Monthly Repository*, NS 9 (1835), 31.
48. Ibid. 33.
49. Taylor, *Eve and the New Jerusalem*, 59–61.
50. Ibid.
51. Ibid. 62–3.
52. See Mary Lyndon Shanley, *Feminism, Marriage and the Law in Victorian England, 1850–1895* (London, 1989), 8.
53. Ibid. 9.
54. Ibid. 36–7.
55. See e.g. Frances Power Cobbe, 'Criminals, Idiots, Women and Minors', *Fraser's Magazine*, 77 (1868), 77–82.
56. Quoted in Francoise Basch, *Relative Creatures: Victorian Women in Society and the Novel, 1837–67* (London, 1974), 20.
57. For Norton's story, see Forster, *Significant Sisters*.
58. Lacey, *Barbara Leigh Smith*, 7–9.
59. Quoted in Shanley, *Feminism, Marriage and the Law*, 27.
60. Norton, *English Laws for Women*, 165.
61. Ibid. 1.
62. *Report of the Married Women's Property Committee Presented at the Final Meeting of their Friends and Subscribers, held at Willis's Room, on Saturday 18th Nov, 1882* (Manchester, 1882), 5–6.
63. Poovey, *Uneven Developments*, 65.
64. Harriet Martineau (1802–1876); see Gillian Thomas, *Harriet Martineau*, Boston, 1980; David, *Intellectual Women*, 1–55; Susan Hoecker-Drysdale, *Harriet Martineau: First Woman Sociologist* (Oxford, 1992).
65. See Valerie Kosse Pichanick, *Harriet Martineau: The Woman and Her Work, 1802–76* (Ann Arbor, 1980) and Gayle Yates (ed.), *Harriet Martineau on Women* (New Brunswick, NJ, 1985).
66. Florence Fenwick-Miller, *Harriet Martineau* (Boston, 1885), 50–5.
67. See Hoecker-Drysdale, *Harriet Martineau*, 143.
68. See Harriet Martineau, *Autobiography*, 2 vols. (London, 1877; repr. London, 1983).
69. See also Mitzi Myers, 'Harriet Martineau's Autobiography: The Making of a Female Philosopher', in Estelle C. Jellinek (ed.), *Women's Autobiography: Essays in Criticism* (Bloomington, Ind., 1980).
70. Mineka, *Dissidence of Dissent*, 168–190.
71. Harriet Martineau, 'Female Education', repr. in Yates, *Harriet Martineau*, 90.
72. Harriet Martineau, 'Political Non-Existence of Women', in id., *Society in America*, 3 vols. (London, 1837), i. 200–8.
73. Ibid. 200.

74. Ibid. 202.
75. Harriet Martineau to E. J. Fox, 13 May 1837, in Valerie Sanders (ed.), *Harriet Martineau: Selected Letters* (Oxford, 1990), 45.
76. Harriet Martineau to unknown recipient, 20 March 1849, in Sanders (ed.), *Martineau: Selected Letters*, 115.
77. Martineau, *Autobiography*, ii. 401.
78. For a discussion of the Convention in relation to the 'woman question', see Midgley, *Women against Slavery*, 158–167.
79. Harriet Martineau's *Autobiography*, iii, quoted Pichanik, *Martineau*, 95.
80. David, *Intellectual Women*, 30–5.
81. Martineau, *Society in America*, i. 198–203.
82. Harriet Martineau, 'The Martyr Age of the United States', *London and Westminster Review*, 32 (1838–9), 1–59.
83. Midgley, *Women against Slavery*, 156–7, Pichanik, *Martineau*, 93.
84. Midgley, *Women against Slavery*, 156.
85. Ibid. 155–6. Sarah Grimke (1792–1873) published her *Letters on the Equality of Sexes, and the Condition of Women* in 1838; see Gerda Lerner *The Grimke Sisters from South Carolina* (Boston, 1967); Hersch, *Slavery of Sex*; Yellin, *Women and Sisters*.
86. Midgley, *Women against Slavery*, 157–8.
87. Martineau, *Society in America*, ii. 330.
88. Ibid. 328.
89. Ferguson, *Subject to Others*, 273–81.
90. Midgley, *Women against Slavery*, 159–167.
91. Harriet Martineau, 'Female Industry', *The Edinburgh Review*, 109 (1859), 293–336.
92. Ibid. 297.
93. Ibid. 300.
94. Ibid. 301.
95. Ibid. 329.
96. Ibid. 335.
97. Harriet Martineau, Letter to the *Daily News*, 28 Dec. 1869, repr. in Yates, *Harriet Martineau on Women*, 252–6.
98. Ibid. 254.
99. Yates, *Martineau*, 243–4.
100. Letter to the *Daily News*, 31 Dec. 1869, signed by Harriet Martineau, Josephine E. Butler, Florence Nightingale, Elizabeth C. Wolstenholme and twenty-four others, and repr. Yates, *Martineau*, 265–7.
101. For feminist reworkings of the model of the family in attempting to find new communities for women, see e.g. Martha Vicinus, *Independent Women: Work and Community for Single Women, 1850–1920* (Chicago, 1985), 35–40.
102. See Barbara Caine, 'Feminism and the Woman Question in Early Victorian England', in id., *Victorian Feminists*, 43–5.
103. For the evangelical impulse within feminism, see Banks, *Faces of*

*Feminism*, 13–27; Rendal, *Origins of Modern Feminism*, 78–101, 322–4.

104. Leonore Davidoff and Catherine Hall, *Family Fortunes: Men and Women of the English Middle Classes, 1780–1850* (London, 1987), 76–106.

105. Catherine Hall, 'Early Formation of Victorian Domestic Ideology', in Sandra Burman (ed.), *Fit Work for Women* (London, 1979), 15–32.

106. Mrs John Sandford, *Woman in Her Social and Domestic Character* (London, 1831), 20.

107. Sarah Ellis, *The Daughters of England* (London, 1844), 216.

108. John Ruskin, 'Of Queen's Gardens', in id., *Sesames and Lilies* (London, 1891), 110–80.

109. J. W. Burgon, BD, *A Sermon Preached before the University of Oxford, June 8, 1884* (London, 1885).

110. Anon., *Woman as She is, and as She Should Be* (London, 1835), 2.

111. Cited in Taylor, *Eve and the New Jerusalem*, 124–5.

112. Anne Richelieu Lamb, *Can Woman Regenerate Society* (London, 1834), 32.

# Chapter 3

1. See Philippa Levine, *Victorian Feminism, 1850–1900* (London, 1987); Olive Banks, *Faces of Feminism: A Study of Feminism as a Social Movement* (Oxford, 1981); Ray Strachey, *The Cause: A Short History of the Women's Movement in Great Britain* (London, 1928; repr. London, 1978).

2. See Jane Rendall, ' "A Moral Engine?" Feminism, Liberalism and the *English Woman's Journal*', in Jane Rendall (ed.), *Equal or Different: Women's Politics 1800–1914* (Oxford, 1987), 112–40; Candida Lacey (ed.), *Barbara Leigh Smith Bodichon and the Langham Place Circle* (London, 1987).

3. Florence Nightingale (1820–1910), see Martha Vicinus and Bea Nergaard, *Ever Yours, Florence Nightingale: Selected Letters* (London, 1989); Elizabeth Fry (1780–1845), see J. Rose, *Elizabeth Fry: A Biography* (London, 1980); Mary Carpenter (1807–1877), see Jo Manton, *Mary Carpenter and the Children of the Streets* (London, 1976); Louisa Twining (1820–1911), see Louisa Twining, *Recollections of Life and Work* (London, 1893); Mary Somerville (1780–1872), see E. C. Paterson, *Mary Somerville* (London, 1979). See e.g. Frances Power Cobbe, 'What Shall we Do with our Old Maids?' *Fraser's Magazine*, 66 (1862), 594–605; Barbara Bodichon, *Reasons For and Against the Enfranchisement of Women* (London, 1872), 9.

4. See e.g. Millicent Garrett Fawcett, *Life of Her Majesty Queen Victoria* (London, Boston, 1895). This biography was part of a series entitled Eminent Women.

5. F. K. Prochaska, *Women and Philanthropy in Nineteenth-Century England* (Oxford, 1980).
6. See esp. Liz Stanley, 'Feminism and Friendship: Two Essays on Olive Schreiner', *Studies in Sexual Politics*, 8 (1995).
7. Lacey (ed.), *Bodichon*, 3–10; Judith Walkowitz, *Prostitution and Victorian Society: Women, Class and the State* (Cambridge, 1980), 113–36.
8. Philippa Levine, *Feminist Lives in Victorian England: Private Roles and Public Commitment* (Oxford, 1990), 60–76.
9. See e.g. Frances Power Cobbe, 'The Claims of Women', in id., *The Life of Frances Power Cobbe by Herself*, 2 vols. (London, 1894).
10. See e.g. Jessie Boucheret and Helen Blackburn, *The Condition of Women and the Factory Acts* (London, 1886).
11. Antoinette Burton, *Burdens of History: British Feminists, Indian Women and Imperial Culture, 1865–1915* (Chapel Hill, NC, 1994).
12. Levine, *Feminist Lives*, 79–102.
13. Mary Lyndon Shanley, *Feminism, Marriage and the Law in Victorian England* (London, 1989), 34–6.
14. K. E. McCrone, 'The National Association for the Promotion of Social Science and the Advancement of Victorian Women', *Atlantis*, 8 (1982), 44–66.
15. Sheila Fletcher, *Feminists and Bureaucrats: A Study in the Development of Girls' Education in the Nineteenth Century* (Cambridge, 1980).
16. Rita McWilliams-Tullberg, *Women at Cambridge: A Men's University—Though of a Mixed Type* (London, 1975).
17. See Shanley, *Feminism, Marriage and the Law*, 22–48.
18. McWilliams-Tullberg, *Women at Cambridge*, 89–96; Barbara Caine, *Victorian Feminists* (Oxford, 1992), 89–91.
19. Leonore Davidoff and Catherine Hall, *Family Fortunes: Men and Women of the English Middle Class, 1780–1850* (London, 1987); Amanda Vickery, 'Golden Age to Separate Spheres? A Review of the Categories and Chronology of English Women's History', *The Historical Journal*, 36 (1993).
20. Davidoff and Hall, *Family Fortunes*, 272–316.
21. See Dorothy Thompson, 'Women, Work and Politics in Nineteenth-Century England: The Problem of Authority', in Rendall (ed.), *Equal or Different*, 57–81; cf. Linda Colley, *Britons: Forging the Nation, 1707–1837* (New Haven, 1992), 244–5.
22. Prochaska, *Women and Philanthropy*; Anne Summers, 'A Home from Home—Women's Philanthropic Work in the Nineteenth Century', in Sandra Burman (ed.), *Fit Work for Women* (London, 1979); Patricia Hollis, *Women in Public: The English Women's Movement, 1850–1900* (London, 1979).
23. The leading feminist journals in this period were *The Englishwoman's Journal* (1858–1864); *The Victoria Magazine* (1864–1880); *The Women's*

*Suffrage Journal* (1870–1890) and *The Women's Review of Social and Industrial Questions.*

24. A good sample of these discussions is available in several collections of documents, see especially Carol Bauer and Lawrence Ritt (eds.), *Free and Ennobled: Source Readings in the Development of Victorian Feminism* (Oxford, 1979).

25. Barbara Leigh Smith, later Bodichon (1872–1891), see Sheila R. Herstein, *A Mid-Victorian Feminist: Barbara Leigh Smith Bodichon* (New Haven, 1985); Bessie Rayner Parkes, later Belloc (1829–1925), see Mrs Belloc Lowndes, *I Too have Lived in Arcadia: A Record of Love and Childhood* (London, 1941). For their friendship, see Jane Rendall, 'Friendship and Politics: Barbara Leigh Smith Bodichon (1827–91) and Bessie Rayner Parkes (1829–1925)', in Susan Mendus and Jane Rendall (eds.), *Sexuality and Subordination* (London, 1989), 136–70.

26. Bessie Rayner Parkes, *Remarks on the Education of Girls, with Reference to the Social, Legal and Industrial Position of Women Today* (London, 1856), repr. in Lacey, *Bodichon.*

27. Herstein, *Mid-Victorian Feminist,* 106–11.

28. Jane Rendall, '"A Moral Engine"? Feminism, Liberalism and the *English Woman's Journal*' in Rendall (ed.), *Equal or Different,* 112–40.

29. Isa Craig (1831–1903); Adelaide Proctor (1825–1864); Maria Rye (1829–1903); Jessie Boucheret (1825–1905). There are no biographies of these women.

30. For the membership of the group and their activities, see Lacey, *Bodichon.*

31. I am indebted to Martha Vicinus for this way of looking at the Langham Place circle.

32. (Sarah) Emily Davies (1830–1921), see Barbara Stephen, *Emily Davies and Girton College* (London, 1927); Caine, *Victorian Feminists,* 54–102.

33. Levine, *Victorian Feminism,* 87.

34. See McCrone, 'The National Association', 44–66.

35. Anna Jameson (1794–1860), see Clara Thomas, *Love and Work Enough: The Life of Anna Jameson* (London, 1967); Mary Howitt (1799–1888), see A. Lee., *Laurels and Rosemary: The Life of William and Mary Howitt* (London, 1955).

36. Strachey, *The Cause,* 89.

37. Mary Howitt, *An Autobiography,* edited by her daughter, Margaret Howitt (London, n.d.); see also Philippa Levine, *Feminist Lives,* 9.

38. Olive Banks, *Becoming a Feminist: The Social Origins of Feminism* (Brighton, 1986).

39. Herstein, *Mid-Victorian Feminist.*

40. See Bessie Rayner Parkes, *Essays on Women's Work* (London, 1865), 55–62.

41. See esp. Cora Kaplan, *Sea Changes: Essays on Culture and Feminism* (London, 1986), 34–50 and Barbara Taylor, 'Mary Wollstonecraft and the Wild Wish of Early Feminism', *History Workshop Journal*, 33 (1992), 197–219.

42. E. J. B., 'Maria Edgeworth', *English Woman's Journal*, 2 (1858), 11.

43. Bessie Raynor Parkes to unknown recipient (n.d.), Bessie Rayner Parkes Papers, Girton College Library, Box V, item 171. I am indebted to Jacqueline Matthews for this reference.

44. Jane Rendall, 'Friendship and Politics: Barbara Leigh Smith Bodichon (1827–91) and Bessie Rayner Parkes (1829–95)', in Susan Mendus and Jane Rendall, *Sexuality and Subordination: Interdisciplinary Studies of Gender in the Nineteenth Century* (London, 1989), 136–70.

45. Faderman, Lilian, *Surpassing Love of Men* (London, 1980); Caine, *Victorian Feminists*, 120–6. Martha Vicinus, 'Lesbian Perversity and Victorian Marriage: The Codrington Divorce Trial', *Journal of British Studies*, (1977) 70–98.

46. Gordon S. Haight, *George Eliot: A Biography* (Oxford, 1968), 176–81.

47. George Eliot, 'Margaret Fuller and Mary Wollstonecraft', *The Leader* (13 Oct. 1855), repr. in Thomas Pinny (ed.), *Essays of George Eliot* (London, 1968), 201.

48. Ibid. 203.

49. For a different reading of Eliot's essay, see Sally Alexander, 'Why Feminism', in id., *Becoming a Woman and Other Essays in 19th and 20th Century Feminist History* (London, 1994), 146–7.

50. Caine, *Victorian Feminists*, 120–30.

51. Lacey, *Bodichon*, 3.

52. Ibid. 7–11.

53. Fulsome tribute was paid to Smith's role in the campaign to improve the lot of married women in the final report of the Married Women's Property Committee, published as a pamphlet: *Report of the Married Women's Property Committee Presented at the Final Meeting of their Friends and Subscribers on 18 November 1882* (Manchester, 1882); see also Caine, *Victorian Feminism*, 204.

54. See Herstein, *Mid-Victorian Feminist*, 106–11.

55. See Gordon S. Haight, *George Eliot and John Chapmen* (New Haven, 1940).

56. Barbara Leigh Smith Bodichon, *An American Diary, 1857–8* (London, 1972), 67.

57. Daphne Bennett, *Emily Davies, and the Emancipation of Women* (London, 1989), 154; cf. Herstein, *Mid-Victorian Feminist*, 112–5. Herstein regards them as a well-suited couple—but bases her account on the American Diary and says nothing about the marriage after the first year.

58. Elizabeth Wolstenholme-Elmy (1834–1913). No biography. See Ellis Ethelmer, 'A Woman Emancipator. A Biographical Sketch', *The Westminster Review*, 145 (1896), 424–8; Sandra Stanley Holton, 'Free Love

and Victorian Feminism: The Divers Matrimonials of Elizabeth Wolstenholme and Ben Elmy', *Victorian Studies*, 36 (1994), 199–222; and Sylvia Pankhurst, *The Suffragette Movement* (London, 1931; repr. London, 1977).

59. Elizabeth Wolstenholme-Elmy, 'Judicial Sexual Bias, II', *Westminster Review*, 149 (March 1898), 282–7.

60. Elizabeth Wolstenholme-Elmy, 'Women's Suffrage', *Westminster Review*, 148 (1897), 357–72.

61. For the fullest discussion of this episode, see Holton, 'Free Love and Victorian Feminism' and Pankhurst, *Suffragette Movement*, 30–3.

62. Holton, 'Free Love and Victorian Feminism'.

63. See pp. 138–9.

64. See Hollis, *Women in Public*; cf. Susan Kingsley Kent, *Sex and Suffrage in Britain, 1860–1914* (Princeton, 1987).

65. Millicent Garrett Fawcett, 'The Future of Englishwomen: A Reply', *The Nineteenth Century*, 4 (1878), 352.

66. There is a useful collection of documents in Jane Lewis (ed.), *Before the Vote Was Won: Arguments For and Against Women's Suffrage* (London, 1987).

67. Josephine E. Butler (1828–1906), see Josephine E. Butler, *An Auto-Biographical Memoir*, ed. G. and L. Johnson (London, 1909); Caine, *Victorian Feminists*, 150–95.

68. Josephine Butler, *Personal Reminiscences of a Great Crusade* (London, 1896), *passim*.

69. See Carole Pateman and Teresa Brennan, ' "Mere Auxiliaries to the Commonwealth": Women and the Origins of Liberalism', *Political Studies*, 27 (1979): Carole Pateman, *The Sexual Contract* (Oxford, 1988), esp. ch. 4; and Zillah Eisenstein, *The Radical Future of Liberal Feminism* (Boston, 1986), 140–3.

70. See Gail Tulloch, *Mill and Sexual Equality* (Brighton, 1989).

71. Millicent Garrett Fawcett, 'The Women's Suffrage Movement', in T. Stanton (ed.), *The Woman Question in Europe* (London, 1888), 4.

72. Josephine Butler to the Rt. Hon. H. A. Bruce, 8 June 1869, NUWSS Papers, M50/2/36, Manchester Public Library.

73. John Stuart Mill, *The Subjection of Women* (London, 1869), repr. in John Stuart Mill and Harriet Taylor, *Essays on Sex Equality*, ed. Alice Rossi (Chicago, 1970), 128–33.

74. Ibid. 136–46.

75. Ibid. 151–6.

76. Ibid. 157–80.

77. Ibid. 320–41.

78. See J. A. Banks and Olive Banks, *Feminism and Family Planning* (Liverpool, 1964), 1–35; cf. Levine, *Feminist Lives*, 42–5.

79. The papers for the Kensington Discussion Society are in the Emily Davies Papers at Girton College, see ED IX/KEN 5.

80. Frances Power Cobbe (1822–1904), see Cobbe, *Life of Frances Power Cobbe*; Caine, *Victorian Feminists*, 103–49; see also Frances Power Cobbe, *The Duties of Women* (London, 1881).
81. See Barbara Caine, 'John Stuart Mill and the English Women's Movement', *Historical Studies* (1978), 52–67.
82. Mill, *Subjection*, 139–40.
83. Caine, 'John Stuart Mill', 59–63.
84. Mill, *Subjection*, 191–2.
85. Ibid. 226–7.
86. Ibid. 168.
87. See Ann Oakley, 'Millicent Garrett Fawcett: Duty and Determination', Dale Spender (ed.), *Feminist Theorists: Three Centuries of Women's Intellectual Traditions* (London, 1983), 226–36; Caine, *Victorian Feminists*, 229–34.
88. Caine, *Victorian Feminists*, 275–82.
89. Josephine Butler et al., *Legislative Restrictions on the Industry of Women, Considered from the Women's Point of View* (London, n.d.).
90. See Butler's speech in the *Report of the Conference of the Association for the Defence of Personal Rights, 14 November, 1871* (Manchester, 1871), 14, Butler Papers, Fawcett Library.
91. For the passage and operation of the acts, see Walkowitz, *Prostitution and Victorian Society*.
92. See Butler, *Auto-Biographical memoir*, 29–31; and Jenni Uglow, 'Josephine Butler: From Sympathy to Theory', in Spender (ed.), *Feminist Theorists*, 147.
93. See e.g. Josephine Butler, 'Letter to the Members of the Ladies' National Association', Aug. 1875, Butler Papers, Fawcett Library.
94. Josephine Butler to the Miss Priestmans, fragment of letter, 5 Aug. 1889, Butler Papers, Fawcett Library; see also Butler, *Personal Reminiscences*, 75–83.
95. Josephine Butler to Mr Edmundson, 28 Mar. 1872, Butler Papers, Fawcett Library.
96. Butler, 'Letter', Aug. 1875.
97. Ibid.
98. Butler, *Personal Reminiscences*, 37.
99. See e.g. Butler, 'Letter', Aug. 1875.
100. Ibid.
101. Josephine E. Butler, *Some Thoughts on the Present Aspect of the Crusade against the State Regulation of Vice* (Liverpool, 1874).
102. Walkowitz, *Prostitution and Victorian Society*, 137–47.
103. Josephine Butler to the Ladies' National Association Executive, 11 Oct. 1877, Butler Papers, Fawcett Library.
104. See her printed letter explaining the objects of the Women's Emancipation Union, May 1895, in the Letters of Mrs Elizabeth Wolstenholme-Elmy, II, British Museum, Add Mss 47450, p. 197.

105. Elizabeth Wolstenholme-Elmy, 'Privilege V: Justice to Women', *Westminster Review*, 152 (1899), 129–40.
106. Frances Power Cobbe, brief note, *Women's Suffrage Journal*, 8 (1877), 139.
107. Walkowitz, *Prostitution and Victorian Society*, 145–7.
108. Cf. Walkowitz, *Prostitution and Victorian Society*, 14–17, 193–200.
109. Josephine E. Butler, *The Education and Employment of Women* (London, 1868), 18.
110. Ibid.
111. Ibid. 20.
112. Josephine Butler to Stanley Butler, 17 June 1895, Butler Papers, Fawcett Library.
113. Caine, *Victorian Feminists*, 66–8; 80–8.
114. Emily Davies, *The Higher Education of Women* (London, 1866; repr. London, 1988), 15–17.
115. Elizabeth Garrett Anderson, 'Sex in Mind and Education: A Reply', *Fortnightly Review*, 21 (1874), 582–94.
116. Millicent Garrett Fawcett, 'The Emancipation of Women', *Fortnightly Review*, ns 50 (1891), 677–8.
117. Fawcett, 'The Future of Englishwomen', 354.
118. Davies, *Higher Education of Women*, passim.
119. Martha Vicinus, *Independent Women: Work and Community for Single Women, 1850–1920* (Chicago, 1985), 129–52; McWilliams-Tullberg, *Women at Cambridge*.
120. McWilliams-Tullberg, *Women at Cambridge*.
121. Quoted in ibid. 77.
122. Muriel Bradbrook, *'That Infidel Place': A Short History of Girton College* (London, 1969); Martha Vicinus, *Independent Women*, 125–40.
123. Josephine Butler to Albert Rutson, 23 May 1868, Butler Papers.
124. Caine, *Victorian Feminists*, 86–8.
125. See Caine, 'John Stuart Mill', 52–67.
126. Lydia Becker (1827–1890), see the 'Biographical Notes and Reminiscences of Miss Becker', in Helen Blackburn, *Women's Suffrage* (London, 1902; repr. New York, 1971), 23–40.
127. Ibid. 28.
128. See esp. *Women's Suffrage Journal*, 2 (Jan. 1871), 1–2; editorial, 2 (July 1871), 74–6.
129. *Women's Suffrage Journal*, 13 (Sept. 1882), 131.
130. *Women's Suffrage Journal*, 9 (Oct. 1878), 172–3.
131. *Women's Suffrage Journal*, 2 (Aug. 1871), 83.
132. *Women's Suffrage Journal*, 14 (Oct. 1883), 176.
133. For Becker's views, see Blackburn, *Women's Suffrage*, 136–7.
134. *Women's Suffrage Journal*, 6 (July, 1875), 94.
135. Elizabeth Wolstenholme-Elmy to Harriet McIlquham, 1 Apr. 1880, Letters of Mrs Elmy, I, British Museum, Add Mss 47449, 21.

136. See Ethelmer, 'A Woman Emancipator', 424–9; Pankhurst, *The Suffragette Movement*, 35–8.
137. Pankhurst, *The Suffragette Movement*, 39.
138. See Walkowitz, *Prostitution and Victorian Society*, 93.
139. Ibid. 141–7.
140. Butler, *Some Thoughts on the Present Aspect of the Crusade*.
141. Anne Wiltsher, *Most Dangerous Women: Feminist Peace Campaigners of the Great War* (London, 1985), 16.
142. Burton, *Burdens of History*, 32.
143. Bodichon, *Reasons For and Against*, 4.
144. Burton, *Burdens of History*, 44–5.
145. Martin Pugh, *The Making of Modern British Politics, 1867–1939* (Oxford, 1982).
146. Marin Pugh, *The Tories and the People, 1880–1935* (Oxford, 1985).
147. Strachey, *The Cause*, 278–81.
148. See also Linda Walker, 'Party Political Women: A Comparative Study of Liberal Women and the Primrose League, 1890–1914', in Jane Rendall (ed.), *Equal or Different*, 165–92.
149. Ibid.
150. Frances Power Cobbe, 'Women in Italy in 1862', *Macmillan's Magazine* (1862), 363–75.
151. Ibid. 373.
152. Frances Power Cobbe, 'Introduction', in Stanton (ed.), *The Woman Question*, p. xvi.
153. See for example Barbara Leigh Smith Bodichon's contribution to the 'Debate on the Industrial Employment of Women at the first Annual Conference of the NAPSS', and Bessie Raynor Parkes 'A Year's experience in Women's Work' given at the 1859 Conference. Transactions of the National Association for the Promotion of Social Science (London, 1858), 531–44 and (London, 1860), 811–19. See also Levine, *Victorian Feminism*, 82–104.
154. Burton, *Burdens of History*, 47.
155. Barbara Ramusack, 'Cultural Missionaries, Maternal Imperialists, Feminist Allies: British Women Activists in India, 1865–1945', in Nupur Chaudhuri and Margaret Strobel (eds.), *Western Women and Imperialism: Complicity and Resistance* (Bloomington Ind., 1992), 119–36.
156. Ibid.; see also Burton, *Burdens of History*, 111–27.
157. Burton, *Burdens of History*, 110.
158. Ibid. 111–12.
159. See also Kumari Jayawardena, *The White Woman's Other Burden: Western Women and South Asia during British Rule* (New York, 1995), 75–90; and Geraldine Forbes, 'Medical Careers and Health Care for Indian Women: Patterns of Control', *Women's History Review*, 3 (1994), 515–30.
160. Burton, *Burdens of History*, 112–3.

161. For detailed analyses of Butler's Indian campaign, see Burton, *Burdens of History*, 127–70.
162. Antoinette Burton, 'The White Woman's Burden: British Feminists and "The Indian Woman"', in Chaudhuri and Strobel (eds.), *Western Women and Imperialism*, 137–57.
163. See Ramusack, 'Cultural Missionaries'; Vron Ware, *Beyond the Pale: White Women, Racism and History* (London, 1992); Nupur Chaudhuri, 'Memsahibs and their Servants in Nineteenth-Century India', *Women's History Review*, 3 (1994), 549–62.
164. Josephine E. Butler, 'Editorial', *Stormbell*, June 1898, cited in Burton, *Burdens of History*, 162.

## Chapter 4

1. R. E. Williams, *A Century of Punch* (London, 1956), *passim*; Frank E. Huggett, *Victorian England as seen by Punch* (London, 1978); Christina Walkley, *The Way to Wear 'Em: 150 Years of Punch on Fashion* (London, 1985).
2. The best analysis of the new kinds of campaigns and of the battle over representation is Lisa Tickner, *Spectacle of Women: The Imagery of the Suffrage Campaign, 1907–1917* (London, 1989).
3. See Lucy Bland, *Banishing the Beast: English Feminism and Sexual Morality, 1885–1914* (Harmondsworth, 1994).
4. Lisa Tickner, 'The Political Imagery of the British Women's Suffrage Movement', in Jane Beckett and Deborah Cherry (eds.), *The Edwardian Era* (London, 1987), 100–16; see also Mrs Humphrey Ward, *Delia Blanchflower* (London, 1915) for a hostile literary representation of suffragettes.
5. See Leslie Parker Hume, *The National Union of Women's Suffrage Societies* (New York, 1982); Sandra Stanley Holton, *Feminism and Democracy: Women's Suffrage and Reform Politics in Britain, 1900–1918* (Cambridge, 1986).
6. Patricia Hollis, *Ladies Elect: Women in English Local Government, 1865–1914* (Oxford, 1987).
7. Brian Harrison, *Separate Spheres: The Opposition to Women's Suffrage in Britain* (London, 1978); John Sutherland, *Mrs Humphrey Ward: Eminent Victorian, Pre-eminent Edwardian* (Oxford, 1990), 299-300.
8. Barbara Caine, *Victorian Feminists* (Oxford, 1992), 240–67; see also Barbara Caine, 'Generational Conflict and the Question of Ageing in Nineteenth and Twentieth Century Feminism', *Australian Cultural History*, 14 (1995) 92–108; Martha Vicinus, *Independent Women: Work and Community for Single Women, 1850–1920* (Chicago, 1985), 146–9.
9. Olive Banks, *Becoming a Feminist: The Social Origins of 'First Wave' Feminism* (Brighton, 1968), 80–4.

10. Philippa Levine, *Victorian Feminism, 1850-1900* (London, 1987); Rosemary Feurer, 'The Meaning of "Sisterhood": The British Women's Movement and Protective Legislation, 1870-1900', *Victorian Studies*, 31 (1988), 233-60; David Rubinstein, *Before the Suffragettes: Women's Emancipation in the 1890s* (Brighton, 1988), 94-102.

11. Jill Liddington and Jill Norris, *One Hand Tied Behind Us: The Rise of the Women's Suffrage Movement* (London, 1978); *Why Working Women need the Vote*, four papers read by members of the Women's Co-op Guild at the Sectional Conferences, 1897, Women's Co-op Guild, Kirby Lonsdale, Westmoreland; Jean Gaffin and David Thoms, *Caring and Sharing: the Centenary History of the Co-operative Women's Guild*, Co-op Union Ltd, Manchester, 1983.

12. Denise Riley, *Am I that Name? Feminism and the Category of 'Women' in History* (Basingstoke, 1988).

13. Antoinette Burton, *Burdens of History: British Feminists, Indian Women and Imperial Culture, 1865-1915* (Chapel Hill, NC, 1994), 1-32.

14. Jill Liddington, *The Long Road to Greenham: Feminism and Anti-Militarism in Britain since 1820* (London, 1989), 59-65.

15. Anna Davin, 'Imperialism and Motherhood', *History Workshop*, 5 (1978); Jane Lewis, *The Politics of Motherhood* (London, 1980).

16. See Lucy Bland, *Banishing the Beast: English Feminism and Sexual Morality, 1885-1914* (London, 1995), 229-31 and Alison Bashford, 'Edwardian Feminists and the Venereal Disease Debate in England', in Barbara Caine (ed.), *The Woman Question in England and Australia* (Sydney, 1995), 58-87.

17. Cicily Hamilton (1872-1952), see id., *Life Errant* (London, 1935); Dora Marsden (1882-1960), see Les Garner, *A Brave and Beautiful Spirit: Dora Marsden 1882-1961* (Aldershot, 1990).

18. Sarah Grand, 'The New Aspect of the Woman Question', *North American Review* (March 1894), 271-5. See also Ellen Jordan, 'The Christening of the New Woman', *Victorian Periodicals Newsletter*, 63 (1983), 19-20; and Rubinstein, *Before the Suffragettes*, 12-37.

19. Sarah Grand (1854-1943), see Gillian Kersley, *Darling Madame: Sarah Grand and Devoted Friend* (London, 1983).

20. Grand, 'The Woman Question', 271.

21. Sarah Grand, *The Modern Man and Maid* (London, 1898), 16.

22. The most extensive discussion of women and parasitism was developed later by Olive Schreiner in *Woman and Labour* (London, 1911; repr. London, 1978).

23. Mona Caird's *The Daughters of Danaus* (London, 1894); Emma Brooke's *A Superfluous Woman* (London, 1894); and Sarah Grand's *The Heavenly Twins* (London, 1893) and *The Beth Book* (London, 1897; repr. London, 1983); Olive Schreiner's *Story of an African Farm* (London, 1893), which was first published under a pseudonym, Ralph Iron, as *An African Farm: a Novel* (London, 1883); Grant Allen's *The Woman Who Did* (London,

1895); George Gissing's *The Odd Women* (London, 1893); and Thomas Hardy's *Jude the Obscure* (London, 1896).

24. Olive Schreiner (1955–1920), see Ruth First and Ann Scott, *Olive Schreiner* (London, 1980).

25. Mona Caird (1855–1932), *The Morality of Marriage and other Essays on the Status and Destiny of Woman* (London, 1897).

26. This was the central theme of Grand's *The Beth Book* and of *The Heavenly Twins*, as also of Brooke's *The Superfluous Woman*. It was taken up also by Christabel Pankhurst (1880–1958), in *The Great Scourge and How to End It* (London, 1913). This issue was also discussed by many moderate and conservative feminists as well; see e.g. Louise Creighton, *The Social Disease and How to Fight it: A Rejoinder* (London, 1914). See also David Mitchell, *Queen Christabel* (London, 1977); Elizabeth Sarah 'Christabel Pankhurst: Reclaiming her Power', in Dale Spender (ed.), *Feminist Theorists: Three Centuries of Women's Intellectual Traditions* (London, 1983).

27. Lucy Bland, *Banishing the Beast*, 146–9, 236–46; Alison Bashford, 'Edwardian Feminists', 62–9; Mary Spongberg, 'The Contagious Diseases Acts Reconsidered (Again)', in Caine (ed.), *The Woman Question*, 27–35.

28. Mary Spongberg, *The Sick Rose: Prostitution and Venereal Disease in British Medical Discourse*, unpublished Ph.D. thesis, Sydney University (1993).

29. Ibid.

30. Alison Bashford, 'Edwardian Feminists', 70–81.

31. Margaret Jackson, *The Real Facts Of Life: Feminism and the Politics of Sexuality* (London, 1994).

32. Caird, *Morality of Marriage*, 311–3.

33. Ibid. 138.

34. G. R. Searle, *Eugenics and Politics in Britain, 1900–1914* (Leyden, 1976); Lucy Bland, ' "Cleansing the Portals of Life": The Venereal Disease Campaign in the Early Twentieth Century', in Mary Langan and Bill Schwarz (eds.), *Crises in the British State 1880–1930* (London, 1985); Greta Jones, *Social Hygiene in Twentieth Century Britain* (London, 1986).

35. Searle, *Eugenics*, 70–8; Bland, *Banishing the Beast*, 222–6.

36. Bland, *Banishing the Beast*, 228.

37. Bashford, 'Edwardian Feminists', *passim*.

38. Havelock Ellis, *Studies in the Psychology of Sex, iii, Analysis of the Sex Impulse, Love and Pain* (Philadelphia, 1903).

39. Ibid.; Bland, *Banishing the Beast*, 258–61.

40. Lilian Faderman, *Surpassing Love of Men* (London, 1981); Sheila Jeffreys, *The Spinster and her Enemies: Feminism and Sexuality, 1880–1930* (London, 1985).

41. See Martha Vicinus, 'Distance and Desire: English Boarding School Friendships, 1870–1920', in Martin Duberman *et al.* (eds.), *Hidden from History: Reclaiming the Gay and Lesbian Past* (New York, 1991).

42. Wollstonecraft's *A Vindication of the Rights of Woman* was issued by T. Fisher Unwin in London in 1891 and as part of the Scott Library in Edinburgh in 1892. See also E. R. Clough, *A Study of Mary Wollstonecraft and the Rights of Woman* (London, 1898); Elizabeth Robbins Pennell, *Mary Wollstonecraft Godwin* (London, 1885).
43. Florence Fenwick-Miller (1854–1935), see id., 'Mary Wollstonecraft and the Vindication of the Rights of Woman', *Woman's Signal*, 12 Aug. 1897, p. 99; see also Pennel, *Mary Wollstonecraft Godwin*, 2–4, both followed the argument first put by Kegan Paul in his Mary Wollstonecraft, *Letters To Imlay*, with prefatory memoir by C. Kegan Paul (London, 1879).
44. Mary Wollstonecraft, *A Vindication of the Rights of Woman*, with an introduction by Millicent Garrett Fawcett (London, 1891), 3.
45. Ibid. 22.
46. Millicent Garrett Fawcett, 'The Woman Who Did', *Contemporary Review*, 23 (1898), 630.
47. See also Bland, *Banishing the Beast*, 3–47, 250–80; and Judith Walkowitz, *City of Dreadful Delight: Narrative of Sexual Danger in Late Victorian England* (London, 1992).
48. Edith Ward, '*Shafts* of thought', *Shafts*, 1 (1892), 2.
49. See Rosemary T. Van Arsdel, 'Mrs Florence Fenwick-Miller and the *Woman's Signal*, 1895–99', *Victorian Periodicals Newsletter*, 14 (1982), 107–17.
50. 'The New Woman', *Woman's Signal* (29 Nov. 1894), 345.
51. Ibid.
52. Emily Burton, 'The New Woman: Ideal and Reality', *Woman's Signal* (30 Apr. 1896).
53. Anon., 'More New Women', *Woman's Signal* (25 Feb. 1897), 118.
54. Florence Fenwick-Miller, 'The Beth Book', *Woman's Signal* (2 Dec. 1897), 354–7.
55. Ibid. 356.
56. Ibid.
57. Florence Fenwick-Miller, 'The Morality of Marriage', *Woman's Signal* (25 Aug. 1898), 115–6.
58. '*The Daughters of Danaus*', *Shafts*, 3 (Apr. 1895), 5–7; (May 1895), 22–4; (June 1895) 36–8.
59. George Bedborough, 'The Legitimation League', *Shafts*, (Apr. 1897), 125.
60. Anon., 'Esther Waters and What it Suggests', *Shafts*, 3 (May 1895), 24–5.
61. See e.g. 'Modern Fiction and the Cause of Woman', *Shafts*, 3 (May 1895), 31–2; (July 1895), 60–2.
62. Alice Grenfell, 'Contemporary Socialists and Women', *Shafts*, 3 (Sept. 1895), 81–2.
63. Anon., 'What the girl says', *Shafts*, 1 (Nov. 1892), 3.
64. Ellis Ethelmer, 'Feminism', *Westminster Review*, 149 (1898), 60–5.
65. Ibid. 63–5.

66. See Christine Collette, 'Socialism and Scandal: The Sexual Politics of the Early Labour Movement', *History Workshop Journal*, 23 (1987); and Ruth Brandon, *The New Women and the Old Men* (London, 1990).

67. See Martin Wright, 'Robert Blatchford, the Clarion Movement, and the Critical Years of British Socialism, 1891–1900', *Prose Studies*, 13 (1990), 74–9; and Norman and Jeanne Mackenzie, *The First Fabians* (London, 1971).

68. See e.g. Virginia Crawford, 'Feminism in France', *Woman's Signal* (16 Sept. 1897). This piece was reprinted from the *Fortnightly Review*. It seems to have been the only discussion of 'feminism' published in the *Woman's Signal*.

69. 'Sydney Smith on Female Education', *Woman's Signal*, 10 (Aug. and Sept. 1898).

70. Thompson had been reviewed earlier by Lydia Becker, in *Women's Suffrage Journal*, 7 (Oct. 1876) 139, but was not republished until the 1890s. See *Woman's Signal*, 10 (Oct. 1898–11 Sept. 1899).

71. *Shafts*, 1 (Feb. 1892), 96.

72. Ignota, 'Women's Suffrage', *Westminster Review*, 148/4 (1897), 358.

73. Harriet McIlquham, 'Mary Astell', *Westminster Review*, 149 (Apr. 1898), 440–9; Harriet McIlquham, 'Sophia: A Person of Quality: The Eighteenth Century Militant Champion of Women's Rights', *Westminster Review*, 150 (Nov. 1898), 533–547; Harriet McIlquham, 'Lady Mary Wortely Montagu and Mary Astell', *Westminster Review*, 151 (1899), 289–99.

74. Dora Marsden, 'Notes of the Week', *The Freewoman* (23 Nov. 1911), 3.

75. Ibid.

76. Dora Marsden, 'The Woman Movement and the "Ablest Socialists"', *The Freewoman*, 2 (1912), 285.

77. 'Commentary on Bondwomen', *The Freewoman* (30 Nov. 1911), 21–2.

78. Christabel Pankhurst (1880–1958), see Mitchell, *Queen Christabel*; Sarah, 'Christabel Pankhurst'.

79. Emmeline Pethick-Lawrence (1867–1954), *My Part in a Changing World* (London, 1938), 158–9.

80. Emmeline Pethick-Lawrence, 'What the Vote Means to Those Who Are Fighting the Battle', *Votes for Women* (Jan. 1908), 49.

81. See Vicinus, *Independent Women*, 247–80; and Sandra Stanley Holton, 'In Sorrowful Wrath: Suffrage Militance and the Romantic Feminism of Emmeline Pankhurst', in Harold Smith (ed.), *British Feminism in the Twentieth Century* (Aldershot, 1990).

82. For an extended discussion of Marsden and the *Freewoman*, see Bland, *Banishing the Beast*, 265–88.

83. For an interesting discussion of the question of bodily purity for the suffragettes, see Vicinus, *Independent Women*, 247–80.

84. Beatrice Webb, 'The Awakening of Women', *New Statesman*, suppl. on the Awakening of Women (2 Nov. 1911).
85. Feurer, 'The Meaning of "Sisterhood"'; Ellen F. Mappen, 'Strategists for Change: Socialist Feminist Approaches to the Problems of Women's Work', in Angela V. John (ed.), *Unequal Opportunities: Women's Employment in England, 1800-1918* (Oxford, 1986), 235-60; Heidi Hartmann, 'Capitalism, Patriarchy and Job Segregation by Sex', in Zillah Eisenstein (ed.), *Capitalist Patriarchy and the Case for Socialist Feminism* (New York, 1981).
86. See e.g. Jane Hannam, *Isabella Ford* (Oxford, 1989), 98-107.
87. Sheila Rowbotham and Jeffrey Weeks, *Socialism and the New Life: The Personal and Sexual Politics of Edward Carpenter and Havelock Ellis* (London, 1977); Stephen Yeo, 'A New Life: The Religion of Socialism in Britain', *History Workshop Journal*, 4 (1977).
88. Levine, *Victorian Feminism*, 105-27; Caine, *Victorian Feminists*, 241-8.
89. David Rubinstein, *A Different World for Women: The Life of Millicent Garrett Fawcett* (London, 1991).
90. See Ellen Mappen, *Helping Women at Work: The Women's Industrial Council, 1889-1914* (London, 1985).
91. Mappen, 'Strategists for Change'.
92. 'Fabian Women's Group', suppl. to *Fabian News* (Feb. 1913), 1; see also Sally Alexander (ed.), *Fabian Women's Tracts* (London, 1988).
93. Margaret Llewellyn Davies, 'Co-operation at the Fountainhead', 1920 typescript in Women's Co-operative Guild Papers, BLPES, Coll. Misc 268 1/24; Jean Gaffin and David Thoms, *Caring and Sharing: The Centenary History of the Co-operative Women's Guild*, Co-op Union Ltd (Manchester, 1983), 3-35.
94. Emma Paterson (1848-1886), see Harold Goldman, *Emma Paterson* (London, 1974).
95. Lady Emily Frances Dilke (1840-1904), see Betty Askwith, *Lady Dilke: A Biography* (London, 1969); Gertrude Tuckwell (1861-1951), see Lucy Middleton (ed.), *Women in the Labour Movement* (London, 1977).
96. Mary Macarthur (1880-1921), see Mary Agnes Hamilton, *Mary Macarthur: A Biographical Sketch* (London, 1925).
97. Deborah Thom, 'The Bundle of Sticks: Women, Trade Unionists and Collective Organization before 1918', in John (ed.), *Unequal Opportunities*, 265-77.
98. For a discussion of the term, see Naomi Black, *Social Feminism* (Ithaca, NY, 1989).
99. Feurer, 'Meaning of "Sisterhood"'; B. Caine, 'From a "fair field and no favour" to Equal Employment Opportunity', *Refractory Girl*, 30 (1987), 36-40; Levine, *Victorian Feminism*, 105-27; Norbert Soldon, *Women in British Trade Unions* (Dublin, 1978), 23-40; Rubinstein, *Before the*

*Suffragettes*, 94–134.

100. For the views of some of the mid-Victorian feminists who entered into this argument, see Jessie Boucheret, Helen Blackburn and some others, *The Condition of Women and the Factory Acts* (London, 1886) and Helen Blackburn and Nora Vigne, *Women Under the Factory Acts* (London, 1903).

101. Beatrice Webb, 'Women and the Factory Acts', Fabian Tract No. 67 (London, 1895), 5; see also B. L. Hutchins and A. Harrison, *A History of Factory Legislation* (London, 1911), 36–54.

102. Margaret Llewellyn Davies (1861–1944) 'Why Working Women need the Vote', paper no. 4, read at Southern Sectional conference of the Women's Co-operative Guild, London, 15 March 1897, Co-operative Guild Papers, Why Working Women need the Vote, four papers read by members of the Women's Co-op Guild at the Sectional Conferences, 1897, Women's Co-op Guild, Kirby Lonsdale, Westmoreland.

103. Millicent Garrett Fawcett, 'Mr Sidney Webb's Article on Women's Wages', *Economic Journal*, 2 (1892), 173–6.

104. Webb, 'Women and the Factory Acts', 4–6.

105. For recent work which supports Fawcett's views, see Hartmann, 'Capitalism, Patriarchy and Job Segregation by Sex'; and Solden, *Women in British Trade Unions, passim*.

106. See e.g. Josephine E. Butler *et al.*, *Legislative Restrictions on the Industry of Women, Considered from the Women's Point of View* (London, n.d.), 8.

107. Margaret Macdonald (1870–1911), Letters and papers of Mrs J. R. Macdonald, iii, 'The Licensing Bills of 1901–2 and the Employment of Barmaids', fo. 62, British Library of Political and Economic Science.

108. Levine, *Victorian Feminists*, 120–3; see also letter from M. F. King, Secretary of the Barmaids' Defence Association to Margaret Macdonald, 28 March 1907, Macdonald Papers, iii, fo. 61.

109. See Carol Dyhouse, *Feminism and the Family in England, 1880–1939* (Oxford, 1989), 86–91.

110. Sally Alexander (ed.), *Fabian Women's Tracts* (London, 1987); her Introduction, 'The Fabian Women's Group 1908–1952', is reprinted in Sally Alexander, *Becoming a Woman and Other Essays in 19th and 20th Century Feminism* (London, 1994), 149–58.

111. Clementina Black, *Married Women's Work* (London, 1915; repr. London, 1983), 4–6.

112. Ada Nield Chew (1870–1945), see Dorris Nield Chew, *Ada Nield Chew: The Life and Writings of a Working Woman* (London, 1982), 28–9.

113. Ada Nield Chew, 'The Problem of the Married Woman Worker', *The Common Cause* (6 March 1914), repr. in Chew, *Ada Nield Chew*, 230–4.

114. Selena Cooper (1864–1946), see Jill Liddington, *The Life and Times of a Respectable Rebel* (London, 1984).

115. Liddington and Norris, *One Hand Tied Behind Us*, 124–42.

116. Quoted in Lucy Middleton, 'Women in Labour Politics', in id., *Women in the Labour Movement*, 25–6.
117. See Alexander (ed.), *Fabian Women's Tracts*, pp. i–vii.
118. Banks, *Becoming a Feminist*, 80–4.
119. See Jean Gaffin, 'Women and Co-operation', in Middleton (ed.), *Women in the Labour Movement*, 114.
120. Davies, 'Co-operation at the Fountainhead'.
121. Margaret Llewellyn Davies, 'Introduction', in *Working Women and divorce: an account of the evidence given on behalf of the Women's Co-op Guild before the Royal Commission on Divorce* (London, 1911), 4–5.
122. Ibid.
123. Gaffin and Thoms, *Caring and Sharing*, 48–51.
124. Eva Gore-Booth (1870–1926); Esther Roper (1868–1938), see Lewis Gifford, *Eva Gore-Booth and Esther Roper: A Biography* (London, 1980).
125. Ada Nield Chew (1870–1945), see Chew, *Ada Nield Chew*; Hannah Mitchell (1876–1956), see Hannah Mitchell, *The Hard Way Up: The Autobiography of Hannah Mitchell, Suffragette and Rebel* (London, 1968); Selena Cooper (1864–1946), see Liddington, *Life and Times of a Respectable Rebel*; Sarah Reddish (1850–1925), no biography.
126. Quoted in Liddington and Norris, *One Hand Tied Behind Us*, 182.
127. Liddington, *Life and Times*, 159–75.
128. Holton, *Feminism and Democracy*, 53–75.
129. Ibid. 55–6.
130. Liddington and Norris, *One Hand Tied Behind Us*, 200–15.
131. Tickner, *Spectacle of Women, passim*.
132. Sylvia Pankhurst, *The Suffragette Movement* (London, 1911; repr. London, 1978), 167–8.
133. Annie Kenney (1879–1953), see Annie Kenney, *Memories of a Militant* (London, 1924).
134. Millicent Garrett Fawcett, *What I Remember* (London, 1925; repr. Westport, Conn., 1976), 182.
135. For the relationship between the Liberals and the women's suffrage campaign, see David Morgan, *Suffragists and Liberals: The Politics of Woman Suffrage in Britain* (Oxford, 1975), 23–39.
136. For somewhat differing accounts of the militants, see Andrew Rosen, *Rise Up Women! The Militant Campaign of the Women's Social and Political Union, 1903–1914* (London, 1974); Pankhurst, *Suffragette Movement*.
137. Hume, *National Union of Women's Suffrage*.
138. Fawcett, *What I Remember*, 184.
139. Hume, *National Union of Women's Suffrage Societies*, 229–31.
140. See Lisa Tickner's brilliant discussion of this subject in id., *Spectacle of Women*.
141. Brian Harrison, *Separate Spheres: The Opposition to Women's Suffrage in Britain* (London, 1978).

142. Liddington and Norris, *One Hand Tied Behind Us*.
143. Holton, *Feminism and Democracy*, 48–51.
144. Rosen, *Rise Up Women!*, 50–8; Vicinus, *Independent Women*, 250–1.
145. Charlotte Despard (1844–1939), see Andro Linklater, *An Unhusbanded Life: Charlotte Despard: Suffragette, Socialist, Sinn Feiner* (London, 1980); Margaret Mulvihill, *Charlotte Despard: A Biography* (London, 1989); Edith Howe-Martin (1875–1954), see Pamela Brooks, *Women at Westminster* (London, 1967).
146. Theresa Billington-Grieg, *The Non-Violent Militant* (London, 1987), 106.
147. Flora Drummond (1879–1949), see Pankhurst, *Suffragette Movement*, 265–6.
148. Theresa Billington-Grieg, *The Militant Suffrage Movement: Emancipation in a Hurry* (London, 1911), repr. in Billington-Grieg, *Non-Violent Militant*, 186–90.
149. Ibid. 141–2
150. Hume, *National Union of Women's Suffrage Societies*, 63–4.
151. Holton, *Feminism and Democracy*, 69–75.
152. Hume, *National Union of Women's Suffrage Societies*.
153. Helena Swanwick (1864–1939), see id., *A Woman's World* (London, 1968); Catherine Marshall (1880–1961); Kathleen Courtney (1878–1974). Sandra Holton, *Feminism And Democracy*, 1–15.
154. Caine, *Victorian Feminists*, 264–5; Holton, *Feminism and Democracy*, 76–115.
155. For a discussion of the role and importance of the different suffrage organizations, see Constance Rover, *Women's Suffrage and Party Politics in Britain, 1866–1914* (London, 1967); Andrew Rosen, *Rise Up Women* (London, 1974); Jill Liddington and Jill Norris, *One Hand Tied Behind Us. The Rise of the Women's Suffrage movement* (London, 1978) and Sandra Holton, *Feminism and Democracy*. Pankhurst (1882–1960), see Richard Pankhurst, *Sylvia Pankhurst, Artist and Crusader: An Intimate Biography* (London, 1979); Patricia W. Romero, *E. Sylvia Pankhurst: Portrait of a Radical* (New Haven, 1987).
156. Martha Vicinus, *Independent Women*, 262–73; Jane Marcus, *Suffrage and the Pankhursts* (London, 1987), Introduction.
157. Cecily Hamilton, Life Errant (London, 1935), 70–4; see also Brian Harrison, 'The Act of Militancy: Violence and the Suffragettes, 1904–14' in id., *Peaceable Kingdoms: Stability and Change in Modern Britain* (Oxford, 1982), 26–81 and Sandra Stanley Holton, ' "In sorrowful wrath": Suffrage militancy and the romantic feminism of Emmeline Pankhurst', in Harold L. Smith (ed.), *British Feminism in the Twentieth Century* (London, 1990), 7–24.
158. Harrison, *Separate Spheres*, 75; Antoinette M. Burton, 'The White Woman's Burden: British Feminists and "The Indian Woman" ', in Nupur

Chandhuri and Margaret Strobel (eds.), *Western Women and Imperialism: Complicity and Resistance*, (Bloomington, Ind., 1992), 132–8.

159. Quoted in Burton, *Burdens of History*, 3.

160. Mrs Wolstenholme-Elmy, 'Woman's Franchise: The Need of the Hour', *Westminster Review*, 148 (1897), 357–72.

161. Burton, *Burdens of History*, 172.

162. Fawcett, *What I Remember*, 149, Josephine Butler, The Native *Races and the War* (London, 1900).

163. See NUWSS Minute Books for Executive Committee, 5 Oct. 1899, NUWSS Collection, Fawcett Library, A1/1 1899–1903.

164. Liddington, *Long Road to Greenham*, 46–53.

165. Millicent Garrett Fawcett, 'Report on the Concentration Camps in South Africa by the Committee of Ladies appointed by the Secretary of State for War containing Reports on the Camps in Natal, the Orange River Colony and the Transvaal', London, 1902. Fawcett's own copy of the report, containing many photographs, is in the Fawcett Library. See also Caine, *Victorian Feminists*, 213–4.

166. Anne Wiltsher, *Most Dangerous Women: Feminist Peace Campaigners of the Great War* (London, 1985), 18.

167. Barbara Caine, 'Vida Goldstein and the British Militant Campaign', *Women's History Review*, 4 (1994).

168. For a discussion of the complex relationship between British feminism and imperialism, see Barbara N. Ramusack and Antoinette Burton, *Feminism, Imperialism and Race: A dialogue between India and Britain*, a special issue of *Women's History Review*, vol. 3, no. 4 (1994). See also Ian Tyrrell, *Women's Empire; Woman's World: The Women's Christian Temperance Union in International perspective, 1880–1930* (Chapel Hill, 1991), 180–5 and *The Woman Voter*, 18 (6 Apr. 1991).

169. Note dated Tuesday 21 March, Goldstein Collection, Rischbieth Papers, Australian National Library, 2004/4/23.

170. Florence Fenwick-Miller, 'Our Sisters in India', *Woman's Signal* (10 Mar. 1898), 48.

171. Burton, 'White Woman's Burden', 137–55.

172. Mineke Bosch and Annemarie Kloosterman (eds.), *Politics and Friendship: Letters from the International Woman Suffrage Alliance, 1902–1942* (Columbus, Oh., 1990), 15.

173. Ibid. 12.

174. 'Conference Report', *Jus Suffragii*, 7 (1913), 3. This was the first English edition of the journal.

175. Liddington, *Long Road to Greenham*, 67–75.

176. Charlotte Perkins Gilman (1860–1935), see id., *The Living of Charlotte Perkins Gilman* (Madison, 1935); M. A. Hill, *Charlotte Perkins Gilman: The Making of a Radical Feminist* (Philadelphia, 1980).

177. *The Vote*, 4 (1909), 79.

## Chapter 5

1. Dale Spender, *There's Always Been a Women's Movement This Century* (London, 1984).

2. See esp. Johanna Alberti, *Beyond Suffrage: Feminists in War and Peace, 1914–1928* (London, 1989); Brian Harrison, *Prudent Revolutionaries: Portraits of British Feminists between the Wars* (Oxford, 1987); Carol Dyhouse, *Feminism and the Family in England, 1880–1930* (Oxford, 1989); Martin Pugh, *Women and the Women's Movement in Britain, 1914–1959* (London, 1992); Susan Kingsley Kent, *Making Peace: The Reconstruction of Gender in Interwar Britain* (Princeton, 1993).

3. See David Doughan, *Lobbying for Equality: British Feminism, 1918–1968* (London, 1980).

4. Harold L. Smith, 'British Feminism in the 1920s', in id. (ed.), *British Feminism in the Twentieth Century* (Aldershot, 1990), 47. See also Susan K. Kent, 'The Politics of Sexual Difference: World War I and the demise of British feminism', *Journal of British Studies*, 27 (1988), 238–40.

5. Eleanor Rathbone, 'Apologia Pro Vita Nostra', 24 February 1926, in *Milestones: Presidential Addresses at the Annual Council Meetings of the NUSEC* (Liverpool, 1929), 32.

6. See e.g. Mrs Pethwick-Lawrence's Presidential Address at the Twenty-Second Annual Conference of the Women's Freedom League, 'Dare to be Free', *The Vote*, 30 (1929), 121–2.

7. See Lucy Bland, 'Marriage Laid Bare: Middle-Class Women and Marital Sex, c.1880–1914', in Jane Lewis (ed.), *Labour and Love: Women's Experience of Home and Family, 1850–1940* (Oxford, 1986); Sheila Jeffreys, *The Spinster and Her Enemies: Feminism and Sexuality, 1880–1930* (London, 1985); Susan Kingsley Kent, 'Gender Reconstruction After the First World War', in Smith (ed.), *British Feminism*, 66–83.

8. Jeffreys, *The Spinster*, 123–4, 189; but see also Deborah Gorham, '"Have we really rounded Seraglio Point?": Vera Brittain and Inter-War Feminism', in Smith (ed.), *British Feminism*, 97–9.

9. See e.g. the discussion in *Time and Tide* (12 Mar. 1926), 243.

10. See Alberti, *Beyond Suffrage*, 164–74.

11. Virginia Woolf, *Three Guineas* (London, 1938; repr. Harmondsworth, 1979), 117; Winnifred Holtby, *Women and a Changing Civilization* (London, 1935; repr. Chicago, 1978).

12. Alberti, *Beyond Suffrage*, 164–7; Hilary Land, 'Eleanor Rathbone and the economy of the family', in Smith (ed.), *British Feminism*, 104–23.

13. Virginia Woolf, *A Room of One's Own* (London, 1928); Holtby, *Women and a Changing Civilization*, 1–7.

14. Cicely Hamilton, 'The Backwash of Feminism', *Time and Tide* (8 Sept. 1922).

15. See Denise Riley, *Am I that Name? Feminism and the Category of 'Women' in History* (London, 1988).
16. Barbara Caine, *Victorian Feminists* (Oxford, 1992), 230–8.
17. Margaret Cole (1893–1980), *Marriage, Past and Present* (London, 1938), cited in Dyhouse, *Feminism and the Family*, 182. See also Margaret Cole, *Growing Up into Revolution* (London, 1949).
18. See e.g. 'The Solicitation Laws', *The Woman's Leader* (30 May 1924), 145; 'The Report of the Street Offences Committee', *The Woman's Leader* (25 Jan. 1929), 396.
19. Barbara Brookes, 'The Illegal Operation: Abortion, 1919–1939', in the London Feminist History Group, *The Sexual Dynamics of History* (London, 1983), 165–76.
20. Maude Royden, *Sex and Commonsense* (London, 1922); Dora Russell, *Hypatia: Or Women and Knowledge* (London, 1925).
21. 'Women in Council', *The Woman's Leader* (4 Mar. 1921), 84.
22. 'The Second Front', *The Woman's Leader* (12 May 1920), 125.
23. See esp. the collection of essays, Margaret Randolph Higonnet *et al.* (eds.), *Behind the Lines: Gender and Two World Wars* (New Haven, 1987); Sandra Gilbert, 'Soldier's Hearts: Literary Men, Literary Women, and the Great War', *Signs*, 8 (1983); and Kent, 'Gender Reconstruction'.
24. See e.g. David Mitchell, *Women on the Warpath* (London, 1965); and Arthur Marwick, *Women at War, 1914–18* (London, 1977), cf. Gail Braybon, *Women Workers in the First World War* (London, 1981).
25. Sylvia Pankhurst, *The Homefront* (London, 1932; repr. London, 1985), 38.
26. Martin Pugh, *Women's Movement*, 7–9.
27. See Braybon, *Women Workers*; Pugh, *Women's Movement*, 25–9.
28. Lady Gertrude Mary Denman (1884–1954), see Gervas Huxley, *Lady Denman GBE, 1884–1954* (London, 1961).
29. See Carol Twinch, *Women on the Land* (Worcester, 1990).
30. Pugh, *Women's Movement*, 13.
31. Vera Brittain (1893–1970), *Testament of Youth* (London, 1933; repr. 1978), 103–4; see also Hilary Bailey, *Vera Brittain* (Harmondsworth, 1987).
32. See esp. the collection of essays, Higonnet *et al.*, *Behind the Lines*.
33. See Elaine Showalter, *The Female Malady* (London, 1987), and Eric Leed, *No Man's Land: Combat and Identity in World War I* (Cambridge, 1979).
34. See Sandra Gilbert, 'Soldier's Hearts'.
35. Ibid.
36. Braybon, *Women Workers*, 2–21; Pugh, *Women's Movement*, 6–34.
37. Pugh, *Women's Movement*, 72–90; Kent 'Gender Reconstruction'.
38. 'A New Attitude', *Time and Tide* (15 June 1923), 609.
39. Jane Lewis, *Women in England, 1870–1950* (Brighton, 1984), 3–7.

40. See Martin Pugh, 'The Cult of Domesticity in the 1930s', in id., *Women and the Women's Movement*, 209–34.
41. Dyhouse, *Feminism and the Family*, 104–6; the treatment of this theme in women's fiction is discussed at some length in Nicola Beauman, *A Very Great Profession: The Woman's Novel, 1914–39* (London, 1983).
42. Gorham, 'Vera Brittain and Inter-War Feminism'.
43. 'Women in Council', *The Woman's Leader* (4 Mar. 1921), 84.
44. Hamilton, 'Backwash of Feminism', 858. Ray Strachey (1887–1940), see Barbara Strachey, *Remarkable Relations: The Story of the Pearsall Smith Family*, (London, 1980) and Harrison, *Prudent Revolutionaries*, 152–83.
45. Lady Rhondda, 'At the Half-Way House', *Time and Tide* (21 Jan. 1921), 54.
46. Ibid.
47. Alberti, *Beyond Suffrage*, 74.
48. National Union of Societies for Equal Citizenship, Annual Report (1919), 14–17.
49. Alberti, *Beyond Suffrage*, 91–2.
50. 'The New Group', *Time and Tide* (25 Feb. 1921), 176.
51. Harold Cox, 'Birth Control and Women's Liberty', *The Woman's Leader* (22 Apr. 1921), 182.
52. Dora Russell, *The Tamarisk Tree* (London, 1985), i. 176.
53. Janet Chance (1885–1953), *The Cost of English Morals* (London, 1931), 41–3.
54. Ibid.
55. Eva Hubback (1886–1949); for a very different view of Hubback, see Harrison, *Prudent Revolutionaries*, 273–300.
56. 'Final Agenda, NUSEC Annual Council Meeting, 1931', NUSEC Papers, Fawcett Library.
57. Report of the council meeting of NUSEC for 1929, published as 'Equal Citizenship', *The Woman's Leader* (15 Mar. 1929), 44–5.
58. Eleanor Rathbone (1872–1946) was an MP, representing the Combined English universities, from 1929 until her death. Her major book, *The Disinherited Family* (London, 1924) expressed her views on the need for family endowment—a measure which she saw come into effect with the Family Allowances Bill of 1945. See Mary Stocks, *Eleanor Rathbone: A Biography* (London, 1949) and Harrison, *Prudent Revolutionaries*, 99–124.
59. 'What is Feminism?', *The Woman's Leader* (17 July 1925), 195.
60. Eleanor Rathbone, 'The Old Feminism and the New', Presidential Address at the Annual Meeting of NUSEC, 11 March 1925, in Eleanor Rathbone, *Milestones* (Liverpool, 1929), 29.
61. Lady Rhondda (Margaret Haig Thomas) (1883–1958), see Lady Rhondda, *This Was My World* (London, 1933); Winnifred Holtby (1898–1935), see Vera Brittain, *Testament of Friendship: The Story of Winnifred Holtby* (London, 1980).

62. 'The "New Feminism"', *Time and Tide* (5 Mar. 1926), 220.
63. 'Miss Rathbone', *Time and Tide* (12 Mar. 1926), 243.
64. See also Joan Scott, 'Deconstructing Equality-versus-Difference: Or the Uses of Post Structuralist Theory for Feminism', *Feminist Studies*, 14 (1988).
65. Vera Brittain, 'Woman's Place, no. IV: The Passing of the Married Woman's Handicaps', *Time and Tide* (25 Nov. 1927), 1054.
66. The best discussion of this question is provided by Dyhouse in her *Feminism and the Family*; but see also Beauman, *A Very Great Profession*, for a discussion of the ways in which marriage and independence were dealt with in women's novels.
67. 'Making History', *The Woman's Leader* (1 Apr. 1927). As was so often the case, the actual history of feminism expounded in the 1920s was quite incorrect—thus this article goes on to say: 'It is to the everlasting credit of our honoured leader, Dame Millicent Garrett Fawcett, that she came down on the right side and gave her support as a young suffragist to Mrs Butler, realizing that the degradation of women implicit in the State regulation of vice was gnawing at the core of the woman's movement.'
68. Eleanor Rathbone, 'Apologia', in id., *Milestones*, 33.
69. Rhondda, *This Was My World*, 299.
70. Winnifred Holtby, 'Feminism Divided', *Time and Tide* (6 August 1926), 714.
71. Rathbone, *Milestones*, 2. For recent discussions of Rathbone and the question of feminism and welfare, see Jane Lewis, 'Feminism and Welfare', in Juliet Mitchell and Ann Oakley (eds.), *What is Feminism?* (London, 1986), 88–94 and Hilary Land, 'Eleanor Rathbone and the economy of the family', in Smith (ed.), *British Feminism*, 104–23.
72. Ray Strachey (ed.), *Our Freedom and its Results* (London, 1936), 123.
73. See e.g. Vera Brittain, 'Opportunity and Importunity', *Time and Tide* (1 Aug. 1924), 737; 'The Civil Service and the Sex Disqualification (Removal) Act', *Time and Tide* (17 Aug. 1928), 825.
74. First Annual report of the Open Door Council, 5 May 1926 to 4 Apr. 1927, Fawcett Library.
75. Ibid.
76. Pugh, *Women's Movement*, 93.
77. 'Statement by the Eleven Resigning Officers and Members of the NUSEC Executive Committee', *The Woman's Leader* (11 Mar. 1927), 38.
78. Eleanor Rathbone, 'The Economic Man and the Equalitarian Woman', *The Woman's Leader* (18 Mar. 1927), 45–6.
79. 'The Message of Our Conference', *The Vote* (19 Apr. 1929), 124.
80. Cicely Hamilton, 'The Return to Femininity', *Time and Tide* (12 Aug. 1927), 737.
81. Riley, *Am I that Name?*, 67–98.
82. Anne Phillips, *Engendering Democracy* (Cambridge, 1991), 60–91; Carole Pateman, *The Sexual Contract* (Oxford, 1988).

83. Eleanor Rathbone, 'Retrospect and Prospect', in id. *Milestones*, 12.
84. Ibid. 13–14.
85. 'The Weekly Crowd', *Time and Tide* (12 Mar. 1926), 243.
86. Cicely Hamilton, 'The Common Sense Citizen', *Time and Tide* (6 May 1921), 421–2; (26 May 1921), 469–70; (3 June 1921), 521–2; (17 June 1921), 569–70.
87. Winnifred Holtby, 'Feminism divided', *Time and Tide* (6 Aug. 1921), 715.
88. 'The Woman Voter', *Time and Tide* (30 Nov. 1923), 1191–2.
89. 'Dare to be Free', *The Vote*, 30 (19 Apr. 1929).
90. Pugh, *Women's Movement*, 50.
91. See the private memo explaining the 'Proposed Lines of Expansion for the NUSEC', Dec. 1928, NUSEC Papers, B3/1, Fawcett Library. See also 'Townswomen's Guilds', *The Woman's Leader* (6 Sept. 1929), 235.
92. Ibid.
93. 'The Townswoman', *The Woman's Leader* (16 Aug. 1929), 218.
94. Pugh, *Women's Movement*, 100–2.
95. 'The Sex Disqualification (Removal) Bill', *Time and Tide* (26 May 1922), 491–2.
96. Oxford did choose, granting women admission to degrees in 1920; Cambridge, however, held out until 1948.
97. 'This Session's Work from the Feminist Standpoint', *Time and Tide* (14 Aug. 1925), 787–8.
98. Smith, 'British Feminism in the 1920s', in id. (ed.), *British Feminism*, 51–2.
99. Alberti, *Beyond Suffrage*, 96.
100. Pugh, *Women's Movement*, 244.
101. Ibid. 172.
102. Ibid. 126–8.
103. Lady Rhondda, 'The Woman Voter', *Time and Tide* (30 Nov. 1923), 1193.
104. Pugh, *Women's Movement*, 128–9.
105. Marion Phillips (1881–1932), see Lucy Middleton (ed.), *Women in the Labour Movement* (London, 1977); Ethel Snowden (1880–1951); Mary MacArthur (Arabella) Susan Lawrence (1871–1947), see Harrison, *Prudent Revolutionaries*.
106. Russell, *Tamarisk Tree*, 172.
107. 'The Trade Unions Grow Up', *Time and Tide* (16 Sept. 1927), 816. 'Party Women and New Voters', *Time and Tide*, 15 May.
108. Pugh, Women's Movement, 125–36.
109. 'The Disinherited Family', *The Woman's Leader* (28 March 1924).
110. 'Not a Feminist Tract', *The Woman's Leader* (10 Jan. 1930), 383.
111. Elisabeth Woodbridge, 'Speaking for Women', *The Yale Review*, 19 (1930), 628.

112. Extract from Strachey quoted in *The Diary of Virginia Woolf*, v, *1936–41*, ed. Anne Olivier Bell (London, 1984), 147.
113. See e.g. Virginia Middleton, '*Three Guineas*: Subversion and Survival in the Professions', *Twentieth Century Literature*, 28 (1982), 407.
114. Woolf, *Three Guineas, passim*.
115. Ibid. 184.
116. Philippa Strachey (1872–1968) was the Secretary of the London National Society for Women's Service; see Harrison, *Prudent Revolutionaries*, 151–83.
117. Woolf, *Diary*, v. 147.
118. Rebecca West, 'Equal Pay for Men and Women Teachers', *Time and Tide* (9 Feb. 1923), 142.
119. Woolf, *A Room of One's Own*, 37.
120. Ibid. Eleanor Rathbone also used a mirror image to explain why men objected to women's economic independence, preferring to see themselves as self-sacrificing in the ways they provided for wives and children; Rathbone, *The Disinherited Family*, 273.
121. See Woolf, *A Room of One's Own*, 37.
122. Rebecca West, 'On A Form of Nagging', *Time and Tide* (31 Oct. 1923), 1052–3. This article also discussed the different values placed on men's everyday pursuits, as compared with those of women—and on the ways in which male nagging served to disguise from women the values which men were attempting to impose on them.
123. Rathbone, *The Disinherited Family*, 81.
124. Anne Martin, 'Woman's Inferiority Complex' (from the *New Republic*), *Time and Tide* (4 Aug. 1922), 734; see also Holtby, *Women and a Changing Civilization*, 97–104.
125. Eleanor Rathbone, 'The "New Feminism" of the NUSEC', *Time and Tide* (12 Mar. 1926), 254.
126. Alison Oram, 'The Spinster in Inter-War Feminist Discourses', *Women's History Review*, 1 (1992), 413–34.
127. Ibid. 422.
128. Holtby, 'Are Spinsters Frustrated', in id., *Women and a Changing Civilization*, 125–32.
129. Holtby, 'Feminism Divided', 714.
130. Ibid.
131. 'What is Feminism', *The Woman's Leader* (23 Mar. 1928). 55.
132. I. B. O'Malley, 'What is Feminism', *The Woman's Leader* (23 Mar. 1928), 59.
133. Winnifred Holtby, *Virginia Woolf. A Critical Memoir* (Chicago, 1978), 161–80.
134. See esp. Mary Sargent Florence, Catherine Marshall, and C. K. Ogden, in Margaret Kamester and Jo Vellacot (eds.), *Militarism versus Feminism: Writings on Women and War* (London, 1987).

135. See e.g. Vera Brittain, 'Feminism at Geneva', *Time and Tide* (25 Jan. 1929), 92.
136. See e.g. 'League of Nations: Traffic in Women Report', *The Woman's Leader* (27 Jan. 1927), 411.
137. Ibid.
138. Brittain, 'Feminism at Geneva', 92.
139. Ibid.
140. 'The Women's Programme', *The Woman's Leader* (22 Mar. 1919), 51.
141. Eleanor Rathbone, 'The Women of India', *The Woman's Leader* (20 June 1930), 151.
142. Antoinette M. Burton, 'The White Woman's Burden: British Feminists and "The Indian Woman"', in Nupur Chaudhuri and Margaret Strobel (eds.), *Western Women and Imperialism* (Bloomington, Ind., 1992), 137–57.
143. Katharine Mayo, *Mother India* (London, 1927), esp. 60–8.
144. Barbara Ramusack, 'Cultural Missionaries, Maternal Imperialists, Feminist Allies: British Women Activists in India, 1865–1945', in Chaudhuri and Strobel (eds.) *Western Women and Imperialism*, 119–36.
145. Ibid. 129; see also Stocks, *Rathbone*.
146. Ramusack, 'Cultural Missionaries', 133.
147. 'Our Programme', *The Woman's Leader* (6 Apr. 1930), 26.
148. See e.g. 'Women Slaves in the British Empire', report of a conference held on 12 February 1930, *The Woman's Leader* (21 Feb. 1930), 22.

## Chapter 6

1. See e.g. Sheila Rowbotham, 'Women's Liberation and the New Politics' (1969), in Michelene Wandor (ed.), The *Body Politic: Writings from the Women's Liberation Movement in Britain 1969–1972* (London, 1972), 16.
2. David Doughan, *Lobbying for Equality: British Feminism, 1918–1968* (London, 1980).
3. Olive Banks, *The Politics of British Feminism, 1918–1970* (Aldershot, 1993), 21–2.
4. Six Point Group, Annual Report, 1945–1946, 1, Papers of the Six Point Group, Fawcett Library.
5. Banks, *Politics of British Feminism*, 21–2.
6. Birmingham Feminist History Group, 'Feminism as Femininity: The Nineteen-Fifties', *Feminist Review*, 3 (1979), 48.
7. Dale Spender, *There's Always Been a Women's Movement This Century* (London, 1984).
8. Martin Pugh, *Women and the Women's Movement in Britain, 1914–1959* (London, 1992), 284. See also Alan Sinfield, 'What happened to femi-

nism', in id., *Literature, Politics, and Culture in Postwar Britain* (Oxford, 1989), 203–7.

9. See e.g. Judith Hubback, *Wives Who Went to College* (London, 1957), 1–12.
10. Jane Lewis, *Women In Britain since 1945*, Institute of Contemporary British History (Oxford, 1992), 30–9.
11. Cynthia Harrison, *On Account of Sex: The Politics of Women's Issues, 1945–1968* (Berkeley, 1988), pp. x–xii.
12. Arthur Marwick, *Women at War, 1914–18* (London, 1977); see also Pugh, *Women's Movement*, 271–5.
13. Gail Braybon and Penny Summerfield, *Out of the Cage: Women's Experience in Two World Wars* (London, 1987); Penny Summerfield, 'Women, War and Social Change: Women in Britain in World War II', in Arthur Marwick (ed.), *Total War and Social Change* (New York, 1988), 95–118; Harold L. Smith, 'The Effect of the War on the Status of Women', in id. (ed.), *War and Social Change: British Society in the Second World War* (Manchester, 1986), 209–29.
14. Summerfield, 'Women, War and Social Change', 98–101.
15. Denise Riley, 'Some Peculiarities of Social Policy Concerning Women in Wartime and Postwar Britain', in Margaret Randolph Higgonet *et al.* (eds.), *Behind the Lines: Gender and the Two World Wars* (New Haven, 1987), 260–71, esp. 261.
16. Marilyn Lake, 'Female Desires: The Meaning of World War Two', *Australian Historical Studies*, 24 (1990), 267–84.
17. Braybon and Summerfield, *Out of the Cage*, 159–60.
18. Penny Summerfield and Nicole Crocket, 'You Weren't Taught that with the Welding: Lessons in Sexuality in the Second World War', *Women's History Review*, 1 (1992), 435–54.
19. But see Harold L. Smith, 'The Womanpower Problem in Britain during the Second World War', *Historical Journal*, 27 (1984).
20. Leila J. Rupp, *Mobilising Women for War: German and American Propaganda* (Princeton, 1978).
21. Braybon and Summerfield, *Out of the Cage*, 230–6.
22. Braybon and Summerfield, *Out of the Cage*, 237–9; Riley, 'Peculiarities of Social Policy', 261–3.
23. Pugh, *Women's Movement*, 275–9.
24. Banks, *Politics of British Feminism*, 18–20.
25. Pugh, *Women's Movement*, 275–9; see the Six Point Group Annual Reports for 1940–1945 for a year-by-year summary of their activities, Six Point Group Papers, Fawcett Library.
26. Harold L. Smith, 'The Issue of "Equal Pay for Equal Work" in Great Britain during World War II', *The Journal of Modern History*, 53 (1981), 656–7; Pugh, *Women's Movement*, 279–80.
27. Smith, 'The Womanpower Problem', 928–31.
28. Ibid.

29. Pugh, *Women's Movement*, 278.

30. See pp. 192–4.

31. Smith, 'The Issue of "Equal Pay"', 657–9.

32. For details of women's wages, see the Report of the Conference on Women's Work and Wages held at Caxton Hall, 7 October 1942, by the Fabian Women's Group, in Fabian Women's Group papers, H 3611, Nuffield College.

33. Smith, 'The Issue of "Equal Pay"', *passim*.

34. Pugh, *Women's Movement*, 279.

35. Six Point Group, Annual Report (1943–4), 14–15.

36. Pugh, *Women's Movement*, 299.

37. Banks, *Politics of British Feminism*, 22.

38. Pamela Brookes, *Women at Westminster: An Account of Women in the British Parliament, 1918–1966* (London, 1967), 137–8.

39. Banks, *Politics of British Feminism*, 21–2.

40. Six Point Group Annual Report (1945–6), 1.

41. Ibid.

42. Dora Russell, *The Tamarisk Tree*, iii, *Challenge to the Cold War* (London, 1985), 113–17.

43. See also Mary Stott, *Before I Go* (London, 1985), 25–32.

44. Hubback, *Wives Who Went to College*, 82.

45. Ibid. 79.

46. Olwen Campbell (ed.), *The Feminine Point of View* (London, 1952), 14.

47. Ibid. 30–2.

48. Six Point Group, Report of Honorary Secretary given at the AGM on 16 Oct. 1952, Fawcett Library.

49. Six Point Group, Minutes of the Executive Committee Meeting of 7 July 1980, in Papers of Hazel Hunkins-Hallinan, Fawcett Library.

50. Six Point Group, Minutes of the Executive Committee Meeting of 7 July 1980, in Papers of Hazel Hunkins-Hallinan, Fawcett Library.

51. Mary Holland, 'The Feminine Condition', *The Spectator* (23 Oct. 1965), 553.

52. Alva Myrdal, *Nation and Family: The Swedish Experiment in Democratic Family and Population Policy* (New York, 1941), cited in Jane Lewis, 'Myrdal, Klein, *Women's Two Roles* and Postwar Feminism, 1945–1960', in Harold L. Smith (ed.), *British Feminism in the Twentieth Century* (Aldershot, 1990), 170.

53. Jane Lewis, *Women In Britain since 1945: Women, Family, Work and the State in the Post-War Years* (Oxford, 1992), 20–2.

54. Ibid.

55. Ibid. 16–18.

56. Ibid. 17.

57. Jane Lewis, *The Politics of Motherhood* (London, 1980).

58. Lewis, *Women in Britain*, 16–25.

59. Sinfield, *Literature, Politics and Culture*, 207.

60. Marjorie Ferguson, *Forever Feminine: Women's Magazines and the Cult of Femininity* (London, 1983), 54.
61. John Bowlby, *Maternal Care and Maternal Health*, World Health Organization (Geneva, 1951).
62. Margaret Mead, 'Some Theoretical Considerations on the Problem of Mother–Child Separation', *American Journal of Ortho-Psychiatry*, 24 (1954), 471–83.
63. Barbara Wootton, 'Theories of the Effects of Maternal Separation or Deprivation', in id., *Social Science and Social Pathology* (London, 1959), 154–5.
64. Sinfield, *Literature, Politics and Culture.*
65. Ibid.; see also Lewis, *Women In Britain*, 19–20.
66. Alva Myrdal and Viola Klein, *Women's Two Roles: Home and Work* (London, 1956), p. ix.
67. Lewis, 'Myrdal, Klein, *Women's Two Roles*', 167.
68. Myrdal and Klein, *Women's Two Roles*, p. xiii.
69. Viola Klein, *The Feminine Character: history of an ideology* (London, 1946; repr. London, 1975). For a discussion of their relationship, see Lewis, 'Myrdal, Klein', *passim.*
70. Myrdal and Klein, *Women's Two Roles*, 6.
71. Ibid. 8.
72. Ibid. 10–15.
73. Ibid. 24.
74. Ibid. 27.
75. Ibid. 128.
76. Ibid. 51–74.
77. This was the title of a talk given on the BBC in 1955. See Florida Scott-Maxwell, 'The Feminine Paradox', *The Listener* (22 Sept. 1955), 464–7.
78. Roger Fulford, *Votes for Women* (London, 1957).
79. Mary Stocks, 'The Suffrage Movement: Triumph and tragedy', *Manchester Guardian* (12 Apr. 1957), 10–11.
80. Barbara Bliss, 'Militancy: The Insurrection that Failed', *Contemporary Review*, 201 (1962), 309; see also Anon., 'Women on the War Path', *The Times Literary Supplement* (12 Apr. 1957).
81. See Barbara Wootton, *In a World I Never Made: Autobiographical Reflections* (London, 1967), 149.
82. Margaret Cole, 'The Woman's Vote: What has it Achieved?', 38 *Political Quarterly* (1962), 74.
83. Lena Jeger MP, 'The Woman's Vote: Has it Made Any Difference?', *New Statesman* (16 Feb. 1968), 198–9.
84. Wootton, *In a World I Never Made*, 155–7.
85. This 'lively-to-a-fault series of girls only arguments', was discussed by John Holmstrom in 'New Woman', *The Listener* (1 Oct. 1964), 509–10.
86. Hannah Gavron, *The Captive Wife: Conflicts of Housebound Mothers* (London, 1966).

87. Ibid. 12.
88. Ann Oakley, 'New Introduction' to Hannah Gavron, *The Captive Wife* (London, 1983), pp. ix–xi.
89. Gavron, Captive *Wife*, 144.
90. Angela Neustater, *Hyenas in Petticoats: A Look at Twenty Years of Feminism* (Harmondsworth, 1989), 5.
91. See e.g. Marghanita Laski, 'The Case for Abortion', *New Statesman* (18 Mar. 1966): 'What Women Want; *Economist* (6 July 1968), 12: Woman's place in the world half a century after the vote,' *The Listener* (4 Apr. 1968), 425–9.
92. Juliet Mitchell, 'Women: the Longest Revolution', *New Left Review* (Nov./Dec., 1966), 2–65.

# Afterword

1. Sheila Rowbotham, *The Past is Before Us: Feminism in Action Since the 1960s* (London, 1989), 248.
2. Angela Neustatter, *Hyenas in Petticoats: A Look at Twenty Years of Feminism* (Harmondsworth, 1989), 23.
3. 'Women's liberation', *Red Rag*, 1 (1972) 2.
4. The first Four Demands are reprinted in Michelene Wandor (ed.), *Once a Feminist: Stories of a Generation* (London, 1990), 242–3.
5. Lynne Segal, *Is the Future Female?: Troubled Thoughts on Contemporary Feminism* (London, 1987), 57.
6. Rosalind Delmar argued a different case, seeing equal pay, equal education and job opportunity, and 24-hour day nurseries as 'three historic demands developed within socialist women's movements', to which had been added one new demand: free abortion and contraception; Ros Delmar, 'Oppressed Politics', *Red Rag*, 2 (1973) 8–9.
7. That History Workshop that was so closely connected with women's liberation also serves to illustrate the central importance of history in the British left in the 1960s. Although there were left-wing and Marxist literary and political theorists, anthropologists, and sociologists in the 1960s, no other discipline established an organization comparable to History Workshop in terms of its capacity to connect academic scholarship with popular beliefs and ideas or with local and national political developments.
8. See interview with Juliet Mitchell in Wandor (ed.), *Once a Feminist*, 110–11; Sally Alexander, *Becoming a Woman and Other Essays in the 19th and 20th Century Feminist History* (Virago, 1994), 233–4; Carolyn Steedman, 'Raymond Williams and History', Raymond Williams Memorial Lecture, Summer, 1993.
9. Sheila Rowbotham, *Hidden from History* (London, 1973).
10. Juliet Mitchell, *Women's Estate* (Harmondsworth, 1971), 76–83.

11. Ibid. 80–1.
12. 'Miss World', in Michelene Wandor (ed.), *The Body Politic: Writings from the Women's Liberation Movement in Britain, 1969–1972* (London, 1972), 254.
13. See e.g. the Belsize Women's Group, 'Nine Years Together', in Marsha Rowe (ed.), *Spare Rib Reader* (Harmondsworth, 1982), 563.
14. See e.g. Mitchell, *Woman's Estate*, 12.
15. 'What Emily Did', *Spare Rib*, 1 (1972), 12–14.
16. See e.g. Sheila Rowbotham, 'A Serious Proposal to the Ladies', *Spare Rib*, 2 (1972), 8.
17. See e.g. feature 'Decades', including interviews of Hazel Hunkins-Hallinan by Amanda Sebestyen, *Spare Rib*, 100 (1980), 7–12.
18. Sheila Rowbotham, 'Women's Liberation and the New Politics', (1969), in Wandor (ed.), *The Body Politic*, 16.
19. Mitchell, *Women's Estate*, 19–20.
20. Ibid. 50–3.
21. Ibid. 36.
22. Rowbotham, *Hidden from History*, 20–5.
23. Rowbotham, 'Women's Liberation', 15.
24. Rowbotham, *Hidden from History*, 77–89.
25. Ibid. The bibliography refers to the collection of essays Strachey edited, *Our Freedom and its Results* (London, 1936), but not to *The Cause*.
26. Rowbotham, *The Past is Before Us*.
27. Wandor (ed.), *Once a Feminist*, 8.
28. Rosalind Delmar, 'What is Feminism?' in Wandor (ed.), *The Body Politic*, 116–23.
29. See Rosalind Delmar, 'Introduction', in Shulamith Firestone, *The Dialectic of Sex* (London, 1979), 2.
30. See Juliet Mitchell, in Wandor, *Once a Feminist*, 107–10; Michelene Wandor, 'Where to next?' *Spare Rib*, 105 (1981), 40–1.
31. See Segal, *Is the Future Female?*, 43–54; Rowbotham, *The Past is Before Us*; Catherine Hall, in Wandor (ed.), *Once a Feminist*, 171–80.
32. See e.g. Amanda Sebestyen, *'68, '78 '88: From Women's Liberation to Feminism* (Bridport, Dorset, 1989).
33. Rowbotham. 'The Beginning of Women's Liberation in Britain', repr. in Wandor (ed.), *Once a Feminist*, 14–27; Mitchell, *Woman's Estate*, 84–7.
34. Mitchell, *Women's Estate*, 86.
35. Segal, *Is the Future Female?*, 43–55.
36. See e.g. Gail Philpott, 'Consciousness Raising: Back to Basics', *Spare Rib*, 92 (1980), repr. in Rowe (ed.), *Spare Rib Reader*, 285–6.
37. Sheila Jeffreys, 'Therapy: Reform or Revolution', *Spare Rib*, 96 (1978), 21.
38. Sheila Rowbotham, in Wandor (ed.), *Once a Feminist*, 23.
39. See e.g., Debbie Cameron, 'Telling it Like it Wasn't: How Radical Feminism became History', *Trouble and Strife*, 27 (1993), 11–15.

40. Amanda Sebestyen, *Feminist Practices*, (London, 1980), 22.
41. See e.g. 'Lesbian Radical Feminism: The Only Radical Feminism?', *Trouble and Strife*, 3 (1983), 6–7.
42. 'Straight Women', *Women's Liberation Newsletter*, 63 (1974).
43. Segal, *Is the Future Female?*, 55; Catherine Hall, in Wandor (ed.), *Once a Feminist*, 173.
44. Hazel Carby, 'White Woman Listen! Black Feminism and the Boundaries of Sisterhood', in Centre for Contemporary Studies, *The Empire Strikes Back: Race and Racism in 70s Britain* (London, 1982).
45. Ibid. 214.
46. Ibid. 219.
47. Ibid. 228–32.
48. Letter from Amina Mama, *Feminist Review*, 14 (1984), 100–1.
49. See *Feminist Review*, 17 (1984), ed. Valerie Amos, Gail Lewis, Amina Mama and Pratibha Parma.
50. See *Spare Rib*, 101 and 107 (1982), and 123 and 132 (1984).
51. See e.g. 'Women Speak Out Against Zionism', *Spare Rib*, 121 (1984); correspondence entitled 'About Anti-Semitism', *Spare Rib*, 123 (1984); Dena Attar, 'An Open Letter on Anti-Semitism and Racism', *Trouble and Strife*, Winter (1983).
52. See also Michelle Barrett and Mary McIntosh, 'Ethnocentrism and Socialist-Feminist Theory', *Feminist Review*, 15 (1985), 23–48.
53. Maxine Molyneux discusses this process in 'Where to next?', *Spare Rib*, 105 (1982), 40.
54. The most influential statement of this position is that of Denise Riley in id., *Am I that Name?*, *passim*.
55. 'Editorial', *m/f*, 2 (1978), 2–3; see also Parveen Adams, 'The Subject of Feminism', *m/f*, 2 (1978), 43–61.
56. This view was first put by Juliet Mitchell in id., *Psychoanalysis and Feminism* (London, 1974).

# Select Bibliography

## Unpublished Papers

Autograph Collection of Letters, Fawcett Library, City of London Polytechnic, London.

Letters and papers of Mrs J. R. Macdonald, iii, 'The Licensing Bills of 1901–2 and the Employment of Barmaids', British Library of Political and Economic Science.

Papers of the National Union of Women's Suffrage Societies (NUWSS), Manchester Public Library.

Six Point Group Papers, Fawcett Library.

The Bodichon Papers, Girton College Archives, Cambridge.

The Butler Papers, Fawcett Library, City of London Polytechnic, London.

The Cobbe Papers, Huntington Library, Los Angeles.

The Davies Papers, Girton College Archives, Cambridge.

The Fawcett Papers, Fawcett Library, City of London Polytechnic, London.

The Letters of Mrs Elizabeth Wolstenholme Elmy, British Museum, Add Mss 47449–47451.

The Papers of Hazel Hunkins-Hallinan, Fawcett Library.

The Papers of Teresa Billington-Greig, Fawcett Library.

The Papers of the National Union of Women's Suffrage Societies, Fawcett Library.

The Papers of the Open Door Council, Fawcett Library.

The Papers of the Status of Women Committee, Fawcett Library.

Women's Co-operative Guild Papers, British Library of Political and Economic Science, Coll. Misc 268 1/24.

## Newspapers and Journals

*Feminist Review*
*The Monthly Repository*
*The Englishwoman's Journal*
*Journal of the Vigilance Association for the Defence of Personal Rights*
*Jus Suffragii*
*Spare Rib*
*The Freewoman*
*The Vote*
*The Woman's Leader*
*Time and Tide*

*Woman's Signal*
*Women's Liberation Newsletter*
*Women's Suffrage Journal*
*m/f*
*Trouble and Strife*
*Women's Liberation Newsletter*
*Outwrite*
*Feminist Review*
*Shafts*

## Books and Articles

ADAMS, PARVEEN, 'The Subject of Feminism', *m/f*, 2 (1978), 43–61.
ALBERTI, JOHANNA, *Beyond Suffrage: Feminists in War and Peace, 1914–1928* (London, 1989).
ALEXANDER, SALLY, *Women's Work in Nineteenth Century London: A Study of the Years 1820–1850* (London, 1983).
—— (ed.), *Fabian Women's Tracts* (London, 1988).
—— *Becoming a Woman and Other Essays in the 19th and 20th Century Feminist History* (London, 1994).
ANG, IEN, 'I'm a Feminist but . . . : "Other" Women and Postnational Feminism', in Barbara Caine and Rosemary Pringle (eds.), *Transitions: New Australian Feminisms* (Sydney, 1995).
ARMSTRONG, NANCY, *Desire and Domestic Fiction: A Political History of the Novel* (New York, 1987).
BANKS, J. A., and BANKS, OLIVE, *Feminism and Family Planning* (Liverpool, 1964).
BANKS, OLIVE, *Faces of Feminism: A Study of Feminism as a Social Movement* (Oxford, 1981).
—— *Becoming a Feminist: The Social Origins of Feminism* (Brighton, 1986).
—— *The Politics of British Feminism, 1918–1970* (Aldershot, 1993).
BARRETT, MICHELLE, and MCINTOSH, MARY, 'Ethnocentrism and Socialist-Feminist Theory', *Feminist Review*, 15 (1985).
BASCH, FRANCOISE, *Relative Creatures: Victorian Women in Society and the Novel, 1837–67* (London, 1974).
BASHFORD, ALISON, 'Edwardian Feminists and the Venereal Disease Debate in England', in Barbara Caine (ed.), *The Woman Question in England and Australia* (Sydney, 1995).
BATTERSBY, CHRISTINE, *Gender and Genius* (London, 1990).
BAUER, CAROL, and RITT, LAWRENCE (eds.), *Free and Ennobled: Source Readings in the Development of Victorian Feminism* (Oxford, 1979).
BEAUMAN, NICOLA, *A Very Great Profession: The Woman's Novel, 1914–39* (London, 1983).

BENNETT, DAPHNE, *Emily Davies and the Emancipation of Women* (London, 1989).

BERG, MAXINE, *The Age of Manufactures, 1700–1820* (London, 1985).

BILLINGTON, LOUIS, and BILLINGTON, ROSAMUND, '"A Burning Zeal for Righteousness": Women in the British Anti-Slavery Movement, 1820–1860', in Jane Rendell (ed.), *Equal or Different: Women's Politics, 1800–1914* (Oxford, 1987).

BLACK, NAOMI, *Social Feminism* (Ithaca, NY, 1989).

BLACKBURN, HELEN, *Women's Suffrage: A Record of the Women's Suffrage Movement in the British Isles with Biographical Sketches of Miss Becker* (London, 1902; repr. New York, 1971).

BLACKBURN, HELEN, and VIGNE, NORA, *Women Under the Factory Acts* (London, 1903).

BLAND, LUCY, 'The Married Woman, the "New Woman", and the Feminist: Sexual Politics of the 1890s', in Jane Rendall (ed.), *Equal or Different: Women's Politics, 1800–1914* (Oxford, 1987).

—— *Banishing the Beast: English Feminism and Sexual Morality, 1885–1914* (London, 1995).

BODICHON, BARBARA LEIGH SMITH, *An American Diary, 1857–8* (London, 1972).

—— *Reasons, For and Against the Enfranchisement of Women* (London, 1872).

BOSCH, MINEKE, and KLOOSTERMAN, ANNEMARIE (eds.), *Politics and Friendship: Letters from the International Woman Suffrage Alliance, 1902–1942* (Columbus, Oh., 1990).

BOUCHERET, JESSIE, and BLACKBURN, HELEN, *The Condition of Women and the Factory Acts* (London, 1886).

BRADBROOK, MURIEL, *That Infidel Place: A Short History of Girton College* (London, 1969).

BRANDON, RUTH, *The New Women and the Old Men* (London, 1990).

BRAYBON, GAIL, *Women Workers in the First World War* (London, 1981).

—— and SUMMERFIELD, PENNY, *Out of the Cage: Women's Experience in Two World Wars* (London, 1987).

BRINDENTHAL, R. and KONNZ, C. (eds.), *Becoming Visible: Women in European History*, 2nd edn. (Boston, 1987).

BRITTAIN, VERA, *Testament of Youth* (London, 1933; repr. 1978).

BURMAN, SANDRA (ed.), *Fit Work for Women* (London, 1979).

BURNEY, FANNY, *The Wanderer* (London, 1988).

BURTON, ANTOINETTE, 'The White Woman's Burden: British Feminists and "The Indian Woman"' in Nupur Chaudhuri and Margaret Strobel (eds.), *Western Women and Imperialism: Complicity and Resistance* (Bloomington, Ind., 1992).

—— *Burdens of History: British Feminists, Indian Women and Imperial Culture, 1865–1915* (Chapel Hill, NC, 1994).

Select Bibliography

BUTLER, JOSEPHINE E., *The Education and Employment of Women* (London, 1868).

—— (ed.), *Woman's Work and Woman's Culture* (London, 1869).

—— *Some Thoughts on the Present Aspect of the Crusade against the State Regulation of Vice* (Liverpool, 1874).

—— 'Sursum Corda: Annual Address to the Ladies' National Association' (Liverpool, 1891).

—— *Recollections of George Butler* (Bristol, 1892).

—— *Personal Reminiscences of A Great Crusade* (London, 1896).

—— *The Native Races and the War* (London, 1900).

—— *An Auto-Biographical Memoir*, ed. George and Lucy Johnson (London, 1909).

—— et al., *Legislative Restrictions on the Industry of Women, Considered from the Women's Point of View* (London, n.d.).

BUTLER, MARILYN, *Romantics, Rebels and Reactionaries: English Literature and its Background, 1760–1830* (Oxford, 1981).

CAINE, BARBARA, 'John Stuart Mill and the English Women's Movement', 18 *Historical Studies* (1978).

—— 'Feminism and Political Economy in Victorian England—or John Stuart Mill, Henry Fawcett and Henry Sidgwick Ponder the "Woman Question"', in Peter Groenewegen (ed.), *Feminism and Political Economy in Victorian England* (Aldershot, 1994).

—— *Victorian Feminists* (Oxford, 1992).

—— 'Feminism and Ageing', *Australian Cultural History*, 8 (1995).

—— 'Women's Studies: Feminist Traditions and the problems of history', in Barbara Caine and Rosemary Pringle (eds.), *Transitions: New Australian Feminisms* (Sydney, 1995).

CAIRD, MONA, *The Daughters of Danaus* (London, 1894).

—— *The Morality of Marriage and Other Essays on the Status and Destiny of Women* (London, 1897).

CAMPBELL, OLWEN (ed.), *The Feminine Point of View* (London, 1952).

CARBY, HAZEL, 'White Woman Listen! Black Feminism and the Boundaries of Sisterhood', in Centre for Contemporary Cultural Studies, *The Empire Strikes Back: Race and Racism in 70s Britain* (London, 1982), 212–35.

CHANCE, JANET, *The Cost of English Morals* (London, 1931).

CHAUDURI, NUPUR, and STROBEL, MARGARET (eds.), *Western Women and Imperialism* (Bloomington, Ind., 1992).

COBBE, FRANCES POWER, 'What Shall we Do with our Old Maids?', *Fraser's Magazine*, 66 (1862), 594–605.

—— 'Women in Italy in 1862', *Macmillan's Magazine*, 6 (1862), 363–75.

—— 'Criminals, Idiots, Women and Minors', *Fraser's Magazine*, 77 (1868), 77–82.

—— *The Duties of Women* (London, 1881).

COLE, MARGARET, *Growing Up into Revolution* (London, 1949).

COLE, MARGARET, 'The Woman's Vote: What Has It Achieved?', *Political Quarterly*, 38 (1962).

COLLETTE, CHRISTINE, 'Socialism and Scandal: The Sexual Politics of the Early Labour Movement', *History Workshop Journal*, 23 (1987).

COLLEY, LINDA, *Britons: Forging the Nation, 1707–1837* (New Haven, 1992).

COTT, NANCY, *The Bonds of Womanhood. 'Woman's Sphere' in New England, 1780–1835* (New Haven, 1977).

—— *The Grounding of Modern Feminism* (New Haven, 1987).

CUTTING, ROSE MARIE, 'Defiant Women: The Growth of Feminism in Burney's Novels', *SEL* 17 (1977).

DAVID, DEIRDRE, *Intellectual Women and Victorian Patriarchy: Harriet Martineau, Elizabeth Barrett Browning, George Eliot* (London, 1987).

DAVIDOFF, LEONORE, and HALL, CATHERINE, *Family Fortunes: Men and Women of the English Middle Class, 1780–1850* (London, 1987).

DAVIES, EMILY, 'The Women's Suffrage Movement', reprinted from the Girton Review for the Lent and Easter Terms, 1905, by the Central Society for Women's Suffrage (London, n.d.), 3–5.

—— *The Higher Education of Women* (London, 1866; repr. London, 1988).

DAVIES, MARGARET LLEWELLYN, 'Why Working Women need the Vote', paper read at Southern Sectional conference of the Women's Co-operative Guild, London, 15 March 1897, in Co-operative Guild Papers, *Why Working Women Need the Vote*, four papers read by members of the Women's Co-op Guild at the Sectional Conferences (Kirby Lonsdale, Westmorland, 1897).

DAVIN, ANNA, 'Imperialism and Motherhood', *History Workshop*, 5 (1978).

DELMAR, ROSALIND, 'What is Feminism?', in Juliet Mitchell and Ann Oakley (eds.), *What is Feminism?* (London, 1986).

DOODY, ANNE, *Frances Burney: The Life in the Works* (New Brunswick, NJ, 1988).

DOUGHAN, DAVID, *Lobbying for Equality: British Feminism, 1918–1968* (London, 1980).

DYHOUSE, CAROL, *Feminism and the Family in England, 1880–1930* (Oxford, 1989).

EISENSTEIN, ZILLAH, *The Radical Future of Liberal Feminism* (Boston, 1986).

ELIOT, GEORGE, 'Margaret Fuller and Mary Wollstonecraft', *The Leader*, 13 October 1855, repr. in Thomas Pinny (ed.), *Essays of George Eliot* (London, 1968).

ELLIS, SARAH, *The Daughters of England* (London, 1844).

EPSTEIN, JULIA, *The Iron Pen: Frances Burney and the Politics of Women's Writing* (Madison, 1989).

ETHELMER, ELLIS, 'A Woman Emancipator: A Biographical Sketch', *Westminster Review*, 145 (1896).

—— 'Feminism', *Westminster Review*, 149 (1898).

FADERMAN, LILIAN, *Surpassing Love of Men* (London, 1980).

FAWCETT, MILLICENT GARRETT, 'The Future of Englishwomen: A Reply', *The Nineteenth Century*, 4 (1878), 347–57.

—— 'The Emancipation of Women', *Fortnightly Review*, NS 5 (1891), 677–8.

—— 'Mr Sidney Webb's Article on Women's Wages', *Economic Journal*, 2 (1892), 173–6.

—— 'The Woman Who Did', *Contemporary Review*, 23 (1898).

—— *Report on the Concentration Camps in South Africa by the Committee of Ladies appointed by the Secretary of State for War containing Reports on the Camps in Natal, the Orange River Colony and the Transvaal* (London, 1902).

—— *What I Remember* (London, 1925; repr. Westport, Conn., 1976).

FENWICK-MILLER, FLORENCE, *Harriet Martineau* (Boston, 1885).

FERGUSON, MARJORIE, *Forever Feminine: Women's Magazines and the Cult of Femininity* (London, 1983).

FERGUSON, MOIRA, *Subject to Others: British Women Writers and Colonial Slavery, 1670–1834* (New York, 1992).

FEURER, ROSEMARY, 'The Meaning of "Sisterhood": The British Women's Movement and Protective Legislation, 1870–1900', *Victorian Studies*, 31 (1988).

FIRESTONE, SHULAMITH, *The Dialectic of Sex* (London, 1979).

FLETCHER, SHEILA, *Feminists and Bureaucrats: A Study in the Development of Girls' Education in the Nineteenth Century* (Cambridge, 1980).

FLIEGELMAN, JAY, *Prodigals and Pilgrims: The American Revolution against Patriarchal Authority, 1750–1800* (Cambridge, 1982).

FORBES, GERALDINE, 'Medical Careers and Health Care for Indian Women: Patterns of Control', *Women's History Review*, 3 (1994), 515–30.

FORSTER, MARGARET, *Significant Sisters: The Grassroots of Active Feminism, 1830–1930* (Harmondsworth, 1986).

FRAISSE, GENEVIEVE, *Muse de la raison: La Democratie exclusive et la differences des sexes* (Aix-en-Provence, 1989).

—— and PERROT, MICHELLE (eds.), *A History of Women: Emerging Feminism from Revolution to World War* (Cambridge, Mass., 1993).

FREEMAN, JO, *The Tyranny of Structurelessness* (New York, 1972).

GATENS, MOIRA, *Feminism and Philosophy* (Oxford, 1991).

GAVRON, HANNAH, *The Captive Wife: Conflicts of Housebound Mothers* (London, 1966).

GEORGE, MARGARET, *One Woman's 'Situation': A Study of Mary Wollstonecraft* (Urbana, Ill., 1970).

GILBERT, SANDRA, 'Soldier's Hearts: Literary Men, Literary Women, and the Great War', *Signs*, 8 (1983).

GODWIN, WILLIAM, *Memoirs of the Author of The Rights of Women* (London, 1796), repr. in Mary Wollstonecraft and William Godwin, *A Short Residence in Sweden* and *Memoirs of the Author of the Rights of Women*, ed. Richard Holmes (Harmondsworth, 1787).

GODWIN, WILLIAM, (ed.), *The Posthumous Works of Mary Wollstonecraft Godwin* (London, 1798; repr. Clifton, 1972).

GRAND, SARAH, *The Heavenly Twins* (London, 1893).

—— 'The New Aspect of the Woman Question', *North American Review* (March 1894).

—— *The Beth Book* (London, 1897; repr. London, 1983).

—— *The Modern Man and Maid* (London, 1898).

GRIMKE, SARAH, *Letters on the Equality of Sexes, and the Condition of Women* (Boston, 1838).

GROENEWEGEN, PETER (ed.), *Feminism and Political Economy in Victorian England* (Aldershot, 1994).

HABERMAS, JURGEN, *The Structural Transformation of the Public Sphere* (Oxford, 1984).

HAIGHT, GORDON S., *George Eliot and John Chapmen* (New Haven, 1940).

—— *George Eliot: A Biography* (Oxford, 1968).

HALL, CATHERINE, *White, Male and Middle Class: Explorations in Feminism and History* (London, 1992).

HAMILTON, CICELY, *Life Errant* (London, 1935).

HAMMERTON, JAMES A., *Cruelty and Companionship: Conflict in Nineteenth-Century Married Life* (London, 1992).

HARRISON, BRIAN, *Separate Spheres: The Opposition to Women's Suffrage in Britain* (London, 1978).

—— *Prudent Revolutionaries: Portraits of British Feminists Between the Wars* (Oxford, 1987).

HARRISON, CYNTHIA, *On Account of Sex: The Politics of Women's Issues, 1945–1968* (Berkeley, 1988).

HAYS, MARY, *Emma Courtney* (London, 1796; repr. London, 1987).

—— *A Victim of Prejudice* (London, 1799; repr. New York, 1976).

HERSCH, BLANCHE GLASSMAN, *The Slavery of Sex: Feminist-Abolitionists in America* (Urbana, Ill., 1978).

HERSTEIN, SHEILA R., *A Mid-Victorian Feminist: Barbara Leigh Smith Bodichon* (New Haven, 1985).

HIGGONET, M. R., JENSON, J., MICHEL, S., and WEITZ, M. (eds.), *Behind the Lines: Gender and the Two World Wars* (New Haven, 1987).

HILL, BRIDGET, *The Republican Virago: The Life and Times of Catherine Macaulay, Historian* (Oxford, 1992).

HOECKER-DRYSDALE, SUSAN, *Harriet Martineau: First Woman Sociologist* (Oxford, 1992).

HOLCOMBE, LEE, *Victorian Ladies at Work: Middle-Class Working Women in England and Wales, 1850–1914* (Newton Abbott, 1973).

HOLLAND, MARY, 'The Feminine Condition', *The Spectator*, 23 October 1965, p. 553.

HOLLIS, PATRICIA, *Women in Public: The English Women's Movement, 1850–1900* (London, 1979).

HOLMES, RICHARD, *Footsteps: Adventures of a Romantic Biographer* (London, 1985).

HOLTBY, WINNIFRED, *Women and a Changing Civilization* (London, 1935; repr. Chicago, 1978).

HOLTON, SANDRA STANLEY, *Feminism and Democracy: Women's Suffrage and Reform Politics in Britain, 1900–1918* (Cambridge, 1986).

—— 'In Sorrowful Wrath: Suffrage Militance and the Romantic Feminism of Emmeline Pankhurst', in Harold Smith (ed.), *British Feminism in the Twentieth Century* (Aldershot, 1990).

—— 'Free Love and Victorian Feminism: The Divers Matrimonials of Elizabeth Wolstenholme and Ben Elmy', *Victorian Studies*, 36 (1994), 199–222.

HOWITT, MARY, *An Autobiography*, ed. by her daughter, Margaret Howitt (London, n.d.).

HUBBACK, JUDITH, *Wives Who Went to College* (London, 1957).

HUFTON, OLWEN, *Women and the Limits of Citizenship in the French Revolution* (Toronto, 1992).

HUGHES, PETER, and WILLIAMS, DAVID (eds.), *The Varied Pattern: Studies in the Eighteenth Century* (Toronto, 1971).

HUME, LESLIE PARKER, *The National Union of Women's Suffrage Societies* (New York, 1982).

HUNT, LYNN, *The Family Romance of the French Revolution* (London, 1992).

HUTCHINS, B. L., and HARRISON, A., *A History of Factory Legislation* (London, 1911).

JAYAWARDENA, KUMARI, *The White Woman's Other Burden: Western Women and South Asia during British Rule* (New York, 1995).

JEFFREYS, SHEILA, *The Spinster and Her Enemies: Feminism and Sexuality, 1880–1930* (London, 1985).

JELLINEK, ESTELLE C. (ed.), *Women's Autobiography: Essays in Criticism* (Bloomington, Ind., 1980).

JOHN, ANGELA V. (ed.), *Unequal Opportunities: Women's Employment in England, 1800–1918* (Oxford, 1986).

JOHNSON, CLAUDIA, *Equivocal Beings: Politics, Gender, and Sentimentality in the 1790s: Wollstonecraft, Radcliffe, Burney, Austen* (Chicago, 1995).

JORDAN, ELLEN, 'The Christening of the New Woman', *Victorian Periodicals Newsletter*, 63 (1983), 19–20.

JORDANOVA, LUDMILLA, *Sexual Visions* (London, 1990).

KAMESTER, MARGARET, and VELLACOT, JO (eds.), *Militarism versus Feminism: Writings on Women and War* (London, 1987).

KAPLAN, CORA, *Sea Changes: Essays on Culture and Feminism* (London, 1986).

KENNEDY, ELLEN, and MENDUS, SUSAN (eds.), *Women in Western Political Philosophy Kant to Nietzsche* (Brighton, 1988).

KENT, SUSAN KINGSLEY, *Sex and Suffrage in Britain, 1860–1914* (Princeton, 1987).

—— 'The Politics of Sexual Difference: World War I and the Demise of British Feminism', *Journal of British Studies*, 27 (1988), 238–40.

KESSLER-HARRIS, ALICE, *Out to Work: A History of Wage-Earning Women in the United States* (New York, 1982).

KILHAM, JOHN, *Tennyson and The Princess: Reflections of an Age* (London, 1958).

KOWALESKI-WALLACE, ELIZABETH, *Their Father's Daughters: Hannah More, Maria Edgeworth and Patriarchal Complicity* (New York, 1991).

LACEY, CANDIDA (ed.), *Barbara Leigh Smith Bodichon and the Langham Place Circle* (London, 1987).

LAKE, MARILYN, 'Female Desires: The Meaning of World War Two', *Australian Historical Studies*, 24 (1990), 267–84.

LANDES, JOAN, *Women and the Public Sphere in the Age of the French Revolution* (Ithaca, NY, 1987).

LAQUEUR, THOMAS, *Making Sex, Body and Gender from the Greeks to Freud* (Cambridge, Mass., 1990).

LEVINE, PHILIPPA, *Victorian Feminism, 1850–1900* (London, 1987).

—— *Feminist Lives in Victorian England: Private Roles and Public Commitment* (Oxford, 1990).

LEWIS, JANE, *The Politics of Motherhood* (London, 1980).

—— *Women in England, 1870–1950* ( Brighton, 1984).

—— (ed.), *Labour and Love: Women's Experience of Home and Family, 1850–1940* (Oxford, 1986).

—— (ed.), *Before the Vote Was Won: Arguments For and Against Women's Suffrage* (London, 1987).

—— *Women in Britain since 1945: Women, Family, Work and the State in the Post-War Years* (Oxford, 1992).

LIDDINGTON, JILL, *The Long Road to Greenham: Feminism and Anti-Militarism in Britain since 1820* (London, 1989).

—— and NORRIS, JILL, *One Hand Tied Behind Us: The Rise of the Women's Suffrage Movement* (London, 1978).

LONDON FEMINIST HISTORY GROUP, *The Sexual Dynamics of History* (London, 1983).

McBRIDE, THERESA, *The Modernization of Household Service in England and France, 1820–1920* (New York, 1976).

McCRONE, K. E., 'The Assertion of Women's Rights in Mid-Victorian England', *Canadian Historical Association Historical Papers* (1972), 39–53.

—— 'The National Association for the Promotion of Social Science and the Advancement of Victorian Women', *Atlantis*, 8 (1982), 44–66.

McILQUHAM, HARRIET, 'The Enfranchisement of Women: An Ancient Right, a Modern Need', paper read to the Bedminster (Bristol) Habitation of the Primrose League, 11 December 1891, Women's Emancipation Union (n.d.).

MACKENZIE, NORMAN and MACKENZIE, JEANNE, *The First Fabians* (London, 1971).

McWilliams-Tullberg, Rita, *Women at Cambridge: A Men's University—Though of a Mixed Type* (London, 1975).

Martineau, Harriet, *Society in America*, 3 vols. (London, 1837).

—— 'The Martyr Age of the United States', *London and Westminster Review*, 32 (1838–9).

—— 'Female Industry', *The Edinburgh Review*, 109 (1859).

—— *Autobiography*, 2 vols. (London, 1877; repr. London, 1983).

Marwick, Arthur, *Women at War, 1914–18* (London, 1977).

Mayo, Katharine, *Mother India* (London, 1927).

Mellor, Anne K., *Romanticism and Gender* (New York, 1993).

Mendus, Susan and Rendall, Jane (eds.), *Sexuality and Subordination* (London, 1989).

Middleton, Lucy (ed.), *Women in the Labour Movement* (London, 1977).

Middleton, Virginia, '*Three Guineas*: Subversion and Survival in the Professions', *Twentieth Century Literature*, 28 (1982).

Midgley, Claire, *Women against Slavery: The British Campaigns, 1780–1870* (London, 1992).

Mill, James, 'An Essay on Government', published in the supplement to the *Encyclopaedia Britannica* (London, 1821; repr. Cambridge, 1937).

Mill, John Stuart, *Essays on Some Unsettled Questions of Political Economy* (London, 1874).

—— and Mill, Harriet Taylor, *Essays on Sex Equality*, ed. Alice S. Rossi (Chicago, 1970).

Mineka, Frances E., *The Dissidence of Dissent: The Monthly Repository, 1806–1838* (New York, 1972).

Mitchell, David, *Women on the Warpath* (London, 1965).

Mitchell, Juliet, 'Women: The Longest Revolution', *New Left Review*, November/December (1966).

—— *Women's Estate* (Harmondsworth, 1971).

—— *Psychoanalysis and Feminism* (London, 1974).

—— and Oakley, Ann (eds.), *The Rights and Wrongs of Women* (Harmondsworth, 1976).

Myers, Mitzi, 'Harriet Martineau's Autobiography: The Making of a Female Philosopher', in Estelle C. Jelinek (ed.), *Women's Autobiography: Essays in Criticism* (Bloomington, Ind., 1980).

—— 'Reform or Ruin: "A Revolution in Female Manners"', in Harry C. Payne (ed.), *Studies in Eighteenth Century Culture* (Madison, 1982).

Myers, Sylvia Harcstark, *The Bluestocking Circle: Women, Friendship and the Life of the Mind in Eighteenth-Century England* (Oxford, 1990).

Myrdal, Alva, *Nation and Family: The Swedish Experiment in Democratic Family and Population Policy* (New York, 1941).

—— and Klein, Viola, *Women's Two Roles: Home and Work* (London, 1956).

Neustater, Angela, *Hyenas in Petticoats: A Look at Twenty Years of Feminism* (Harmondsworth, 1989).

NEWBURY JO VELLACOT, 'Anti-War Suffragists', *History*, 62 (1977), 411–25.

NORTON, CAROLINE, *English Laws for Women in the Nineteenth Century*, privately printed (London, 1854).

OFFEN, KAREN, 'Defining Feminism: A Comparative Historical Approach', *Signs*, 14 (1988).

ORAM, ALISON, 'The Spinster in Inter-war Feminist Discourses', *Women's History Review*, 1 (1992).

PANKHURST, RICHARD, 'Anna Wheeler: A Pioneer Socialist and Feminist', *Political Quarterly*, 25 (1954).

PANKHURST, SYLVIA, *The Suffragette Movement* (London, 1931; repr. London, 1977).

—— *The Homefront* (London, 1932; repr. London, 1985).

PATEMAN, CAROLE, *The Sexual Contract* (Oxford, 1988).

—— *The Disorder of Women* (London, 1989).

—— and BRENNAN, TERESA, ' "Mere Auxiliaries to the Commonwealth": Women and the Origins of Liberalism', *Political Studies*, 27 (1979).

PAYNE, HARRY C., *Studies in Eighteenth Century Culture* (Madison, 1982).

PENNELL, ELIZABETH ROBBINS, *Mary Wollstonecraft Godwin* (London, 1885).

PETHICK-LAWRENCE, EMMELINE, *My Part in a Changing World* (London, 1938).

PHILLIPS, ANNE, *Engendering Democracy* (Cambridge, 1991).

PICHANICK, VALERIE KOSSE, *Harriet Martineau: The Woman and Her Work, 1802–76* (Ann Arbor, 1980).

PINCHBECK, IVY, *Women Workers and the Industrial Revolution* (London, 1930; repr. 1981).

PINNY, THOMAS (ed.), *Essays of George Eliot* (London, 1968).

POOVEY, MARY, *The Proper Lady and the Woman Writer: Ideology as Style in the Works of Mary Wollstonecraft, Mary Shelley and Jane Austen* (Chicago, 1985).

—— *Uneven Developments: The Ideological Work of Gender in Mid-Victorian England* (London, 1989).

PROCHASKA, F. K., *Women and Philanthropy in Nineteenth Century England* (Oxford, 1980).

PROCTOR, CANDICE E., *Women, Equality, and the French Revolution* (New York, 1990).

PUGH, MARTIN, *The Making of Modern British Politics, 1867–1939* (Oxford, 1982).

—— *Women and the Women's Movement in Britain, 1914–1959* (London, 1992).

PUJOL, GENEVIEVE, *Feminism and Antifeminism in Political Economy* (Toronto, 1992).

QUATAERT, JEAN, and BOXER, MARILYN (eds.), *Connecting Spheres: Women in the Western World, 1500 to the Present* (New York, 1987).

RAMUSACK, BARBARA, 'Cultural Missionaries, Maternal Imperialists,

Feminist Allies: British Women Activists in India, 1865–1945', in Nupur Chaudhuri and Margaret Strobel (eds.), *Western Women and Imperialism: Complicity and Resistance* (Bloomington, Ind., 1992).

—— *Western Women and Imperialism: Complicity and Resistance* (Bloomington, Ind., 1992).

RATHBONE, ELEANOR, *The Disinherited Family* (London, 1924).

—— *Milestones* (Liverpool, 1929).

RENDALL, JANE, *The Origins of Modern Feminism: Women in Britain, France and the United States, 1760–1860* (London, 1985).

—— (ed.), *Equal or Different: Women's Politics, 1800–1914* (Oxford, 1987).

—— 'Virtue and Commerce: Women in the Making of Adam Smith's Political Economy', in Ellen Kennedy and Susan Mendus (eds.), *Women in Western Political Philosophy: Kant to Nietzsche* (Brighton, 1988).

—— 'Friendship and Politics: Barbara Leigh Smith Bodichon (1827–91) and Bessie Rayner Parkes (1829–95)', in Susan Mendus and Jane Rendall, *Sexuality and Subordination: Interdisciplinary Studies of Gender in the Nineteenth Century* (London, 1989), 136–70.

RHONDDA, VISCOUNTESS, *This Was My World* (London, 1933).

RICHELIEU LAMB, ANNE, *Can Woman Regenerate Society?* (London, 1834).

RILEY, DENISE, 'Some Peculiarities of Social Policy Concerning Women in Wartime and Postwar Britain', in Margaret Randolph Higgonet *et al.* (eds.), *Behind the Lines: Gender and the Two World Wars* (New Haven, 1987).

—— *Am I that Name? Feminism and the Category of 'Women' in History* (Basingstoke, 1988).

ROWBOTHAM, SHEILA, 'Women's Liberation and the New Politics' (1969), in Michelene Wandor (ed.), *The Body Politic: Writings from the Women's Liberation Movement in Britain, 1969–1972* (London, 1972).

—— *Hidden from History* (London, 1973).

—— *The Past is Before Us: Feminism in Action Since the 1960s* (London, 1989).

ROWE, MARSHA (ed.), *Spare Rib Reader* (Harmondsworth, 1982).

ROYDEN, MAUDE, *Sex and Commonsense* (London, 1922).

RUBINSTEIN, DAVID, *Before the Suffragettes: Women's Emancipation in the 1890s* (Brighton, 1988).

RUSKIN, JOHN, *Sesames and Lilies* (London, 1891).

RUSSELL, DORA, *Hypatia: Or Women and Knowledge* (London, 1925).

—— *The Tamarisk Tree* (London, 1985).

SANDERS, VALERIE (ed.), *Harriet Martineau: Selected Letters* (Oxford, 1990).

SANDFORD, MRS JOHN, *Woman in Her Social and Domestic Character* (London, 1831).

SAPIRO, VIRGINIA, *A Vindication of Political Virtue: The Political Theory of Mary Wollstonecraft* (Chicago, 1972).

SARAH, ELIZABETH, 'Christabel Pankhurst: Reclaiming her Power', in Dale Spender (ed.), *Feminist Theorists* (London, 1983).

SCHOFIELD, MARY ANNE, and MACHESKI, CECILIA, *Fetter'd or Free? British*

*Women Novelists, 1670–1815* (Athens, Oh., 1986).

SCOTT, JOAN, 'Deconstructing Equality-versus-Difference: Or the Uses of Post Structuralist Theory for Feminism', *Feminist Studies*, 14 (1988).

—— and TILLY, LOUISE, 'Women's Work and the Family in Nineteenth-Century Europe', *Comparative Studies in Society and History*, 17 (1975), 36–64.

SEBESTYEN, AMANDA, *Feminist Practices* (London, 1980).

—— (ed.), *'68, '78, '88: From Women's Liberation to Feminism* (Bridport, Dorset, 1988).

SEGAL, LYNNE, *Is the Future Female?: Troubled Thoughts on Contemporary Feminism* (London, 1987).

SHANLEY, MARY LYNDON, *Feminism, Marriage and the Law in Victorian England, 1850–1895* (London, 1989).

SHIMAN, LILLIAN LEWIS, *Women and Leadership in Nineteenth-Century England* (New York, 1992).

SHORTER, EDWARD, *The Making of the Modern Family* (London, 1976).

SHOWALTER, ELAINE, *The Female Malady* (London, 1987).

SINFIELD, ALAN, *Literature, Politics and Culture in Postwar Britain* (Oxford, 1989).

SMITH, HAROLD L., 'The Issue of "Equal Pay for Equal Work" in Great Britain during World War II', *The Journal of Modern History*, 53 (1981), 652–72.

—— (ed.), *British Feminism in the Twentieth Century* (Aldershot, 1990).

SOLDON, NORBERT, *Women in British Trade Unions* (Dublin, 1978).

SPACKS, PATRICIA MEYER, *Imagining a Self: Autobiography and the Novel in Eighteenth-Century England* (Cambridge, Mass., 1976).

SPENCER, JANE, *The Rise of the Woman Novelist from Aphra Behn to Jane Austen* (Oxford, 1986).

SPENDER, DALE, *Feminist Theorists: Three Centuries of Women's Intellectual Traditions* (London, 1983).

—— *There's Always Been a Women's Movement This Century* (London, 1984).

SPIES, S. B., *Methods of Barbarism: Robertson and Kitchener and Civilians in the Boer Republic: January 1900–May 1902* (Cape Town, 1976).

STANTON, T. (ed.), *The Woman Question in Europe* (London, 1888).

STANLEY, LIZ, 'Feminism and Friendship: Two Essays on Olive Schreiner', *Studies in Sexual Politics*, 8 (1995).

STEBBINS, EMMA (ed.), *Charlotte Cushman: Her Letters and Memories of Her Life* (Boston, 1879).

STEPHEN, BARBARA, *Emily Davies and Girton College* (London, 1927).

STOCKS, MARY, *Eleanor Rathbone: A Biography* (London, 1949).

—— 'The Suffrage Movement: Triumph and Tragedy', *Manchester Guardian* (12 April 1957), 10–11.

STONE, LAWRENCE, *The Family, Sex and Marriage in England, 1500–1800* (London, 1977).

Stott, Mary, *Organization Women: The Story of the Townswomen's Guilds* (London, 1978).

Strachey, Ray, *The Cause: A Short History of the Women's Movement in Great Britain* (London, 1928; repr. London, 1978).

—— *Millicent Garrett Fawcett*, London, 1931.

—— (ed.), *Our Freedom and its Results* (London, 1936).

Summerfield, Penny, and Crocket, Nicole, 'You Weren't Taught That with the Welding: Lessons in Sexuality in the Second World War', *Women's History Review*, 1 (1992), 435–54.

Taylor, Barbara, *Eve and the New Jerusalem: Socialism and Feminism in the Nineteenth Century* (London, 1983).

—— 'Mary Wollstonecraft and the Wild Wish of Early Feminism', *History Workshop Journal*, 33 (1992).

Thompson, William, *Appeal of One-Half of the Human Race, Women, against the Pretensions of the other Half, Men, to retain them in political and thence in civil and domestic Slavery; in Reply to a paragraph of Mr Mill's celebrated 'Article on Government'* (London, 1825; repr. London, 1983).

Tickner, Lisa, *Spectacle of Women: The Imagery of the Suffrage Campaign, 1907–1917* (London, 1989).

Todd, Janet, *The Sign of Angelica: Women, Writing and Fiction, 1660–1800* (London, 1989).

—— and Butler, Marilyn (eds.), *The Works of Mary Wollstonecraft* (London, 1989).

Tomalin, Claire, *The Life and Death of Mary Wollstonecraft* (London, 1974).

Tulloch, Gail, *Mill and Sexual Equality* (Brighton, 1989).

Twinch, Carol, *Women on the Land* (Worcester, 1990).

Tyrrell, Ian, *Woman's Empire; Woman's World: The Women's Christian Temperance Union in International Perspective, 1880–1930* (Chapel Hill, NC, 1991).

Van Arsdel, Rosemary T., 'Mrs Florence Fenwick-Miller and the *Woman's Signal*, 1895–99', *Victorian Periodicals Newsletter*, 14 (1982), 107–17.

Vicinus, Martha, *Independent Women: Work and Community for Single Women, 1850–1920* (Chicago, 1985).

—— 'Distance and Desire: English Boarding School Friendships, 1870–1920', in Martin Duberman *et al.* (eds.), *Hidden from History: Reclaiming the Gay and Lesbian Past* (New York, 1991).

—— 'Lesbian Perversity and Victorian Marriage: The 1864 Codrington Trial', *Journal of British Studies*, 36 (1997), 70–98.

Vickery, Amanda, 'Golden Age to Separate Spheres? A Review of the Categories and Chronology of English Women's History', *The Historical Journal*, 36 (1993).

Walkowitz, Judith R., *Prostitution and Victorian Society: Women, Class and the State* (Cambridge, 1980).

—— *City of Dreadful Delight: Narrative of Sexual Danger in Late Victorian England* (London, 1992).

WANDOR, MICHELENE (ed.), *The Body Politic: Writings from the Women's Liberation Movement in Britain, 1969–1972* (London, 1972).

—— (ed.), *Once a Feminist: Stories of a Generation* (London, 1990).

WARDLE, RALPH M. (ed.), *Collected Letters of Mary Wollstonecraft* (Ithaca, NY, 1972).

WARE, VRON, *Beyond the Pale: White Women, Racism and History* (London, 1992).

WEBB, BEATRICE, 'Women and the Factory Acts', Fabian Tract No. 67 (London, 1895).

WEIR, ANGELA, and WILSON, ELIZABETH, 'The British Women's Movement', *New Left Review*, 148 (1984).

WILTSHER, ANNE, *Most Dangerous Women: Feminist Peace Campaigners of the Great War* (London, 1985).

WOLLSTONECRAFT, MARY, *Mary: A Fiction* (London, 1789).

—— *A Vindication of the Rights of Men* (London, 1790), in Janet Todd and Marilyn Butler (eds.), *The Works of Mary Wollstonecraft* vol. v (London, 1989).

—— *A Vindication of the Rights of Woman* (1791), in Todd and Butler (eds.), *Works of Mary Wollstonecraft*, vol. v.

—— *Maria, or the Wrongs of Woman* (London, 1798).

—— *A Vindication of the Rights of Woman: With Strictures on Political and Moral Subjects*, 3rd edn. (London, 1844).

—— *Letters To Imlay*, with prefatory memoir by C. Kegan Paul (London, 1879).

—— *A Vindication of the Rights of Woman*, with an introduction by Millicent Garrett Fawcett (London, 1891).

WOLSTENHOLME-ELMY, ELIZABETH, 'Women's Suffrage', *Westminster Review*, 148/4 (1897).

—— 'Judicial Sexual Bias, I', *Westminster Review*, 149 (February 1898).

—— 'Judicial Sexual Bias, II', *Westminster Review*, 149 (March 1898).

—— 'Privilege V: Justice to Women', *Westminster Review*, 152 (1899).

WOOLF, VIRGINIA, *A Room of One's Own* (London, 1929).

—— *Three Guineas* (London, 1938; repr. Harmondsworth, 1979).

—— *The Diary of Virginia Woolf*, iii, *1925–30*, ed. Anne Olivier Bell (London, 1980).

—— *The Diary of Virginia Woolf*, v, *1936–41*, ed. Anne Olivier Bell (London, 1984).

WOOTTON, BARBARA, *Social Science and Social Pathology* (London, 1959).

—— *In a World I Never Made: Autobiographical Reflections* (London, 1967).

WRIGHT, MARTIN, 'Robert Blatchford, the Clarion Movement, and the Critical Years of British Socialism, 1891–1900', *Prose Studies*, 13 (1990).

YATES, GAYLE GRAHAM (ed.), *Harriet Martineau on Women* (New Brunswick, NJ, 1985).

YEATMAN, ANNA, 'Interlocking Oppressions', in Barbara Caine and Rosemary Pringle (eds.), *Transitions: New Australian Feminisms* (Sydney, 1995).

YELLIN, JEAN FAGIN, *Women and Sisters: The Antislavery Feminists in American Culture* (New Haven, 1989).

ZONANA, JOYCE, 'The Sultan and the Slave: Feminist Orientalism and the Structure of *Jane Eyre*', *Signs*, 18 (1993).

# Index

# Index

# Index

Myrdal, Alva 240
   and Klein, Viola *Women's Two Roles: Home and Work* 245–8, 252

National Association for the Promotion of Social Science 91, 94, 126
National Council of Women's Citizen's Associations 201
National Federation of Women Workers 150
National Union of Societies for Equal Citizenship (NUSEC) 174, 184, 185, 186, 187, 188, 190, 192, 193, 195–6, 198, 201–2, 205, 209, 221
National Union of Women's Suffrage Societies (NUWSS) 124, 153, 157, 158, 160–2, 164, 165, 166, 169, 179, 183, 184, 248, 262
Newnham College 116
Nightingale, Florence 57, 88, 97
North of England Society for Women's Suffrage 156
Norton, Caroline 57, 66–70, 95
   *English Laws for Women in the Nineteenth Century* 69, 95

Oakley, Anne 252
O'Malley, I. B. 216
Open Door Council 225, 229, 231
Oram, Alison 215
Owenites 54–6, 60, 61
Oxford University 116, 203

Pankhursts, the 134, 159, 160, 162, 163, 166, 167, 204, 259
Pankhurst, Christabel 136, 145, 146, 157, 159, 160, 163, 259, 260, 262
Pankhurst, Emmeline 163, 248, 260, 262
Pankhurst, Sylvia 122, 166, 178, 262
Parkes, Bessie Rayner 93–5, 97–8, 99
Parliamentary politics:
   women Members of Parliament 229–34
Pateman, Carole 197
Patterson, Emma 149
Paul, Kegan 102
peace movement 217
Pennell, Elizabeth Robins 139
pensions 187, 203
Pethick-Lawrence, Emmeline 145–6, 163, 166, 238
Pethick-Lawrence, Fred 163, 166
philanthropy 54, 89, 107, 126, 127, 179
   'women's mission' 82, 84–5
Phillips, Anne 197

Phillips, Marion 195, 207, 208
Picton-Turvervill, Edith 206
Political Economy 21, 33, 72, 75
political thought:
   citizenship 18–19, 92, 200–2
   reform 57, 91, 175, 196
Primrose League 124, 206
Poovey, Mary 15, 36, 37, 45, 69
Proctor, Adelaide 94
prostitution 106, 111–12, 177, 218, 221
psychoanalysis 270
*Punch* 131
Pugh, Martin 173, 206, 208, 223–4

Queen Victoria 88

race 35, 77, 90, 125–30, 267
   imperialism 123, 133, 137, 168–72, 219–21, 253, 256, 268
   'feminist orientalism' 90
Radcliffe, Ann 44, 45
Raeburn, Antonia 259
Ramusack, Barbara 219, 221
rape 271
Rathbone, Eleanor 174, 176, 183, 184, 185, 187, 188, 189, 190, 191, 192, 195–6, 198–9, 201, 209, 213, 214, 215, 219, 220–1, 230, 236, 246
*Red Rag* 256, 263
Reddish, Sarah 155, 156
Reid, Elizabeth 77
Rendall, Jane 97
Rhondda, Lady 183, 184, 185, 188–9, 189, 191, 199, 206–7, 238
Richardson, Samuel 44
Riley, Denise 197, 227
Roper, Esther 156
Rousseau, Jean Jacques 27, 30–3, 36
   *Emile* and 'Sophie' 17
   sexual difference and 15, 17–18
Rowbotham, Sheila 257, 258, 260, 261–1, 265
Royden, Maude 177, 215
Ruskin, John 85, 143
Ruskin College:
   History Workshop 257
   Women's Conference 256, 263, 264
Russell, Dora 177, 185, 208, 223, 234–5, 251, 260
Rye, Maria 94

Sandford, John (Mrs) 84
Schreiner, Olive 136, 142, 172